W9-ABG-361

"A Poet and a filthy Play-maker"

AMS Studies in the Renaissance: No. 14
ISSN: 0195–8011

Other Titles in This Series:

1. Hilton Landry, ed. *New Essays on Shakespeare's Sonnets.* 1976.
2. J. W. Williamson. *The Myth of the Conqueror: Prince Henry Stuart, a Study of 17th Century Personation.* 1978.
3. Philip C. McGuire and David A. Samuelson, eds. *Shakespeare: The Theatrical Dimension.* 1979.
4. Paul Ramsey. *The Fickle Glass: A Study of Shakespeare's Sonnets.* 1979.
5. n.p..
6. Raymond C. Shady and G. B. Shand, eds. *Play-Texts in Old Spelling: Papers from the Glendon Conference.* 1984.
7. Mark Taylor. *Shakespeare's Darker Purpose: A Question of Incest.* 1982.
8. Kenneth Friedenreich, ed. *"Accompaninge the players": Essays Celebrating Thomas Middleton, 1580–1980.* 1983.
9. Sarah P. Sutherland. *Masques in Jacobean Tragedy.* 1983.
10. Margaret Loftus Ranald. *Shakespeare and His Social Context: Essays in Osmotic Knowledge and Literary Interpretation.* 1987.
11. Clifford Leech. *Christopher Marlowe: Poet for the Stage.* Ed. Anne Lancashire. 1986.
12. Clifford Davidson, C. J. Gianakaris, and John H. Stroupe, eds., *Drama in the Renaissance: Comparative and Critical Essays.* 1986.
13. Georgianna Ziegler, ed. *Shakespeare Study Today: The Horace Howard Furness Memorial Lectures.* 1986.
15. W. R. Streitberger. *Edmond Tyllney, Master of the Revels an Censor of Plays.* 1986.
17. Donald K. Anderson, Jr., ed. *"Concord in Discord": The Plays of John Ford, 1586–1986.* 1987.
19. Herbert Berry, *Shakespeare's Playhouses.* Illus. by C. Walter Hodges. 1987.
20. Nancy Klein Maguire, ed. *Renaissance Tragicomedy: Explorations in Genre and Politics.* 1987.
22. Clifford Davidson. *The Guild Chapel Wall Paintings at Stratford-upon-Avon.* 1988.

"A Poet and a filthy Play-maker,"
New Essays on Christopher Marlowe

Edited by
Kenneth Friedenreich, Roma Gill,
and Constance B. Kuriyama

AMS Press, Inc.
New York, N. Y.

Library of Congress Cataloging-in-Publication Data

A Poet and a filthy play-maker.

(AMS studies in the Renaissance, ISSN 0195-8011; no. 14)

Bibliography: p.

Includes index.

1. Marlowe, Christopher, 1564-1593—Criticism and interpretation. I. Friedenreich, Kenneth, 1947-   II. Gill, Roma. III. Kuriyama, Constance Brown, 1942-   . IV. Series.

PR2674.P64 1988   822'.3   85-47999

ISBN 0-404-62284-4

AMS PRESS, INC.
56 East 13th Street
New York, N.Y. 10003

Manufactured in the United States of America

Contents

Preface

Few authors have stimulated as vigorous debate about the merits of his achievement as Christopher Marlowe. This does not mean that critics and interpreters of his work cannot find a significant place for him in his time. Rather, Marlowe's contribution to literature is at once so original and the course of his career so difficult to chart that he never fails to challenge, for good or ill, the imagination of reader and playgoer. Indeed, even Marlowe's very name could provoke heated attacks from his puritan and philistine enemies, such as the one which (ironically) has provided the title for this volume, Edmunde Rudierde's *The Thunderbolt of Gods Wrath against Hard-Hearted and stiffe-necked sinners* (London, 1618). The decade and a half since Marlowe's death had not diminished the attackers' venom:

> We read of one *Marlin*, a *Cambridge* Scholler, who was a Poet, and a filthy Play-maker, this wretch accounted that meeke seruant of God *Moses* to be but a Coniurer, and our sweete Sauiour but a seducer and a decieuer of the people.

It is clear that audiences experience a dramatic poet of such intensity and concentration of power that it is still difficult to imagine him engaging in all matter of other business, not all of it savory or well documented. His plays form a patchwork canon from the standpoint of a modern editor's methods; fraught with major problems, one cannot but take a strong stand regardless of the choices one elects. In other places I have decried the lack of genuine interest from the vantage of scholars in Marlowe's abilities as a dramatist. Only in the past decade, perhaps, with an increasing number of realizations of the plays, has the community of Marlowe's interpreters accepted the truth that his plays possess—albeit in varying degrees—a theatrical dimension possessed of its own powerful structure and logic. The following essays do not, of course, simply call attention to Marlowe's dramatic skill. They span a wide and challenging range of topics, giving considerable fresh insight to much of the acknowledged Marlowe canon. Certainly, too, the reader will have cause to take strong issue with some of these interpretations and will perhaps feel called upon to challenge other assertions made concerning Marlowe's career, associations, reputation, and wanderings. But that seems less a hazard than testimony to the vitality of our subject.

The present collection contains twenty-four new essays. Many of them saw first light at Marlowe Society of America meetings during the past few years. Of these the predominant number formed a central part of the first international Marlowe Society Conference held at the University of Sheffield in mid-July, 1983. For the vision and energy going into that effort, we owe collectively a debt of thanks to MSA founder and president, Professor Jean Jofen, Baruch College of the City University of New York, for conceiving and coordinating that conference. Indeed, that site and success of the meeting depended, too, on Professor Jofen's co-chair, Professor Roma Gill. The remaining dozen or so pieces were commissioned as part of my Marlowe commemorative volume, and in as much as several of these also emerged as MSA presentations at first blush, it seemed very right to put all of the efforts into one volume.

Editorial prejudices dictate the sequence of essays, beginning with those dealing with Marlowe's literary relations and critical reputation. This includes essays by Kenneth Muir, Norman Rabkin, Kay Stanton, James A. Riddell, John T. Shawcross, and Lois Potter. The three following essays focus on dramatic language with a concentration in the ways these show Marlowe making deliberate, far-reaching improvements in the state of theatrical art, particularly in *Dido, Queen of Carthage* and *Tamburlaine*. These essays include those by J. W. Van Hook, Matthew N. Proser, and Jill L. Levenson. Innovation seems the theme—though not always expressed in complete harmony—in the essays dealing with *The Jew of Malta* by Thomas Cartelli, Edward L. Rocklin, and Coburn Freer respectively. These teach us much about the play and the paths Marlowe opened up to his theatrical successors. Having always felt that *Doctor Faustus* and *The Jew of Malta* are proximate in time of composition and (no pun) in spirit, three essays about this perennial classic follow. The first of these by Thomas Pettitt, rich and suggestive, relates quite well to the dramaturgical considerations in those essays about *The Jew of Malta* and his follows appropriately. The succeeding two essays by King-Kok Cheung and Kay Stockholder address singular cruces in the interpretation of this drama, that by Marlowe's means, has his figure and his conflict brought into the mainstream of Western culture. The essays on drama end with three concerning *Edward II*, by Claude J. Summers, Sara Munson Deats, and collaboration by David Bevington and James Shapiro. three unquestionably confirm the eminence with which the contemporary public now regards this play. Happily, all of the dramas in the canon are represented by the collective effort although in one's own quest for completeness (an editorial phobia) a self-contained paper on *The Massacre at Paris* would have been welcome.

Succeeding papers turn to non-dramatic works and to biographical issues. Two essays by Robart A. Logan and William L. Godshalk neatly complement one another as they offer interpretations of *Hero and Leander*. James Shapiro and Roma Gill, writing on Marlowe's translation of Lucan and the topic of his translations in general, contrast with one another, but illuminate this realtively darker corner of the Marlovian enterprise. It makes good sense, too, that we should learn that in this aspect of his art Marlowe cut with a two-edge blade between tradition and innovation. Last, two papers address the well-documented but nonetheless vexing circumstances leading up to and following immediately at Marlowe's death. Written by two of this collection's editors respectively, the essays remind us that in approaching the four-hundredth anniversary of those events, Marlowe's hold upon our imaginations grips stronger than ever. Further, when we think just how briefly Marlowe flourished to fasten this hold, his accomplishment looms greater still.

—Kenneth Friedenreich

Notes on Contributors

DAVID M. BEVINGTON, Professor of English at the University of Chicago, has edited *The Macro Plays* (1972), *Medieval Drama* (1975), a *Bibliography of Shakespeare* (1978), and *The Complete Works of Shakespeare* (1980). His book-length critical studies include *From "Mankind" to Marlowe* (1962), *Tudor Drama and Politics* (1968), and *Action Is Eloquence: Shakespeare's Language of Gesture* (1984).

THOMAS CARTELLI, Assistant Professor of English and Drama at Muhlenberg College, has published articles on Shakespeare, dramatic theory, and Ben Jonson and currently is working on a book-length study, "Marlowe, Shakespeare, and the Psychology of Theatrical Experience."

KING-KOK CHEUNG, Assistant Professor of English at UCLA, has written articles on Marlowe, Shakespeare, Milton, and Asian-American writers.

SARA MUNSON DEATS, formerly a professional actress and director, is Professor of English at the University of South Florida and has published articles on Marlowe, Shakespeare, Lyly, Jonson, and Marston.

COBURN FREER is Professor of English at the University of Georgia. He is the author of *The Poetics of Jacobean Drama* (1981) and *Music for a King* (1972), a study of George Herbert.

KENNETH FRIEDENREICH taught at several universities before becoming Executive Director of The Association for Human Achievement. His books include *Tercentenary Essays in Honor of Andrew Marvell* (1977), *Henry Vaughan* (1978), *Christopher Marlowe: An Annotated Bibliography of Criticism since 1950* (1979), *"Accompaninge the Players": Essays in Honor of Thomas Middleton* (1983).

ROMA GILL, Christopher Marlowe Research Professor in the University of Sheffield, has published on a number of English Renaissance writers, but her chief interest has been in the editing of sixteenth- and seventeenth-century drama. She is editor of the Oxford School Shakespeare and is at work on a new three-volume edition of The Complete Works of Christopher Marlowe to be published by Oxford University Press.

W.L. GODSHALK is Professor of English at the University of Cinncinnati and General Editor of the Garland Shakespeare Bibliographies; he has written books on Shakespeare, Marlowe, and James Branch Cabell.

CONSTANCE BROWN KURIYAMA is the author of Hammer or Anvil: Psychological Patterns in Christopher Marlowe's Plays (1980). An Associate Professor of English at Texas Tech University, she is currently at work on a biography of Marlowe.

JILL L. LEVENSON, Professor of English at Trinity College, University of Toronto, has published editorial and bibliographical research on English Renaissance drama, as well as theater history. Currently she has completed a study of Romeo and Juliet for the University of Manchester Shakespeare in Performance series and an edition of Romeo and Juliet for Oxford University Press.

ROBERT A. LOGAN, Associate Professor of English at the University of Hartford, is currently at work on Marlowe's influence on Shakespeare, Shakespeare's kinetic characterizations and the psychology of a reader's or viewer's responses, and recent trends in Marlowe criticism.

KENNETH MUIR, King Alfred Professor of English Literature at Liverpool, Emeritus, was editor of Shakespeare Survey for many years and is the current chairman of the International Shakespeare Association. He has directed a number of Shakespeare's plays and acted in others—one of his roles was Doctor Faustus. He has edited five of Shakespeare's plays and written on the tragedies, comedies, sonnets, and sources. His most recent books are King Lear: Critical Essays (1984) and a collection of his own dramatic essays.

THOMAS PETTITT is a lecturer at the English Department, Odense University, Denmark. His research and publishing is devoted to tracing the development of early English traditional culture (particularly ballads and folk drama) and its interaction with the literary history of the period. He is co-author of The Ballad as Narrative (1982).

LOIS POTTER, Senior Lecturer in English at The University of Leicester, is one of the General Editors of the Revels History of Drama in English. She has published books on Shakespeare and Milton and currently is writing a book on the literature of the Interregnum.

MATTHEW N. PROSER, Professor of English at the University of Connecticut, has written primarily on Shakespeare and also on Marlowe, the modern novel, and contemporary drama. He has published a book on Shakespeare's tragedies, *The Heroic Image* (1965) and currently is working on a psycho-biographical study of Marlowe's creative process.

NORMAN Rabkin, Professor of English, University of California at Berkeley, is the author of *Shakespeare and the Common Understanding* (1967) and *Shakespeare and the Problem of Meaning* (1981). He is co-editor of *Shakespeare's Contemporaries: Modern Studies in English Renaissance Drama* (1961) and of *Drama of the English Renaissance* (1976); he is the editor of *Twentieth-Century Interpretations of "The Duchess of Malfi"* 1968) and of *Reinterpretations of Elizabethan Drama: Selected Papers from the English Institute* (1969).

JAMES A. RIDDELL, Professor of English at California State University, Dominguez Hills, has published a number of articles, chiefly on English Renaissance literature and on early English lexicography.

EDWARD L. ROCKLIN, is an Assistant Professor of English at Columbia University. His essay on *The Jew of Malta* grew out of his dissertation on the disabler in Marlowe and Shakespeare. Currently he is working on a study tentatively called "Transforming Figures: Overreacher, Disabler, Inheritor, and Enabler in Shakespearean Dramaturgy."

JAMES SHAPIRO is an Assistant Professor of English at Columbia University. He has written on Renaissance drama and versification and currently is at work on a book on "Marlowe and the Problem of Influence."

JOHN T. SHAWCROSS, Professor of English at the University of Kentucky, has written widely about many facets of Renaissance literature. He is the editor of *The Complete Poetry of John Donne* and *The Complete Poetry of John Milton,* and *Milton: The Critical Heritage* and the author of *With Mortal Voice: The Creation of "Paradise Lost."*

KAY STANTON, Associate Professor of English at California State University of Fullerton, has presented many conference papers, both in the United States and England, and has published articles on Shakespeare and on Milton. At present she is at work on a book on *As You Like It*.

KAY STOCKHOLDER is Associate Professor of English at the University of British Columbia; her article in this volume was generated from her work in progress, "Dream Works: Lovers and Families in Shakespeare's Plays."

CLAUDE J. SUMMERS, Professor of English at the University of Michigan—Dearborn, has published essays on Marlowe, Shakespeare, Donne, Herbert, Herrick, and Vaughan and is the author of *Chrostopher Marlowe and the Politics of Power* (1974).

J. W. VAN HOOK teaches at the University of Arkansas. His main research interest is in Renaissance and seventeenth-century poetic theory.

Marlowe and Shakespeare

KENNETH MUIR

A few months before Leslie Hotson discovered that Marlowe had been killed by a future churchwarden, Clemence Dane, better known as a novelist, wrote a verse play entitled *Will Shakespeare* in which Marlowe is killed by his great rival. Although literally untrue, the act has a certain symbolic value: it could be said that the most important event in Shakespeare's career took place in Eleanor Bull's tavern at Deptford. For the next few years, Shakespeare was without a serious rival. Some months earlier, Robert Greene's voice from the grave (or Chettle's imitation of it) had warned Marlowe of the Upstart Crow. Shakespeare, like Marlowe, was born in 1564; and if he had been the victim of a brawl in 1593, he would have been regarded not as one of the greatest dramatists of the world, but merely as one of the most promising among a number of Elizabethans—the author of *Henry VI, The Comedy of Errors*, and a handful of other plays. Now his predecessors and rivals vanished from the scene. Greene, Kyd, and Peele died of poverty, torture, and the pox. Lyly's vogue having passed, he lapsed into silence. Lodge was metamorphosed into a respectable physician, author of an admirable treatise on the plague (advocating isolation hospitals and cleanliness), and into the learned translator of Seneca and Josephus. The upstart crow was left; and there may well have been complaints among the critics that he was sadly lacking in originality. Whereas Lyly, Kyd, Greene, Peele, and Marlowe had all produced work which was unlike anything which had been written before, all Shakespeare had

1

done had been to imitate them all, throwing Latin comedy into the bargain.

His biggest debt, of course, was to Marlowe. Everyone knows that he took over and modified Marlovian verse, so as to make it better able to express subtleties of characterization. Marlowe's tragic heroes, larger than life as they are, influenced Shakespeare's; but he soon realized, as Marlowe himself did in *Edward II*, that it was not enough for the dramatist to speak only through the protagonist: it was necessary to bring all his characters, or as many as possible, to life.

All poets are influenced by their contemporaries in one way or another—even Hopkins and Emily Dickinson. Eliot and Yeats learned some vital lessons from Pound; Auden learned from Graves and Eliot; Pinter is a rib taken out of Beckett's side; and Larkin had to shake off what to him was the baleful influence of Yeats. So if Shakespeare was influenced by Marlowe, Marlowe was equally influenced by Shakespeare. Marlowe, too, modified the drumming decasyllabon, so that Faustus's final soliloquy is more daringly irregular than any verse written by Shakespeare before the end of the sixteenth century; and the verse of *Edward II* is much closer to ordinary speech than that of *Tamburlaine*. He too learned to depict characters other than his protagonists. And if *Richard II* is indebted to *Edward II*, as everyone admits, *Edward II* was equally indebted to *Henry VI*, and possibly to *Richard III*, though I am less certain than the Arden editor that the play was written in 1591.

The interrelationship between Marlowe and Shakespeare has been brilliantly charted by F. P. Wilson and Nicholas Brooke, so I need not go over this familiar ground. Shakespeare was clearly fascinated by the Machiavels in Marlowe's plays, and I would make only two qualifications. Although Shakespeare condemns, and compels his audience to condemn both Aaron and Richard III, audiences always respond positively to their vitality; on the other hand, Marlowe, who is thought to condone Barabas and Mortimer, if not Guise, shows nevertheless in *Edward II* that the followers of Machiavel are all converted or destroyed. Gaveston begins by exploiting the King's love and ends with disinterested affection. Spencer and Baldock, who begin as hardheaded careerists, end by thinking more of Edward's fate than of their own:

> *Spencer.* O is he gone? is noble Edward gone?
> Parted from hence, never to see us more!
> Rent sphere of heaven, and, fire, forsake thy orb!

> Earth, melt to air! Gone is my sovereign,
> Gone, gone, alas! never to make return.
> *Baldock*. Spencer, I see our souls are fleeted hence.
> We are deprived the sunshine of our life.
> Make for a new life, man. Throw up thy eyes,
> And heart and hand to heaven's immortal throne
> Pay nature's debt with cheerful countenance.
> Reduce we all our lessons unto this:
> To die, sweet Spencer, therefore live we all:
> Spencer, all live to die, and rise to fall.

They have learned the lesson Duke Vincentio tries to instill into the condemned Claudio. On the other hand, the Machiavellians in the play go to their deaths unredeemed: Mortimer is ruined by his failure to realize the integrity of the young prince; Lightborn—his name an echo of Lucifer— is himself murdered; Matrevis's reward is permission to fly to the savages; Warwick is beheaded. The followers of Machiavel are either converted or destroyed.

* * *

Marlowe and Shakespeare came from roughly the same social stratum and went to the same kind of grammar school; however, they differed so much in temperament and experience that, even if Marlowe were not the only major poet whose cause of death was certified by a coroner's jury, it would still be difficult to believe—though not all find it impossible—that he survived to become the author of most of Shakespeare's plays. The facts of Shakespeare's life are meager and ambiguous: he never saw the inside of a prison and therefore had no dossier. The anecdote about his forestalling Burbage at an assignation is no more than *ben trovato*; and the legacy of the second-best bed tells us nothing about the success or failure of his marriage. Several contemporaries refer to him as "gentle," and his pursuit of a coat of arms suggests that he would not have disapproved of this epithet. We are told that his conversation was witty, but we know nothing of what he said. We cannot imagine him acting as a spy, or going to prison for brawling, or shocking his associates by blaspheming, or spending his last day on earth in the company of a confidence trickster, a spy, and a pickpocket, though we could imagine him in the company of Falstaff.

Yet we can count Marlowe lucky to have been killed by Ingram

Frizer! He otherwise would have been burnt at the stake and shared the fate of Kett. He had been accused of atheism by Robert Greene, and less than three weeks before his death, Kyd's arrest led to an inquiry into the opinions of his fellow-lodger and fellow-dramatist. I agree with Kocher that Kyd's accusations are substantially supported by the evidence of Baines. Kyd, clearly terrified, was anxious to distance himself from Marlowe's character and opinions. He was, said Kyd, "intemperate and of a cruel heart," and he was in the habit of "attempting sudden privy injuries to men," as in his final brawl with Frizer. Not merely was he an atheist, but also a persistent propagandist for the cause. In spite of the appalling risk, "almost into every company he cometh, he persuades men to atheism, willing them not to be afeard of bugbears and hobgoblins, and utterly scorning both god and his ministers": The "first beginning of religion was only to keep men in awe"; "there were people living in the world before Adam"; "St. Paul was a timorous fellow in bidding men to be subject to the magistrates"; "all Protestants were hypocritical asses"; "the angel Gabriel was bawd to the Holy Ghost"; and Jesus had sexual relations both with the woman of Samaria and with St. John the Evangelist. Apart from these religious comments, Marlowe indulged in other scandalous talk. He said that he had as much right to coin as the Queen of England; he advised people to go to King James, and he declared that those who loved not boys and tobacco were fools. The remark about tobacco, if not the other, would have alienated James. But counterfeiting, treason, homosexuality, and blasphemy were all capital offenses: the only question was whether hanging, beheading, or being burnt at the stake was the most appropriate punishment.

Now many of these things may have been said to shock people, and some of them may have been invented to suit his reputation as the author of *Tamburlaine* or *Doctor Faustus*. "Atheist" was a term as elastic as "red" in McCarthy's America or as "Marxist" in Thatcher's Britain. I believe that a truer guide to Marlowe's private opinions may be found in the passages he copied from *The Fall of the Late Arrian*. These consisted of all the key passages, and they suggest that his sympathies were with the Socinians. John Assheton, the late Arrian, had sought to demonstrate that Jesus was a man, with man's infirmities, "subject to the passions of man, as hunger, thirst, weariness and fear." "And to believe, forsooth, that this nature, subject to these infirmities and passions is God, or any part of the divine essence, what is it other but to make God mighty and of power of th'one part, weak and impotent of th'other part—which thing to think were madness and folly." "If Jesus Christ, even he which was born of Mary was God, so shall he be a visible God comprehensible and mortal, which is not counted God with me quoth great Athanasius of Alexandria." Assheton, interrogated by Cranmer, retracted; but Marlowe, if we may judge from his table talk, went a good deal further than Assheton in his satirical remarks. Yet through a character, he continued to speak of the god that

> sits on high and never sleeps,
> Nor in one place is circumscriptible.

Some have argued that Marlowe was perfectly orthodox in his religious ideas. I think it would be more accurate to say that a former theological student would necessarily be aware of theological issues, and that he would make use of them not out of personal conviction, but because of dramatic logic. A man who makes a pact with the devil has, dramatically speaking, to suffer damnation. Nevertheless Marlowe reminds me of a Graham Greene character who, having been brought up a Catholic, and having lost his faith, continually hankers after lost certainties. This would account for the extraordinary poignancy of Mephistophilis's lament:

> Why, this is hell, nor am I out of it.
> Think'st thou that I who saw the face of God
> And tasted the eternal joys of heaven,
> Am not tormented with ten thousand hells
> At being deprived of everlasting bliss?

His theological training is perhaps the thing which most distances Marlowe from Shakespeare. Although it has been argued that in *Measure for Measure* Shakespeare showed awareness of the Catholic, the Anglican, and the Calvinistic conceptions of Grace; although Elizabeth Pope, in a well-known essay, argued that in that play Shakespeare's commentary on the Sermon on the Mount was more impressive, more Christian indeed, than that of contemporary theologians; and though Roy Battenhouse and others have suggested that he knew his St. Augustine, and like him condemned the unfortunate Lucrece, yet the

general impression we get of his work is surely quite different. It is true
that Berowne and his creator exhibit surprising knowledge of the controversy about the translation of *agape*; and that, as Noble has shown,
Shakespeare was acquainted with nearly all the books of the Bible and
could assume that his audience—churchgoers perforce—were similarly acquainted. He possessed a copy of the Geneva Bible. He had read
several works by Erasmus—*The Praise of Folly*, the *Adagia*, the *Colloquia*,
and even the *De conscribendis epistolis*—but not, as far as we know, his
more theological writings.

Shakespeare, at least in his early plays, seems to have conformed
without difficulty, but so undogmatically that it is impossible to tell
from his plays whether he was a secret sympathizer with the old religion, or whether he preferred the Hooker line (accepting it hook, line,
and sinker!). He had at least read Hooker's masterpiece. I have
suggested elsewhere (*Jadavpur University Essays and Studies*, 1981) that at
the end of the sixteenth century a change came over Shakespeare's religious views. Although there are evil characters in most of his early
plays, these are all recognized as exceptions and aberrations—Shylock, Richard III, Don John. In the plays written after 1600, Shakespeare seems to have abandoned belief in the natural goodness of man,
becoming much more aware of his depravity. The noble characters
have to operate in a corrupt world. When Troilus assures Cressida that
he does not doubt her constancy, he adds significantly:

> But something may be done that we will not:
> And sometimes we are devils to ourselves
> When we will tempt the frailty of our powers.

The words remind us of St. Paul's confession: "I do not the good thing
that I would, but the evil which I would not, that I do." In the scene
where Troilus witnesses Cressida's surrender to Diomed, he contrasts
the bonds of heaven uniting him to Cressida, with the bonds of hell,
five-finger-tied, tying her to Diomed. As we know from Chaucer's Parson, these were Looking, Touch, Foul Words, Kissing, and Copulation.

Measure for Measure takes its title from the Sermon on the Mount. It is
concerned with sin, grace, and forgiveness, the liberty on which virtue
depends, and the licence into which it may degenerate. Its central action is the fall of Angelo, who confesses:

> Alack, when once our grace we have forgot,
> Nothing goes right: we would and we would not.

Once again Shakespeare seems to be echoing the Pauline confession.

Bertram's basic sin, from which all others spring, is self-love; and Parolles, the tempter, urges him to follow his own desires. Lavache, the most pessimistic of Shakespeare's Fools, continually returns to the idea of damnation, the primrose way to the everlasting bonfire. He sings a ballad of Helen of Troy, and alters the refrain from one *bad* in ten to one *good* in ten. Two anonymous lords, acting as chorus, comment on Bertram's depravity. "As we are ourselves," says one, "What things we are!" "Merely our own traitors," replies the other. Bertram's admitted valor will be offset by the shame earned by his sexual behavior. The other spokesman sums up the matter:

> The web of our life is of a mingled yarn, good and ill together. Our virtues would be proud if our faults whipped them not; and our crimes would despair if they were not cherished by our virtues.

He is not suggesting that Bertram is exceptionally wicked, quite the contrary. It is mankind as a whole, including themselves, they are deploring. This view of human depravity is not, of course, confined to Shakespeare. It is the stock-in-trade of preachers of all denominations; and it spread from them to secular writers in the last years of Elizabeth's reign—in Fulke Greville's choruses and verse treatises, for example. One expects it in tragedy which depends on human frailty and on the wickedness of society; what is significant in Shakespeare's case is that this somber view of mankind invades his comedies too.

There is another way in which Shakespeare's position was modified before the end of the century. Although Tillyard doubtless exaggerated the extent to which the histories were a vehicle for Tudor propaganda and an expression of the uniformity of the Elizabethan world picture, it is undoubtedly true that Shakespeare, along with most of his fellow-countrymen, appears to have regarded civil war as the worst of secular evils, and therefore to have given a supernatural sanction to the maintenance of order. One cannot imagine Marlowe adopting such a line; even before the end of Elizabeth's reign, Shakespeare himself had reservations. The last eulogies on order are spoken by a devious Archbishop and the fox, Ulysses. After that, Shakespeare ceased not only to personify order but also to associate it with cosmic order. Instead, we have devastating remarks about the unacceptable face of order—authority. Claudio refers bitterly to authority as a demi-god; his sister derides "Man, proud man, / Dressed in a little brief authority," and behaving as a tyrant; while Lear tells us why the great image of authority is "A dog's obeyed in office."

It has been argued by William Elton in *King Lear and the Gods* that Shakespeare's skepticism went further than this, and that in this play,

> By depicting a superstitious pagan progressing toward doubt of his gods, Shakespeare secured for the play the approbation of the less speculative devout, who saw in its direction the victory of the True Faith. . . . Moreover he obtained for it the interest of those more troubled and sophisticated auditors who were not to be stilled by pious assurances in the unsteady new world of the later Renaissance.

Elton implies that Shakespeare shared those doubts, as perhaps he did for the duration and purposes of the play. He was content (as Keats said) to be in mysteries, doubts, and fears, without any irritable reaching after fact and reason. Prayers in *King Lear* receive only dusty answers, and the innocent suffer with the guilty. Wilde's Miss Prism boasted that in her sentimental novel abandoned in the pram, "the good ended happily, the bad unhappily: that is what fiction means." But not the kind of fiction represented in *King Lear*: tragedy is impossible if rewards and punishments are dealt out according to deserts. Poetic justice and great tragedy are incompatible.

It should be remembered, moreover, that both Catholics and Protestants held profoundly pessimistic views about life in this world. Henry Smith, the silver-tongued preacher, declared: "Many are the troubles of the righteous, for they must be made examples of patience, they must suffer their hell here." Although Shakespeare does not pretend that Cordelia's sufferings will be compensated in an afterlife, the ethical teaching of Jesus is everywhere apparent in the play. It fulfills the function of parabolic art which "teaches us to unlearn hatred and to learn love," as Auden said in an early essay.

Most critics assume that Marlowe could never have reached that kind of maturity; but we ought continually to remind ourselves that he was still in his twenties when he died—a reminder that some Shakespearians neglect. One critic who is, I think, in need of this reminder, is Wilbur Sanders who devotes his book, *The Dramatist and the Received Idea*, to the daring proposition that Shakespeare is a better dramatist than Marlowe, who has been absurdly overrated. It is certainly fair to discuss the relative merits of *Edward II, Richard III,* and *Richard II* since all three plays were written in the same two or three years. But is it really fair to accuse Marlowe of jingoism in *The Massacre at Paris* without mentioning the treatment of St. Joan in *Henry VI* or of the French in *Henry V*? Or without making allowances for the fact that *The Massacre* is a bad quarto? In these circumstances, a more valid comparison would be with *The Contention*. Even less justifiable is the comparison of *Doctor Faustus* with *Macbeth*. Here again is the failure to recognize openly that the text of *Doctor Faustus* is mangled; and here again is the absurdity of comparing the work of a man of twenty-eight with that of a man of forty.

When he comes to consider the play in detail, Mr. Sanders becomes even more eccentric. He refers to the lines where Mephistophilis speaks of being deprived of the joys of heaven, but he does not quote them because they might upset his argument. He objects to the conflict in the play between this conception of hell and the physical tortures elsewhere described; but whereas Shakespeare is tacitly commended for appealing on more than one level, Marlowe is condemned for doing the same thing. Mr. Sanders complains that in the appearance of Helen, the humanist and the moralist are at war; yet it could be retorted that the greatness of the play depends on the tension between humanist and moralist. It would be as absurd to complain that Milton gives Comus some of the best poetry in his masque.

An earlier critic, Una Ellis-Fermor, made a related complaint about the address to Helen. She expressed indignation that Marlowe had included this symbol of beauty among the wiles of the tempter, and she accused him of apostasy. She responded to the beauty of the poetry and was apparently unaware that the figure of Helen was the devil in disguise. Yet it was perfectly appropriate that Marlowe should express in the speech his own love of classical literature and the quintessence of beauty which no virtue can digest into words because, as Shelley said, "the mind in creation is like a fading coal."

Mr. Sanders was right to praise the wonderful prose scene in which Faustus says farewell to the scholars; but he spoils this hint of generosity by using it to denigrate the final soliloquy of the hero. He complains of the hectic tone—not inappropriate to the situation, one would have thought—of the "essentially undirected energies" of the verse, of what he calls a perfunctory line ("That Faustus may repent and save his soul") and of the air of contrivance in the lines:

> Fair nature's eye, rise, rise again, and make
> Perpetual day; or let this hour be but
> A year, a month, a week, a natural day.

Mr. Sanders asks, "Do we *need* the repeated 'rise'? Would it matter if the month or the week were omitted?" What Mr. Sanders would regard as virtues in a Shakespeare play are dismissed as blemishes because Marlowe was responsible. He even asks whether one can be entirely happy about the line:

> See, see where Christ's blood streams in the firmament.

He suggests that this soliloquy is an actor's vehicle. "It looks like fine thumping drama, but once one tries to speak it, it becomes embarrassingly stagey." It is surely odd to blame a speech in a drama for being an actor's vehicle, and very odd that Mr. Sanders should say that the lines have "gestural implications which are incipiently comic and depend for their functioning upon an actor who can emotionally intimidate an audience, as apparently Alleyn succeeded in doing." This is surely absurd. I have seen several amateur performances of the play in which the actor, though falling below professional standards, was able to move the audience by the virtue inherent in the words. Mr. Sanders imagines that the element of artificiality in the speech prevents us from being taken into the hero's consciousness, but there is an element of artificiality in all poetic drama. Finally he declares that the quotation from Ovid ("O lente, lente currite noctis equi"), though much admired by literary critics, "is at best a distraction in its self-conscious sophistication, and at worst an obtrusion of a somewhat pedantic Marlowe." It is difficult to imagine a more insensitive criticism of the speech, and it fails even as a one-sided attack because it conflicts with the natural reactions of the ordinary playgoer, and even of the ordinary lover of poetry. It appears to demand of poetry the limitations of naturalism, and this is the more absurd in that Mr. Sanders made no such demand when he wrote his first-rate chapter on *Macbeth*.

* * *

That Marlowe was less than thirty when he died makes it pointless to speculate on how he might have developed. He was, perhaps, the sort of poet who inevitably dies young. On the other hand, *Hero and Leander,* left unfinished at his death, and probably written in his last year, is strong evidence that he was continuing to develop. Unlike his previous work, the poem is a model of control, a blend of sensuous beauty and wit. It might be cited as a perfect illustration of Milton's famous aside about poetry, that it was simple, sensuous and passionate, but with the addition of a subtle irony which Milton did not bargain for. With this poem in mind, it would be absurd to say that Marlowe could not have written satisfactory comedies; and those who think that his missionary fervor would never have permitted him to be fair to his opponents, should remember that the author of *The Necessity of Atheism* ended up by writing *The Triumph of Life.*

In one respect, perhaps, Marlowe could not have been a serious rival to Shakespeare, the respect in which Shakespeare was unique—his use of "conflicting impressions" of his characters to create the illusion of life. Falstaff—this was Morgann's example—is depicted as a *miles gloriosus,* a jester, a realist, a good companion, a thief, a confidence trickster, a whoremaster, and a Lollard; and we believe in him not despite these conflicting impressions, but because of them. Another example is Iago, who is motivated by his resentment of Cassio's promotion, by jealousy of Emilia, by his lust for Desdemona, by his love of power, and by his being a demi-devil anxious to destroy a happy marriage and bring about the damnation of Othello; he is even, perhaps, a racist.

When, however, Marlowe tries to set up such conflicting impressions, he leaves us dissatisfied. One can accept that the barbarous and bloody Tamburlaine might worship Zenocrate's beauty—in its fine excess it is what we might expect; but when he laments the inadequacy of poetry fully to express the poet's vision, one cannot help feeling that this is an intrusion of Marlowe himself:

> If all the pens that ever poets held
> Had fed the feeling of their masters' thoughts,
> And every sweetness that inspir'd their hearts,
> Their minds and muses on admired themes;

> If all the heavenly quintessence they still
> From their immortal flowers of poesy,
> Wherein as in a mirror we perceive
> The highest reaches of a human wit;
> If these had made one poem's period,
> And all combin'd in beauty's worthiness,
> Yet should there hover in their restless heads,
> One thought, one grace, one wonder, at the least,
> Which into words no virtue can digest.

That Marlowe himself realized that these lines were out of character can be seen from those that follow, in which Tamburlaine comments on the unseemliness of his effeminate musings, although he defends them on the ground that love inspires the desire for glory. In an earlier speech, after his treatment of Cosroe, Tamburlaine justifies his behavior by the example of Jupiter; but the sweet fruition of an earthly crown, as many critics have recognized, comes as a strange climax to the praise of knowledge, which would seem to be more appropriate to a Faustus, or to a Marlowe:

> Our souls whose faculties can comprehend
> The wondrous architecture of the world,
> And measure every wandering planet's course,
> Still climbing after knowledge infinite
> And always moving as the restless spheres.

But if the speech astonishes us on the lips of Tamburlaine, it might seem to be equally inappropriate in the mouth of his creator, the secret agent. It would be as astonishing to hear that an employee of the F.B.I. had written *The Waste Land,* or that one of Smiley's people had written *Four Quartets*.

Marlowe's Mind
and the
Heart of Darkness

NORMAN RABKIN

The pun of my title intends a paradox which will be the subject of my brief essay, a paradox that I hope to glorify rather than to resolve.

I begin with an anecdote. Several years ago, frustrated by one of the famous cruces in Marlowe—I can't remember now whether it was the sublime bathos of Tamburlaine's ending his most intoxicatingly inspiring speech with "the sweet fruition of an earthly crown" or Faustus's inability to remember the second half of any biblical text he quoted—I remarked to the late C. L. Barber that Marlowe must be the stupidest of our great poets.[1] He responded, with the kind of dialectical shock and impassioned thought that made conversation with him always so exciting, that he had been just about to say that the more he read and studied Marlowe the more convinced he became that every line of his best work simply bowled him over with the power and richness of intellect that produced it.

The dilemma posed by that conversation is represented in two of the best books about Marlowe that I have ever read, both written almost simultaneously and almost diametrically opposed to one another. I refer to Judith Weil's *Christopher Marlowe: Merlin's Prophet*[2] and Constance Brown Kuriyama's *Hammer or Anvil: Psychological Patterns in*

Christopher Marlowe's Plays, published in 1980.[3] Together they deepen
the problem suggested by my conversation with Barber so profoundly
that I want, all too briefly, to summarize them, restricting their analyses of particular plays, for the sake of economy and clarity, to *Tamburlaine* and *Doctor Faustus.*

Judith Weil's subtitle, "Merlin's Prophet," borrowed from
Rabelais, suggests, as she explains, that Marlowe is a conscious
"rhetorical provocateur" (p. 1). Through his skill as a playwright,
Marlowe gives an "impression of a personality"; recognizing this fact,
we must revise some of the questions we are used to asking about him.
"Instead, for example, of asking why he was a rebellious free-thinker,
we must ask why he wanted some of his contemporaries to *believe* he
was a rebellious free-thinker" (p. 2). As her argument develops, Weil
insists always on Marlowe's intentionality, his control of himself as
well as of his audience. Employing a deliberately "ironic style,"
Marlowe resembles Erasmus, to whom the book repeatedly compares
him, and the fact that he hides always behind an ironic mask calls into
question even, in Weil's words, "common assumptions about his personal knavery" (p. 2). If Marlowe's heroes strike their audiences as
patently foolish or misguided in their aspirations, it is those
"characters then, but not Marlowe, who fail to criticize their visions
when they attempt to turn them into actions" (p. 19).

Treating the *Tamburlaine* sequence as a single work, Weil shrewdly
adopts Sidney's distinction between the poet and the historian in order
to make sense of the play's apparent contradictions between heroic
afflatus and satirical deflation. Tamburlaine, she argues, is "the Poet
who constantly uses his own 'best wisdom' in order to frame himself
as an example, but Marlowe is "the Historian who chronicles the gradual unbridling of wickedness in his warrior-poet and repeatedly hints
that Tamburlaine is foolish" (p. 106). The plays are undeniably complex because Marlowe's attitude is complex and he is writing tragedies
rather than "moral allegories" (p. 107), and in some splendid analyses
she displays the "verbal storm of contradictory attitudes [that] swirls
furiously about Tamburlaine himself " (p. 105), describing the work
as a "baffling . . . combination of Christian allegory, based upon apoc-
alyptic allusions, with tantalizing references to classical gods, heroes,
and monsters," "a whirlwind of possibilities" (*loc. cit.*). But for all the
complex irony of the repeated contrast between the strength which
Tamburlaine imagines and proclaims and his essential weakness, such

antinomies are, in Weil's view, the product of consciously ironic design: "Marlowe often organizes his discourse [note the word] so as to
throw weight upon critical statements which undercut or puncture
more poetic ones" (p. 111).

As for *Faustus*, the notorious theological complexities of that play are
the result of "Marlowe's strategy" (p. 73); "We can surmise, I think,"
she says, "that Marlowe deliberately sought to gain sympathy for
Faustus by means of a speech which subtly exposes him" (p. 74); "the
fifth act . . . is calculated [again, note the word], I think, to acquaint
the audience with the fatal ignorance which abides within the hero's
knowledge" (p. 72). Marlowe, in short, resembles Erasmus in devising
an ironic encomium to folly in order to undermine his own construction, and the perplexing bits of evidence that make it possible to see
Faustus either as archetypal Promethean hero—Faustian man—or as
consistent fool, as proof of the freedom of human will or as refutation of
that notion, represent for Weil both a consistent theological position
obscured by Marlowe's ironic stance and a carefully constructed theatrical design. "Marlowe may adhere to Augustine's psychology of sin,"
Weil observes. "I doubt that he can fully have shared Augustine's—or
St. Paul's—anti-intellectual bias" (p. 51). Thus, as she can speak of the
"fundamental thematic order" and the "great dialectical vigour" (p.
117) of the Tamburlaine plays, she sees Marlowe's "ironic art" (p.
174) in control of *Doctor Faustus*. I could not hope to sum up Weil's
thesis better than she does herself:

> Marlowe's merciful treatment of his characters suggests that they
> are obsessively self-bound. But it also implies that all are, like
> Faustus, potentially amiable, open, responsible, and capable of us-
> ing their extraordinary freedom to change themselves.   (p. 176)

Weil's verb "obsessively" is the link between her book and Kuriyama's; it is also the mark of their difference from one another. For it is
Kuriyama's thesis that Marlowe, rather than his characters, is obsessive. To be more precise, the plots, action, imagery, and symbolism of
Marlowe's plays reveal him incontrovertibly, as do the facts of his life,
to be the creature of his own psychology. His personality is identical to
those of groups of homosexuals studied in 1962 and 1967; the studies
examined their parents and their relations with them, their sexual

identification, their relation to authority, and their anal-phallic aggressive tendencies. Such a description of Kuriyama's thesis betrays
the critical subtlety with which she develops both her psychoanalytic
argument and her readings, her superb attentiveness to detail, and the
delicacy as well as the force of her book, and I shall do her even more
injustice than I did Weil in summarizing her arguments as decorum
requires. But, for all the virtues I have just indicated, her thesis is
nevertheless bold enough to justify such reduction. A characteristic instance is her summary of her own brilliant and subtly argued account
of *Tamburlaine*:

> Tamburlaine as a whole is ethically, thematically, and causally
> incoherent. . . . If I were asked to reconstruct hypothetically, on
> the basis of such evidence, the authorial mental state that might
> produce such a conjunction of concepts and feelings, I would have
> to say that it was probably one of intense conflict of a marked ho-
> mosexual character. I would add that if we are willing to entertain
> this hypothesis, and assume that the play is indeed a tentative
> symbolic working out of a homosexual conflict, we will find that
> the hypothesis has value both as a coherent description and as a
> means of resolving some of the most difficult problems of interpre-
> tation.   (pp. 18-19)

These problems include such as the following:

> The play represents two views of man's situation. Either he is total-
> ly in control or he is totally controlled. Either he holds the fates fast
> bound in iron chains or he is totally at the mercy of capricious,
> irrational forces that make him a king one day and a slave the next.
> . . . In relation to his fate he is either master or slave, hammer or
> anvil.   (p. 17).

At the outset Kuriyama derides the "blithe unanimity" with which
Marlowe's plays were [interpreted as] primarily an expression of their
author's unorthodox beliefs" (p. 1), and, as if answering Weil, she argues that "it is fatal to approach [*Tamburlaine*] with the conviction that
the author is a totally conscious creator, or that his works are shaped
exclusively by the philosophical systems or values of his age" (p. 8).
The *Tamburlaine* plays, like all the others, are "symbolic attempts to
resolve emotional conflicts that characteristically accompany a partic-

ular homosexual adaptation" (p. 44). To give Kuriyama her full due as a critic who is now, as it happens, studying Renaissance philosophy, she acknowledges that Marlowe's "exceptional intelligence enables him eventually to put enough distance between himself and his hero that he loses considerable faith in Tamburlaine" (p. 44); but the burden of her analysis, even of the plays' theology, is its psychoanalytic portrait of Marlowe.

And so it is with *Doctor Faustus*. To be sure, she acknowledges that the play "draws on so many orthodox ideas, extensively and redundantly catalogued in scholarly articles, that the orthodoxy of [its] basic premises can hardly be denied" (p. 95), but her explication primarily sees *Doctor Faustus* as "still another reenactment of the Marlovian son's confrontation with the hostile, threatening father" (p. 116).

> In *Doctor Faustus* . . . we have still another version of the same pathological and destructive father-son relationships that characterize *Tamburlaine,* and once again, an examination of a relationship symbolically represented in the play accounts more satisfactorily for what we find on the surface than do attempts to explain the play in terms of Renaissance theology. . . . In fact, it is possible to read Faustus' history as an elaborate metaphor for homosexuality, operating simultaneously on various levels of meaning, which permits the expression of complex and conflicting attitudes toward a homosexual adaptation.   (p. 116)

I must repeat that my oversimplification of their arguments has made both Weil and Kuriyama sound more doctrinaire and narrow-minded than either is. In fact, writing unaware of the other's work in progress, each concedes something to the other's position: Weil insists that critics who discuss only Marlowe's "intellectual control of his art sometimes seem to have neglected his air and fire" (p. 5); and Kuriyama suggests that Marlowe "remained a scholar by temperament" (p. 226) and that his "rejection of authority . . . led him to raise questions that others preferred to ignore, and because of his searching intelligence his writing still retains much of its power to jolt and unsettle" (p. 227). More striking than that is their fundamental agreement, arrived at across a seemingly unbridgeable gap, on the essential qualities of Marlowe's best plays, their complex expression of conflicted attitudes toward their great protagonists. As interpretations of the plays, Weil's and Kuriyama's are far more similar than dissimilar.

But their differences are disturbing. For Kuriyama there is virtually nothing but the strange personality of Christopher Marlowe, using his plays to resolve emotional conflicts over which he had no control; for Weil there is scarcely a person behind the plays, only the simulacrum of a personality artfully constructed to preside over the consciously designed encomia to late sixteenth-century folly.

Who is right? If one of these persuasive critics is telling the story as it should be told, must not the other be entirely wrong? I shall answer not with the dissertation I am tempted to offer, but with a single word: no. I promised a paradox, and this is it. In the drama of the English Renaissance—as, one might venture to say, in all the crucial moments of the world's literature—circumstances have so conspired that it becomes possible, even inevitable, that as they express their own private and obsessive conflicts the greatest writers simultaneously involve themselves in the major intellectual and social conflicts of their day. If *Faustus* or *Tamburlaine* suggests unresolvable polarities between attitudes toward authoritarian power in the state or the heavens, we need only remind ourselves that these plays were staged toward the end of Elizabeth's increasingly authoritarian reign and only a half-century before a revolution that, at least for two decades, would deny the validity of royal power itself; and that they breathed the air of a religious controversy no less ferocious or fundamental. I have argued elsewhere that it is the very genius of Elizabethan and Jacobean drama to have found, by the accidents of its birth and growth, a medium in which the personal conflicts of a group of supreme artists—pre-eminently Shakespeare, of course—found a public language and a sympathetic audience who recognized in the dramatization of those conflicts the reflection of their own concerns.[4]

"By the accidents of birth and growth"—I need only point to a few familiar phenomena: the rhetorical structure of debate that Joel Altman has so persuasively shown to have been built into the foundations of sixteenth-century theater;[5] the contradictory impulses yoked together in the marriage of native and classical traditions and conventions; the centrifugal force apparent even in the mysteries and moralities caused by the increasingly discrepant desires to entertain and to instruct; the not always covert admiration of playwrights as well as audiences for villains ostensibly designed for condemnation; and the powerful, mysterious, often clearly eccentric personalities of dramatists like Marlowe, Kyd, Jonson, Webster, and—dare I say it?—Shakespeare. Thus, if for the most personal of reasons, Marlowe is ulitmately unable to decide whether to present Faustus as a foolish sinner needlessly earning eternal damnation or an admirable rebel against a relentlessly cruel and nemesis-like divinity, his confusion dresses itself in the robes of the theological debates of his day and expresses itself, as Shakespeare's more modulated ambivalences will, in a dramaturgy that cannot be reduced to simple answers and that is both uniquely personal and magnificently public.

The issues raised by these two books and by my juxtaposition of them are too large for full resolution here, but since I have focused my discussion of the two books on their analyses of two plays, it might be appropriate to suggest how the authors' opposed interpretations can be supported by a kind of analysis that is committed to the methodology of neither. In the case of *Tamburlaine*, I have demonstrated elsewhere the crucial significance of what at the beginning of this essay I referred to as a notorious problem in the interpretation of the play, the shocking conclusion of the hero's grandest statement of his splendid aspiration in a mundane line that seems to undercut everything that has preceded it.[6] As an economical way to get at the heart of the play's problematic, I shall briefly rehearse my argument here.

> The thirst of raigne and sweetnes of a crown,
> That caused the eldest sonne of heavenly Ops,
> To thrust his doting father from his chaire,
> And place himselfe in the Emperiall heaven,
> Moov'd me to manage armes against thy state.
> What better president than mighty Jove?
> Nature that fram'd us of foure Elements,
> Warring within our breasts for regiment,
> Doth teach us all to have aspyring minds:
> Our soules, whose faculties can comprehend
> The wondrous Architecture of the world:
> And measure every wandring plannets course:
> Still climing after knowledge infinite,
> And alwaies mooving as the restless Spheares,
> Wils us to weare our selves and never rest,
> Untill we reach the ripest fruit of all,
> That perfect blisse and sole felicitie,
> The sweet fruition of an earthly crown.
>   (ll. 836–880)

Any sensitive reader of the play, and any knowledgeable reader of its criticism, recognizes the problem: the speech boldly begins with a reminder of the significance of man's creation in God's image, moves from praise of aspiration in both aspects of life, active and contemplative, in language glorifying the soul and the universe, only to end in apparently bathetic anticlimax. The critical argument, which I shall not catalogue here, ranges from guesses that by the end of the speech Tamburlaine is worn out to suggestions that Marlowe is definitely blasphemous (a conclusion hardly supported by what happens to the hero in the second Part of the play) to other suggestions that the playwright uses the end of the speech as a way of demonstrating the *hero's* blasphemy and thus, as such critics would have it, of consistently denigrating Tamburlaine, setting him up as a cautionary example of the Christian version of hubris.[7]

Judith Weil, who writes as convincingly about this speech as she does about all of Marlowe, argues that the lines, like the discrepancy between the hero's aspirations and his achievements, exemplify the "disproportions" between character and dramatic action [that] create instability in all of Marlowe's plays" (p. 16); Constance Kuriyama argues that the "ambiguity" of the speech is characteristic of Marlowe's own ambivalent attitude toward authority, both defiantly challenging that paternal power and terrified by the effrontery of his rejection of it (p. 10). Clearly both Weil's and Kuriyama's views can be reconciled: Marlowe's personal conflict about authority, his desire to rebel against it and his knowledge that that rebellion is necessarily self-destructive, is consistent with the picture of an artist in control of his work, filling such a speech as we are glancing at with the lore of a multitude of Renaissance writers, creating a hero whose true power for an audience lies precisely, as both Weil and Kuriyama would agree, in his inscrutable ambiguity. And the questions aroused by his ambiguity, as I suggested at the outset, are just the questions about the relation of man to secular and divine authority that are at stake in the years of Marlowe's pre-eminence on the stage.

The combination of a knowledge of the theological and humanistic issues involved in *Doctor Faustus* and of a design so perfect that it won the praise of Goethe, even in the butchered state in which the text survives, with the most mystifying ambivalence continues to produce a flood of controversialist criticism that seems unstanchable. The perhaps unresolvable issues that divide critics of the play have definitively been made clear in one of the few truly indispensable pieces of Marlowe criticism, the late Max Bluestone's "*Libido Speculandi*: Doctrine and Dramaturgy in Contemporary Interpretations of Marlowe's *Doctor Faustus*."[8] What Bluestone shows is the impossibility of deciding whether Marlowe advocates or condemns his hero's rebellion, whether he believes that salvation is possible up to the last moment or implacably denied from the first, whether God is a loving father or an overbearing bully. If such questions agonize Marlowe, other literature of the period would suggest that he is not alone; one need only think of the similar theological questions aroused, argued about by critics, never resolved, torturous to audience as to critics and *dramatis personae* as presumably to the author himself, in *King Lear*; one might look forward a few decades to *Paradise Lost*. Once again, Weil's carefully presented argument that the ambiguity that makes *Faustus* a powerful and disturbing drama is not in any way contradictory of Kuriyama's thesis that the play acts out Marlowe's anguished personal tragedy.

To end where I began: reading Marlowe in the years since my conversation with Barber, I have found myself inclining, despite all of the above, toward his view—that is, toward admiring the intellectual brilliance which Judith Weil celebrates and even Constance Kuriyama acknowledges; and I had planned to end my essay with that confession. And then, in the moment of writing my peroration, I turned over *Hammer or Anvil* and reread Barber's jacket blurb, a characteristically astute and eloquent bit of criticism which suggests that perhaps he was simultaneously moving toward my abandoned corner: Kuriyama's book, he says, is a

> very interesting, self-consistent account of the poet's development as a man, and as an artist using and interacting with his art; there are many places where its account is moving, indeed awesome, in penetrating formulation of the predicament animating the works and the changing attitude expressed and embodied in them towards [now he quotes Kuriyama] "the psychological and intellectual cul-de-sac which Marlowe flailed about in."

It is the particular pleasure of the study of great literature that in the last analysis there is no last analysis: between the mind and the heart of darkness we do not ultimately have to choose.

NOTES

1. *Tamburlaine*, l. 880. My text for Marlowe is C. F. Tucker Brooke, ed., *The Works of Marlowe* (Oxford: Clarendon Press, 1910).

2. Judith Weil, *Christopher Marlowe: Merlin's Prophet* (Cambridge: Cambridge University Press, 1977).

3. Constance Brown Kuriyama, *Hammer or Anvil: Psychological Patterns in Christopher Marlowe's Plays* (New Brunswick, N.J.: Rutgers University Press, 1980).

4. Norman Rabkin, "Stumbling Toward Tragedy," in Coppélia Kahn and Peter Erickson, eds., *'Shakespeare's Rough Magic': Essays in Honor of C. L. Barber* (Newark, Del.: University of Delaware Press, 1985).

5. Joel B. Altman, *The Tudor Play of Mind: Rhetorical Inquiry and The Development of Elizabethan Drama* (Berkeley and Los Angeles, Cal.: University of California Press, 1978).

6. "Stumbling Toward Tragedy."

7. The explanation that what Havelock Ellis called the "Scythian bathos" of the end of the speech should be attributed to the hero's exhaustion can be found in Una Ellis-Fermor, ed., *Tamburlaine the Great*, in R. H. Case, general editor, *The Works and Life of Christopher Marlowe* (London: Methuen, 1930), p. 113; one instance among many of the view that Marlowe consciously presents a derogatory view of Tamburlaine as blasphemous can be found in Roy W. Battenhouse, *Marlowe's Tamburlaine: A Study in Renaissance Moral Philosophy* (Nashville, Tenn.: Vanderbilt University Press, 1941).

8. In Norman Rabkin, ed., *Reinterpretations of Elizabethan Drma: Selected Papers from the English Institute* (New York and London: Columbia University Press, 1969), pp. 33–88.

Shakespeare's Use of Marlowe
in *As You Like It*

KAY STANTON

In *As You Like It*, Shakespeare unmistakably invokes Christopher Marlowe, with Phebe directly quoting *Hero and Leander*, I. 176: "Dead shepherd, now I find thy saw of might, / 'Who ever loved that loved not at first sight?'" (III.v.81–82).[1] The play creates an appropriate context for these lines by being self-consciously "literary" throughout, referring to kinds of artistic creation and to specific modes of poetic expression. Shakespeare alludes obliquely to Chaucer, Sidney, and others, and directly to Ovid. But Marlowe is recalled most often and most strikingly. Besides Phebe's lines above, other references to Marlowe occur in Rosalind-as-Ganymede's condemnation of the chronicler of Hero and Leander's story (IV.i.97-106), and in Touchstone's complaint about being struck "more dead than a great reckoning in a little room" (III.iii.14-15).[2] This last instance is actually a portmanteau reference, since it is both a biographical allusion to the manner of Marlowe's death and a literary allusion to a similar line in *The Jew of Malta:* "Infinite riches in a little room" (I.i.37).[3] The ambiguities in Shakespeare's use of Marlowe recapitulate the subtleties of Shakespeare's analysis of poets and poetry in *As You Like It*.

I shall examine the problem of how Shakespeare uses Marlowe, and whether his references to Marlowe are meant as tribute or ridicule. My position is that they are both: because they can survive ridicule, they demonstrate the highest possible tribute that one great poet can offer another. Furthermore, Shakespeare's treatment of Marlowe is intimately bound up with his treatments of Ovid, Chaucer, Sidney, and the aesthetic philosophers, as well as his references to himself and to poetry itself. The implications of these allusions reveal themselves gradually and build a powerful statement on what poetry is or should be and what great poets are.

Shakespeare's play establishes and continually repeats a pattern of poetic outpouring followed by undercutting or qualification. Charles the wrestler's poetic lines about Arden (I.i.120-125), alluding to Robin Hood and the Golden Age, evoke traditions of romantic legend and pastoral innocence, but our first glimpses of the forest contrast those traditions to the reality of the exiles' state. Yet despite these harsh conditions, characters often wax poetic in Arden. Duke Senior makes sweet the "uses of adversity" in a blank verse speech that poeticizes nature (II.i.1-18). The "woeful pageant" of the starving and desperate Orlando provokes Jaques to utter one of the most memorable blank verse poetic speeches in the Shakespeare canon, the Seven Ages speech (II.vii.139-166)). Both of these blank verse poetic speeches are undercut, however. After Amiens remarks that the Duke translates the "stubbornness of fortune" into a sweet style, the First Lord then recounts Jaques's indictment of the Duke as usurper of the forest. When Orlando carries in the ancient servant Adam, his action directly contradicts Jaques's conclusion in the Seven Ages speech that in old age a man is "sans everything."

Poetry fares worst when characters use it to express love. Rosalind, Celia, Touchstone, and Jaques unmercifully mock Orlando's love poetry. The disdainful Phebe ridicules and rejects the pastorally poetic lovemaking of Silvius. When the cynical Touchstone succumbs to love and writes poetry, Audrey frustrates him by her lack of understanding. Satire or other means of qualification counterpoints every poem and even every poetic sentiment.

In this play, the greatest English poet seems to criticize not only the specific poetic efforts of his characters, but also poetry itself. Touchstone and Rosalind, the two characters with the most intelligence and pithiest judgment, both possess some qualifications to speak about poetry, since Touchstone composes verse and Rosalind is the subject of every poem given in the play.[4] In analyzing poetry, both allude to Marlowe and to other poets, and both come to the same conclusion: poetry lies.

Among the verse-makers of the play, Touchstone is the only one who self-consciously defines himself in terms of a poetic heritage. Through puns, he comically compares Ovid's plight as a misunderstood poet to his own: he is with Audrey and her goats, "as the most capricious poet, honest Ovid, was among the Goths" (III.iii.7-9). The pun on goats-Goths connects to a pun on "capricious," deprived from Latin "caper," male goat; thus "capricious" connotes "lecherous." By making these associations, Touchstone does here what he does habitually: he brings down to his level those greater than himself. Ovid was exiled among the Goths for the "immorality" of his verses; the lecherous versifier Touchstone is among the goats by his choice of a goat-girl as lust-object. Touchstone's mention of Ovid leads to his reference to Marlowe: "When a man's verses cannot be understood, nor a man's good wit seconded with the forward child, understanding, it strikes a man more dead than a great reckoning in a little room." Marlowe is metaphorically even "more dead" by misunderstanding than by the "great reckoning" that led to his actual death. The reference to Marlowe follows easily after that to Ovid, since Ovid influenced Marlowe, Marlowe translated Ovid, and Marlowe, like Ovid, suffered for the "immorality" of his work. Through the links established by these references, Ovid, Marlowe, and Touchstone are all three struck dead by misunderstanding. But if Touchstone can put himself into the company of Ovid and Marlowe, so certainly could Shakespeare. His own contemporaries considered him to be in the tradition of Ovid, and Marlowe definitely influenced him. Thus Touchstone's remarks about poets and poetry also apply ultimately to Shakespeare himself.

Although Shakespeare often writes jokingly if not disparagingly of poets, he at least as often allows characters to be "poetic" without undermining their intentions. In *As You Like It*, however, no one is allowed to be "poetic," and that is different from Shakespeare's usual practice. Here, also, he focuses more on the subject of poetry than he does elsewhere and is most "self-consciously" literary in his allusions. Not only bad poets are ridiculed, but also great ones, because verse is the medium through which the criticism is expressed. Shakespeare manages to be anti-pastoral within a pastoral and to be anti-poetic while being poetic, such that the effect produced is of a poetic pastoral. This amazing feat seems to be accomplished *because* he has already applied the strongest kind of poetic criticism to himself and still has chosen poetry (poetic drama). Thus he, more than anyone else, knows what it means to be a poet and what tests determine poetry's greatness. He then applies tests to Marlowe, Ovid, and others, as well as to himself, in the play.

Because poets "die" by misunderstanding, they seem to deserve sympathy—until Touchstone tells Audrey what being "poetical" means: "the truest poetry is the most feigning; and lovers are given to poetry; and what they swear in poetry, it may be said, as lovers, they do feign" (III.iii.19-22). Commentators often read these lines as referring to the recent debate on the truth of poetry carried on between Stephen Gosson and Sir Phillip Sidney, and discussed by numerous others.[5] However, Touchstone's position on this question is complicated by means of a pun on "feign," pretend, and "fain," desire.[6] Thus the "truest poetry" both desires the most and pretends the most. Lovers are given to poetry because they "fain," desire consummation with the beloved. To make what they desire come true, poet–lovers "feign." They pretend in swearing the truth of whatever needs to be said to seduce the love object. By his punning commentary on the most controversial literary question of the day, Touchstone identifies himself with the aesthetic philosophers, just as he had linked himself with Ovid and Marlowe. But through his analysis, lofty aesthetic principles come down to sex.

In practical application of his aesthetic theory, Touchstone wishes that Audrey were "poetical," because she swears she is "honest." The use of "honest" here harks back to and redefines "honest Ovid." Because "honest Ovid" is a poet, he is a liar, as are Marlowe, Touchstone, Shakespeare, and every other poet. Furthermore, "honesty" for all love poets is a guise for sexual libertinism. But one more twist complicates Touchstone's analysis. By comparing himself to Ovid and other feigning poets while he poetically addresses his beloved, Touchstone condemns everything he says here as a lie, by his own definition.

Since Touchstone is a professional fool, the reliability of his aesthetic evaluation may be suspect; yet the sensible Rosalind essentially seconds his position. Physically disguised as the male Ganymede, Rosalind further poses as "Rosalind" to "cure" Orlando of love. When she states that, in the person of "Rosalind," she will not have him, Orlando swears, "Then, in my own person, I die" (IV.i.93), thereby illustrating Touchstone's definition of poetical feigning. As a purgative to this poetical oath, Rosalind tells Orlando to "die by attorney," because, since the world began, "there was not any man died in his own person, videlicet, in a love cause"(IV.i.96–97). Those who reputedly died for love, like Troilus and Leander, did not do so in their own persons, but by "attorney," the substitute selves created for them by "foolish chroniclers." These chroniclers are poets, who weave "lies" when reporting on real, unpoetic lives. Because such poeticizing is unrealistic, it is "foolish." Thus Rosalind associates poetry with both feigning and folly, restating the message of the fool, Touchstone.

Again like Touchstone, Rosalind uses literary allusion to strengthen her point. Chaucer is presumably the "foolish chronicler" of the Troilus story, Marlowe of the Hero and Leander. But just as Touchstone's allusions ultimately include Shakespeare himself, so do Rosalind's. *As You Like It* was registered in 1600 and Shakespeare's version of *Troilus and Cressida* in 1603; Shakespeare probably knew when composing *As You Like It* that he would himself soon become a "foolish chronicler" of the Troilus story. Also, *As You Like It* was most likely still performed at the Globe after he had written *Troilus and Cressida*. Therefore, through Rosalind, Shakespeare calls not only Chaucer and Marlowe foolish liars, but also himself.

Several complexities emerge from Rosalind's allusion to the chroniclers of the Troilus story. In his *Troilus and Creseyde*, Chaucer self-consciously and continually refers to his sources, previous chroniclers of the story. On the one hand, past versions restrict him, because he must repeat unpleasant details of the story that they report. For example, he urges that female readers not be angry with him because of Creseyde's infidelity; they can read of her sins in other books. On the other hand, the work of others frees him to concentrate on the parts of the story that most interest him; he directs those who wish to learn more of Troilus's battles to Dares, who relates them all. In his apostrophe to his book, he tells it not to envy any other poem, but to be humble before them all, and to kiss the steps where Vergil, Ovid, Homer, Lucan, and Statius walk. Thus Chaucer follows in the steps of Ovid and others, just as Touchstone does. But Chaucer elevates his predecessors; Touchstone makes his descend. In his *Troilus and Cressida,* Shakespeare will not refer directly to Chaucer or his other sources; however, he will alter and use a famous line from Marlowe.[7]

After Chaucer notes briefly that Achilles killed Troilus, he dwells on the idea that love was responsible for Troilus's undoing, and he presents Troilus's example as a warning for young lovers. In Chaucer, then, Troilus dies for love and is "one of the patterns of love," so Chaucer undoubtedly fits Rosalind's depiction of a "foolish chronicler." But Shakespeare's Troilus will follow the patterns of Paris and Menelaus more than he will strike a pattern for himself. Although Rosalind states here that "Troilus had his brains dashed out with a Grecian club" (IV.i.97–98), in Shakespeare's *Troilus and Cressida,* Troilus will not die at all, by love or otherwise.

This passage where Rosalind discusses feigning chroniclers also involves complications in its allusion to Marlowe. A particular oddity in this allusion lies in Rosalind's assertion that "Leander, he would have lived many a fair year, though Hero had turned nun" (IV.i.100–101). In Marlowe's rendering of the story, Hero already is a nun when she meets Leander—a nun of Venus—and Hero's role as Venus's nun suggests sexual licentiousness rather than chastity. This word play on "nun" is connected to Touchstone's pun on "honest," forming another link between the speeches.

One more dimension to the reference to Marlowe is that just as Marlowe adds allusions to Ganymede in his story, in *As You Like It* another Ganymede alludes to Marlowe. In Marlowe's poem, men often mistake Leander for a woman because of his beauty, but homosexual Neptune mistakes the youth for a homosexual Ganymede. Many characters in Shakespeare's play mistake Rosalind for a man, but heterosexual Phebe mistakes her for a heterosexual Ganymede. Leander and Rosalind, then, each become unwilling objects of same-sex lust because each is thought to be a suitably sexed Ganymede. Leander's difficulty in escaping Neptune's lustful embrace in the Hellespont may foreshadow Marlowe's planned treatment of Leander's end. Leander might indeed have died for love: not because of his own love for Hero, but because of Neptune's unrequited homosexual love for him. Within the part of the poem Marlowe completed, however, Leander rejects homosexual temptation to consummate his love with Hero. Rosalind's use of her bisexual identity as Ganymede-"Rosalind" to "cure" Orlando of love for Rosalind may be a test of Orlando's sexual bonding. Although he plays at love with Ganymede, Orlando ultimately rejects his male "Rosalind" for his female love.

In her condemnation of the chroniclers of the Troilus and Leander stories, then, Rosalind introduces allusions that complicate her point more than they reinforce it. The feignings of Chaucer and Marlowe in her account lead to the feignings of Shakespeare and of herself. Maura Slattery Kuhn proposes that Rosalind's statement "But these are all lies" ultimately means not only that poetry lies, but also that Rosalind's own interpretations of Troilus's and Leander's deaths are deliberate lies.[8] If Rosalind lies in calling chroniclers' stories lies, she again echoes Touchstone, who "lies" while calling poets liars. Besides, just as Audrey cannot comprehend Touchstone's remarks on poetry, so Orlando misses Rosalind's meaning. As soon as Rosalind declares that "Men have died from time to time and worms have eaten them, but not for love" (IV.i.106-108), Orlando swears, "I would not have my right Rosalind of this mind, for I protest her frown might kill me." The message that poetry lies fails to convince its audiences.

In between these two allusive passages is Phebe's couplet invoking Marlowe and quoting from *Hero and Leander*. Phebe's use of allusion differs somewhat from that of Touchstone and Rosalind. Their references to Marlowe are oblique, but Phebe's is direct. Touchstone and Rosalind set their allusions into a context critical of poetry, but Phebe alludes by means of poetry—a rhymed couplet. Touchstone and Rosalind use allusion wittily, whereas Phebe is entirely serious. But through its own complexities, Phebe's allusion, like theirs, becomes a comment on the interrelationships among poetry, feigning, and death.

Before Phebe meets Ganymede, she has basically the same attitude that Touchstone and Rosalind have—that poetic sentiments of lovers are lies. In response to Silvius's poetic protestations of love for her, she, like Rosalind, insists that unrequited love cannot kill a lover, and she, like Touchstone, reveals the feigning-faining beneath lovers' poetic oaths (III.v.1-34). Yet when Ganymede chides her for such chiding, she falls in love. She proclaims that she now recognizes the truth behind Marlowe's "saw," and therefore quotes it. Alexander Leggatt suggests that Phebe mocks the convention of love by taking it too literally, but that once she sees Ganymede, she is "forced to acknowledge the truth behind the cliché."[9] Rosalind's position, however, essentially is that the clichés are lies, while Touchstone's is that the truths are lies. Touchstone and Rosalind use their allusions to support their position that poetry lies, whereas Phebe uses hers to trumpet her departure from that stance. To Touchstone and Rosalind, Marlowe is one of the poet-liars; to Phebe, Marlowe represents the epitome of poetic truth in love.

As a result of her "conversion" to love, Phebe realizes that only poetry can truly articulate her feelings. But Phebe's love is based upon a lie: that Ganymede is a man. Once again, Marlowe is associated with a lie. In the context of *Hero and Leander,* the line about "love at first sight" is "true"; in Phebe's situation, "love at first sight" becomes a lie. Thus because Phebe fains, desires love of Ganymede, she is given to poetry, which feigns. Marlowe typifies for Phebe the "truest poet," but in application to her situation, he is the "most feigning." Phebe's couplet, then, demonstrates Touchstone's theory.

As does Touchstone, Phebe composes verse when she falls in love. Before Touchstone writes love verses to Audrey, he parodies one of Orlando's love poems to Rosalind. Although his lines to Audrey are not quoted in the play, his parody is, and it is half again as long as Orlando's original. Touchstone is thus a derivative poet and a lying chronicler. He turns Orlando's "true" chronicle of his love into a bawdy burlesque. He identifies Ovid and Marlowe as his poetic forebears, but then uses them to support his stand that the underlying motive of all love poetry is seduction. Phebe, too, is a derivative poet. She makes her rhymed couplet by adding a line of her own to Marlowe's line. Later, she writes a poem to Ganymede that is a blatantly sexual offer of herself. If Phebe gleans a truth about poetry and love from Marlowe, it is essentially Touchstone's point that poetry is a vehicle for sex. She does not praise Marlowe so much as she exploits him.

Not only does Phebe single out Marlowe as her spokesman, but also she pictures him as a "Dead shepherd." Her choice and depiction of Marlowe have provoked critical commentary. To Eamon Grennan, Phebe's invocation implies that "the dead Marlowe was the shepherds' poet in residence."[10] James Smith states that "no incongruity is intended or feared from [Marlowe's] introduction with fleece and crook: the [pastoral] tradition being rich enough to absorb him, vigorous enough to assert even beside him its actuality."[11] These commentators forget, however, that by writing "The Passionate Shepherd to His Love," Marlowe put *himself* into the pastoral tradition. [12] As this poem was and is one of Marlowe's best known, there is little incongruity in his being addressed as "shepherd." But if Phebe gives him the label "shepherd" *because* of the poem, she suggests the problem of the audience's taking a poet's persona for himself. On the other hand, she may associate herself with Marlowe in order to make the identification of her feelings by his words more complete. She is a shepherdess, so Marlowe is a shepherd, because he has written what she feels. She projects her life of pastoral artifice upon the poet in order to impart the relevance of his words to her situation. In doing so, she again parallels Touchstone, who aligns himself with Ovid and Marlowe and thus distorts their work.

By referring to Marlowe as the "Dead shepherd," Phebe may be doing more than mourning his passing. She may be distinguishing him from Silvius, a living pastoral shepherd. Although every word that Silvius speaks is pastorally poetic, he does not quote or write poetry himself, unlike his counterpart in Lodge's *Rosalynde*. Once Phebe has quoted the "Dead shepherd" Marlowe, however, she more willingly listens to Silvius's conventionally poetic speech. Silvius is appointed as the spokesman of love in V.ii. 87-115, and Rosalind, Orlando, and Phebe all quote Silvius's vows of service, observance, and faith. Silvius, then, seems to be recognized as an authority on pastoral poetic expression by the other characters in the play. They borrow from him, just as Phebe borrows from Marlowe when she first falls in love. Possibly Silvius does not write poetry because he sees himself (as perhaps other characters see him) as being a character *in* poetry, rather than as a composer *of* it. He *is* poetic, and is, in his limited way, inspiring, but he lacks the originality, love of composition, and desire for recognition that even such a poor poet as Orlando has. But the living shepherd Silvius still bears similarity to the "Dead shepherd" Marlowe. Being dead, Marlowe has become a synthesis of his characters and verse. He can no longer compose, so he now speaks only through his personae and the characters in his works.

Irony accompanies Phebe's use of Marlowe. In the mouth of a character who unwittingly falls in love with one of her own sex, the line about "love at first sight" is comical. Marlowe's statement becomes a joke; its poetic truth on the experience of love is not only undercut, but contradicted. If Phebe can be mistaken in a first sight that provokes love, so could others who could quote the line. But the love between most of the couples in the play begins at first sight. Although some deception accompanies the courtship of each couple, all of the first-sight lovers except for Phebe marry their choices. The character most struck by the *poetic truth* of love at first sight is the only one frustrated by it. Other characters feel love at first sight and react accordingly, but she is the only one to *analyze* it in terms of poetry. Phebe takes a "foolish chronicler" too seriously; but when she learns the truth behind the feigning of Ganymede, she learns to accept the true, if poetically trite, lover Silvius. The love associated with the "Dead shepherd" gives way to the reliable love of the living shepherd.

Part of Phebe's problem in her allusion may lie in her faulty understanding of Marlowe. Marlowe's development of the "mighty line" was a tremendous achievement in English literature, but Phebe refers to Marlowe's "saw of might." Since a saw is a proverbial, thus hackneyed, expression, Phebe suggests that she knows Marlowe's line by its frequent quotation, not by its context. If Marlowe *were* the shepherds' "poet in residence," as stated by Grennan, Phebe would know that in *Hero and Leander,* the classical Ganymede is discussed as a homosexual. Although Marlowe's line about love at first sight does refer to heterosexual love between Hero and Leander, Neptune falls in love with Leander at first sight too, thinking him to be Ganymede. If Phebe had read *Hero and Leander,* her first sight of an effeminate shepherd boy named Ganymede should have led to an informed guess that "he" was homosexual, not a potential heterosexual lover for herself. In a sense, the "Dead Shepherd" Marlowe is "struck dead" by Phebe's misunderstanding.

Numerous commentators have analyzed Shakespeare's motives for referring to Marlowe. Anne Righter reasons that because Shakespeare's allusions are so deeply embedded in their context, "one almost wonders if they were intended to evoke the image of Marlowe for the playgoers at The Globe, or whether they represented some purely private rite of memory."[13] The richly allusive plays of other playwrights of this period suggest that the audiences did understand and appreciate allusion, so Shakespeare could have made his private mourning for Marlowe public through Phebe's invocation. But Frederick S. Boas poses an important question on this point: "The passage is generally quoted as an affectionate tribute of Shakespeare to Marlowe, but would he have put this into the mouth of the fickle Phebe?"[14] One could pose a similar question regarding Shakespeare's choice of a professional fool for apparent tributes to Ovid and Marlowe. Shakespeare seems to ridicule the very poets who most obviously influenced him. Grennan suggests that, like Spenser with his invocations of Chaucer and Vergil, Shakespeare establishes a "literary pedigree" for himself by alluding to Ovid and Marlowe. Such allusions underline "the intensely literary nature of the pastoral as it self-consciously incorporates the author's literary ancestors." Because "both Marlowe and Shakespeare were indelibly associated in the literary mind with Ovid," Shakespeare's "literary pedigree" is "historically respectable (if ironically shaded)."[15] But by its habitual undercutting and satire, *As You Like It* is both a pastoral and an anti-pastoral play. If Shakespeare establishes a "literary pedigree" for himself, he also seems to burlesque it, not just "ironically shade" it. His satiric use of allusion forces us to re-examine and re-evaluate literary history and to test the relative truth of poetry.

Poetry results from the merging of imagination with truth; by its nature it must use "lies." Although Touchstone's and Rosalind's definitions of poetic lies both involve death, the major difference between them is the literal versus the figurative meaning of "die." Rosalind states a literal truth that lovers do not die of love; Touchstone presents a figurative truth that poets die by misunderstanding. Both are true, and both are lies. Lovers cannot die from their emotions, although their emotions can lead them into suicidal situations, as with Troilus, or dangerous situations, as with Leander, so they can, indirectly, die of love. Poets do not literally die from misunderstanding, but those poets who are read achieve a kind of immortality; they live past their actual lives, although they "die" in the larger sense if they are misunderstood or forgotten. Phebe's couplet involves both sides of the paradox formed by Touchstone's and Rosalind's positions. Marlowe is literally "dead," but when Phebe quotes his line, he lives, even if he is only partially understood.

Just as Marlowe is and is not "dead," so he is and is not a liar. Rosalind points to Marlowe and Chaucer as examples of poetic liars, and a lie inspires Phebe's quotation of Marlowe, yet Touchstone calls the "truest poets" the "most feigning." Thus Ovid, Chaucer, and

Marlowe are the "truest poets." Ovid is the great ancient true poet, Chaucer the great Old English true poet, and Marlowe the great modern true poet. Shakespeare undercuts these tributes, but he does not burlesque the poetic masters any more than he does himself. He thereby suggests that all art should be brought to a touchstone and tested, as love should be. True poets, like true love, can survive mocking; Shakespeare's mockery of them and himself leads to a new awareness of true poets' complexities.

All three of the allusions to Marlowe place him in the context of death, feigning, and poetry as he and other great poets are tested through these three interrelated concepts. Poetry involves a complex layering of literal and figurative truth; the allusions to Marlowe recapitulate that layering, adding as well layers of tribute and satire. Marlowe lives through the tests in *As You Like It* and takes his place next to Ovid, Chaucer, and Shakespeare himself.

NOTES

1. Quotations from Shakespeare are from *Shakespeare: The Complete Works*, ed. G. B. Harrison (New York: Harcourt, Brace & World, 1952). The number for Marlowe's line is that assigned by *The Poems: Christopher Marlowe*, ed. Millar Maclure (London: Methuen, 1968).
2. Some editors and commentators have seen references to Ovid, Chapman, and others, as well as to Marlowe, in this line. See Richard Knowles, ed. New Variorum Edition of *As You Like It* (New York: Modern Language Association, 1977), pp. 188–190, for a summary of readings of the line.
3. Quotations from Marlowe's dramatic works are from *Christopher Marlowe: The Complete Plays*, ed. J. B. Steane (Harmondsworth: Penguin Books, 1969).
4. These qualities in Touchstone are lauded by many commentators. See, for example, R. H. Goldsmith, "Touchstone: Critic in Motley," *PMLA*, 68 (1953), 886-894, *passim*.
5. See Alvin Thaler, *Shakespeare and Democracy* (Knoxville: University of Tennessee Press, 1941), p. 218; William Empson, *Some Versions of Pastoral* (London: Chatto & Windus, 1950), p. 138; Howard C. Cole, "The Moral Vision of *As You Like It*," *College Literature*, 3 (1976), p. 26; and Knowles, pp. 190-191.
6. The Folio (as reprinted in Knowles) uses both spellings: "the truest poetrie is the most *faining*"; "what they swear in Poetrie, may be said as Lovers, they do *feigne*" (italics mine).
7. Shakespeare changes Marlowe's "Was this the face that launch'd a thousand ships, / And burnt the topless towers of Illium?" (*Doctor Faustus*, xiii. 112-13) to "Why, she is a pearl, / Whose price hath launched above a thousand ships, / And turned crowned kings to merchants" (II.ii. 81-83).

8. Maura Slattery Kuhn, "Much Virtue in 'If,'" *Shakespeare Quarterly*, 28 (1977), 48.

9. Alexander Leggatt, *Shakespeare's Comedy of Love* (London: Methuen, 1974), p. 207.

10. Eamon Grennan, "Telling the Trees from the Wood: Some Details of *As You Like It* Re-examined," *English Literary Renaissance*, 7 (1977), 203.

11. James Smith, "*As You Like It*," *Scrutiny*, 9 (1940), 27.

12. Shakespeare has Sir Hugh Evans sing part of this poem in *The Merry Wives of Windsor* (III.i. 17-29).

13. Anne Righter, *Shakespeare and the Idea of the Play* (New York: Barnes & Noble, 1952), p. 155.

14. Frederick S. Boas, *Queen Elizabeth in Drama: and Related Studies* (London: George Allen & Unwin, 1950), p. 59.

15. Grennan, p. 204.

Ben Jonson and "*Marlowes* mighty line"

JAMES A. RIDDELL

I

Jonson alludes to Marlowe a number of times over a rather long period, seeming sometimes to have a high opinion of his predecessor, sometimes a low one. On occasion it appears difficult, perhaps impossible, to tell what Jonson's opinion is. That modern critics should have varying interpretations of Jonson's attitude is not surprising: critical insights tend not to concur under the best of circumstances, and when critics are dealing with something that has seemed so elusive as Jonson's attitude towards Marlowe, some confusion is bound to ensue. I think that a measure of order is introduced when one realizes that a good deal of the elusiveness lies not in Jonson's changing his opinion or in his being confused about it, but in his habit of balancing it. In Marlowe Jonson found much to admire and much to fault, and in his judgments of Marlowe never lost sight of either possibility. Furthermore, it seems that Jonson rarely, if ever, referred to Marlowe (or possibly to anybody) without bothering to judge him.

I suspect that Edmund Wilson's notorious claim about Jonson's attitude toward Marlowe still has a good deal of currency: "The . . . filthy travesty of Marlowe's *Hero and Leander* [in *Bartholmew Fair*] in terms of bankside muck has an ugliness which makes one suspect that Jonson took an ugly delight in defiling a beautiful poem which he could not hope to rival."[1] Wilson may be extreme here, but he does call atten-

37

tion to the conjunction of two of the best known works of the two poets; it is as good a place as any to begin.

Before turning to *Bartholmew Fair,* however, I would like to note a reference to *Hero and Leander* in an early play by Jonson, *Every Man in his Humour,* which was first acted in 1598, the year of the earliest printings of *Hero and Leander.* When in the play the poet-ape Matheo claims that he was written, "extempore," some lines that he has filched (with slight alterations) from Marlowe, it is clear from the context that the lines are understood to be good ones, and well known. They stand in contrast to another of Matheo's thefts, a contrast that is present in the first (quarto) edition (1601), but which is much emphasized in Jonson's revision of the play for the folio (1616).[2] Matheo (quarto) or Mathew (folio) has no idea whether he is stealing good or bad verse, but we should know. At the end of the quarto version of the play Matheo cites some lines from Daniel, lines that apparently provoked Jonson's contempt, although, it seems, not quite so apparently as Jonson would have liked. In the revised version Jonson took pains to make clear that the lines from Daniel were introduced for their ineptness. Instead of Mathew reciting a passage in a straightforward fashion, as is done in the quarto, in the folio the passage is changed for the worse, which impels a character to exclaim: *"A Parodie! a parodie!* with a kind of miraculous gift, to make it absurder then it was."[3] Jonson makes no such changes in lines quoted from Marlowe or in characters' reaction to them. There seems to have been no danger that an audience would misconstrue Jonson's low opinion for a high opinion, because in the case of Marlowe the only possibility was that Matheo was stealing lines that were much too good for him to have written. The lines being too good for a fool to have written does not prove that Jonson thought they were good, but it does confirm that he did not judge them to be bad.

More of Jonson's judgment can be inferred from the way he employs *Hero and Leander* in *Bartholmew Fair.* The puppet show which is performed near the end of *Bartholmew Fair* has for its subject a conflation of the Hero-Leander and Damon-Pythias stories. They are presented as parodies, specifically of Marlowe and of Richard Edwardes, but parodies in quite different meanings of the word. The parody of Edwardes is of a very direct kind. Jonson travesties Edwardes's style, the ill-kept poulter's measure, the forced rimes. Short passages from each are enough to demonstrate.

Edwardes:

> But now for to be briefe, the matter to expresse,
> Which here wee shall present: is this *Damon* and *Pithias*.
> A rare ensample of Frendship true, it is no Legend lie,
> But a thinge once donne in deede as Hystories doo discrie.[4]

Jonson:

> Gentles, that no longer your expectations may wander,
> Behold our chief Actor, amorous *Leander*,
> With a great deale of cloth, lap'd about him like a Scarfe,
> For he yet serves his father, a Dyer at *Puddle* wharfe.
> (V.iv.116-119)

In the case of Marlowe, however, Jonson's object of ridicule is not *Hero and Leander*, but rather a "modern" incapacity to understand the kind of poem that Marlowe wrote, so that the object of the ridicule is not the object of the parody. The character in the play who claims responsibility for the alteration of the Hero and Leander story, John Little-Wit, explains what he has done:

> I have onely made it a little easie, and *moderne* for the times; . . . As, for the *Hellespont* I imagine our *Thames* here; and then *Leander*, I make a Diers sonne, about *Puddle-wharfe*: and *Hero* a wench o' the *Banke-side*, who going over one morning, to old fish-street; *Leander* spies her land at *Trigsstayers*, and falls in love with her: Now do I intoduce *Cupid*, having *Metamorphos'd* himselfe into a Drawer, and hee strikes *Hero* in love with a pint of *Sherry*, and other pretty passages there are . . . that will delight you . . . and please you of judgement. (V. iii. 120-130)

It is not only the audience of fair-goers in the play who are being ridiculed; by extension any audience whose "judgement" can appreciate only that which is "moderne" is also being ridiculed. A parallel to this can be found in the long scatalogical poem with which Jonson ends his book of *Epigrammes*. "The Famous Voyage," as Peter Medine has demonstrated, is a "*modern* Epigram" (Medine's emphasis), a mock epic contrived to reflect the values of depraved times, a poem that is corrupt both in content and form.[5] The puppet play of Hero and Leander is not so coarse as "The Famous Voyage," but it is as coarse as might have been possible in a work meant for public performance. In it, as in "The Famous Voyage," Jonson satirizes current manners and current taste. It is, in short, what Little-Wit called it, "*moderne* for the times." Thus, although Edwardes is the object of parody, Marlowe is not. In fact, Marlowe is being praised to some degree, as he is the author of a work that is too good for its audience, a work, we may suppose, something like Jonson's own, written according to "the old way, and the true,"[6] though it does seem unlikely that Jonson would rank Marlowe with himself.

II

No date had been assigned to Jonson's "An Ode. To Himself" (*Underwood*, XXIII), although modern editors suggest a comparison between this poem and another of Jonson's, "Ode to Himself," on the failure of *The New Inn* in 1629.[7] Whether it belongs to so late a period in Jonson's life or to the time of *Poetaster* (1602), as Gifford supposes,[8] it does bring together Jonson, Ovid, and Marlowe in a way that suggests a particular way that Jonson associated himself and Marlowe as poets. The first two lines of *Underwood* XXIII echo the beginning of Ovid's *Amores*, I, xv, and the poem concludes with Jonson's advice to himself to "sing high and aloofe, / Safe from the wolves black jaw, and the dull Asses hoofe." Both refer specifically to *Poetaster*, either the play itself or the "Apologeticall Dialogue," which was written early but which was not published until the folio of 1616.[9] In the case of the two conclusions, the words are virtually the same; when writing one Jonson indisputably has the other in mind. With the references to Ovid, we cannot be absolutely sure. However, *Poetaster* and *Underwood* XXIII both are written about what it means to be a poet; both allude to a well-known elegy of Ovid written on just the same theme. That both have the same conclusion gives support to the notion that Jonson had a number of the same things in mind when he wrote each.

But where does Marlowe come in? The first words in the first scene of *Poetaster* are spoken by Ovid, who has just finished writing an elegy (I, xv). Forty lines farther into the scene, Ovid recites the entire poem, which in the event is Jonson's redaction of Marlowe's translation. Though Marlowe is, of course, not mentioned in the play, Jonson's version is so close to his that no one who knew the earlier version could mistake the allusion. And no one who knew the earlier version *well* could fail to understand that Jonson had improved it.[10] The close association between the two versions was known to some of Jonson's contemporaries as the next edition of Marlowe's *Ovids Elegies* included a copy of Jonson's version taken from the printed text of *Poetaster*.[11]

Critics do not agree about Jonson's presentation of the character of Ovid any more than they agree about the quality of Jonson's improvements on Marlowe's translation.[12] Because the character of Horace in the play has always been understood to be the representative of Jonson himself,[13] Horace's attitude towards Ovid is thought to be about the same as Jonson's. It is my contention that the Horace/Jonson appraisal of Ovid is close to Jonson's appraisal of Marlowe, that while Jonson did not think of Marlowe as among the best of poets (perhaps because he was not among the best of men [preface to *Volpone*]), he was nonetheless a *poet*, and therefore akin to Jonson. Once having noted a close connection between Marlowe and Elegy I, xv, Jonson could scarcely ignore the implications of associating himself with that same elegy. Even in the unlikely case that events were the other way around, that is, if *Underwood* XXIII were written before *Poetaster,* Jonson could not ignore the association.

What part of my argument assumes, of course, is that Marlowe's translation of Elegy I, xv was well enough known that at least some of Jonson's audience would recognize it. There were at least two editions of Marlowe's translations of the *Amores* printed in the several years before *Poetaster* was first performed.[14] That Jonson's redaction was printed directly following Marlowe's original in subsequent editions shows that the association was certainly known, though how widely and how early cannot be determined. As Jonson was scarcely unwilling to translate poetry himself, his inclusion of a close but improved version of a translation by a very popular poet must have been done for some reason. The only reason that makes any sense is that he was saying something about Christopher Marlowe. That he chose to improve the translation suggests that Marlowe, poet though he was, was perhaps not close enough to his classical antecedent that his efforts were entirely satisfactory; they were good enough to be admired, but not so good as to be beyond mending.

There were attempts in the past to identify Ovid in *Poetaster* with one

or another of Jonson's contemporaries, most often with John Donne.[15]
The play does invite such speculation, given the association of Horace
with Jonson and of Crispinus and Demetrius with Marston and
Dekker. Where such identifications went wrong was in their reliance
upon coincidences of biographical detail, such as Ovid's romantic intrigue wih Julia, a woman above his station, and John Donne's with
Anne More. What should be the main consideration is the kinds of
writing for which characters in *Poetaster* were responsible, which, in the
case of Crispinus and Demetrius, is the cause of their censure in the
play. Marlowe's verse, like Ovid's, is flamboyant, popular, sensuous,
and at times indecent. It is also poetry. It wins Jonson's admiration,
but this side (occasionally rather far this side) of idolatry.

III

The commentary in *Volpone* and *The Alchemist* is oblique but discernible. Since Eliot observed more than half a century ago that "Jonson is
the legitimate heir of Marlowe," it has been widely acknowledged that
there certainly is a connection between the language of Marlowe and
that of Jonson, particularly in the speech of Volpone and Sir Epicure
Mammon.[16] But Jonson was not an heir who merely accepted his legacy. Jonson employs overblown verse (it is, by the way, always blank
verse), to subvert what his characters think that they are saying: their
grandiloquence carries its own condemnation with it. Harry Levin noticed much the same thing. He says: "Jonson unquestionably inherited
Marlowe's rhetoric of enticement; but, whereas most of Marlowe's
characters take the proffered jewels and delicacies at their face value,
Jonson's characters employ them as Barabas did—to ensnare and delude" (pp. 148-49). Levin's point is excellent, but I wish to amend it,
for I think that one more consideration can be added.

Jonson doesn't simply appropriate Marlowe's gorgeous language;
he exaggerates it into something grotesque. One may compare Faustus
and Sir Epicure Mammon.

Faustus:

> Sweet *Hellen* make me immortall with a kisse:
> Her lips sucke forth my soule, see where it flies.
> Come *Hellen*, come, give me my soule againe,

> Here will I dwell, for heaven is in these lippes,
> And all is drosse that is not *Helena.*
> I will be *Paris,* and for love of thee,
> In stead of *Troy* shall *Wittenberg* be sack't,
> And I will combat with weake *Menelaus,*
> And weare thy colours on my plumed crest.
> Yea, I will wound *Achilles* in the heele,
> And then returne to Hellen for a kisse.[17]

Sir Epicure Mammon:

> I will have all my beds, blowne up; not stuft:
> Downe is too hard. And then, mine oval roome,
> Fill'd with such pictures, as Tiberius tooke
> From Elephantis: and dull Aretine
> But coldly imitated. Then, my glasses,
> Cut in more subtill angles, to disperse,
> And multiply the figures, as I walke
> Naked betweene my *succubae.*
>
> (II.ii.41-48)

Eliot quotes just this passage, but breaks off at the end of line 47 ("as I walke"). This was done, I suppose, for reasons of delicacy; however, the omission is an unfortunate one because with the four words curtailed, the luxuriousness of Mammon's bloated imagination has to be guessed at—or looked up. "Imagination" is the crucial term. In the context of the play Faustus's Helen is "real," a part of the fiction. Mammon's succubae are the creatures of his own perverse creation. Mammon's expansiveness makes Faustus's rapture seem tame in comparison, as though nothing in reality could support the outrageous diction (along this line, it might be noted, one succubus is adequate for Faustus). Mammon continues in his catalogue of delights:

> I my selfe will have
> The beards of barbels, serv'd, in stead of sallades;
> Oild mushromes; and the swelling unctuous paps
> Of a fat pregnant sow, newly cut off,
> Drest with an exquisite, and poynant sauce.
>
> (ll. 81-85)

There is no tether, nor could there be, for unreality is essential to Mammon's distortions. In part of *Volpone,* also, there is an essential unreality, but only in part. Here I disagree somewhat with Levin, who says: "The luxuries of *Volpone,* though tainted, are perfectly tangible; those of *The Alchemist* do not really exist" (p. 149). In the seduction scene with Celia, Volpone's diction is as tetherless as that of Mammon.

Volpone:
> A gem, but worth a private partimony,
> Is nothing: we will eate such a meale.
> The heads of parats, tongues of nightingales,
> The braines of peacocks, and of estriches
> Shall be our food: and , could we get the phoenix,
> (Though nature lost her kind) shee were our dish.

(III.vii. 200-205)

It is in scenes like the first in the play that one finds the "tangible" luxuries that Levin identifies. But even here there is considerable distance from Marlowe. The greed of Barabas is merely greed; with Volpone it becomes blasphemy. Barabas would have "men of judgment" to "inclose / Infinite riches in a little room." Volpone's gold is his "saint," to whom he can say: "Haile the worlds soule, and mine." In each of these examples what should be noted is that Jonson goes well beyond Marlowe, he overreaches the overreacher.

What is important here is not the ways that some characters affect others in the plays, but the ways they indulge their own fantasies. In the passages just cited Jonson's characters don't so much "ensnare and delude" others (as Levin sees Barabas doing), they delude themselves. There is no one taken in when Volpone deifies his gold; Celia is repelled rather than attracted; Mammon doesn't convince anyone beyond himself. The self-deception responsible for and heightened by such inflated language carries with it an implicit stricture, not only of the characters but also of the Marlovian source of the language they speak. It is stricture, however, not condemnation. Jonson may chide Marlovian excess, but when it is inflated into folly by characters in *Volpone* and *The Alchemist,* we can see that it is the corruption of the character's imaginations that is responsible for their particular speech. Marlowe remains in the background, to be blamed perhaps, but not himself to be mocked as were, say, Edwardes or Daniel or Marston.

IV

Thus one finds both the parody of Marlowe's gorgeousness in *Volpone* and *The Alchemist* and the ridiculing of thise who can understand Marlowe only in parody in *Bartholmew Fair*. One finds also the measured judgment of an English Ovid, a poet given to excess, but still a poet. Such a view is perfectly consistent with the ambiguity (praise touched with irony) found in Jonson's famous description in the second half of: "Or sporting *Kid*, or *Marlowes* mighty line." Herford and Simpson call this Jonson's "finest single touch of criticism" (XI, 145). They then go on to lament: "In such a context one cannot but regret the inane joke on the name of Kyd." I think that they give Jonson both too much credit (for generosity) and too little (for lapsing in decorum). The appelation "sporting *Kid*" should put us on notice that "mighty line" is not meant to be taken simply as compliment. Jonson is jesting here, as he is in the previous verse when he says that Shakespeare "didst our *Lily* out-shine." "Mighty" does mean "powerful, potent, strong," but it also means "of huge proportions, massive, bulky." It carries the implication of "cumbersome" or "overblown" as well as "forceful."[18]

Jonson's meaning was accurately perceived, I think, by the author of an early reference to Jonson's assessment of Marlowe, one W. C., who saw through the press a posthumous edition of the poems of William Bosworth in 1651. R. C. praises Bosworth for the astuteness of his imitations and for the variety of poets he followed. On one point R. C. says:

> The strength of his fancy, and the shadowing of it in words he takes from Mr. *Marlow* in his *Hero* and *Leander,* whose mighty lines Mr. *Benjamin Johnson* (a man sensible enough of his own abilities) was often heard to say, that they were Examples fitter for admiration than for parallel, you shall find our Author every where in this imitation.[19]

Even if the antecedent for "whose" were not Marlowe (as it almost certainly is) but rather *Hero and Leander*, R. C.'s *general* application of the term "mighty lines" to any of Marlowe's work would be reasonable enough. And "mighty lines" can come from no place else in Jonson than from the Shakespeare poem. This passage was sufficient to con-

vince Thomas Warton that "Marlowe was a favorite with Jonson."[20]
Although today one might be reluctant to reach the same conclusion
on no more than the same evidence, and although "favorite" might
seem to require the kind of qualification R. C. himself makes
("Examples fitter for admiration than for parallel"), Warton was
probably right about Jonson's attitude towards *Hero and Leander* and,
by extension, towards Marlowe the Poet.

NOTES

1. Edmund Wilson, *The Triple Thinkers* (London: John Lehmann, 1952), p. 217. Recently Wilson's essay had been cited with a number of reservations, but still with
   condiserable approbation by E. Pearlman, "Ben Jonson: An Anatomy," *English
   Literary Renaissance*, 9 (1979), 364-394.
       Jonas Barish considers that in the instance of *Hero and Leander* there is a great
   deal more distance between the two poets: "*Hero and Leander* [is] only very roughly
   after Marlowe; . . . from the looseness of the imitation of Marlowe, it can be
   assumed that Jonson is burlesquing the theme rather than any particular version
   of it" ("*Bartholomew Fair* and Its Puppets," *Modern Language Quarterly*, 20 [1959],
   13, 13n.). Most critics simply note the parody, *e.g.*: Eugene Waith "The Poet's
   Morals in Jonson's *Poetaster*," *Modern Language Quarterly*, 12 (1951), 13-19; E.
   B. Partridge, *The Broken Compass* (London: Chatto & Windus, 1958), pp. 235f.
   Alan C. Dessen, in passing, agrees with the position that I shall take that Jonson
   does not object to the subject matter of *Hero and Leander* but to the "reduction" of it
   (*Jonson's Moral Comedy* [Evanston: Northwestern University Press, 1971], p. 224).

2. The nature of the revisions is analyzed by Jonas Barish, *Jonson and the Language of
   Prose Comedy* (Cambridge, Mass.: Harvard University Press,1960), pp. 130-141.
   See also: H.H. Carter, ed., *Every Man in His Humour*, Yale Studies in English (New
   Haven, Conn.: Yale University Press, 1921), pp. xxxi-lvii; C.H. Herford and
   Percy Simpson, *Ben Jonson*, I (Oxford: Clarendon Press, 1925), 358-370; J.W.
   Lever, ed., *Every man in His Humour* (Lincoln: University of Nebraska Press, 1971),
   xx-xxiv; A. Richard Dutton, "The Significance of Jonson's Revisions of *Every Man
   in His Humour*," *Modern Language Review*, 69 (1974), 241-249.

3. V.v. 26-27. Herford and Simpson, *Ben Jonson*, III (1927). All references to Jonson
   are to this edition; i/j and u/v have been regularized to conform with modern
   practice. The passages stolen from Marlowe appear at III.iv.60-64, 72-73
   (quarto) and at IV.ii.41-45, 48-49,54-55 (folio).

4. Richard Edwardes, *Damon and Pithias* (1571). These lines, and a half-dozen more,
   are cited by Herford and Simpson, X, 210-211.

5. "Object and Intent in Jonson's 'Famous Voyage,' " *Studies in English Literature*, 15
   (1975), 109-110.

6. This is from Jonson's Epigram 18, alluded to by Medine (p. 110).

7. Herford and Simpson, XI, 61; Ian Donaldson, ed., *Ben Jonson: Poems* (London:
   Oxford University Press, 1975), p. 167n.

8. William Gifford, ed., *The Works of Ben Jonson* (1816), VIII, 383-384.

9. The "Apologeticall Dialogue" has one more reference to *Amores*, I, xv [ii. 123-124]. It is here noted; it has no bearing on my argument.

10. All who comment on the two versions agree that Jonson's is the more correct. Some, like Millar Maclure (ed., *The Poems of Christopher Marlowe*, Revels Plays [London: Methuen, 1968], pp. 140n.-141n.), suggest that Jonson's may be better; others, like J. B. Steane (*Marlowe: A Critical Study* [Cambridge: Cambridge University Press, 1964], p. 281), contend that Marlowe's is "more vigorous" and "may well in fact be found preferable to the 'mature' product." See also: U.M. Ellis-Fermor, *Christopher Marlowe* (London: Methuen, 1927), pp. 13-14; Eric Jacobsen, *Translation, a Traditional Craft*, Classica et Mediaevalia. Dissertationes VI (Copenhagen: Gyldendal, 1958), pp. 184-186; Roma Gill, "Snakes Leap by Verse," in *Christopher Marlowe*, ed. Brian Morris (New York: Hill and Wang, 1969), pp. 149-150.

It has been claimed, beginning with Gifford, that both versions were written by Jonson (*The Works of Ben Jonson*, II, 397n.-398n.). This view has been endorsed by Herbert S. Mallory (ed. *Poetaster*, Yale Studies in English [New York: Holt, 1905[, pp. xcvi-ciii) and by Josiah H. Penniman (ed. *"Poetaster" by Ben Jonson and "Satiromastix" by Thomas Dekker* [Boston: Heath, 1913], pp. 186-187). More recently, citing Penniman, Joan Carr ("Jonson and The Classics: The Ovid-Plot in *Poetaster*," *English Literary Renaissance*, 8 (1978), 298, 298n.) makes the same argument based on the same assumption: Jonson would not have stooped to using someone else's translation. There are reasons (see below) for rejecting this argument.

11. Fredson Bowers has demonstrated that the text of Jonson's version which appears in the third octavo (O3) edition of Marlowe's *Ovid's Elegies* is from the quarto (Q) *Poetaster* (1602) and not from the folio (1616) ("The Early Editions of Marlowe's *Ovid's Elegies*," *Studies in Bibliography*, 25 [1972], 172). He does not show, however, that it was from the printed rather than a manuscript copy. Thus he does not prove precedence between O3 and Q. There is one bit of evidence to demonstrate that O3 is set from Q, although how long after Q (as Bowers notes) cannot be determined. The evidence comes from a broken ligature. In the Q version of Elegy I. xv all words with a terminal "l" have the letter doubled, with apparently a single exception. In the penultimate line of the poem "funeral" seems to be printed with a single "l". In fact the first half of the ligature "ll" is almost entirely broken away, so that there is a small space between the "a" and the "l," with only a tiny portion of the upper part of the first "l" being printed; the word looks like "funera'l." In O3, a faithful compositor, coming as close as he could to the text of Q, has reproduced this as "funeral," the only word in the O3 version of the poem with a terminal "l" rather that the doubled "ll."

12. Most see Ovid as a good poet but a flawed man. The nature of the flaw is seen as ranging from Ovid's being somewhat weak (J.A. Bryant, Jr., *The Compassionate Satirist: Ben Jonson and His Imperfect World* [Athens, Ga.: University of Georgia Press, 1972], pp. 40-45) to his being "dangerously immoral" (Frank Kermode, "The Banquet of Sense," *Bulletin of The John Rylands Library*, 44 [Sept. 1961], 73). See also: O. J. Campbell, *Commical Satire and Shakespeare's "Troilus and Cressida"* (San Marino, Calif.: Huntington Library, 1938), pp. 113-129; Eugene Waith, "The Poet's Morals in Jonson's *Poetaster*," 13-19; Gabriele Bernhard Jackson,

Visions and Judgement in Ben Jonson's Drama, Yale Studies in English, 166 (New Haven, Conn.: Yale University Press, 1968), pp. 21-30; Joseph A. Dane, "The Ovids of Ben Jonson in *Poetaster* and in *Epicoene," Comparative Drama,* 13 (Fall 1979), 222-234. Earnest W. Talbert ("The Purpose and Technique of Jonson's *Poetaster," Studies in Philology,* 42 [1945], 225-252) sees Ovid as being a good man and good poet; Joan Carr ("Jonson and the Classics . . . " pp. 304-311) sees Ovid as representing a part of Jonson, that part which wants to defend love poetry, but with an "appeal to his audience not to misunderstand poet-satirists like himself as they undertake their morally arduous and even politically dangerous vocation."

13. Beginning, in print, with Dekker's *Satiromastix* (1602).

14. The two extant editions published before *Poetaster* contain only two elegies in Marlowe's translation including I, xv. They were included with epigrams by Sir John Davies, which they followed; their dates are conjectural, the new STC giving (1599?), Fredson Bowers noting: "The date unknown (usually assigned to *ca.* 1594-95)" (Ed. *The Complete Works of Christopher Marlowe,* 2nd ed. [Cambridge: Cambridge University Press, 1981], II, 309). In the third and later editions all of Marlowe's translations are included. In these later editions Davies's epigrams follow the elegies, distinguished merely by a head-title. "The titlepages reflect this different order, obviously an indication of the relative popularity of the two parts" (Bowers, "The Early Editions of Marlowe's *Ovid's Elegies,"* p. 150).

15. Summarized by Mallory in his ed. of *Poetaster,* pp. lxx-lxxii.

16. T. S. Eliot, *The Sacred Wood,* 3rd. ed. (London: Methuen, 1932), pp. 113-114. See also: J. B. Steane, *Marlowe,* pp. 167-168, 176; and (especially) Harry Levin, *The Overreacher: A Study of Christopher Marlowe* (Cambridge, Mass.: Harvard University Press, 1952), 148-149.

17. Bowers, ed., *Marlowe,* lines 1770-1780.

18. T. J. B. Spencer ("Ben Jonson on his beloved, The Author Mr. William Shakespeare," *The Elizabethan Theatre,* IV [1974], 33) comes to the same conclusions. He says that the reference to Kyd "makes it certain that our *Lily out-shine* refers to Mathew 6.28-29." Spencer also suggests a pun on Marlowe's name: "Was Jonson really likely to praise the quality of the writing of *Tamburlaine?* Perhaps Jonson is only enjoying linking together the *low* in Marlowe's surname with the rumbustious eloquence of the mighty monarchs in his plays."

    For the reference to Lily, Ian Donaldson cites both Virgil (*Aeneid,* VI, 708-709 and most cogently, the Cary/Morrison ode *Underwood* 70, 72), where the lily is described as the "plant and flower of light,"

19. *The Chast and Lost Lovers,* "To the Reader" (sig. A4). The parenthetic observation, "a man sensible enough of his own abilities," prompted Saintsbury to observe: "This looks as if R. C. had actually experienced Ben—who had not been more than fourteen years dead at this time" (*Minor Poets of the Caroline Period,* II [Oxford: Clarendon Press, 1906], 527n).

    Herford and Simpson quote a portion of this but omit the reference to *Hero and Leander* and notice of Bosworth's imitation of that poem (XI, 145).

20. *The History of English Poetry, from the Close of the Eleventh to the Commencement of the Eighteenth Century,* III (1781), 436n.

The Rhetoric of Marlowe's Orations

J. W. VAN HOOK

From Tamburlaine's "high astounding terms" to Edward II's graphic demonstrations that "outragious passions cloye my soule," Marlowe's protagonists distinguish themselves by the vigor of their orations. It is surprising, then, that the art by which they construct their speeches has not been more widely studied. *Tamburlaine*'s style alone has received much critical attention, and indeed our understanding of that play's rhetoric has matured greatly since Eliot pronounced it "a pretty simple huffle-snuffle bombast" in his *Sacred Wood*. But our estimation of Marlowe's craftsmanship cannot afford to rest on a thetorical understanding of a single, early work. *Tamburlaine* offers a gorgeous and "copious" display of the tropes and figures its decade was the first to master, extending to the stage the characteristic Elizabethan technical dexterity that poets and romance writers were, in 1587, only beginning to achieve. But the play's style is hardly typical of Marlowe's entire output, which spanned the years, and the stylistic distance, between *The Spanish Tragedy* and *Richard II*.

We might remind ourselves of how great that distance is by contrasting the effect of Faustus's final appeals with those of the similarly frantic rejected lover, Iarbus, in what was probably Marlowe's first play, *Dido, Queen of Carthage*:

> O love, O hate, O cruell womens hearts,
> That imitate the Moone in every chaunge,

49

And like the Planets ever love to raunge:
What shall I do . . . ?[2]

The oxymoron, the apostrophes, the rhyme, and the methodically worked-out simile have little to do with the question Iarbus poses. Except for the fact that they had not yet, six years before the publication of *Astrophel and Stella,* become wholly conventional, such displays have little to recommend them, particularly as dramatic utterance. When we trace how Marlowe's characters handle their tropes and figures, from such beginnings to the great soliloquies of what are commonly considered his last plays, we can better define both the formal characteristics of the mature Marlovian style and the rhetorical impulses which helped fashion it into one of the most readily distinguishable features of Elizabethan drama.[3]

In his later works, Marlowe seems to have anticipated his contemporaries in his impatience with the limited range of tones and manners an ornate style can convey. According to Vere L. Rubel, the century's "copious" or densely figured poets labored to show "the extent of their inventive genius by highly complex combinations, variations, and mutations of the rhetorical features that for generations had been an acknowledged part of the poet's craft."[4] But during the final decade of the century, principles of decorum quickly evolved by which the earlier decorative effusions were brought under control and restrained. Embellishment increasingly had to justify itself by its dramatic appropriateness—by seeming to suggest the way a person so situated as the speaker might actually be expected to express himself—and by the formal criterion of drawing attention to the verse's most significant words and images. Above all, decorum demanded that poets gain more control over their audiences' reactions, so that, as Rosemond Tuve found, mature Elizabethan rhetoric deployed its techniques "with the subtlest possible understanding of their effectiveness upon a reader's sensibilities."[5] Marlowe contributed to this trend toward controlled restraint in the drama in two ways. He found techniques, in the plays which followed *Tamburlaine,* to make his imagery more functional and expressive, so that his characters could begin to reveal their personalities and moods more subtly; and the structure of his orations eventually became, again through his adaptation of rhetorical features, both less static and more complex.

In his earlier plays, both the imagery and the structure of Marlowe's longer speeches were dominated by "amplification," a variety of related techniques for dwelling on, or drawing out, an idea or image. Doctor Johnson reacts like a modern reader against the excesses to which amplification was prone in his "Preface" to *The Plays of William Shakespeare*. That author's "declamations or set speeches are commonly cold and weak," Johnson charges, because "when he endeavoured, like the other tragick writers, to catch opportunities of amplification, and instead of inquiring what the occasion demanded, to show how much his stores of knowledge could supply, he seldom escapes without the pity or resentment of his reader."[6] But whereas Marlowe later developed alternatives to amplification, we will not have a balanced view of his orations until we recognize just how expressive and powerful his early amplified style could be.

It is apparent that rhetoric is to be more than a "cold and weak" vice of style from the first time we hear Tamburlaine's oratory. While still a shepherd, commanding only a gang of highwaymen who are about to be attacked by the combined might of the Persian army, he woos Zenocrate with an overwhelming display of conceits arranged into several different types of amplification:

> Thinke you I way this treasure more than you?
> Not all the Gold in *Indias* welthy armes,
> Shall buy the meanest souldier in my traine.
> *Zenocrate*, lovelier than the love of *Jove*,
> Brighter than is the silver Rhodope.
> Fairer than whitest snow on Scythian hills,
> Thy person is more woorth to *Tamburlaine*,
> Than the possession of the Persean Crowne,
> Which gratious starres have promist at my birth.
> A hundreth Tartars shall attend on thee,
> Mounted on Steeds, swifter than *Pegasus*.
> Thy Garments shall be made of Medean silke,
> Enchast with precious juelles of mine owne:
> More rich and valurous than *Zenocrates*.
> With milke-white Hartes upon an Ivorie sled,
> Thou shalt be drawen amidst the frosen Pooles,
> And scale the ysie mountaines lofty tops:
> Which with thy beautie will be soone resolv'd.
> My martiall prises with five hundred men,
> Wun on the fiftie headed *Vuolgas* waves,

> Shall all we offer to *Zenocrate*,
> And then my selfe to faire *Zenocrate*.
>   (I.ii.84-105)

The rhetorical display in this exuberant passage is stunning in its variety and density, but this should not obscure its conscious control. The scattering of ornate syntactic figures adds to almost every line a note of artifice and design that works to sharpen the flamboyant hyperbole by setting it in relief. The potentially undisciplined personifications of India and the stars are muted unobtrusively by the tropes they are used with: a synecdoche draws our attention to India's capacious arms, and the speaking stars are the less surprising because of the metonymy which domesticates them as dispensers of grace. The minor tropes and figures, then, are both copious and self-effacing, setting the tone for the dominant hyperbolic amplifications without distracting from their hypnotic effect.

The Tudor poet "amplified" by dwelling on what he considered significant detail. In practice, he tended to follow either of two alternative approaches. *Merismus* stresses the importance of a subject by analysing it into its components and dwelling on each of them separately, while *synathroesmus* aims at the same effect by stating a single proposition in several different ways. Not surprisingly, Tamburlaine tries both approaches in his impassioned appeal. The opening comparisons of Zenocrate to Juno, silver, and snow comprise a *synathroesmus* whose encomiastic similes are essentially redundant. The second amplification augments the speaker's offer by a *merismus*, by detailing the trappings of state that his empress will enjoy. Even here, the sly rhetorician avoids empty bombast by the control with which he emphasizes those aspects of his proposal most likely to appeal to the young princess: power (in the Tartars), wealth (in the gems), and repressed sexuality (in the ice and dangerous peaks that seem emblematic of her present virginity). The final amplification, incidentally, follows the order prescribed by one of Marlowe's most characteristic figures, *auxesis*, which places items in an ascending order of importance. Here, Tamburlaine's intended wedding gifts are arranged so as to culminate in the offer she evidently was to consider the ultimate prize, that of "my selfe."

Marlowe was frequently successful, especially in the early plays, at making the copious, amplified style come alive. But amplification, with its expansive, repetitive progress, dictates too many of the poet's choices, and soon becomes, as Shakespeare himself later discovered, too constricting a principle for dramatic orations. Its control over a speech's imagery permitted relatively little scope for nuance, but this was a problem Marlowe never resolved until later in his career. Of more immediate concern, apparently, were the sluggish pace and static organization which amplification entailed.

Marlowe solved this structural problem, ingeniously, by substituting for conventional amplification the more dynamic rhetorical figure of "deliberation" as the organizing principle, or outline, of his longer speeches. Instead of merely repeating or expanding on their ideas, characters using this new figure to guide them could begin to develop trains of thought with more apparent spontaneity, changing course as they considered alternatives and responded to events. Indeed, such fluctuations were called for explicitly by the figure itself.

Deliberation is, in many ways, the most curious of the Tudor rhetorical figures. It appears only once in the handbooks, in Abraham Fraunce's Ramist *Arcadian Rhetorike* of 1558, but its influence on Marlowe's imagination is unmistakable. Like amplification, it proposes an arrangement for long passages, rather than for individual words or phrases. In using it, says Fraunce, the orator progresses through three well-defined phases. To begin, he explains, "we aske and enquire in consultation wise: then when we have thus for a while held the auditors in suspense, we determine of somewhat either more or less contrarie to their expectation."[7] From these rather cryptic suggestions, Marlowe eventually developed such soliloquies as those of Faustus's final hour, or Edward II's abdication of his throne. But the deliberation pattern makes its first, tentative appearance as early as *Tamburlaine*. The most famous of these early attempts at dynamic orations will clearly indicate both the pattern itself and the direction Marlowe had to develop in as he matured in his craft.

Ordinarily, Tamburlaine's inflexible character is adequately expressed in the more conventional, amplified oration. But, of course, even the "Scourge of the imortall God" must change, as he does for instance when he realizes that he can topple Cosroe and assume the crown:

> The thirst of raigne and sweetnes of a crown,
> That causde the eldest sonne of heavenly *Ops*,

> To thrust his doting father from his chaire,
> And place himselfe in the Emperiall heaven,
> Moov'd me to manage armes against thy state.
> What better president than mightie *Jove?*
> Nature that fram'd us of foure Elements,
> Warring within our breasts for regiment,
> Doth teach us all to have aspyring minds:
> Our soules, whose faculties can comprehend
> The wondrous architecture of the world:
> And measure every wandring plannets course:
> Still climing after knowledge infinite,
> And alwaies moving as the restles Spheares,
> Wils us to weare our selves and never rest,
> Untill we reach the ripest fruit of all,
> The perfect blisse and sole felicitie,
> The sweet fruition of an earthly crowne.
>
> (II.vii.12-29)

The copiousness we have learned to recognize as a sign of Marlowe's youthful style is here in abundance. The speech contains three of the main tropes the Renaissance recognized—metaphor, metonymy, and synecdoche—and arranges these into local clusters of hyperbolic amplification. There are, for instance, several extended metaphors—of Tamburlaine as Jove, of the elements as parties in a civil war, and of the restless Ptolemaic universe of the soul. A conventional synecdoche allows "armes" to stand for military force in the same way that the "wandring plannets course" signifies man's potential conquest over even the most abstruse and distant truths. Several metonymies are used here, as well, to substitute "crown" and "throne" for kingship, or the four elements for the turbulent human life they make possible.

Although the speech has its share of localized syntactical figures, its flamboyant display of tropes responds mainly to the dominant organizing figure of deliberation. "What better president than mightie *Jove?*" is the rhetorical question that both sums up the preceding lines and inaugurates the formal deliberative process Fraunce had described. Cosroe had just raised the objection that men's states are, or deserve to be, relatively stable, a position Tamburlaine counters with the hyperbolic images of mutability that end with the phrase, "never rest." In considering the issue in order to hold his auditors in suspense, he makes use of an extensive *merismus* that proudly enumerates the soul's boundless capacities. Finally, after all of this theological and cosmological imagery, Tamburlaine arrives at the conclusion "more or less contrarie" to our expectations, especially if Jove is to be our "president," when he proclaims man's "perfect blisse" to be an "earthly," and not a heavenly, crown.

But if *Tamburlaine*'s early experiments with the deliberation figure represent a structural triumph over the more conventional and static amplifications, they make absolutely no advances in the realm of imagery. The amplifications are still present, cumbersomely enumerating the stages of Jove's rebellion, the mental faculties (of passion, mind, and soul) which drive mankind to aspire, and the potential triumphs open to human knowledge. Jonas Barish points out that such static figures "bend somewhat reluctantly to quick shifts in feeling; they pursue a statelier, more galleon-like course" than actual thought and expression ordinarily take.[8] Until Marlowe could develop a way of handling imagery which managed to be self-consistent without such localized stasis, he clearly was not stylistically mature enough to exploit the potentials which his deliberative structure opened up.

Marlowe's most characteristic innovation in this second respect was to have his speeches actually vary their rhetorical features in response to abrupt changes in a speaker's mood. *The Jew of Malta* and *The Massacre at Paris*, generally assumed to be the plays which directly followed *Tamburlaine*, are full of orations and soliloquies which alternate every few lines between short trope-filled bursts of imaginative introspection and starkly unembellished literal statements about external events. Such speeches naturally pass up the purposiveness which deliberation offers. But they do work out rhetorical means of delineating a wide range of moods and voices, and so constitute a major advance in the adaptation of Elizabethan lyric styles to the stage.

Unfortunately, the texts we have from Marlowe's middle period are among his most corrupt, so the abundant evidence they offer of this stylistic experimentation is fatally suspect. By coincidence, however, one of the soliloquies preserved in what Professor Fredson Bowers asserts to be an undoubtedly "genuine" leaf of the manuscript of *The Massacre* handles rhetoric exactly as I have been suggesting.[9] In the unique case in which we can, Bowers assures us, "recover the exact readings of the author's manuscript," Marlowe's rhetoric carves out the vividly turbulent moods and broken trains of thought of the Duke of Guise at a passionate and critical moment. By killing Mugeroun, he has taken a momentous first step in his quest for power. The crime eliminates at one stroke his wife's lover and the king's minion, and thus serves to announce publicly his own Machiavellian designs.

It is a moment he has prepared carefully, since it means that his standing army is at last ready to challenge the king's. It is strange, then, that this masterful rhetorician should find himself as distant and awkward when the fatal shot is fired as he appears to be in the scene's printed version:

> Lye there the Kings delight, and *Guises* scorn
> Revenge it *Henry* as thou list or dare,
> I did it only in despite of thee.
> (xviii.818-820)

The neat *parison* of the first line seems incongruously balanced and composed for this tense moment, and the apostrophe, though perhaps less out of place, seems wholly uninspired. But perhaps the most disappointing thing about the speech is its brevity: it allows the duke only a few moments to explore his new position before he is interrupted by the entering king.

The careless and fragmented effect Marlowe appears to settle for at this crucial moment is typical of the tone of the whole play in its printed version, so it is doubly significant that the manuscript speech should be as intense and revealing as it is. It sets the duke's three lines within an exuberant and yet disciplined tropal outburst far more appropriate to both the man and the scene:

> thus fall Imperfett exhalatione
> wch our great sonn of fraunce cold not effecte
> a fyery meteor in the fermament
> lye there the kinges delyght and guises scorne
> revenge it henry yf thow liste or darst
> I did it onely in despight of thee
>
>   /verso/
> fondlie hast thow in censte the guises sowle
> y^{t} of it self was hote enoughe to worke
> thy Iust degestione wth extreamest shame
> the armye I have gathered now shall ayme
> more at thie end then exterpatione
> and when thow thinkst I have foregotten this
> and y^{t} thow most reposest one my faythe

then will I wake thee from thie folishe dreame
and lett thee see thie selfe my prysoner

Two sorts of restraint make this rhetorical display more disciplined and expressive than any in *Tamburlaine*. We might notice first that the images are arranged into clusters of three lines each, and that these mark separate stages in the speaker's train of thought. Even the connections between clusters have their psychological interest: the images of astronomy (ll. 1-3) share with those of the digestive processes (ll. 7-9) the common property of heat, while the final cluster of metaphors on sleep (ll. 12-15) refer, like those of the preceding cluster, to unconscious organic processes. The overt connections between these three stages of the Guise's speech, then, might readily have been suggested by a simple process of association of ideas. What the Guise does not realize, of course, is that all three clusters allude as well to subtly ominous portents, referring as they do to meteors, imprisoning dreams (ll. 14-15), and the hell within the Guise's own "sowle" (ll. 7-8). Marlowe's tropes, then, are no less profuse here than they were in the earlier plays, but they are controlled with far more dexterity, ingenuity, and suggestive power.

Evidence of a second sort of rhetorical restraint can be found in the short passages of literal statement which separate the image clusters from one another. These unembellished passages have no connection to the ongoing train of thought to which the more tropal passages testify. Instead, they are interruptions made to indicate both the motive (ll. 4-6) and the significance (ll. 10-11) of the murder which the Guise has just committed. It is important to recognize these interruptions as attempting to signify rhetorically, by their relative absence of tropes, the literal-minded attention to facts which characterizes their contents. By introducing a principle of selection based on verisimilitude, then, lines such as these give Marlowe's more tropal passages a greater significance, as complementary efforts to portray various more imaginatively engaged states of mind.

What distinguishes this speech's dynamic development from that of the deliberation structure proper is its lack of overall direction. The organizing scheme of deliberation formally prescribes the phases of an oration that aims to pose and explore some complex problem. The subtle and expressive control Marlowe begins to exercise over his characters' rhetoric in *The Massacre* simply reflects, in the manuscript speech, the more or less random migrations of an introspective mind as it responds to or considers events. When, in his final two plays, Marlowe manages to harness these subtleties of expressive rhetoric to the task of invigorating deliberation's more purposeful structure, he finally achieves his most mature and impressive orations.

Faustus's final soliloquy is perhaps the best-known of these mature speeches. As deliberation ordains, the speech considers its question with a palpable suspense. It is, of course, the question of Faustus's own fate, and, deluded by his habitual submission to his passions, he fails to resolve it successfully. He pleads throughout for enough time to recant and reform, ironically failing to realize that his hysterical plea is using up precisely that very final chance for repentance he is begging for. Thus his conclusion—"I'le burne my bookes"—is indeed contrary to our expectation, since it resolves his predicament in an irrelevant and ineffectual fashion. By seemingly organizing this intense final scene as a formal deliberation, then, Marlowe is ensuring that it will have the most dramatic and affecting structure his repertoire can provide.

As he had learned to do in *The Massacre at Paris,* Marlowe makes the deliberative framework more vivid by manipulating its imagery in response to Faustus's frantic vacillations of mood. The speech begins with a static amplification device more characteristic of *Tamburlaine*'s style, in the *synathroesmus* that reflects his stunned condition as he dazedly reiterates his desire for more time:

> Stand still you ever moving Spheares of heaven,
> That time may cease, and midnight never come.
> Faire natures eye, rise, rise again, and make
> Perpetuall day: or let this houre be but
> A yeare, a month, a weeke, a naturall day,
> That Faustus may repent, and save his soule.
> *O lente lente currite noctis equi.* . . .
>   (V.ii.1929-1935)

Even by Marlowe's standards, this is an impressively copious display. The first line, for example, begins with an apostrophe, introduces the prolonged *synathroesmus,* and glances toward synecdoche (with the "Spheares of heaven" for the motions of the universe) and metonymy (by which those spheres indicate the passage of time).

But, as Faustus realizes abruptly, his imaginative apostrophes are futile, for

> The Stars move still, Time runs, the Clocke will strike,
> The devill will come, and Faustus must be damned.
> (ll. 1936-1937)

The abrupt change of mood is reflected clearly in the figures, as Faustus switches from the static *synathroesmus* to the more chilling *auxesis* which relentlessly narrows the frames of reference that disclose to him the inescapability of his fate. The panic which this realization causes sets off a long, profusely rhetorical passage, in which the hyperbolical imagery borders on the hallucinatory ("See see where Christs bloud streames in the firmament /. . . Mountains and Hils, come, come, and fall on me"). But he is recalled from his frenzy by the striking of the clock, and the following lines show the pitilessly lucid mood in which he awaits his end:

> Ah Pythagoras Metemsycosis; were that true,
> This soule should flie from me, and I be chang'd
> Unto some brutish beast.
> All beasts are happy, for when they die,
> Their soules are soone dissolv'd in elements,
> But mine must live still to be plagu'd in hell,
> Curst be the parents that ingendred me;
> No *Faustus,* curse thy selfe, curse Lucifer
> That hath depriv'd the of the joies of heaven.
> (ll. 1966-74)

There is a single metaphor in this passage, whereby the watery "soules" of animals dissolve at death, but it is otherwise almost devoid of rhetorical devices. The speaker's imagination pales, it would seem, before the awful fact of his own condemnation.

But when Faustus's clock strikes its last note, he is driven again into a frenzy of terror that his intensified rhetoric reveals. Desperation now elicits a furious series of vain apostrophes, as he grasps in terror for any means out of his predicament:

> It strikes, it strikes; now body turne to aire,
> Or *Lucifer* will beare thee quicke to hell.
> O soule be chang'd into little water drops,

And fall into the Ocean, ne're be found.
My God, my God, looke not so fierce on me;
Adders and serpents, let me breathe a while:
Ugly hell gape not; come not *Lucifer*.
I'le burne my bookes; ah *Mephistophilis*.

                                (ll. 1975-1982)

Even at this almost unbearably anguished moment, Marlowe's craftsmanship is evident. About to be consumed by fire and swallowed up by
earth, Faustus appeals in understated synecdoches to air and water,
Hell's complementary elements, for relief. The very syntax, which is
clogged with caesuras and repeated words, seems to be struggling to
stop the relentless progression of time. In fact, the passage is structurally yet another *synathroesmus*, since it reformulates frantically a single
appeal for escape. But by the fitness and dramatic appropriateness of
the images that go into the amplification, Marlowe manages to make
his figurative infrastructure escape the casual reader's notice.

The Faustus soliloquy seems a logical culmination of Marlowe's experiments with the rhetoric of the dramatic oration. Rhetorically and
imaginatively, it is quite possibly the first mature Elizabethan soliloquy. Its imagery is supple and consummately expressive of the
speaker's surging emotions and subconscious preoccupations. Its
structure is both dramatic and tense, holding the reader in suspense
before Faustus arrives at his unexpected final offer to burn his necromantic books. But Marlowe, whatever credit may be due him for having introduced the dynamic Elizabethan style of oration, handles it
with assurance only in *Faustus* and *Edward II*, so his achievement has
proven easy to overlook. Fortunately, within a year or two of the end of
Marlowe's career, Shakespeare's Richard II was able to speak with a
similarly expressive complexity. With what happy results Marlowe's
successors developed his technical suggestions from that point on is a
matter of common knowledge and delight.

NOTES

1. *The Sacred Wood* (London: Methuen, 1920), p. 88. Works which have shown themselves more sympathetic to the play's rhetoric include Howard Baker's *Introduction to Tragedy* (Baton Rouge: Louisiana State University Press, 1939), pp. 50-59; Harry Levin's *The Overreacher* (Cambridge, Mass.: Harvard University Press, 1952), and Donald Peet's "Rhetoric of Tamburlaine," *ELH*, 26 (1959), 137-55). The only work I know of that treats the rhetoric of all of the plays is Virginia M. Meehan's *Christopher Marlowe, Poet and Playwright* (The Hague: Mouton, 1974).

2. All citations are from Fredson Bowers, ed., *The Complete Works of Christopher Marlowe*, 2 vols. Cambridge: Cambridge University Press, 1973.

3. Speculation about the order in which Marlowe wrote his plays has lost the allure it would once seem to have held. Both internal and external evidence has been repeatedly sifted, without leading to any firm consensus, particularly on *Doctor Faustus* and *The Massacre at Paris*. Nonetheless, since Irving Ribner's 1963 edition of the *Complete Plays*, no one has seriously challenged the working hypothesis that the work falls into the three groups that my essay will speak of: an early *Dido* and *Tamburlaine*, a *Jew of Malta* and a *Massacre at Paris* from about the turn of the decade, and a relatively late *Faustus* and *Edward II*.

4. *The Poetic Diction of the English Renaissance* (New York: Modern Language Association, 1941), p. 275.

5. *The Elizabethan and Metaphysical Imagery* (Chicago: University of Chicago Press, 1947), p. 33.

6. "Preface" to *The Plays of William Shakespeare*, from *The Yale Edition of the Works of Samuel Johnson*, 7, ed. Arthur Sherbo (New Haven, Conn.: Yale University Press, 1968), 73.

7. *The Arcadian Rhetorike* (1588; rpt. Oxford: Luttrell Society, 1950).

8. *"The Spanish Tragedy,"* in *Elizabethan Theatre*, Stratford-upon-Avon Studies, 9, ed. John Russell Brown and Bernard Harris (London: Edward Arnold, 1966), p. 75.

9. Bowers, ed., *Complete Works*, I, 358, is the source for both the cited opinions.

Signs of the Times:
Christopher Marlowe's Decline
in the Seventeenth Century

JOHN T. SHAWCROSS

Millar Maclure, in *Marlowe: The Critical Heritage*, writes: "[W]e find little or no attention given to the text of Marlowe in the century after the Restoration, either in the study or the theatre. Instead we have a set of errors or professions of ignorance, clichés of biography, and snap judgments which make poor reading."[1] This decline in Marlovian appearance and awareness is echoed by the fate of others, like John Donne, Thomas Dekker, and John Webster. The world of literature—of idea and literary performance—had shifted both its theoretical base and its products, and while such matters as Maclure suggests to account for the decline are possibly cogent (like the re-establishment of London theaters after 1660, the influence of Puritan attitudes of the immediate past, the unavailablity of texts, and the assumed remoteness of the pre-Interregnum literary world, except for Shakespeare [2]), the decline which for Marlowe had set in before the closing of the theaters in 1642 is a sign of the shift in the world of literature. The result is the generally unfortunate output of tragic drama in the Restoration and beyond, a dominance of comedic and indeed farcical works, and a poetic which has little of the strength and exuberance of Marlowe's poetry. I do not mean to suggest any condemnation of the

seventeenth-century theater or poetic which grew out of an ethos antithetical to that of the Elizabethan age. It was not until the revival of
individualism toward the end of the eighteenth century that someone
like Marlowe could reassume his major position as an author, dramatist, and poet.

The seventeenth century greeted Christopher Marlowe as "happy in
his buskind muse,"[3] but so given to "Epicurisme and Atheisme" that
he was but "a Poet of scurrilitie, who by giving too large a swinge to his
owne wit, and suffering his lust to have the full raines, fell (not without
just desert) to that outrage and extremitie, that hee denied God and his
sonne Christ."[4] The end of the century saw him either as one "inferior
to *Shakespear*, not only in the number of his Plays, but also in the elegan-
cy of his Style,"[5] or as one who was not "accounted a less Excellent
Poet . . . and the Best of Poets."[6] *Doctor Faustus* was thought of as "a
great noise," as a "Comedy," and as "tragical sport."[7] *Hero and Leander*
was generally praised during the century, and often quoted, imitated,
or alluded to, even while George Chapman's continuation was dismissed. Indeed it is this fragmentary poem that had received most
praise earlier as well. Marlowe's atheism and violent end were especially noted by "Precisians," Anthony Wood tells us in 1691, whose
embellished account thus became the source of knowledge for the
eighteenth century and after, although Theophilus Cibber remained
sceptical.[8] Cibber lists the plays, saying that *Tamerlane the Great* is said
to be the worst of Marlowe's productions, which implies that he himself did not know it, but omits *The Tragedy of Dido, Queen of Carthage*
(perhaps because of Thomas Nashe's hand in it) and includes *Lust's
Dominion; or The Lascivious Queen*. For the latter play he gives a date of
1661 with publication by Francis Kirkman, which was the second issue
of the only surviving text of 1657, whose title page states that the play
was "written by Christofer Marloe, Gent.," although John Day,
William Haughton, John Marston, and Thomas Dekker have also
been credited with collaboration. What Marlowe's name on this play
suggests, regardless of authorship, is that in 1657-61 he was known and
apparently was thought to be a good draw for sales. The play was acted
in 1600 and is apparently the same as *The Spanish Moor's Tragedy*. It was
altered by Aphra Behn as *Abdelazer, or, The Moor's Revenge* (1676),
published in 1677 and 1693. *The Maiden's Holiday*, a comedy, was also

entered in the Stationers' Register by Humphrey Moseley on 8 April 1654, ascribed to "Christopher Marlow and John Day."

Publication of Marlowe's work in the early seventeenth century is actually most significant. The only known printing of *The Jew of Malta* came in 1633, although it was first entered in the Stationers' Register on 17 May 1594. The completed *Hero and Leander*, whose publication may thus have had an assist by George Chapman, appeared eight times through 1637. There were single editions of each part of *Tamerlane the Great* in 1605 and 1606 respectively; and *Doctor Faustus* went through eight editions through 1631, not having been published before 1600, as we all know, and was the only Marlowe work published after the Restoration, in 1663. There were three seventeenth-century editions of *Edward II* (1612 and 1622), one of which is a variant edition. With the encroaching Civil Wars from 1639 onward and the closing of the theaters in 1642, Marlowe's and other playwrights' presences disappeared publicly. We do not have a record of performances of Marlowe's plays during the seventeenth century, although it would seem that *Tamburlaine, Doctor Faustus*, and *The Jew of Malta* remained on the popular stage spasmodically until the closing of the theaters, and *Faustus* was presented in 1662 and 1675.

Tucker Brooke tells us that "It was as the author of *Hero and Leander* and of the *Passionate Shepherd* that Marlowe enjoyed the highest personal reputation in the period immediately following his death,"[9] and Robert Burton's citation in *Anatomy of Melancholy* (1621), John Milton's allusive lines in "L'Allegro" and "Il Penseroso" (1631), R. C.'s recognition of William Bosworth's indebtedness to *Hero and Leander* in *Chast and Lost Lovers* (1651), and Izaak Walton's reference and quotation in *The Compleat Angler* (1653) evidence that. Further corroboration occurs earlier in plays by John Cooke, Ben Jonson, and Richard Brome, among others, and later in the poetry of Charles Cotton and John Wilmot, Earl of Rochester.

Marlowe's contemporary or near contemporary dramatists paid homage through imitation to *Tamburlaine, The Jew of Malta, The Massacre at Paris*, and *Doctor Faustus*. But those who allude to Faustus or Mephistophilis throughout the century seem not to be truly acquainted with Marlowe's play, only with its reputation in the popular mind, bothered by a *"visible apparition of the Devill on the Stage"* in the profane playing of "the *History of Faustus* (the truth of which [William Prynne had] heard from many now alive, who well remember it)."[10] Such allusions are not unlike our contemporary remarks about E. T. or Mr. Spock (even if we have seen neither movie nor television show), or about Willy Loman or the Caretaker by those who do not know the Arthur Miller source or the Pinter play. There are a few allusions to Marlowe and *Tamburlaine* or *Faustus* in the years after the closing of the theaters, but they offer little for the assessment of his reputation. Even Charles Saunders's *Tamerlane the Great* (1681) and Nicholas Rowe's *Tamerlaine* (1702) profess to be unrelated in any way to Marlowe's work. Saunders specifically says he does not know Marlowe and apparently took his plot from a novel called, *Asteria and Tamerlain*, or the *Distressed Lovers* by Mlle. de la Roche Guilhem, published in 1677 in E. C.'s translation, and as *Royal Lovers; or, The Unhappy Prince* in 1680.

We should note that a prose novel entitled, *The Famous and Renowned History of the Two Unfortunate, Though Noble, Lovers, Hero and Leander*, appeared around 1690, and more significantly that *The Historie of the Damnable Life and Deserved Death of Doctor John Faustus*, first published in 1592, reappeared twelve times between 1608 and 1700, with additional abridgments in 1685, 1690, and 1696, and the *Second Report of Doctor John Faustus*, published twice in 1594, was reprinted in 1674, 1680, 1685, and 1687. Doctor Faustus as character and legend was often before the public, though not necessarily or directly through Marlowe's play.

Only the 1663 quarto of *Doctor Faustus*, with its employment of lines from *The Jew of Malta*, as well as entries in the biographical compendia of Edward Phillips, William Winstanley, Gerard Langbaine, and Charles Gildon, already noted, and one imitation offer more than just allusion in the latter part of the century. Undoubtedly, however, some of the numerous jest books, poetic anthologies, and commonplace books of the period record unattributed excerpts, brief imitations, and variously used lines, but until a careful study of these ephemera has been made, we cannot fully assess Marlowe's popular, though not public, presence. We should not be too certain, however, that Marlowe, albeit unrecognized, was not before the seventeenth-century reading audience. The 1663 quarto may have resulted from the stage performance of 1662, and the 1675 stage performance may have occurred because the character and the legend were before the reading public from sources such as we have just described. The reputed near obliteration of Marlowe and his work, however, should disturb us less, I think, than our scholarly and critical hindsight might lead us to believe. Who, pray tell, today reads or perhaps even knows Richard Harding Davis, prolific though he was: more than thirteen journalistic volumes, eleven volumes of short stories, more than fifteen novels, and twenty-five plays; or think of the once popular John Galsworthy as playwright; or even more distressingly, the recent dramatist John Arden (whose plays may occasionally be presented by uncommercial groups and avant-garde companies). Even good authors are often being lost from our own contemporary perspectives, and if we are not losing the authors, we are losing some of their works, like George Bernard Shaw's *The Simpleton of the Unexpected Isles* or *Geneva*. Further, and more importantly, the world of literature had shifted to a different theoretical base, and the contextual world which would sustain literature had likewise altered.

Part of our understanding of this may lie in the one imitation noted before: William Mountfort's *The Life and Death of Doctor Faustus, Made into a Farce. With the Humours of Harlequin and Scaramouche: As they were several times Acted By Mr. Lee and Mr. Jevon, at the Queens Theatre in Dorset Garden. Newly Revived, At the Theatre in Lincolns Inn Fields, With Songs and Dances between the Acts.* The entertainment was produced sometime in the 1680s, perhaps spring 1688, and published in 1697. [11] As Tucker Brooke writes, "About 150 lines of the original verse are retained in broken patches, and the scenes of the Deadly Sins, the Horsecourser, the Hostess and Carter, and Benvolio's revenge are re-worked; but over half the actual lines and the whole of the tone are Mountfort's alone." [12] Anthony Kaufman in his introduction to a facsimile reprint stresses the farcical elements, noting that farce depends on its farceurs, and pointing out the importance of the stage-effect and contemporaneously satiric elements. [13] (One wonders, however, how Kaufman got the strange idea that Marlowe wrote George Chapman's *Bussy D'Ambois*.) Albert S. Borgman believed that what Mountfort did was to add farcical materials to a play that was already verging on slapstick. [14] But this view presupposes that the appearances of the good and bad angels and of Lucifer and Beelzebub, the pageant, the use of spirits and the compact itself, as well as the scene with the Old Man and its contrastive scene with Benvolio, are humorous, even farcical.

Although Professor Borgman was once my teacher, the only factor that I can agree with in his reading of Marlowe is that the playwright did have a mighty line of great verse which Mountfort totally discards. Mountfort in his various plays had learned to steer clear of declamatory lines that sank Indian Emperours and to build an ephemeral reputation on the kinds of things Samuel Pepys adored.

The basis of the humor, one must admit, may exist in the contrastive scenes of Marlowe's play, particularly in the B version of 1616, which some have claimed resulted from other playwrights' additions and tampering, while others have seen the A version of 1604 as a memorial and incomplete text. Perhaps certain comic formulas and standard comic improvisations lie behind parts of Marlowe's text, particularly the B text, but they are meant to contrast with the serious, philosophic main plot and treatment. However, Mountfort's version is decidedly representative of such formulas. There has been a sharp shift to comedic elements and a corresponding loss of the serious, philosophic dimension of the play: biblical contexts are submerged; any kind of allegoric hint disappears; Faustus as victim of *superbia vitae* and example to humankind recedes under the "humours of Scaramouche." There is nothing in Marlowe like Scaramouche's "Why I never said my Prayers in all my Life, but once; and that was when my damn'd wife was sick, that she might dye," which is directed to the male audience and their amours attending the theater with them. It capitalizes on comedy of manners in the way that our contemporary stand-up comics, who josh the audience to take their wives, do. Scaramouche, the cowardly braggart of the *commedia dell'arte* tradition, hopes the Devil will love him because he never saw a church in his life and he never gave alms: "I never gave any thing in my Life, but the Itch once to a pawn-broker." The subplot, indeed, if we can elevate it to such status, exists for its own sake, not as a contrast to the seriousness of what Faustus is engaged in. But the pattern had begun earlier with the buffoonery plays or rather skits of the 1620s, a time when Ben Jonson could not find positive reception for such works as *The Staple of News* or *The New Inn* or *The Magnetic Lady*. Today we forget them along with the actors "upon the Stage writhing and unboning their . . . limmes to all the antick and dishonest gestures of Trinculo's, Buffons, and Bawds; prostituting [themselves] . . . to the eyes of Courtiers and Court-Ladies, with their Groomes and *Madamoisellaes*."[15]

The parade of vices in Mountfort's play employs some of Marlowe's pictures and words, but the amplifications are contemporary for his audience and deflect allegoric attention. For example, Marlowe's Sloth says: "Heigh-ho! I am Sloth. I was begotten on a sunny bank. Heigh-ho, I'll not speak a word more for a king's ransom." Mountfort's Slothe amplifies with some obscene implications: "Hey Ho! I am *Sloth*; I was begotten at Church by a sleepy Judge on a Costermonger's Wife, in the middle of a long Sermon. I am as Lazy as a Fishmonger in the Dog-days or a Parson in *Lent:* I would not speak another Word for a King's Ransom." One wonders whether this Sloth would lead to *desperatio.* In other words, we do not have the Elizabethan reinforcement of the main plot in the subplot, and we do have elements in the main plot that detract from it.

Mountfort's ending, say from the time the clock strikes eleven, is enough to make a serious drama lover and especially a Marlovian cringe and shudder. It exemplifies the formulaic, and specifically in the form of *lazzi* (jests, acts of buffoonery), which involve standard routines common to the comic stage. Faustus's speech is greatly reduced, but for the most part it consists of the words given by Marlowe, and the old man and scholar, or the two scholars, have some similar lines. The Chorus in Marlowe ends the play and presents the moral ending in a couplet: "Whose deepness doth entice such forward wits / To practice more than heavenly power permits." But in the seventeenth-century farcical version, the old man has four lines in typically singsong rhyming couplets, the earmark of much late seventeenth-century verse. The rhythms and alliteration of Marlowe's lines, even those not in blank verse, are simply abandoned for trivializations:

> May this a fair Example be to all,
> To avoid such Ways which brought poor *Faustus*'s Fall.
> And whatsoever Pleasure does invite,
> Sell not your Soul to purchase vain Delight.

The scene changes to Hell, Faustus's limbs come together, and there is a dance and a song. Mountfort has completed his version of Marlowe with a *lazzo*: the bones reunite and join the dance.

Mountfort is not interested in the metaphysical problems that Marlowe is examining. The medievalism that Marlowe's play engages and rejects no longer exists for Mountfort's age as any kind of serious problem. The belief in the strength of the individual so essentially a part of the Renaissance had disappeared into the concept of governmental force, part Hobbesian, part Filmerian. Or else, like Algernon Sidney, the individualistic nonaccepter of political reality was hanged. The emotional appeal of tragedy, which William Wollaston in 1691 defined as that "which teaches us not to over-value or rely upon temporal advantages, by the falls of those who have had the most of them; to be tender-hearted, by using to pity their misfortunes; to be couragieous, by evoking at their patience; and to be humble, by observing what the greatest of men may come to,"[16] was no longer to be seen in the advancement of virtue through the fall of the important, but rather in the pity and patience of a work like Thomas Otway's *Venice Preserv'd* (1682). Wollaston went on to suggest the major genres of the era: "those . . . that tend *to depress and discredit Vice*: as *Comedy*, which presents to view the faults of common Conversations: and *Satyr*, which by its arguments exposes, not so much men, as their unreasonableness and enormities." The sentimental and the comedic could never sustain an Edward or a Barabas. Marlowe was no longer appropriate as a playwright to be imitated, and besides he was a "modern," in an age ostensibly (although I would underscore *ostensibly*) given to imitation and not innovation, to the rules of definition and category (and if demonstrably from the farther past, all the better), to Thomas Shadwell, and Nathaniel Lee (who incidentally did his own *The Massacre of Paris* in between asylum confinements), and William Wycherley. The world of literature had indeed shifted its theoretical base and therefore, the art it produced. It was not only Marlowe whose reputation declined but the value of the Elizabethan Renaissance world. It was a different theater that opened in 1660, and what resurrections of Elizabethan tragic modes there were either failed or were transformed into something like Lee's *The Rival Queens*. I cannot credit much the Puritan attitudes or the supposed remoteness of the pre-Interregnum world for the decline; those are historical pasts rather than present influences. The unavailability of texts was surely a result of the lack of popular demand. Rather I would suggest the change had set in with the rise of the ephemeral theater of the twenties and thirties, the neoplatonic, French courtly, and fleshless works of the thirties and forties, and the development of comedy of manners as we see it beginning with *Much*

Ado About Nothing and proceeding to Congreve. The decline of Marlowe and his plays in the seventeenth century is only one sign of the change of the ideational and literary times.

NOTES

1. Millar Maclure, *Marlowe: The Critical Heritage, 1588-1896* (London: Routledge and Kegan Paul, 1979), Introduction, p. 7.
2. *Ibid.*, p. 8.
3. *The Second Part* of *The Return from Parnassus*, ed. J. B. Leishman (1949), p. 242.
4. Thomas Beard, *The Theatre of Gods Iudgements* (1597), Chapter XXV.
5. William Winstanley, *The Lives of the Most Famous English Poets* (1687), p. 134.
6. Gerard Langbaine, *An Account of the English Dramatick Poets* (1691) citing Ben Jonson (1623) and Thomas Heywood (1635).
7. See Edward Phillips, *Theatrum Poetarum* (1685) and Winstanley; Winstanley; and Phillips and Winstanley, respectively.
8. Theophilus Cibber, *The Lives of the Poets* (1753), I, 85-87.
9. Tucker Brooke, "The Reputation of Christopher Marlowe," *Transactions of the Connecticut Academy of Arts and Sciences*, 25 (1922), 360.
10. William Prynne, *Histrio-Mastix* (1633), Act 6, Scene 9, f. 556.
11. See also Paul W. Miller's introduction to *The Plays of William Mountfort* (New York: Scholars' Facsimiles and Reprints, 1977). Robert D. Hume argues for a date of 1688 in "The Date of Mountfort's *The Life and Death of Doctor Faustus*," *Archiv für das Studium der Neueren Sprachen*, 213 (1976), 109-111.
12. Brooke, p. 386.
13. Anthony Kaufman, ed., *William Mountfort: The Life and Death of Doctor Faustus Made into a Farce (1697)* (Los Angeles, Calif.: William Andrews Clark Memorial Library, 1973).
14. Albert S. Borgman, *The Life and Death of William Mountfort* (Cambridge, Mass.: Harvard University Press, 1935).
15. John Milton, *An Apology Against a Pamphlet* (1642), p. 14.
16. William Wollaston, *The Design of Part of the Book of Ecclesiastes* (1691), pp. 7-8.

Marlowe in the Civil War and Commonwealth: Some Allusions and Parodies

LOIS POTTER

This essay began as an attempt to fill a gap: Miller Maclure's volume on Marlowe in the Critical Heritage series has no entries for the period of the Civil War and Interregnum. Its last prewar reference comes from *Timber,* published in the posthumous 1640 Folio of Jonson's *Works*; the next is the short biography by Edward Phillips in *Theatrum Poetarum Anglicanorum* (1675).[1] The various passages which I have found from the intervening years may not seem, individually, to contribute much to the history of Marlowe criticism. But, as Maclure says, "it is upon these fugitive allusions, often lighthearted, often prejudiced, that so much of the heritage depends."[2] Taken as a whole, moreover, they form a pattern which may be of interest.

One common factor in all the following quotations is their lack of biographical awareness. Apart from Walton, whose quotation of what he called "The Milkmaid's Song" in *The Compleat Angler* is well known, no one who made use of the dramatist's lines or characters in this period seems to have known the name of their author. Plays probably did matter more than playwrights in the popular consciousness: the first two attempts at giving a complete list of published plays (both of which date from 1656) arrange their entries alphabetically by titles, not authors.[3] But the absence of biographical comment is particularly significant for a writer like Marlowe, whose life would have lent itself so well to moralizing comment. By 1633, Prynne's *Histriomastix*, quoted in Maclure, made capital from the appearance of the devil during a performance of *Faustus* but failed to follow this up by describing the diabolical fate of the dramatist himself. It thus seems likely that, by 1642, "Faustus and Mephistophilis, like Barabas in *The Jew of Malta*," had "become stock types unconnected with their creator."[4]

There is a good deal of evidence to supply negative corroboration of this view. Marlowe's name is notably absent from many contexts where one might expect to find a writer of importance. For instance, some prologues, epilogues, and dedications of plays published during this period not only lament the closing of the theaters but list the most admired dramatists whose works have thus become inaccessible. A typical example of this sort of pantheon, with a strong court emphasis, is: "*Johnson, Shakespeare, Goffe*, and *Devenant*, / Brave *Sucklin, Beaumont, Fletcher, Shurley*."[5] John Cotgrave's anthology of passages from plays (*Wit's Treasury*, 1655) deliberately extended its net very widely to draw attention to the vastness of the achievements it was celebrating, but Marlowe is represented by only one quotation—from *The Jew of Malta*—as against 154 from Shakespeare, 112 from Beaumont and Fletcher, and even seven from Tomkis's *Lingua*, a university play.[6] Robert Baron's *Mirza* (1655), a play which acknowledges its debt to Jonson's *Catiline* and imitates its extensive annotations, contains references to Persepolis and to Tamburlaine's treatment of Bajazet, but does not take the opportunity to add a footnote on Marlowe's play. The attribution to him of *Lust's Dominion* (published 1657) and of *The Maiden's Holiday* (never published but entered in the Stationers' Register of 1654, by Moseley, as the work of Marlowe and John Day)[7] further confirm that the author's name and plays had by this time become separated.

Two years before the first play-lists, Edmund Gayton, in *Pleasant Notes upon Don Quixot* (1654), mentioned *Tamburlaine, The Jew of Malta*, and *Faustus* in a long list of plays associated with the popular stage.[8] Gayton, born in 1608, could in theory have seen the Marlowe plays performed or bought copies of them. Yet some of the works mentioned in his list are no longer extant, and it is likely that he knew little of them except their names. The context of his list is a distinction between the crude and barbarous drama of the past, now surviving only in the repertoire of the "terrible teare-throats" of the Red Bull and Fortune, and the more sophisticated drama, the result of a "reformation" by Jonson, Jones, and Beaumont and Fletcher, which he would like to see restored to the stage.[9] His notions of the "old" drama are vague: for instance, he describes a "play of *Adam* and *Eve*" where "the good grandam is brought in with two or three waiting maides attending her, and in Paradise too, when there were but two in all the world."[10] This amusing attempt at theater history may well reflect current opinion: I shall return to it later.

It thus needs to be borne in mind that the quotations which follow are not allusions to Marlowe but to his plays or, more precisely, to some aspects of the plays, probably taken out of context. Many topics which figure in his work were also important to writers of the Civil War: the harm done by bad favorites (sometimes actually called "Gavestons");[11] the political role of the magician-prophet (especially William Lilly); the supposed influence of Machiavelli on contemporary politicians, and the threat from the Turks (the first English translations of *The Prince* and *The Koran* were published in 1640 and 1649 respectively). I have tried to avoid confusing references to Marlowe's subject matter with genuine references to his work, but it must be admitted that some of my examples are rather problematic.

1. From Thomas Herbert, *News Newly Discovered. In a pleasant Dialogue betwixt Papa the false Pope, and Benedict an honest Friar.* 1641. (British Library, E.1102.3; Wing H1530)

This is an anti-Catholic pamphlet, one of many dating from the first year of the Long Parliament. The "honest friar," who eventually reveals that he has been converted to Protestantism, tells the Pope of the measures currently being taken against Catholics in England. The Pope fulminates:

> Those which were the cause of it,
> I thus curse them with Bell,
> Booke, and Candle, Candle, Booke, and Bell,
> Backewardes and forewardes unto Hell.
> (Sig. A[3])

The curse could of course have been a familiar jingle. But its context—a papal court and a malicious friar—is similar enough to *Faustus* to suggest actual recollection of III.ii.92–93.[12]

The remaining examples are from royalist publications.

2. From *Have Amongst You, My Masters*, an anonymous broadside. 1647. (669.f.11.25; Wing H1159)

> But oh! those subtile men must not
> (Above all others) be forgot,
>   We Jewes of *Malta* call;
> Who lately have a new trick found,
> To make men for their own compound,
>   These get the Devill and all.

This is a reference to the highly unpopular Committees for Compounding, which levied fines on those who had borne arms against Parliament and were willing to pay in order to avoid confiscation of the whole estate. There is an obvious parallel between this "trick" and the one played by Ferneze on the Jews of Malta. But here it is the tricksters, not their victims, who are described as Jews. This may reflect vagueness about the plot of the play, or the fact that the expression had come to be used loosely (many people still think that the title of *The Merchant of Venice* refers to Shylock). The author may also be making the familiar association between the Puritans and the Chosen People.[13]

3. From "J. A. Rivers" [John Abbott], *Devout Rhapsodies: in Which, is Treated, of the Excellencie of Divine Scriptures*. 1647. (E.413.16, Wing A67)

This is a series of sermons in verse, by a royalist who says that he wrote in prison, "to divert my minde from too serious thoughts of publick and private calamities" (A2^r). The fifth sermon, which deals with the war in heaven, thus describes Lucifer:

> The Armies ordered, and in mutuall view,
> The grant [*sic*] Commander of the Traytruous [*sic*] crue
> Himselfe advances, and at every straine,
> Presents Goliah, or fierce *Tamerlaine*.
>
> (p. 29)

I include these lines somewhat tentatively: Tamberlaine may be as untheatrical a comparison as Goliath. But there may have been some recollection in the author's mind of the prebattle exchanges of defiance between Tamburlaine and his opponents. The passage is also interesting in the light of what is sometimes suggested about the influence of Marlowe on Milton's Satan.

4. From *The Levellers Levell'd. Or, The Independents Conspiracie to root out*

Monarchie, by "Mercurius Pragmaticus" (usually attributed to March-amont Nedham). 1647. (E. 419.4; Wing N394)

This set of extracts, like the next, is taken from a miniature play published under the name of one of the illegal royalist news-sheets of the period. The latter were normally quartos of a single gathering; this play is a double number, running to fourteen pages in all, but the need to save space has forced the author or compositor to present verse as though it were prose. The same is true of Nos. 5 and 7, below. Literary allusion is commonplace in pamphlet literature; to write in dramatic form was itself an act of defiance, since Parliament's antitheatrical leg-islation had been renewed in July 1647 (this playlet dates from early December). The sheer multiplicity of possible sources makes it difficult to say whether or not anything is specifically Marlovian in origin as opposed to atmosphere. As the parallels are more convincing when seen as a whole, I shall quote even passages which, on their own, I would ignore. For instance, a stage direction from Act III describes "Orlotto" (Lilly, whose predictions had tended to be favorable to Parliament) as having "*a* Iacobs *stafe, a Globe and Booke.*" That this corresponds pretty closely to the image of Faustus on the 1616 and lat-er editions of the play may not mean much, since all magicians must have looked much the same. Orlotto's style, moreover, is quite un-Marlovian.

The language given to John O'London (a caricature of the Leveller Lilburne) is another matter:

> Wee'l cut our safety through their Coates of Steele, and write our Lawes (as *Draco* did) in bloud: I that have dar'd for to encounter death, when Leggs and Armes did quarrell in the Aire, shot off from maimed trunkes, and hewed my passage through an host of Royallists, have been a perfect Traytour against my Prince, and stood as sole Antagonist against all Law, will lead you Gentlemen through all assaies, and make my way with fire and vinegar over the frozen Alpes of *Highgate* Hill, not [sic] put Armour off till I do strike my sword on *London*-stone, and be proclaimed Lord of *London.*
>
> (Act IV, p. 12)

> What direfull Planet is't that thwarts my hopes? did I but know I'de scale *Joves* starry roofe, there seize upon't, and throw it down from thence, like Lucifer from Heaven.
>
> (Act V, p. 13)

The most obvious, pervasive influence is that of Shakespeare's Jack
Cade, but the first speech opens with an echo of *The White Devil* and is
followed shortly by a borrowing from *Richard III*: "You know tomor-
row is a busie day" (p. 13). The author did not need to know the
prologue to *The Jew of Malta* to be aware that

> laws were then most sure
> When like the Draco's they were writ in blood.
>   (20-21)

Nor did he need to draw on *II Tamburlaine* for the limbs quarrelling in
the air or the threats to storm heaven (III. 98-102; V. iii. 46-63). So
many heroes, villains, and tyrants had already imitated the Marlovian
style—Chapman's *Bussy D'Ambois*, for instance, appeared in a revised
edition in 1641—that it is impossible to say whether the model is being
followed at first or second hand.

5. From *Crafty Cromwell*: Part One is attributed to "Mercurius
Melancholicus," Part Two to "Mercurius Pragmaticus." 1648. (E.
426.17; Wing C6772.)

The second scene of Part One, probably meant to parody the opening of *Catiline*, introduces the Ghost of Pym:

> From the black Lake that runs round *Erebus* I come, permitted by
> the King of Flames, to visit those that my Co-partners were, when
> I was clothed in flesh . . . pale *Cynthia* mounted in her silver
> Waine, now takes her progresse by the milkie way, and now
> *Aldeboran* is mounted high, above the shinie Cassiopeia's Chaire.
>   (Act II, sig. A4)

The speech ends with Pym drawing a curtain to reveal the sleeping
Cromwell—a device, again, probably taken from *Catiline*, though it
had been used earlier by Marlowe. The most interesting borrowing in
the speech is the last phrase quoted; it is taken from *The Faerie Queene* (I.
iii.16), a work from which Marlowe had also plagiarized.[14]

However, there is an odd conjuncture of images at this period which
might be taken to indicate some recollections of *Tamburlaine*. Part Two
gives the stage direction, "*Rainsborow* drawne in a Chariot, Six Trum-
peters sounding before him" (Act III). There is an immediate topical
source for this episode. Rainsborough was a Leveller who had just been
appointed Vice-Admiral of the Navy. *A New Magna Charta*, a pamphlet

published in the same week as Part Two of *Crafty Cromwell*, described him on his way to take up the new post, "in a Coach and four horses, with a trumpeter and some troopers riding before and after it, sounding the trumpet in every towne and village as they passed."[15] But this (possibly fictitious) example of overweening pride seems to have awakened memories of the most famous stage chariot. *A New Magna Charta* was dated 17 February by the collector George Thomason; the number of *Mercurius Melancholicus* dated 12-19 February provides my next Marlowe allusion.

6. From *Mercurius Melancholicus*, No. 25, 12-19 February 1648. (E. 427. 23)

> But who are these? foure Parliament-men, that now are got into *Charles* his *Waine*; drive on Carr-man . . . :
>
> > Hollo ye pampered Jades of *Asia*,
> > What can ye draw but thirty miles a day,
> > Having so brave a Coach-man as old *Mildmay*?
> > Young *Crook-back'd Veine*, and *Challenore*,
> > With ill-lookt *Martyn*, that so loves a Whore?
> > These are the Chariters of great *Britaines Waine*,
> > Laugh, if you see them over-turne againe.

Mercurius Melancholicus was probably the most scurrilous of the royalist news-sheets, and these lines are typical of its manner. Two famous stage-tyrants are used as models for some of the leading Parliamentarians. Vane is compared with Richard III in another news-sheet, *Mercurius Aulicus*, a few weeks later; the same author probably had a hand in both.[16] The pun on Charles's Wain is widely used in the period, not surprisingly (it features, for instance, in Martin Parker's ballad, "When the King Enjoys His Own Again"). As for the *Tamburlaine* lines, I suspect that they were best known through their occurrence in the mouth of Ancient Pistol.

This is typical of the way in which Shakespeare's heroes come increasingly to dominate the field of literary allusion and even parody. Richard III, in Shakespeare's version, was as much a model for the stage tyrant in Milton's *Eikonoklastes* as in *The Levellers Levell'd* and *Crafty Cromwell*.[17] Once Cromwell had assumed the title of Lord Protector the comparison became inevitable. A pamphlet of 1657, sometimes attributed to William Prynne, discusses his reluctance to be

made king in the context of *King Richard the Third Revived*.[18] The first
Restoration biography of Cromwell contrasts his unremarkable birth
with the prodigies recorded of Richard. Though the book is called *Fla-gellum*, its author shows no interest in Marlowe's 'Scourge of God'
hero.[19] Yet there are many parallels that could have been drawn be-tween Tamburlaine and Cromwell, if anyone had remembered
Marlowe's play: in particular, the unbroken succession of military vic-tories. Cromwell even had a coaching accident in 1654, when the
horses ran away with him, but the various poems commemorating his
lucky escape stick to Hippolytus, Phaeton, and Charles's Wain.[20]

The final extract shows Cromwell and his chaplain Hugh Peters in a
relationship which is directly indebted to that of Richard III and
Buckingham but also, directly or indirectly, to that of Barabas and Ith-amore. It comes from the longest and most ambitious of the topical
royalist pamphlet plays.

7. From *The Famous Tragedy of King Charles I*. 1649. (Wing F384)

Peters. Most Valiant, and invincible Commander, whose Names's as
    terrible to the *Royallists* as e're was Huniades to the *Turkes*, or *Talbot* to
    the *French*; thy Nose, like a bright Beacon, sparkling still (the *Ætna*,
    that doth fame our English world) hangs like a Comet o're thy dread-full face, denouncing death & vengeance.
    . . . thou hast not slaine but tane the Kingly *Lyon*, and like great
    Tamburlaine with his *Bajazet* canst render him within an Iron-Cage a
    spectacle of mirth, when e're thou pleasest.

Cromwell. Thou art that Load-stone, which shall draw my sense to any
    part of policy i' the Machiavelian world, we two (like *Mahomet* and his
    pliant *Monke*) will frame an *English Alchoran*, which shall be written
    with the self-same pensil great *Draco* grav'd his Lawes.

(I.i. pp. 3-4)

While the passage is full of Marlovian echoes, it is possible to find
other sources for each of them. The joke about Cromwell's nose (ubiq-uitous in this period) naturally suggests Barabas, but what lies behind
both figures is a folktale bogeyman; Cromwell himself was later to be-come a character in the mummers' plays.[21] It has already become clear
that Tamburlaine, Bajazet, and Draco could have an independent ex-

istence. The reference to the Koran is part of a royalist argument that the licensing of the first English translation of this work, early in 1649, proved the essentially non-Christian nature of the new government. The link with Machiavellianism was, of course, a common accusation on both sides. What makes the passage a candidate for inclusion here is not, then, any one allusion, but the combination of so many of them, and the presence of the mock-heroic style.

The Famous Tragedy also offers a clue as to why that style was chosen, and how it was meant to be taken. At one point, Peters says, "But Noble Sir, this Colloquie is too poor, if we consider our most high resolves, our language should be like the Lawes we meane to give, awfull and to be wonder'd at by mortals" (p. 3). The bombastic rhetoric of the stage tyrant functions both socially and politically. On one level, it ridicules characters whose aspiring minds are reflected in aspiring vocabularies; it will be noticed that high astounding terms are never given to sympathetic characters. (The absence of a language fit for true heroism was a problem for these dramatists, and would continue to be a problem after the Restoration.) But the fact that the style was old-fashioned may also be significant. Supporters of Parliament claimed to be restoring a freedom that had previously existed, rather than introducing new ideas. The reign of Elizabeth I was often cited as a time of Protestant purity and harmony between ruler and subject. In this context, Edmund Gayton's pseudohistory of a stage "reformed" by Jones and Jonson can be seen as an implicit contrast between their true reformation and the false one attempted in his own time. According to royalist satire, the idealized past which the caricatured revolutionaries are trying to restore was grotesque and primitive. In a state of nature, as conceived in dramatic terms, speeches are nasty, brutish, and long.

NOTES

1. Millar Maclure, ed., *Marlowe, The Critical Heritage 1588-1896* (London, Boston, and Henley: Routledge and Kegan Paul, 1979).
2. *Ibid.*, 7.
3. The lists, appended to *The Careless Shepherdess* and *The Old Law*, are reprinted in full in W. W. Greg, *A Bibliography of the English Printed Drama to the Restoration*, 4 vols. (London: The Biblographical Society, 1939-1955), III, 1319-1362.
4. Maclure, 48.
5. 'Prologue to the Gentry,' from *The Famous Tragedy of King Charles I* (1649).

6. For a discussion of Cotgrave's anthology and full statistics on its contents, see G. E. Bentley, "John Cotgrave's *English Treasury of Wit and Language* and the Elizabethan Drama," *Studies in Philology*, XI (1943), 186-203.

7. See Greg, *Bibliography*, II (1951), 993.

8. Book IV, 272-273.

9. Book I, 24, and IV, 272.

10. Book IV, 272.

11. *E.g.*, a character in Part Two of *Crafty Cromwell* says that Charles I has had too many Gavestons (I.i. p. 5).

12. Quotations from Marlowe's plays are taken from E. D. Pendry and J. C. Maxwell ed., *Complete Plays and Poems* (London, Melbourne and Toronto: Dent, 1976).

13. This last point was suggested by Thomas Pettit when this paper was given at the 1983 Marlowe Society conference in Sheffield.

14. The Spenser borrowing was pointed out to me by T. W. Craik at the Sheffield conference.

15. Attributed to William Prynne. E. 427.15; Wing P4020.

16. His soul is said to be 'as aspiring as his shoulders'; he "looks as like *Richard* the third, as if he were spit out of his mouth." *Mercurius Aulicus*, No. 6 (29 March 1648).

17. Milton compares his religious hypocrisy to Charles I's prayers and meditations in *Eikon Basilike*. See *Eikonoklastes, Complete Prose Works*, Vol. II.

18. E. 896.5*.

19. James Heath, *Flagellum, or the Life and Death, Birth and Burial of O. Cromwell the late Usurper Faithfully Described* (London, 1663). Wing HI328.

20. See Marvell's "First Anniversary" and George Wither's *Vaticinium Casuale, a Rapture Occasioned by the late miraculous deliverance of his highness the Lord Protector from a desperate danger* (1655).

21. Marion Jones has drawn my attention to a number of folk-play references to Oliver Cromwell with a face of brass.

Dido Queene of Carthage
and the Evolution of Marlowe's
Dramatic Style

MATTHEW N. PROSER

In *The Shape of Time* George Kubler speaks of an artist's "biological opportunity," the circumstantial coming together of an individual's "temperament and training" and a specific moment—"early, middle, or late"—in the development of his tradition. Kubler calls this moment an artist's "entrance" into his tradition and the point at which he assumes his "position" in it.[1] *Dido Queene of Carthage* (written before 1586/7) and *Tamburlaine I and II* (written Summer/Autumn 1587)[2] are ordinarily considered early works of Marlowe. As such, they appear to illustrate a crucial dividing point in Marlowe's development as a dramatist and in the role he was to play in the coming age of great Elizabethan drama. Each work manifests a group of specific leanings or tendencies, either of which might have been fulfilled by Marlowe contingent upon the movement of popular taste, the general pressure of English stage history, and the focus of Marlowe's authorial sensibility. Each play also shows solid examples of the other's tendencies, so that we are always assured that both pieces are by the same author.[3]

Two distinct lines of production can be distinguished in Marlowe's works. One derives from classical influence and inclines toward the lyrical and narrative. The other stems from Medieval and Renaissance backgrounds and is wholly dramatic. In the first category are the translations of Book I of Lucan's *Pharsalia* and Ovid's *Amores* and *Hero and Leander*.[1] Attached to this group, however, would also appear to be the Dido play. Connections are the drama's classical background and subject, its obvious dependency on the Vergilian narrative,[5] its theme of love, and finally, significant tonal and stylistic features. The second category comprises Marlowe's more familiar works: *Tamburlaine, The Massacre at Paris, The Jew of Malta, Doctor Faustus,* and *Edward II*. This group includes Marlowe's major productions, the plays that helped give body and shape to the developing tradition of Elizabethan drama—the works for which Marlowe justly won his fame.[6]

Formalistically, Elizabethan drama is sprawling and episodic, an agglomeration of contradictory tendencies held together by the English genius for incorporation and a late attachment to medieval forms and techniques.[7] Considering Marlowe's reputation as a crucial English playwright establishing important dramaturgic bridgeheads for the Elizabethan stage, his *Dido Queene of Carthage* is remarkable in its "neoclassical" sense of balanced structuring and orderly containment of events. Of course it may be said that Marlowe's dependency on his primary source, Vergil's *Aeneid* (Books I, II, and IV especially) obviated the necessity of his working out a plot line of his own. On the other hand, some of Marlowe's changes or additions, such as the institution of an un-Vergilian affection by Anna for Iarbas or the triple suicide at the play's end, effectively modify the Vergilian narrative; so does the tone of various sections concerning the play's divine figures, these being inherited from Vergil as well. Such portions often carry a satiric or sensual Ovidian quality. Mary E. Smith has said that *Dido*'s tone "resembles that of Ovid and Homer more"[8] than that of Vergil, and that "in the ironical sophistication of the classic Ovid, Marlowe found a spirit closely akin to his own."[9] This "Ovidian spirit" and Marlowe's impulse toward innovation along a number of dramatic avenues, including structure, may, with other possibilities to be later brought forward, help to account for *Dido*'s interesting combination of Elizabethan, classical, and neoclassical qualities.

Of course, *Dido Queene of Carthage* is not Marlowe's only literary production with a traditional story line, Ovidian influence, and intimations of classical shapeliness. Another is *Hero and Leander*, which Marlowe executes in a style balancing light lyricism with irony and urbane wit. *Hero and Leander* uses Ovid's *Heroides* as one of its sources, although, as William Keach suggests, it is really the spirit of the *Amores* and the *Ars Amatoria* which exerts a stronger influence.[10] Once again, as in the case of *Dido Queene of Carthage*, the poem's Ovidian features are tied to a shapely progression of episodes.[11] These are molded on a superstructure of glittering heroic couplets that reflect a quality of control and rational intelligence far less visible in the strenuous progressions of *Tamburlaine I and II* or the cataclysmic emotional descent of *Doctor Faustus*. Again, such phenomena in *Hero and Leander* suggest a neoclassical dimension to Marlowe's talents which may seem surprising, although it is quite readily apparent in the well-known "Passionate Shepherd" lyric as well.

This classic Ovidian spirit, to use Smith's terms, observable in various of Marlowe's works, is not absolutely consistent. Still, one would not be entirely wrong in pointing out such general features as urbanity, wit, satiric impulse, and, of course, eroticism, along with mythological interest, lyricism, shapeliness, and a peculiar combination of emotional sophistication and clarity. All these are attributes of Ovid's classically civilized and knowing consciousness.[12] In *Dido* the Ovidian influence is felt in Marlowe's tongue-in-cheek view of the gods (and sometimes of Aeneas), and in various notable scenes and speeches involving such figures as Jupiter, Dido, and Cupid-Ascanius.[13]

In both *Hero and Leander* and *Dido Queene of Carthage*, the linkage of Ovidian features to the practice of structural control may hint at neoclassical standards which after an Italian inception come to their most extreme fulfillment in the rigors of the French style: "consciousness, rationality, moderation, order, clarity."[14] Marlowe can scarcely be accused of fulfilling these completely. Nevertheless, one might add to the list polish, charm, and grace, in addition to stress on technique and artifice; classical subject matter and proportion; and, in the drama, declamation, balance as a formal technique, and, if not outright obedience to the unities and proprieties, then a general sense of containment—an aura of poised and deliberate restraint.

Marlowe's urbane, skillful, and playfully satiric tendency may be poised against the "romantic" side Mario Praz found in him, with all its rebellious fire.[15] Smith notices this urbane quality in *Dido* too: "Nothing serious or sacred has been able to escape the clutches of Marlowe's mischievous and yet savage humor. . . ."[16] But along with wit and satire, Marlowe has converted his narrative and mainly linear source into a true system of dramatic stresses and balances almost as a neoclassical dramatist might. It is not the play's construction alone that makes *Dido* seem slow and unelectrifying to some contemporary readers. Rather it is the play's classical subject matter, its stylization and appreciable regularity, and its basically declamatory nature. In short, *Dido* is not to all contemporary tastes, nor would it have been fully to the taste of the uneducated or uninitiated at the public playhouses. Indeed, it appears that the play was written for presentation at court first, and thereafter at the private playhouses by "the Children of her Maiesties Chappell." Such productions were notable for their elegance, sophistication, and stylization.[17]

Dido Queene of Carthage is an adroitly organized system of counterweighted scenes and relationships, all thematically attached to the central plot concern—the conflict between Dido's imperious passion for Aeneas and the Trojan's divinely appointed obligations and ambitions. The central conflict is communicated by the main characters, who themselves are placed in conflict with each other and with aspects of their own natures. Dido must negotiate a passion that she senses will ultimately destroy her; Aeneas must trim his vacillating instincts to determine just what kind of use he will make of the importunate queen. The play's divine figures are not mere decorations, any more than they are in *The Aeneid*. They play significant roles in inciting feelings and actions, such as Dido's passion or Aeneas's departure for Italy. The gods themselves appear on the stage, revealed in their own passions and conflicts, as in Jupiter's flirtation with Ganymede, or the animosity between Venus and Juno. This divine frame amplifies (sometimes comically) the play's main theme of ironic and tragic passion while augmenting its sense of dramatic containment by implying limits to the universal forces. These limits are brought forward in the very human manipulativeness and perversion shown in some of the gods, namely Venus and Jupiter. Within this frame and linked to the larger tragic action depend a number of subsidiary and reflective plot elements: Iarbas's rejected passion for Dido and Anna's unrequited affection for Iarbas (the larger subplot components) immediately come to mind. But other smaller actional kernels consist of Venus's use of Cupid (disguised as Ascanius) to trigger the love affair of Dido and Aeneas, and the perverse flirtation between Cupid and Dido's nurse.

Contrastively, Aeneas's masculine subordinates are used to help motivate the "war" side of Marlowe's epical drama, *i.e.* the Vergilian issue
of Aeneas's divine appointment with a Roman destiny. The scenic construction of *Dido Queene of Carthage* is a system of intermeshed units,
large and small wheels, all moving the play's main action either dramatically or thematically, or both. This main action at its broadest is
the sacrificial destruction of Dido in the name of love, for the sake of
Aeneas and his heroic role. At times Marlowe identifies with Aeneas,
at others with Dido; at times he is ironic and detached, at others satiric,
and at yet others heroic and grandiose.

Of course the play also contains many examples of Marlowe's Renaissance exuberance and Romantic excess, *e.g.* Aeneas's wildly violent
evocation of the fall of Troy with its "young infants swimming in their
parents' blood" and the townsfolks' "headless carcasses piled up in
heaps" (II.i.193,194). And this *grand guignol* is outdone by the ghastly
description of Priam's murder (II.i.235-258) in which Neoptolemus
cuts off old Priam's hands as he pleads for his life, and then rips the
reverend father "from the navel to the throat" (l. 255). The outrageous
description of old Hecuba caught by the heels and "swung . . . howling
in the empty air" (II.i.247-248) combines horror with a kind of black
humor. Images like these are bound to work against the play's opposed
qualities of restraint and containment, although, in fact, they are reminiscent of such classical models as Euripides and Seneca. Other instances cannot claim such distinguished antecedents, for example,
Ganymede's early complaint to Jupiter, telling how Juno "reached
him" so hard a rap for spilling wine that "blood run down" his ears
(I.i.8). Dido's more Tamburlainean moments also threaten to burst
the play's retaining seams—"How now, Gaetulian," she bullies Iarbas, "are ye grown so brave / To challenge us with your comparisons? / Peasant, go seek companions like thyself . . . " (III.iii.19-21).
Her final instructions to Iarbas in this scene, who is ordered by Dido to
go "unto the house" (III.iii.62), are actually laughable. Even the style
in which the goddesses Juno and Venus address each other (*haute imperious fishwife*) violates the dignity and grandeur one would expect in
such classical figures. Witness Marlowe's conscious, abrasive mockery: "Avaunt, old witch," shrills Venus to Juno, and threatens to tear
out her eyes and "feast the birds with their blood-shotten balls"
(III.ii.34-35). Finally, intrusions such as the odd little scene of flirta

tion between the Nurse and Cupid-Ascanius (IV.v) may reveal thematic parallels, but in fact, even if this interlude is rationalized as "comic relief," it nevertheless breaks into the action in a manner more Elizabethan than "Neoclassical."

All these examples must be acknowledged, along with their mitigating, grotesque, and loosening effects. Such elements vary and complicate the tone of the play and show the imperfections (or ineptitudes) attached to its efforts at balance and restraint. Yet, these admissions having been made, the main lines of *Dido*'s construction remain surprisingly regular, clear, suggestively extended, and cleverly articulated. Such attributes, along with the play's Ovidian features, manage to create an overall impression. Marlowe was not to manage such structural sophistication again until *Edward II*.

But if *Dido Queene of Carthage* is neoclassically oriented, it is also fresh and innovative in this tendency. Marlowe's development of a love subplot revolving around Anna and Iarbas was, according to Roma Gill, decisive in transforming the piece from narrative to dramatic form.[18] What is more, according to Smith this balancing element seems to have been one of Marlowe's unique contributions to earlier versions of the legend, particularly those Renaissance Dido plays written in Italy, France, and England.[19]

Although McDiarmid found possible links between the declamatory poetry of Robert Garnier in *Porcie*, *Les Juives*, and *Cornélie* and *Tamburlaine*'s ranting style,[20] Smith acknowledges no debt to the French or English tradition of Dido plays, particularly Jodelle's *Didon se sacrifiant* (1558) and Gager's *Dido* (1583).[21] But Smith sees "six points of resemblance between Marlowe's *Dido* and the Italian plays, some of which lead into, but stop short of, Marlowe's contributions.[22] Of these, the complication of Iarbus's devotion to Dido and his jealousy of Aeneas "figure prominently in all three of the Italian Dido plays": Pazzi's *Dido in Carthagine* (1524), Giraldi-Cinthio's *Didone* (c. 1543), and Dolce's *Didone* (1547). In Vergil's *Aeneid*, Iarbas is rejected and the jealousy is implicit; but in Marlowe, as derived from his Italian forebears, the jealousy is explicit and Iarbas's role is made a vital one. However, it is Marlowe himself who reshapes Anna's suicide in Dolce's play into a tragic reflection of Dido's own self-destruction for a frustrated passion. Marlowe has Anna destroy herself at the funeral pyre for Iarbas's sake after both Dido and Iarbas have already taken the same course, and for similar reasons.[23] Interestingly, it is Anna's words that conclude the play: "Now, sweet Iarbas, stay! I come to thee!" Two of Marlowe's key changes—the creation of the Anna-Iarbas subplot and the triple suicide in the last scene—swing our attention away from Dido's Vergilian dignity in a tragic death willed her by the gods to a perception of the tragic nature of love in the lives of all the play's principals. True, as Roma Gill humorously indicates, "diversifying the interest in this way, Marlowe not only makes drama out of epic but, playing with fire, leads tragedy into comedy" (or comes dangerously close to doing so). On the other hand, Marlowe's amplification of Anna's role and complication of it with that of Iarbas does "create additional conflict," whether "wet-handkerchiefed" or not.[24] The upshot, Italian derivations notwithstanding, is as D. C. Allen rightly states: " . . . the alteration of plot and temperance of the English poet suggest that he was feeling his way toward the neo-classical technique of Corneille and Racine."[25]

Or might have done, had his course not been deflected toward another kind of drama, another kind of style. Art critic Meyer Shapiro acknowledges the possibility that a creator may have two sides to his personality, one of which usually dominates. However, the second side may reveal itself more clearly under certain circumstances. For instance, an artist's "drawings or sketches" may be "more advanced than the finished paintings and suggest another side of his personality."[26] Shapiro brings forward the example of Picasso and points out that in his case "two styles—Cubism and a kind of classicizing naturalism—were practiced at the same time."[27] Perhaps Marlowe would have been perfectly capable of practicing both his styles at the same time also; or perhaps *Dido* is like the case of an artist's "drawings or sketches" that "suggest another side of his personality" and another stage of development and achievement, one picked up again in *Hero and Leander*, if it was his final work. Whatever the case, works like *Dido* and the translations from Ovid are earlier ones; thus it would appear that Marlowe professionally moved away from the Ovidian and neoclassical tendencies revealed in these pieces toward something more native and robust that was more like his own dominant personality. This shift can be readily seen in the change that comes to Marlowe's poetic style, not only his dramatic structure, in *Tamburlaine*.

Self-evidently, the Ovidian spirit is strong in the translations of the *Elegies*:

> If she be tall, she's like an Amazon,
> And therefore fills the bed she lies upon;
> If short, she lies the rounder; to say troth,
> Both short and long please me, for I love both.
> I think what one undeck'd would be, being dress'd;
> Is she attir'd? then show her graces best.
> A white wench thralls me, so doth golden yellow;
> And nut-brown girls in doing have no fellow.
>
> (*Elegies*, II.iv.33-40)[28]

Here a lighthearted facetiousness enlivens the verse, as in the poetry of a later Romantic, Byron.[29] Equally, in comparison with the wide-ranging hyperboles of *Tamburlaine*, some of *Dido*'s appear neoclassically restrained, even refined:

> But bright Ascanius, beauty's better work
> Who with the sun divides one radiant shape,
> Shall build his throne amidst those starry towers
> That earth-born Atlas, groaning, underprops.
> No bounds but heaven shall bound his empery,
> Whose azured gates, enchasèd with his name,
> Shall make the morning haste the gray uprise
> To feed her eyes with his engraven fame.
>
> (I.i.96-103)[30]

Though uncoupleted, the lines are Drydenesque. Jupiter's appreciative predictions concerning Ascanius are grandiose in content but are limited by endstopped lines and irregular rhyme. Tucker Brooke remarks that in *Dido* "rime is relatively more frequent than in any other of Marlowe's plays (over 100 verse) . . . ."[31] The technique produces a kind of calculated rhetorical quality which colors the resonance of the verse. This "crafted" aspect of Marlowe's technique in *Dido* takes on an etched or lapidary aura with the use of images and terms like "starry towers," "azured gates," and "enchasèd with his name." By the same token, "Popeian" rhythmic manipulations also make their contribution.[32] For instance, Marlowe interjects the word "groaning" to modify "earth-born Atlas" in the fourth line of the excerpt, a move that lays great emphasis on the word intellcctually and on its sound onomatopoeically, while at the same time it stabilizes rhythmically the final word "underprops" at the endstop, also reinforcing its meaning, so that "sound appears to imitate the sense."[33]

There are, however, other instances of such strategies in *Dido Queene of Carthage*. At I.i.72-81 Venus speaks of Aeneas with an artificial yet Ovidian sensuousness, lapsing, if bathetically, into couplets:

> Ay me! The stars surprised, like Rhesus' steeds
> Are drawn by darkness forth Astraeus' tents.
> What shall I do to save thee, my sweet boy,
> Whenas the waves do threat our crystal world,
> And Proteus, raising hills of floods on high,
> Intends ere long to sport him in the sky?
> False Jupiter, reward'st thou virtue so?
> What, is not piety exempt from woe?
> Then die Aeneas in thine innocence,
> Since that religion hath no recompense.

Dido, on her part, approaches Aeneas with lush blandishments that rival the pastoral enticements of the passionate shepherd and match the rosy imagistic sumptuousness in passages of *Hero and Leander*.

> I'll give thee tackling made of rivelled gold,
> Wound on the barks of odoriferous trees,
> Oars of massy ivory, full of holes
> Through which the water shall delight to play.
> Thy anchors shall be hewed from crystal rocks,
> Which, if thou lose, shall shine above the waves;
> The masts whereon thy swelling sails shall hang
> Hollow pyramides of silver plate;
> The sails of folded lawn, where shall be wrought
> The wars of Troy, but no Troy's overthrow.
>   (III.i.115-124)

It is difficult to say what precisely Marlowe had in mind here. There is a certain amount of humor in these absurdly useless, tinselly nautical objects. Dido's overripe Cleopatran aestheticism refines and reduces Aeneas's ship to a delectable bauble reshaped specifically for ef- feminizing and self-indulgent pleasure.[34] Oars of "massy ivory, full of holes" can scarcely be expected to transport anything but a self-reflex- ive imagination awash in sensual impressions. Impotence in these im- ages is tricked out in a kind of artistic *chic* by Dido, Carthage Queene. Also, the near-rhyme and assonance (*gold-holes, trees-play, waves-plate,* etc.) along with the pulsing suggestions of syntactic repetition ("Thy anchors," "The masts," "The sails") give the passage an artificial, stylized effect, which when linked with the satiric frivolousness of the images, creates a sensation somewhat akin to that of a slightly campy rococo. Equally, Aeneas's passionately apprehensive outcry upon his first attempt to leave Carthage is led into by lines that seem wrought by a jeweler or silversmith for an Italian courtier of the *cinquecento*:

> Her silver arms will coll me round about
> And tears of pearl cry, "Stay, Aeneas, stay."
> Each word she says will then contain a crown,
> And every speech be ended with a kiss.
> I may not dure this female drudgery.
> To sea Aeneas! Find out Italy!
>
> (IV.iii.51-56)

In spite of Aeneas's threatened, slightly aggrieved tone, the poetry has the effect of a delightfully executed statuette, a replica miniature. The words almost appear to be the things they represent (the tears of pearl "cry" and Dido's every word will "contain a crown"); and the couplet with which the passage concludes helps lend this curious yet technically eye-catching piece of rhetoric a sort of winning charm.

Tamburlaine's typical lines, on the other hand, seem much more unvarnished and immediate when compared to the technical self-consciousness demonstrated in the speeches in *Dido*. And this is all the more remarkable since *Tamburlaine*'s verse is scarcely plain and unadorned! Consider, for instance, Tamburlaine's "working words" to Zenocrate at the end of Part I:

> As Juno, when the giants were suppressed,
> That darted mountains at her brother Jove,
> So looks my love, shadowing in her brows
> Triumphs and trophies for my victories;
> Or as Latona's daughter, bent to arms,
> Adding more courage to my conquering mind.
> To gratify thee, sweet Zenocrate,
> Egyptians, Moors, and men of Asia,
> From Barbary unto the Western Indie,
> Shall pay a yearly tribute to thy sire;
> And from the bounds of Afric to the banks

       Of Ganges shall his mighty arm extend.
                          (V.ii.447-458)

As in the first passage taken from *Dido* ("But bright Ascanius, beauty's better work"), this too concerns itself with the overwhelming of boundaries: in the first case by Ascanius's "empery" and reputation; in the second by the power delegated through Tamburlaine's conquests to Zenocrate's father, the Soldan of Egypt. The expanse and breadth of these will "gratify . . . sweet Zenocrate." The lines from *Dido* demonstrate a dynamic of potential expansion tempered by the limits imposed through versification; but those from *Tamburlaine* reveal a broader, looser accumulation of terms and impressions whose power overshadows questions of technique. In the epic simile that opens the *Tamburlaine* illustration, the striking impact of the "shadowing in her brows" metaphor in the third line prevents any automatic response as to a merely ritualized epic convention. This is the kind of effect we more customarily associate with Marlowe. Here the playwright's rendition of a classical convention paradoxically achieves a romantic effect. The listing of heroic conquests which follows moves with typical Marlovian pace and grandeur. "Triumphs and trophies" will amplify Tamburlaine's "victories" (1.4 above); "courage" is added to his "conquering mind." Through Tamburlaine's conquests "Egyptians, Moors, and men of Asia" will all be corralled under the sway of the Solden of Egypt's "mighty arm," along with a wide range of territories from "Barbary unto the Western Indie," and from "the bounds of Afric to the banks / Of Ganges. . . ." The lines at first move sinuously, but then straighten out, cumulatively working their way forward to a kind of biblically cadenced closure: "And from the bounds of Afric to the banks / Of Ganges shall his mighty arm extend." The total effect is one of language imperialistically incorporating power over the very specifics it means to evoke. Tamburlaine's "working words" are a steady march of conquest in blank verse unblocked by rhyme or insistently endstopped lines.[35] Enjambment helps open the rhythmic pulses to the rich sense of expanding majestical solemnity Marlowe wishes to convey.

    In each of these modes, then, the more stylized sort exemplified at points by *Dido* and the more passionate, instinctive sort characteristic of *Tamburlaine*, Marlowe early on showed considerable talent. Whether he is metrically trimming Aeneas's faithless sails or marching in iambs to Persepolis, Marlowe reveals alternative sides to his poetical and dramatic gifts, indeed, to his nature, one major difference between these styles being the way he releases his feeling. *Dido*'s style shows signs of control and wit, a rationalistically oriented urbanity, and a neoclassical respect for balance and limits, and these in a variety of scenes and passages. Yet such are actually the reflections of a subordinate dimension of Marlowe's personality. Alternatively, *Tamburlaine* shows throughout a freer, more expansive style, and an even more volatile one—his more natural vein. Feeling, rather than technical intelligence or cleverness, is more completely the guiding principle. Feeling effects a liberation of the psyche and allows a display of Marlowe's startling vigor. This liberation permits unrestricted amplitude and experimentation in which passion shapes the poetry and form, not vice versa. Each of these early styles of Marlowe reflect at once a part of his personality and a historic opportunity for the development of English verse drama. Marlowe's preference for his native tradition rather than for the continental one carried both the playwright and his stage toward a moment of unique theatrical accomplishment in the western world.

NOTES

1. George Kubler, *The Shape of Time: Remarks on the History of Things* (New Haven: Yale University Press, 1962), p. 7.

2. These dates are taken from Irving Ribner's Introduction to *The Complete Plays of Christopher Marlowe* (New York: Bobbs-Merrill Co., Inc., 1963), p. xxi. They are the more or less generally accepted ones. Ribner's estimate is in line with that of scholars who place the play in the latter part of Marlowe's Cambridge period, e.g. C. F. Tucker Brooke, ed., *The Life of Marlowe* and *the Tragedy of Dido Queen of Carthage* (London: Methuen & Co., Ltd., 1930), p. 115 and H. J. Oliver, ed., Revels Plays, *"Dido Queen of Carthage" and "The Massacre at Paris"* (Cambridge, Mass.: Harvard University Press, 1968), p. xxvi. T.M. Pearce rather unconvincingly puts the play after *Tamburlaine* (1587) in "Evidence for Dating Marlowe's *Tragedy of Dido*," in *Studies in English Renaissance Drama in Memory of Karl Julius Holzknecht* (New York: New York University Press, 1959), pp. 232-233. Pearce is effectively answered by Oliver, pp. xxvi-xxvii.

3. Tucker Brooke, ed., pp. 116-117, remarks that "in style *Dido* resembles *Tamburlaine*. The great majority of the verses are regular decasyllables, end-stopped, which

close with a long polysyllabic word so often as to constitute a distinct mannerism." But the quantity of rhyme Tucker Brooke indicates in *Dido* as well as the rareness of run-on lines and feminine endings are features strikingly prevalent that help shade the tone of the play differently from that of *Tamburlaine,* while never leaving us with the feeling that *Dido* was mainly the work of another author. As to this question of authorship: the 1594 quarto gives the play as "written by Christopher Marlowe, and Thomas Nash, Gent." Nashe's name occurs in smaller print. Oliver, pp. xxii-xxv, notes that most commentators have "brushed aside" the linkage of Marlowe's and Nashe's names as co-authors of *Dido,* although he is unwilling to do so. Roma Gill's views represent the position of most contemporary scholars: "Despite the uncertainty of some of its parts, and the joint attribution to Nashe, the whole is essentially Marlovian in its energy and its odd mingling of the tragic and the comic." [Introduction to the Oxford paperback edition of *The Plays of Christopher Marlowe* (London: Oxford University Press, 1971), p. xii.]

4. Una Ellis-Fermor, *Christopher Marlowe* (London: Methuen & Co., Ltd., 1926), p. 21, feels that *Hero and Leander* is a final work of Marlowe (the more popular view). Millar Maclure's Revels Plays Introduction to *The Poems* (London: Methuen & Co., Ltd., 1968), also acknowledges the work's control and elegance as symptoms of a late work, but then mentions the possibility that it is an earlier production from the Cambridge period which "was interrupted by writing for the stage" (p. xxv). For further discussion of the early-late controversy, see John Bakeless, *The Tragicall History of Christopher Marlowe,* 2 vols. (Cambridge, Mass.: Harvard University Press, 1942), II, 99-101 and L. C. Martin, ed. Introduction to *Marlowe's Poems* (London: Methuen & Co., Ltd., 1931), pp. 3-4. My own opinion is that the Ovidian influence is so strong that it is very possible that earlier versions were written during the *Elegies-Dido* period and were reworked at Scadbury during the time just prior to the poet's death.

5. See Tucker Brooke, cited above, on the matter of Marlowe's debts and additions regarding the Vergil (pp. 117-118). See also Pearce's "Evidence for Dating . . . *Dido,*" pp. 232-233 which finds there are eight lines of *The Aeneid* quoted in Latin, 194 "very near to straight translations" and 410 "re-expressed in English." For further descriptions of Marlowe's changes and additions see H. J. Oliver's introduction to the Revels *Dido,* pp. xxxiii-xxxvi; R. E. Knoll, *Christopher Marlowe* (New York: Twayne Publishers, Inc., 1969), pp. 32-35; Constance B. Kuriyama, *Hammer or Anvil: Psychological Patterns in Christopher Marlowe's Plays* (New Brunswick, N. J.: Rutgers University Press, 1980), pp. 55, 63-64; and Mary E. Smith, *Love Kindling Fire: A Study of Christopher Marlowe's "Tragedy of Dido Queen of Carthage"* (Salzburg, Austria: Institut für Englische Sprache und Literatur, Universität Salzburg, 1977), pp. 22-72.

6. Ellis-Fermor finds the *Elegies* and *Pharsalia* translations and *Dido* "preliminary to Marlowe's real work" (p. 22). She goes on to say: "In fact, the most immediately noticeable thing about the next group of plays is the change of tone that accompanies the now definite purpose of his thought."

7. R. M. Frye, "Ways of Seeing in Elizabethan Drama and Elizabethan Painting," *Shakespeare Quarterly,* 31(1980), 328-335, 341-342, and *passim.*

8. Mary E. Smith, *Love Kindling Fire,* p. 103. Ellis-Fermor (p. 11) refers to an "Ovidian" phase of which the translations of the *Elegies* are a part. J. B. Steane,

Marlowe: A Critical Study (Cambridge: Cambridge University Press, 1964), p. 291, notices that the *Elegies* call to mind not only *Hero and Leander* but also *Dido*.

9. Mary E. Smith, *Love Kindling Fire*, p. 145.

10. William Keach, *Elizabethan Erotic Narratives* (New Brunswick, N.J.: Rutgers University Press, 1977), p. 11. Keach feels Marlowe takes from *Heroides* only "a few descriptive details."

11. Louis L. Martz believes the 1598 wholly Marlovian text is a complete poem which closes intentionally on the fulfillment of the lovers. Despite the traditional assumption that Marlowe's love poem was unfinished and thus invited Chapman's additions, Martz offers the suggestion that Marlowe created *Hero and Leander* in a three part form like a medieval triptich. See Introduction, pp. 3-4, p. 13 of Martz's edition of the facsimile first edition of *Hero and Leander* (Washington, D. C.: Folger Shakespeare Library, 1972).

12. See Steane, pp. 289-297.

13. The most important Ovidian scenic elements occur in I.i; II.i. 304-322; III.i.; and IV.v. Important speeches reflecting Ovidian sensuousness are at I.i.34-49; III.i.80-95; III.i.115-132; IV.i.2-10.

14. Colin Martindale, *Romantic Progression: The Psychology of Literary History* (London: John Wiley & Sons, 1975), p. 56.

15. Mario Praz, "Christopher Marlowe," *English Studies*, 13 (1931), 215-218.

16. Smith, *Love Kindling Fire*, p. 157.

17. See Oliver, ed., pp. xxvi-xxvii and Smith, *Love Kindling Fire*, p. 166.

18. Roma Gill, "Marlowe's Vergil: *Dido Queen of Carthage*," *Review of English Studies*, N.S., 28 (1977), p. 146.

19. Mary E. Smith, "Marlowe and Italian Dido Drama," *Italica*, 53 (1976), 232.

20. M. D. McDiarmid, "The Influence of Robert Garnier on some Elizabethan Tragedies," *Études Anglaises, Grande-Bretagne, États-Unis*, 2 (1958), 291-293.

21. Smith, "Marlowe and Italian Dido Drama," p. 231. For discussion of the European tradition of Dido plays, see Robert Turner, *Didon dans la Tragédie de la Renaissance* (Paris, 1926). In the English tradition of Dido plays, Oliver also points out "Halliwell's *Dido*, acted before the queen at Cambridge in 1564" and even earlier, "John Rightwise's version acted for Wolsey, probably in 1532" (p. xxxix).

22. Smith, "Marlowe and Italian Dido Drama," p. 232. These include "the jealousy of Iarbas, the weak nature of Aeneas's character, the role of Achates, the image of the serpent, and the allusions to Scythia." Finally, there is Anna's suicide. Of these, the most influential is the explicit jealousy of Iarbas, because it lays the groundwork for Marlowe's version of the character (p. 226). See also p. 232 for a breakdown of the resemblances between the Italian plays. Smith makes a reasonable case for Marlowe's familiarity with Dolce's *Didone*.

23. *Ibid.*, pp. 233-234, 226.

24. Gill's remarks, pp. 146 and 153. She also notices that Marlowe has developed Anna from a "mere confidante" to a "rudimentary character, cherishing the pangs of dispriz'd love for her sister's unwanted suitor and . . . offering herself as a substitute in his affections" (p. 146).

25. D. C. Allen, "Marlowe's Dido and the Tradition," *Essays on Shakespeare and Eliza-*

bethan Drama in Honor of Hardin Craig, ed. Richard Hosley (Columbia, Missouri: University of Missouri Press, 1962), p. 65. Allen discusses the tradition of Dido and Aeneas characterization, especially in the Middle Ages and Renaissance. So does Smith in *Love Kindling Fire*, summing up on pp. 23-24.

26. Meyer Shapiro, "Style," *Anthropology Today* (Chicago: University of Chicago Press, 1953), p. 293.

27. *Ibid.*, p. 294.

28. *The Poems*, ed. Millar Maclure, cited above, p. 150.

29. Elizabeth Bieman, "Comic Rhyme in Marlowe's *Hero and Leander*," *English Literary Renaissance*, 9 (1979), 69-77, supposes that Marlowe's use of multisyllabic rhymes in his couplets for comic effect derives from the technique of the Italian Poet Pulci, and is the first use of its kind in English, anticipating Byron.

30. Quotations from *Dido Queene of Carthage* are taken from Ribner's *The Complete Plays of Christopher Marlowe*, cited above in note 2.

31. Tucker Brooke, ed., p. 116. Oliver remarks that A. W. Verity in *The Influence of Marlowe on Shakespeare's Earlier Style* (Cambridge: Cambridge University Press, 1886), pp. 29, 70-71, felt significance in Marlowe's use of couplets in *Dido*. He suggested "that Marlowe was writing the play at the same time as *Hero and Leander*, leaving both unfinished at his death . . ." (Oliver, p. xxviii). Oliver also notices the quantity of end-stopped lines and the lack of feminine endings in *Dido*. Steane, p. 286, offers that in fact Marlowe created the English "Augustan" couplet in his translation of the *Elegies*.

32. Steane, p. 286, refers to such devices in the *Elegies*.

33. Oliver remarks in a general way: "Marlowe is experimenting in *Dido* with all kinds of variation, and particularly with the omission of one syllable from the decasyllabic line, to throw greater emphasis on an important word or otherwise indicate a special intonation," p. xxviii.

34. See Kuriyama, cited above, on Dido as an effeminizing female, p. 73. D. C. Allen, on the other hand, finds this aspect as part of the tradition of Dido presentation (p. 60). It goes, of course, all the way back to Vergil.

35. Oliver makes the clear stylistic distinction between *Dido* and *Tamburlaine* in the following manner: " . . . the prevailing impression must be that Marlowe when he composed *Dido* was writing mostly in single lines, whereas even in *Tamburlaine* he was writing in what must have been called verse-paragraphs," p. xxviii.

"Working Words":
The Verbal Dynamic of *Tamburlaine*

JILL L. LEVENSON

With characteristic flourish, Swinburne describes the verse of Marlowe's first well-known play as a crashing bore: " . . . the stormy monotony of Titanic truculence . . . blusters like a simoom through the noisy course of its ten fierce acts."[1] This generalization sweeps into the open a verbal feature of *Tamburlaine* observed by a number of more recent literary critics. As tragical discourse, Marlowe's portrayal of Tamburlaine evinces a quality of sameness which affects all of the personae and speeches. This uniformity, which challenges the auditor to distinguish among "the re-echoing captains and rhetorical kings,"[2] has been traced to various sources. T. B. Tomlinson attributes it to Marlowe's prosody: "The lines move with a firm deliberation which Marlowe applies equally to *any* situation, any imagery. The fabric of the verse—the denotative imagery, the rigid control—is the same in those speeches on Damascus as it was when Tamburlaine saw only the lyrical beauty of Zenocrate. . . . "[3] Donald Peet explains it as a rhetorical effect:

> The techniques of amplification . . . are quite impersonal; they may be effectively employed by any speaker without being significantly modified to reflect his individual nature. Relying almost exclusively upon these techniques, Marlowe thus was unable

to distinguish his characters from one another by varying the tone, structure, or style of their individual speeches. Every one of his characters must amplify all of the time; and every one of them must amplify in very much the same manner. As a result, they all tend to talk alike.[4]

Clifford Leech has found a reflection of it in the structures of the two plays, citing parallel incidents between and even within them.[5]

Doubtless Marlowe's prosodic, rhetorical, and dramaturgic strategies account in large part for the consistency of *Tamburlaine*. But the ultimate source of the plays' continuity—an element of each aesthetic maneuver—has to be the most basic units of the dramas' composition: the words and the patterns of their distribution. In *Tamburlaine*, the characters share not only formal modes of expression, but the expressions themselves. From Mycetes to Zenocrate, the personae employ the same lexicon, a collection of words both idiosyncratic and relatively large. Obviously Marlowe does not adjust this body of language to produce subtle characterizations; yet he does vary the texture of language in *Tamburlaine* as a whole by means of sound effects and visual imagery. The diction seems to intensify or relax, heighten into aria or subside into recitative[6], according to the playwright's manipulation of sounds: " . . . spuming rhetorics of foam and eddy: in sibilants, gutturals, dentals, and explosives; in long vowels, double vowels, and especially *o* and *u* vowels."[7] While the sound effects change from moment to moment, words materialize as stage images at irregular intervals. Marlowe uses properties and costumes symbolically, and as a result the words they body forth acquire emblematic associations.[8]

The paper which follows will first describe Marlowe's lexicon for *Tamburlaine*, illustrating how the characters share it, and then demonstrate the use of sounds and sights to vary the effects of diction. From this textual evidence, the concluding section will argue that Marlowe achieves contrast in unity which requires the kind of attention that William Empson recommends for Spenser: "The size, the possible variety, and the fixity of . . . [the poetic units] give something of the blankness that comes from fixing your eyes on a bright spot; you have to yield yourself to it very completely to take in the variety of its movement. . . . "[9]

I

Whatever the original publisher cut out, the extant *Tamburlaine* plays boast large vocabularies. Part One numbers 3,271 different words in a total of 17,781; the basic vocabulary therefore constitutes 18.4 percent of the whole text. Similarly, the lexical statistics for Part Two enumerate 3,281 different words in 18,135, or 18.09 percent of the entire text. Except for *Edward II*, Marlowe's other plays employ comparable or even larger vocabularies.[10] By comparison, the lexicons of Shakespeare's dramas rarely equal those of Marlowe's: for a sample, the vocabulary of *Richard II* makes up 14.45 percent of the text; *Hamlet*, 15.9 percent; *King Lear*, 16.51 percent; *The Winter's Tale*, 15.94 percent.[11]

Despite its large vocabulary, *Tamburlaine* gives the impression of repeating itself. Marlowe arranges his many different words in about a dozen large clusters, motifs easier to perceive in these verbally dense texts than the individual notes which compose them. A sensitive listener, Moody E. Prior classifies some of the recurrent tropes in Part One:

> . . . the figures of speech which appear most frequently and which are used with most consistency are drawn from a limited and fairly definite range of categories—the gods of classical mythology, principally Jove; jewels, treasure, and precious stones and metals; stars, planets, and other heavenly bodies. Dozens of instances of these are dispersed throughout the play. In addition to these principal ones, considerable use is made of references to and analogies drawn from elemental forces of nature and features of the classical underworld, and of historical and geographical references.[12]

These categories appear in both parts of *Tamburlaine*. As Harry Levin corroborates, exotic proper nouns—1,410 of them altogether—richly emboss the texts; "[m]ore than a third of these, 545, gain peculiar stress by coming at the end of a line. This means that 12 per cent of the lines of the two plays terminate with such a colourful polysyllable." Levin also notices how Marlowe relies on nature for metaphors, and he points out as well how the dramatist uses enumeration and absolute terms ("all," "every") to amplify his protagonist.[13] Moreover, Part Two frequently displays allusions to myth, treasure, astronomy, history, and the classical underworld.

If figurative language and unusual words appear conspicuously grouped in both parts of *Tamburlaine,* perhaps the rest of Marlowe's vocabulary sets them into relief.[14] Most of the verbs—and many of the nouns—come from a stock of familiar, often monosyllabic words. For example, commonplace terms related to war are predictably abundant in this dramatic history of a conqueror: *e.g.,* variants of "conquer" and "conquest" occur seventy times; "sword(s)," sixty-six times; "blood," forty-six times; "war(s)," forty-four times; "field(s)," thirty-nine times; "host(s)," thirty-one times. Analogously, both plays depend on a large body of terms related to kingship: "king," recurs 103 times by itself and ninety-two times as parts of other words ("kings," "kingdom," "kingdoms," "kingly"); "crown" is repeated as a noun or verb eighty-six times; and a variety of related words such as "royal," "throne," and "highness" round out the motif. Other groups of commonplace words denote colors, parts of the body, digestion, fire, intent, and processes of thought (*e.g.* variants of "conceit" and "conceive," "think," "know"). The verb "make," in the sense of "cause," appears 107 times.

Further, *Tamburlaine* draws upon a collection of unadorned words prominent throughout Marlowe's canon, terms which may be collocated with "sight." In his dissertation on Marlowe's stage technique, George B. Shand demonstrates the high frequency of words linked with vision by providing a count of such items as "sight" as a noun (fifty-six), "behold" and "beheld" (forty-four), "eye" as a noun and verb (ninety-seven), "look" as a verb (103), "see" as a verb (372), "stare" (five), "gaze" (eleven), "view" as a noun and verb (thirty), and "perceive" (eleven). He connects these verbal allusions with Marlowe's "close attention to the visual effects of his plays on stage."[15] As scholars have remarked, The Prologue to the first part of *Tamburlaine* explicitly directs the audience's attention to the visual component of the drama: "View but his picture in this tragic glass . . . " (l. 7),[16] and both texts make heavy demands upon words from this lexical set: "see(st)" occurs eighty-eight times; "look(s)" as a verb and noun, fifty-five; "eye(s)" as a verb and noun, thirty-two. Simultaneously, the two plays rely on the matching audile set also introduced in The Prologue to Part One: " . . . you shall hear the Scythian Tamburlaine / Threat'ning the world with high astounding terms . . . " (ll. 4-5). A sizable group of words denotes listening and speaking, and the term which occurs most often among them is "word(s)" (twenty-eight times).

The unique diction of *Tamburlaine* seems to result from the continual juxtaposition of the exotic with the commonplace and from Marlowe's unwavering reliance on a limited number of verbal sets. All of the characters share this diction; every speech of more than a few lines sets trope against topos within the bounds of particular verbal motifs. Since this linguistic compound occurs throughout both plays, one kind of illustration should suffice to represent the whole. I shall focus on the way personae describe one another, because most of the characters engage in verbal portraiture at some point in the dramatic narrative.

Peristasis takes the form of blazon, anatomizing the person of the subject into the bodily parts which form one of Marlowe's image clusters. Whoever the speaker or subject, the descriptions combine terms for physical attributes in metaphoric arrangements with words from other lexical sets. These combinations may produce a sketch from only a feature or two, as Techelles and Theridamas delineate Tamburlaine (Part One: I.ii.52-57 and 154-160), or as Tamburlaine portrays Theridamas (Part One: I.ii.164-170) and himself (Part Two: III.ii.117-129). When formulated as extensive catalogues, they tend to portray human figures as emblematic compositions: so Menaphon describes Tamburlaine (Part One: II.i.7-30); Bajazeth, his sons (Part One: III.iii.103-111); Tamburlaine, his sons (Part Two: I.iv.21-34); and First Physician, the dying Tamburlaine (Part Two: V.iii.82-97). The repetition of these stylized accounts generates echoes. Both Tamburlaine and Theridamas display aspiring miens, expressive brows, and martial physiques. If Tamburlaine compares with Atlas and Achilles, Bajazeth's sons challenge Hercules. He exhibits large limbs, wide shoulders, and strong arms and fingers; they brandish " . . . hands . . . made to gripe a warlike lance, / . . . shoulders broad, for complete armor fit, / . . . [and] limbs more large and of a bigger size / Than all the brats y-sprung from Typhon's loins, . . . " (Part One: III.iii.106-109). Descriptions of the beloved—Zenocrate's of Tamburlaine (Part One: III.ii.47-52), Tamburlaine's of Zenocrate

(Part One: III.iii.117-123; V.ii.72-87 and 447-452), Theridamas's of Olympia (Part Two: IV.iii.28-32)—offer mythical or classical frames of reference for extraordinary looks and eyes. Although they vary in length and bias, therefore, descriptions in *Tamburlaine* share the same format and verbal clusters. Like the rest of these two plays, even the smallest verbal portraits blend motifs from the basic stock:

> *Second Virgin*
> . . . Grant that these signs of victory we yield
> May blind the temples of his conquering head
> To hide the folded furrows of his brows,
> And shadow his displeased countenance
> With happy looks of ruth and lenity.
>
> (Part One: V.i.55-59)

II

T. S. Eliot appreciates not only the economies of Marlowe's blank verse, but also Spenser's influence on it: "There had been no great blank verse before Marlowe; but there was the powerful presence of this great master of melody immediately precedent; and the combination produced results which could not be repeated."[17] Various critics have argued that Marlowe borrowed lines from Spenser now and then,[18] but Eliot—referring to *Tamburlaine*—suggests a larger correspondence: "Marlowe gets into blank verse the melody of Spenser. . . . "[19] When Marlowe's verse in *Tamburlaine* rings Spenserian, the resemblance probably derives, at least in part, from a technique the two poets share: both equip metrically regular units of verse with a remarkable variety of sound effects. Like the Spenserian stanza, Marlowe's "mighty line" imposes a number of constraints on rhythm and accent. It advances predictably iambic and end-stopped, with regular pauses after each second foot; and it favors trim syntax and rhetorical balance. Yet John Bakeless concludes rightly that ". . . no one line sounds exactly like any other. . . . "[20] Spenser performed like auditory feats with both sound effects and diction: for instance, "The aural texture of the *Cantos* runs the gamut from the consonantal Billingsgate of 'this off-scum of that cursed fry' (7.6.30.1), to the lyric vowel sequence of 'Out of her bowre, that many flowers strowes' (7.6.41.5)."[21] As we have seen, however, Marlowe works his diction within a tight compass, and in effect he conjures mainly with pitch and the quality of sounds.

Marlowe's phonetic experimentation has already received scholarly attention. In his article about the playwright's use of vowel sounds, Ants Oras studies echoes which accelerate the verse, reinforce the terminal effects of lines, and generally create a sense of patterns emerging from the text, dissolving into other patterns, and re-emerging with added vigor: "Intensity, impulsively kindling into even greater intensity, seemingly on an ever ascending scale, appears . . . typical of his art, at least in *Tamburlaine*."[22] Harry Morris finds in "Marlowe's Poetry" careful organization of consonants as well as vowels: Mycetes lisps in sibilants, for example, whereas Tamburlaine vaunts in plosives, dentals, and gutturals.[23] In broader terms, critics generally recognize the numerous repetitions of sounds which affect Marlowe's rhythms and distinguish his verse—poetic or rhetorical devices extending from alliteration, rhyme, and assonance to polyptoton, chiasmus, and anaphora. But they have not noticed that in *Tamburlaine* this panoply of audile repetitions varies in concentration and pitch from moment to moment. As a result of this variation, words from a dozen or so lexical groups recur in perpetually changing auditory contexts. Marlowe plays his lexicon for *Tamburlaine* in many different keys, and aural modulations in both parts—like the dramas' linguistic compounds—occur everywhere in the texts. I shall illustrate them briefly by analyzing two sets of short passages, each set focusing on common subject matter and therefore on related lexical clusters as well as variations in sound. (The phonetic symbols employed in this demonstration can be found in Helge Kökeritz, *Shakespeare's Pronunciation* [New Haven and London: Yale University Press and Oxford University Press, 1953].)

In Part One, two accounts of Tamburlaine's white emblems produce distinctive timbres. An anonymous Messenger delivers one:

> The first day when he pitcheth down his tents,
> White is their hue, and on his silver crest
> A snowy feather spangled-white he bears,
> To signify the mildness of his mind
> That, satiate with spoil, refuseth blood . . .
>
> (IV.i.50-54)

Throughout this passage a number of sounds interweave: *f, t, th,* various sibilants, *ɛ, uɪ, ɪ.* Alliteration on *s* in accented syllables within and between lines, and on *m* similarly in line 53, makes the passage irregularly emphatic; the pitch rises occasionally on *ɛɪ* or *iɪ* notably in the fourth line. Whereas the Messenger repeats only the key word "white," Tamberlaine stress the central terms of his dialectic, "they" and "my":

> They know my custom; could they not as well
> Have sent ye out when first my milk-white flags,
> Through which sweet Mercy threw her gentle beams,
> Reflexing them on your disdainful eyes,
> As now . . . ?
>
> (V.ii.4-8)

Tamburlaine's rhetorical question, consistently high-pitched, interweaves sounds less than it concentrates effects in individual lines or repeats them to link consecutive ones. So the first line repeats "they" and the *k* sound; and the second uses *æ* from "as" in "have" and "flag," repeats "my," and alliterates *f* and *m.* With the third line, the intricacies of sound in this passage heighten: line 6 plays on "Through"/ "threw"; picks up the *iɪ* of "ye" in "sweet"; alliterates "sweet" with "sent" in the previous line; and repeats *ɛn* from "sent" in "gentle" as well as *ĕr* from "first" in "mercy" and "her." The closing participial phrase echoes the *ɛɪ* and *iɪ* sounds which opened the passage.

In Part Two, first Tamburlaine and then Theridamas relate similar fantasies about beloved women who have just died. When Tamburlaine imagines Jove courting Zenocrate, different configurations of sounds again distinguish individual lines or connect pairs of lines:

> For amorous Jove hath snatched my love from hence,
> Meaning to make her stately queen of heaven.
> What god soever holds thee in his arms,
> Giving thee nectar and ambrosia,
> Behold me here, divine Zenocrate. . . .
>
> (II.iv. 107-111)

Here the first line produces assonance on λ and *æ,* alliteration on *h,* and sibilance; but the second, changing tone color, emphasizes the stronger *ɛ,* k, t, and introduces itself with alliteration on *m* (and a trochee). This passage contains words that verge on rhyme ("Meaning"/"queen") or rhyme imperfectly ("soever"/"nectar"), in addition to polyptoton ("holds"/"Behold"). In lines 109 and 110, Tamburlaine repeats the *o* ("soever," "holds," "ambrosia") from line 107 ("Jove"); and he echoes the *ī* of line 108 ("stately") when he repeats "thee" (109, 110) and introduces its rhyming partner "me" (111). By comparison, Theridamas's poetry—a description of Dis courting Olympia—modulates sound for a subdued effect:

> Infernal Dis is courting of my love,
> Inventing masks and stately shows for her,
> Opening the doors of his rich treasury
> To entertain this queen of chastity. . . .
>
> (IV.iii.93-96)

Although Theridamas borrows several words from Tamburlaine's conceit, he voices them differently in lines pitched lower and containing an imperfect end-rhyme. He repeats mild sounds—*l*, *ę*, *n*—throughout this passage; and he balances like syllables against each other at the beginnings and ends of lines ("Infernal" / "Inventing," "treasury"/"chastity"), as well as in participles. In conjunction, the sounds and balance give a decorous edge to the expression of Theridamas's grief.

Sound effects in *Tamburlaine* change not only in quality, but also in quantity. In some speeches, the patterns of repetition maintain such high degrees of intricacy that they are difficult to analyze and to pronounce. The lengthy exchanges between Zabina and Bajazeth before their suicides—passages dotted with rhetorical figures of iteration—crowd rhyme, assonance, alliteration, and consonance into little rooms. As a result, their deliveries require oratorical skill:[24]

> *Zabina.* Then is there left no Mahomet, no God,
> No fiend, no fortune, nor no hope of end
> To our infamous, monstrous slaveries?
> Gape earth, and let the fiends infernal view
> A hell as hopeless and as full of fear
> As are the blasted banks of Erebus,
> Where shaking ghosts with ever-howling groans
> Hover about the ugly ferryman

To get a passage to Elysium!

(Part One: V.ii.176-184)

But despair is not the only inspiration for demanding verbal arias: the Soldan of Egypt pronounces two on his way to battle with Tamburlaine (Part One: IV.iii. 1-22 and 28-42); the Second Virgin of Damascus directs a solo on the theme of pity toward Tamburlaine (Part One: V.i.48-61); Techelles and Tamburlaine exchange the crown of Fez in duet (Part Two: I.vi.11-29); and Orcanes expresses his fury at the death of Sigismund in a virtuoso speech (Part Two: II.iii.14-30). Sometimes the intricacies occur in short passages:

> *Magnetes.* And since we have arrived in Scythia,
>   Besides rich presents from the puissant Cham,
>   We have his highness' letters to command
>   Aid and assistance if we stand in need.
> *Tamburlaine.* But now you see these letters and commands
>   Are contermanded by a greater man. . . .
>
> (Part One: I.ii.17-22)

Moreover, they do not always play a part in serious moments; so Cosroe dies straightforwardly:

> My bloodless body waxeth chill and cold,
> And with my blood my life slides through my wound;
> My soul begins to take her flight to hell
> And summons all my senses to depart.
> The heat and moisture which did feed each other,
> For want of nourishment to feed them both,
> Is dry and cold; and now doth ghastly death
> With greedy talents gripe my bleeding heart
> And like a harpy tires on my life.
>
> (Part One: II.vii.42-50)

On the whole, sound effects in *Tamburlaine* seem to change from line to line or passage to passage, and their intensity waxes and wanes. No readily identifiable pattern appears to govern the aural component of the play. Almost every character expresses himself in a range of speeches from recitative to aria; and the verbal mode does not relate inevitably to the events which provide its context. If any principle con-

trols the sound of *Tamburlaine*, perhaps variety is its key. Marlowe's
two-part drama resonates like a brilliant Spenserian *tour de force* which
exploits all the potentialities of its chosen verse. Possibly a younger art
form offers the best analogy for *Tamburlaine*: opera is a "type of drama
in which all or most characters sing and in which music constitutes a
principal element having its own unity."[25] In this early play, all of the
characters speak blank verse endless in its modulations, and the constantly changing sound effects may be in themselves an autonomous
design in Marlowe's composition.

III

"His peculiarly musical verse and his emblematic presentation of the
action . . . are in accord with current standards of decorum and signif-
icancy. And they document the shift from an aural to a visual culture
taking place during the early Renaissance."[26] With slight adjustment,
S. P. Zitner's statement about Spenser applies to Marlowe, who performed the role of a dramatic innovator who preserved. According to
Levin, Marlowe's incorporation of spectacle into the dramatic action—a novel synthesis in an age which had separated the visual from
the audile in tragedy—vitally influenced the shape of his narrative
form and (after the mighty line) attracted audiences. "But his audacity
lay in taking a metaphor and acting it out, in turning a manner of
speaking into a mode of action, in concretely realizing what had there-
tofore subsisted on the plane of precept and fantasy."[27]

Consequently, the vocabulary of *Tamburlaine* not only passes
through countless auditory variations, but also materializes—at
irregular but carefully orchestrated intervals—on the stage. For obvious reasons, Marlowe rarely bodies forth his more exotic verbal
clusters: allusions to classical myth, heavenly bodies, and elemental
forces of nature would have taxed even his ingenuity. Although treasure (Part One: I.ii) and a map (Part Two: V.iii) do appear at critical
points to embody key motifs, Marlowe depends on oratorical devices to
represent the abstractions, to "set things before the eyes" in Aristotle's
sense.[28] In contrast, the stock of familiar words in *Tamburlaine* becomes
tangible in the drama's most conspicuous properties. For instance, the
term "crown," repeated dozens of times, takes shape from the begin-

ning of Part One in the court of Mycetes and remains in sight through most of the action of both plays. Similarly, the audience views a number of "thrones" or emblematic seats of power in the course of events. As the dramatic narrative advances, ordinary words denoting weapons, color, the human body, digestion, and fire come to life, at different instants, on the stage.

Both Shand and Judith Weil have carefully studied how these motifs come to life. In the earlier analysis, Shand discusses all of the stage properties in *Tamburlaine*, but he concentrates on the most significant ones: for Part One, "crowns, thrones, weapons and human bodies treated as inanimate objects, . . ." as well as dress; for Part Two, the same properties and, in addition, the symbols of physical decay made concrete in Zenocrate's deathbed, hearse, memorial, and the fire set by Tamburlaine. Shand interprets the effects of these stage properties as they counterpoint stage action and speech; moreover, he attends to the emblematic implications of several episodes such as the footstool scene, Tamburlaine's costume change, the display of crowns, and the climactic appearance of the chariot drawn by the pampered jades of Asia.[29] In a complementary manner, Weil focuses on these symbolic passages, explicating a number of them to show how emblematic language and stage images work together in *Tamburlaine*.[30] Since this visual aspect of the play has already received comprehensive scholarly treatment, the following paragraphs will simply mention or review two emblematic features especially pertinent to the verbal dynamic.

First, Weil makes and illustrates the important point that "in the *Tamburlaine* plays, meanings of allusions tend to emerge in a cumulative, incremental manner."[31] In effect, the plain words in the text acquire frames of reference and symbolic complexity when they appear concretely on the stage. Sometimes the process of metamorphosis takes place through spectacle. For instance, the crown and throne both appear in dramatic scenes which pictorialize the *de casibus* motif, tableaux which add connotations of mortality to denotations of power. At other times, individual characters explicate simple words before, during, or after their transformations into emblematic stage properties and thus heighten the commonplace with symbolism: Tamburlaine's colors deepen in this fashion, as we have seen. In some cases, Marlowe's sources provided emblematic definitions: Tamburlaine's colors and Bajazeth's cage had already appeared with explications. But in other cases, the playwright created emblems, among them Tamburlaine's physical person. Earlier in this paper I referred to the verbal portraits of Tamburlaine which recur throughout both plays; these culminate in Theridamas's version for Olympia (Part Two: III.iv.45-67). As Weil says: "Such portraits are emblematic; they appear to grow from an intellectual analysis of Tamburlaine's qualities, and the presentation of these qualities in images is a way of symbolizing his spirit, not of recording actual physical traits."[32] Thus the character of Tamburlaine becomes an emblem of himself, and once anatomized, the various parts of his body also become emblematic:

> *Tamburlaine.* Hold thee, Cosroe; wear two imperial crowns.
>   Think thee invested now as royally,
>   Even by the mighty hand of Tamburlaine,
>   As if as many kings as could encompass thee,
>   With greatest pomp, had crowned thee emperor.
>   (Part One: II.v.1-5)

> Not now, Theridamas; her·[Zabina's] time is past.
>   The pillars that have bolstered up those terms
>   Are fall'n in clusters at my conquering feet. . . .
>   So from the East unto the furthest West
>   Shall Tamburlaine extend his puissant arm.
>   (Part One: III.iii.228-230,246-247)

> My stern aspect shall make fair Victory,
>   Hovering betwixt our armies, light on me,
>   Loaden with laurel wreaths to crown us all.
>   (Part Two: III.v.162-164)

In one episode of Part Two cited above, Tamburlaine arranges himself as a physical emblem for his sons:

> View me, thy father, that hath conquered kings, . . .
>   Quite void of scars and clear from any wound,
>   That by the wars lost not a dram of blood,
>   And see him lance his flesh to teach you all.
>   *He cuts his arm.* . . .
>   Come, boys, and with your fingers search my wound,
>   And in my blood wash all your hands at once,
>   While I sit smiling to behold the sight.
>   (III.ii.110-114,126-128)

Second, Marlowe introduces emblematic motifs by design. On the one hand, symbols of kingship appear from the opening scene and therefore accompany their verbal motifs throughout the play. On the other, the remaining emblems occur first in the language, as if Marlowe were carefully preparing for their reception as consummate, material images on the stage. In the second act of Part One, for example, the motif of fire and burning becomes apparent verbally, and it threads its way through the drama until the town where Zenocrate died burns in Part Two: III.ii. Allusions to food and feeding enter the text in Act III of Part One, becoming the center of the action in the banquet scene of Act IV and a point of reference for allusions to feasting thereafter. Unlike the play's sound effects, then, its visual component, highly structured, manifests itself in a number of distinctive patterns which sometimes coexist or overlap. And the language of *Tamburlaine*, perceived through both media of sound and sight, resonates differently from moment to moment while the significance of words grows increasingly complex.

CONCLUSION

Marlowe's early play seems monotonous only if we bring to it expectations conditioned by Shakespeare's later drama. So furnished, we notice that the scope of Marlowe's vocabulary fails to equal that of Shakespeare's: *Tamburlaine* wants expressions for family relationships, nature in its seasonal cycles, daily pastimes, aphoristic wisdom, humor, and sex. Moreover, the play barely alludes to mirrors and reflections. If Marlowe holds up a glass, he does not direct it at human nature. On his own terms, he offers a rhetorical and ironic version of history rather than an experiential or philosophical commentary on human relationships; and as The Prologue to the first part says, he builds his creation out of the fundamental materials of theater: "Looks and words, those two components of drama, the blood and the thunder. . . . "[33]

Thus Marlowe confronts us with a presentational—instead of a representational—work of art. Now that critics have learned to appreciate its "looks," perhaps we can cultivate an ear for its sounds. According to the unsympathetic Joseph Hall, *Tamburlaine* in its original performances "ravishe[d] the gazing scaffolders" with its verse. Recent scholarship explains that Elizabethan and Jacobean "[a]udiences could hear the blank verse line emerge and take shape, and their ability to do this gives the point to literally hundreds of speeches and scenes in English Renaissance drama."[34] If we imitate our predecessors in Marlowe's audience, perhaps we can learn to recognize in *Tamburlaine* the brilliant craftsmanship which juxtaposes with stage pictures a composition of words in perpetually changing melody.

NOTES

1. Algernon Charles Swinburne, *The Age of Shakespeare* (London: Chatto & Windus, 1908), p. 1. (The point is repeated on p. 2.)

2. Harry Levin, *Christopher Marlowe: The Overreacher* (London: Faber & Faber Limited, 1961), p. 74. On the likenesses among speeches in *Tamburlaine*, see also David Daiches, "Language and Action in Marlowe's *Tamburlaine*," *More Literary Essays* (Edinburgh: Oliver & Boyd, Ltd., 1968), rpt. in *Christopher Marlowe's "Tamburlaine Part One and Part Two": Text and Major Criticism*, ed. Irving Ribner (Indianapolis and New York: The Odyssey Press [A Division of The Bobbs-Merrill Company, Inc., Publishers], 1974), pp. 331-332; and Judith Weil, *Christopher Marlowe: Merlin's Prophet* (Cambridge: Cambridge University Press, 1977), p. 120.

3. T. B. Tomlinson, *A Study of Elizabethan and Jacobean Tragedy* (Cambridge and Melbourne: Cambridge University Press and Melbourne University Press, 1964), p. 57.

4. Donald Peet, "The Rhetoric of *Tamburlaine*," *ELH*, 26 (June 1959), 151-152. *Cf.* Audrey Ekdahl Davidson and Clifford Davidson, "The Function of Rhetoric, Marlowe's *Tamburlaine*, and 'Reciprocal Illumination,'" *Ball State University Forum*, 22 (Winter 1981), 24-25.

5. Clifford Leech, "The Structure of *Tamburlaine*," *Tulane Drama Review*, 8 (Summer 1964), rpt. in *Christopher Marlowe's "Tamburlaine"*, ed. Ribner, pp. 273-276.

6. For an extensive comparison between musical practice and the rhetoric and structure of *Tamburlaine*, see the Davidsons' article, especially 23-29.

7. Harry Morris, "Marlowe's Poetry," *Tulane Drama Review*, 8 (Summer 1964), 139.

8. For a useful and brief explanation of this effect, see George B. Shand, "Stage Technique in the Plays of Christopher Marlowe," Diss. University of Toronto 1969, pp. 75-77. *Cf.* David Hard Zucker's Introduction to his *Stage and Image in the Plays of Christopher Marlowe*, Elizabethan Studies 7, ed. James Hogg (Salzburg: Institut für Englische Sprache und Literatur, Universität Salzburg, 1972), pp. 1-19.

9. William Empson, *Seven Types of Ambiguity* (London: Chatto and Windus, 1930), p. 45.

10. My calculations are based on the figures in Louis Ule, *A Concordance to the Works of Christopher Marlowe,* The Elizabethan Concordance Series 1 (Hildesheim, New York: Georg Olms Verlag, 1979). *Cf. Doctor Faustus* (1604), 21.24 percent and (1616), 18.49 percent; *Dido, Queen of Carthage,* 20.24 percent; *The Massacre at Paris,* 18.31 percent; *The Jew of Malta,* 16.36 percent; and the exception, *Edward II,* 14.89 percent.

11. My calculations are based on the figures in Marvin Spevack, *A Complete and Systematic Concordance to the Works of Shakespeare,* 9 vols. (Hildesheim: Georg Olms Verlagsbuchhandlung, 1968). *1 Henry VI* (18.58 percent) and *The Tempest* (19.64 percent) are unusual in this respect.

12. Moody E. Prior, *The Language of Tragedy* (Bloomington and London: Indiana University Press, 1966), p. 37. On the classical motifs, see also M. M. Mahood, *Poetry and Humanism* (London: Jonathan Cape, 1950), pp. 55-60.

13. Levin, pp. 61-62; quotation from p. 61.

14. *Cf.* Levin, p. 61, on this point.

15. Shand, pp. 5-6; quotation from p. 6.

16. Citations of *Tamburlaine* come from Ribner's edition, and references appear parenthetically in my text.

17. T. S. Eliot, "Notes on the Blank Verse of Christopher Marlowe," *The Sacred Wood: Essays on Poetry and Criticism,* University Paperbacks 11 (London and New York: Methuen and Barnes & Noble, 1960), pp. 88-89; quotation from p. 89.

18. For a summary account of this scholarship, see W. B. C. Watkins, "The Plagiarist: Spenser or Marlowe?", *ELH,* 11 (December 1944), 249, n. 1.

19. Eliot, p. 91.

20. John Bakeless, *Christopher Marlowe* (London: Jonathan Cape, 1938), p. 283.

21. S. P. Zitner, Introduction to his edition of Edmund Spenser, *The Mutabilitie Cantos,* Nelson's Medieval and Renaissance Library, ed. Geoffrey Shepherd (London, etc.: Thomas Nelson and Sons, Ltd., 1968), p. 65.

22. Ants Oras, "Lyrical Instrumentation in Marlowe: A Step Towards Shakespeare," in *Studies in Shakespeare,* University of Miami Publications in English and American Literature 1, edd. Arthur D. Matthews and Clark M. Emery (Coral Gables, Fla.: University of Miami Press, 1953), p. 80.

23. Morris, 139-140.

24. For some indication of the oratorical skills demanded to enunciate particular sounds, see Mark Van Doren's discussion of *Julius Caesar* in *Shakespeare* (Garden City, N. Y.: Doubleday & Company, Inc., 1939), pp. 153-158.

25. Arthur Jacobs, *A New Dictionary of Music,* Penguin Reference Books R 12 (Baltimore, Md.: Penguin Books, 1965), *s.v.* "opera."

26. Zitner, p. 66.

27. Levin, pp. 66-67; quotation from p. 67. *Cf.* Rosalie L. Colie, *Shakespeare's Living Art* (Princeton, N. J.: Princeton University Press, 1974), pp. 145-146, on Shakespeare's method for achieving a similar effect.

28. Davidson and Davidson, 23.

29. Shand, pp. 77-103; quotation from p. 77. For similar overviews, see also Zucker, chapters I and II, and Felix Bosonnet, *The Function of Stage Properties in Christopher Marlowe's Plays*, The Cooper Monographs on English and American Language and Literature, edd. Rudolf Stamm and Eduard Kolb, Theatrical Physiognomy Series 27 (Basel: Francke Verlag Bern, 1978), chapters II and III.

30. Weil, pp. 125-142.

31. *Ibid.*, p. 125.

32. *Ibid.*, p. 128.

33. Levin, p. 66.

34. Coburn Freer, *The Poetics of Jacobean Drama* (Baltimore and London: The Johns Hopkins University Press, 1981), p. 33; Joseph Hall, *Virgidemiarum* (London, 1597), quoted on p. 28.

Endless Play: The False Starts of Marlowe's *Jew of Malta*

THOMAS CARTELLI

Because the last three acts of *The Jew of Malta* are largely devoted to seemingly arbitrary exercises in sensationalism and intrigue, and because they fail to sustain the standard of seriousness presumably established in the first two acts of the play, they have often been singled out critically to testify to the artistic failure or textual corruption of the original play Marlowe wrote.[1] Taking my own critical precedent from scholars whose interpretations of *The Jew* have been influenced by T. S. Eliot's groundbreaking description of the play as "savage farce," I would suggest that the tendency to discredit the play's second movement is based on a general misreading of the play's first movement and on a more specific failure to recognize that the drama's superficially random mixture of contrasting tone and content has its source in the peculiar theatrical mode within which the play is working.[2]

For lack of a better term, I will (as others have before me) call this theatrical mode a version of burlesque, but will define it (as others have not) as a free-form approach to theatrical representation which encourages the generally unmediated expression of fantasies that more conventional theatrical modes (*e.g.*, tragedy) formally inhibit.[3] All plays, of course, employ the stage as a privileged area, consciously set off from the real world, that liberates both actor and audience from the

117

social constraints of everyday life. But most plays also impose strict limits on the enjoyment of such liberation by means of a formal organization that prevents both actor and audience from "going too far," that defends against the possibility of a collective fantasy getting out of hand.[4] Whereas in these conventional modes of representation, "the dramatist will," as Freud wrote, "provoke not merely an *enjoyment* of the liberation but a *resistance* to it as well," in *The Jew of Malta* Marlowe provokes only minimal resistance to the enjoyment his version of burlesque affords.[5] This is the case because the compositional basis for such resistance—namely, a formal structure of moral restraints—is a conspicuously indeterminate link in the play's dramatic design. In *The Jew* Marlowe does not commit himself to the dramatic economy of checks and balances described by Freud. Instead, he develops a more elusive, more fluid structure for his play that effectively neutralizes audience resistance by failing to provide an unequivocal source of moral gravity that would serve to inhibit audience involvement.[6] In so doing Marlowe offers his audience the prospect of endless play without engendering in that audience the fear of having its collective hand slapped, or of having its licensed fantasies swept back under the rug by a moral or aesthetic authority that recreates its original resistance.[7] In brief, I see *The Jew of Malta* working within—indeed, establishing for itself—a theatrical mode that encourages and facilitates the informal interplay of fantasy instead of the formal imitation of an action, that communicates a sense of shared make-believe without ever really requiring our willing suspension of disbelief.[8] And I would, accordingly, describe its working premises in terms of fluidity of form and content, flexibility of movement and perspective, and an art of characterization that seeks to transcend the limits of economically narrow character definition.[9]

Given the protean logic of Marlowe's dramatic enterprise, we must now ascertain how we, as theatrical outsiders, can respond (and, for that matter, how Marlowe *conditions* us to respond) to a play that is so "pre-eminently a stage-piece" and is, therefore, "only to be understood in terms of its theatrical mode."[10] We can begin by acknowledging that the fluidity of the play's form and content requires a reciprocal fluidity of response on the part of its audience. In order to meet *The Jew* on its own terms, we must ride the play as we ride an unfamiliar rapids, adjusting our positions to fit the contours of its protean shape and texture. Marlowe negotiates our passage through these rapids by inducing us to surrender our preconceived notions about dramatic consistency, our normative assumptions about what does or does not constitute acceptable behavior, and whatever expectations of "high seriousness" of tone and content we bring with us into the theater. He proceeds in this vein by means of an opening series of plot manipulations which produce a constant shifting of dramatic perspective. This shifting of perspective generates, in turn, corresponding shifts in audience response which effectively prevent the audience from narrowly defining and, therefore, limiting the play's theatrical range and interests.

Marlowe's interest in the manipulation of plot for specific theatrical ends is especially obvious in the first movement of the play. In my opinion, this first movement—roughly consisting of Machiavel's prologue, the exposition of Barabas's mercantile aspirations, and the demonstration of Ferneze's politic hypocrisy, followed by Barabas's resolute response—comprises a series of false starts which determines the theatrical orientation of the play as a whole. Instead of establishing a set of expectations which the rest of the play fails to fulfill, the opening scenes establish a pattern of discontinuity which disarms the audience of conventional expectations of logical development and accommodates it to the acquired freedom of the play's burlesque mode. This movement proceeds by channeling Machiavellism and related issues into a deliberately ambiguous process of dramatic give-and-take in which the audience plays a responsive role, and culminates by giving the audience dramatic license to roam at will through all the novel precincts of theatrical experience that the play explores. The invitation to enter these precincts is offered—and the process that makes it unlikely that we will refuse the invitation begins—when Machiavel enters and brings the drama to life.

Machiavel appears onstage to establish relations between the play and its audience, to set a prevailing tone and supply a point of interpretive contact. Like the insidiously attractive Gaveston who plays a similar role in what amounts to the prologue of *Edward II*, Machiavel brings to bear on play and audience alike a particular style and set of associations which remain resonant throughout the production and influence the way we respond to the dramatic proceedings. There is, to start with, something casual, disarming, and "ingratiating" about his first remarks and the manner in which he broaches them, "a suggestion of private knowledge shared by the few who happen to be in the theatre"[11]:

> Albeit the world think Machiavel is dead,
> Yet was his soul but flown beyond the Alps,
> And, now the Guise is dead, is come from France
> To view this land and frolic with his friends.
> To some perhaps my name is odious,
> But such as love me guard me from their tongues,
> And let them know that I am Machiavel,
> And weigh not men, and therefore not men's words.
>   (Prologue, 1-8)[12]

Machiavel's ingratiating style virtually requires the instinctive admission of shared hypocrisy by pragmatic men who know the way the world works and revel in their respective disclosures. Cutting right to the heart of what often disguises men's hidden desires and doubts, he challenges the audience to come out of the closet of its observance of custom, form, and superstition in order to "frolic" with him in a temporary release from civilized obfuscation:

> Admired I am of those that hate me most.
> Though some speak openly against my books,
> Yet will they read me and thereby attain
> To Peter's chair; and, when they cast me off,
> Are poisoned by my climbing followers.
> I count religion but a childish toy
> And hold there is no sin but ignorance.
> Birds of the air will tell of murders past;
> I am ashamed to hear such fooleries.
>   (Prologue, 9-17)

At the same time the vision of the world he offers the audience is palpably sensationalized. When, for instance, Machiavel says that lapsed Machiavellians, upon casting him off, "Are poisoned by my climbing followers," he presents a cynically pragmatic picture of man as a small but ambitious backstabber, an opportunistic competitor for the highest anthill of power, that has as much currency in popular caricatures of Medicean intrigue as in commonly perceived political fact. He thus reminds the audience that his status as an indifferent arbiter of reality, who turns all our pretty fictions about honor and position to critical account, is coextensive with the distorting sensationalism of his theatrical self-presentation. The avowedly authoritative approach he brings to bear on the subjects of religion, ignorance, and superstition—each of which is addressed in the same incisive and unanswerable manner—is, in other words, as much a theatrical style as it is a philosophic position. And, ultimately, it is Machiavel's style, not his position, which induces the audience to suspend its common-sense discriminations between fact and fantasy, and to enter more fully into the spirit of the proceedings.

This becomes increasingly obvious when Machiavel intensifies his attack on cultural shibboleths in his analysis of the relation between power and the right to govern:

> Many will talk of title to a crown:
> What right had Caesar to the empery?
> Might first made kings, and laws were then most sure
> When, like the Draco's, they were writ in blood.
> Hence comes it that a strong built citadel
> Commands much more than letters can import;
> Which maxim had Phalaris observed,
> H'had never bellowed in a brazen bull
> Of great one's envy. O' the poor petty wights
> Let me be envied and not pitied.
>
> (Prologue, 18-27)

It is Machiavel's knowing insistence on his position—"Might first made kings"—that brings his message across to the audience, the self-consciously theatrical manner in which he broaches it that persuades the audience to accede imaginatively to its cynical truth. Machiavel's method here is closely akin to an aggressive brand of seduction. He intimidates the audience into letting down its conventional guards of repression and restraint by appealing to its pride about being up-to-date and worldly. Whatever one's normative persuasion, no one wishes to be thought a child playing with toys, or guilty of the sin of ignorance; nor does anyone wish to be left out of touch with the feeling of common conspiracy which informs the prologue and, to a great extent, the play. In generating this feeling of common conspiracy, Machiavel encourages the audience (and, significantly, *all* members of

the audience, from professionals who recognize their own cynical practice in Machiavel's speech, to apprentices who can only fantasize their
release from social and religious constraints) to participate vicariously
in the most sensational forms of forbidden behavior under the auspices
of a worldly authority who sanctions their participation with the blessing of common sense.

In the final turn of the prologue, Machiavel, however, pulls his "lecture" up short in order to establish a more problematic connection between himself and the nominal hero of the "tragedy" he is here to introduce:

> But whither am I bound? I come not, I,
> To read a lecture here in Britain,
> But to present the tragedy of a Jew
> Who smiles to see how full his bags are crammed,
> Which money was not got without my means.
> I crave but this: grace him as he deserves,
> And let him not be entertained the worse
> Because he favors me.
>
> (Prologue, 28-35)

Although Barabas does, in the course of the play, make bold statements and perform nefarious deeds which could be construed as
Machiavellian in spirit, neither his words nor his deeds are consistent
with the intellectual content and almost clinical perspective—in short,
the "letter"—of Machiavel's lecture. Barabas is at his most Machiavellian (and I now use the word loosely) only in terms of the sensational *style* of his increasingly arbitrary intrigues, not in the mercantile
pursuit of profit or, for that matter, in the politic pursuit of power
which he attempts to relinquish as soon as he gains it. These obvious
disparities between what Machiavel says about Barabas and what
Barabas does, between Machiavel's systematic philosophy and Barabas's arbitrary exercises in mayhem, are, however, symptomatic of
Marlowe's attempt first to establish and, then, to divert into other
channels the tendentiousness of the Machiavellian letter, while turning
the sensationalism of the Machiavellian spirit to continuing theatrical
account by filtering it through the burlesque abandon of Barabas.
They are also symptomatic of Marlowe's ongoing attempt to condition
his audience to the discontinuities and fractured logic, the ironies and

ambiguities of the kind of play he is actually writing. Marlowe's intentions may be discerned in the studied ambiguity of Machiavel's presentation of "the tragedy of a Jew / Who smiles to see how full his bags are crammed." One need hardly be a scholar to recognize that smiling in prosperity is the perfect precondition for a drastic change in circumstance, or to notice that Machiavel's superficially partisan appeal on behalf of Barabas involves an element of disarming and casual indifference. In such a context, Machiavel's closing request—"And let him not be entertained the worse / Because he favors me"—may be taken as a rather insidious piece of irony in which sympathy is solicited for Barabas by a character whose attachments are notoriously suspect and whose pronouncements are proverbially misleading.

The spirit of irony and ambiguity into which Machiavel initiates us is sustained throughout the early scenes of the play proper, where Marlowe's working logic requires Barabas to be "set up" before being sent off to pursue his comically nefarious intrigues. Machiavel sets the tone by misleadingly implicating Barabas in his philosophy, and Marlowe exploits it by superimposing Barabas's comic exterior (the Jew's prominent "bottle-nose") on the more sober front of a no-nonsense merchant-prince. The audience, which has been conditioned by Machiavel to expect an equally iconoclastic Machiavellian to take his place on stage, seems to get, as Alfred Harbage has noted, a relative innocent in his stead.[13] Far more interested in the poetry of acquisition than in the strategy of power, Barabas presents himself as a supremely competent man of means who, from his island base in Malta, commands much of the trade and profit of the Mediterranean:

> Give me the merchants of the Indian mines
> That trade in metal of the purest mold,
> The wealthy Moor that in the eastern rocks
> Without control can pick his riches up
> And in his house heap pearl like pebble-stones,
> Receive them free and sell them by the weight.
> (I.i.19-24)

Not only do Barabas's interests here seem far removed from the competitive political infighting portrayed in Machiavel's lecture, but he, himself, seems far above the roguish proportions of the character who will later poison a bevy of nuns and effect a series of similarly sensational plots in the course of his exploits. Indeed, as Barabas becomes caught up in describing the glittering inventory of his wealth, the effect is not unlike that elicited by Tamburlaine's hypnotic contemplation of the glories of sovereignty, or the Passionate Shepherd's depiction of an exquisite garden of delights.[14] The difference is that, in this instance, Marlowe is setting his hero up for a fall as pronounced as that presumably suffered by the shepherd upon receipt of the nymph's reply. Marlowe is also setting his audience up by offering it the false scent of Tamburlainean rhetoric, the exciting prospect of "infinite riches," within a dramatic context that will soon transform Barabas's "little room" and everything it represents into the mere backdrop for Barabas's free-form pursuit of theatrical enormity. True to the emerging form of the drama, Marlowe first introduces a Machiavellian atmosphere of criminal complicity and intrigue, then establishes a counter-climate of mercantile idealism for Barabas to inhabit, only to subject both to the shifting perspectives of a burlesque plot, the only real constant in the play.

Once the play is put into motion and its opening speeches cede to a series of dramatic interactions, the peculiar nature of its theatrical orientation becomes more apparent. The most pivotal of these early interactions involves Barabas's first direct confrontation with Ferneze, where the ambiguous role played by Machiavellism makes itself keenly felt (I.ii.38ff). As what amounts to the play's third false start, the Ferneze sequence should check any residual determination we might have to come to terms with the drama in any straightforward manner. Conditioned by the prologue to expect Barabas's victimization of guileless opponents, we are presented, instead, with his own victimization at the hands of another stand-in Machiavel.[15] This turn of events is apt to make the audience feel that it is undergoing some kind of test in applied policy. Despite Machiavel's injunctions on behalf of Barabas (and, perhaps, because of them if they are, in fact, ironic), it may appear to the audience that identifying with Barabas is not really the best policy to pursue. Gracing Barabas "as he deserves" may, in short, prove to be as ill-advised a pursuit as the statement is ambiguous. By validating several different interpretations of Machiavel's advocacy and invalidating an exclusive commitment to either of the characters involved, Marlowe keeps his audience off balance, prevents it from making easy associations or stock responses. He tests the audience by providing a dramatic analogue to the subversively appealing aphorisms of the prologue which is apparently meant to separate the dispassionate men from the compassionate boys, but complicates the test by having it superficially redound against the credit of the nominal hero of the piece, whom we were previously enjoined to favor and with whom we are subsequently encouraged to identify.

Having been pushed off the center stage of Machiavellian practice, Barabas does not, in his ensuing intrigues, attempt to reclaim that ground as his own by imitating the prosaic hypocrisy of Ferneze. Instead, Barabas "rouses" himself to a resolve of burlesque aggression that exploits the more sensational aspects of Machiavel's earlier theatrical appeal:

> Daughter, I have it. Thou perceiv'st the plight
> Wherein these Christians have oppressed me.
> Be ruled by me, for in extremity
> We ought to make bar of no policy.
> |(I.ii.270-273)

Policy is the Machiavellian code word which at first sight seems to identify and encapsulate Barabas's decision to match ruthlessness with ruthlessness.[16] But his adoption of the word and its suggestion of purposeful activity does not suddenly transform Barabas into a card-carrying Machiavellian, either in terms of the philosophic position of the prologue, or of the applied philosophy of Ferneze. Barabas only superficially identifies himself with a program of action which, if taken too literally, distorts what he is actually about; he conveniently mimics the characteristic idiom of Ferneze, but never reveals any theoretical interest in the Machiavellian letter as it is represented in the prologue. He is, however, clearly interested in exploiting the Machiavellian spirit to effect his own, far from philosophic ends, and will, from this point forward, attempt to transform the exercise of policy into an occasion to make fantastic pastime of the freedom of the stage (see, e.g., II.i,) where Barabas's first act of policy eventuates in the comic elation of a successful siege of a floorboard in a nunnery).

Barabas's exuberance in going on to pursue intrigue for its own sake, and his free-spiritedness in reveling in his exploits beyond the immediate needs of respective situations, encourage the audience also to subordinate its critical faculty to an equally "radical will to play."[17] The false starts of the play's first movement serve to stimulate the audience's active engagement in this interplay of fantasy by repeatedly denying the audience what Norman Holland calls the "conscious, intellecting" satisfactions of art of a conspicuously Apollonian persuasion.[18] Once this denial is accomplished—that is, once the play persuades the audience of its own freedom from the formal dramatic constraints that provoke audience resistance—the audience is licensed to pursue its "most primitive form of gratification" which is equivalent, in Holland's terms, to a regression into fantasy.[19] Since this denial coincides structurally with the dramatic reduction of Ferneze—the play's only potential source of moral authority—to the same level over which he presumes to preside, both play and audience are left to proceed in the absence of anything (short of dramatic closure) that might constrain or confine the imaginative commerce between them. With this manifest break from any claim to high seriousness, *The Jew* effectively sunders the deceptively formative bonds of its false starts, demonstrating in the process that such a play can only be defined in terms of what it does, not in terms of what it should do, only pretends to do, or does not attempt to do at all.

NOTES

1. For a fine summary of textual approaches to the play, see H. S. Bennett, ed., *The Jew of Malta and The Massacre at Paris* (1931; rpt. New York: Gordian Press, 1964), pp. 15-19. The most extreme dismissal of the last three acts, equal to a consignment to oblivion, is offered by F. P. Wilson, *Marlowe and the Early Shakespeare* (Oxford: Clarendon Press, 1953), p. 65. A far more reasonable, although still prejudicial, approach to *The Jew's* "structural complications" is taken by Wilbur Sanders in his chapter on the play in *The Dramatist and the Received Idea* (Cambridge: Cambridge University Press, 1968), pp. 38-60.

2. See J. B. Steane, *Marlowe: A Critical Study* (Cambridge: Cambridge University Press, 1964), pp. 166-203; Nicholas Brooke, "Marlowe the Dramatist," *Elizabethan Theatre*, Stratford-upon-Avon Studies, 9 (1964), pp. 95-96; and Stephen J. Greenblatt, "Marlowe, Marx, and Anti-Semitism," *Critical Inquiry*, 5:2 (1978), 305.

3. The term "burlesque" is, admittedly, a loose one and has often been used in an unsystematic manner in critical attempts to categorize *The Jew*. J. B. Steane employs the term with precision and to good advantage in his splendid chapter on the play (see previous citation). But his association of burlesque with "farcical action, roughly colloquial speech, and caricatured *personae*," hence, with a general

"lowering of tone" (p. 186), is very different from the definition broached here.

4. See the interpretation of artistic form as defense advanced by Norman Holland in *The Dynamics of Literary Response* (New York: Oxford University Press, 1968), which is nicely summarized in the following: "In effect, the literary work dreams a dream for us. It embodies and evokes in us a central fantasy; then it manages and controls that fantasy by devices that, were they in a mind, we would call defenses, but, being on a page, we call 'form'" (p. 75).

5. Sigmund Freud, "Psychopathic Characters on the Stage," *Standard Edition, Vol. VII* (London: Hogarth Press, 1956), p. 309.

6. Although it may be argued that what Harry Levin—in *The Overreacher* (Boston: Beacon Press, 1964)—terms the play's "overplot," presided over by Ferneze, provides just the kind of formal restraint I find lacking, Levin himself contends that, morally speaking, all of the play's interconnected plots "operate on the same level," a fact which, he concludes, "is precisely what Marlowe is pointing out" (p. 67). In other words, whatever formal restraint is discerned as potential in the play's overplot is neutralized by the fact that Marlowe makes no moral distinctions between the competitive malefactors who inhabit every level of the play.

7. It may, of course, be contended that the formal closure of *The Jew* does, indeed, sweep the audience's fantasies back under the rug by returning both audience and play to a sense of normative order and proportion. With Ferneze's cunning defeat of Barabas, the devil is effectively put back in his pot and the reign of pious surfaces is renewed. But in burlesque of this variety, the imaginative traffic between audience and play is not terminated by dramatic closure. In the first place, the criminal spirit of Barabas lives on through Ferneze himself, the more reserved Machiavellian who serves as his prosaic heir-apparent, hence, as a bridge or intermediary between burlesque and the real world outside the theater to which the audience is returning. Barabas's anarchic spirit endures as well in the audience's conditioned perception of the tenuousness of the hold exercised over its collective drives and fantasies by civilized restraints. In this respect, closure simply slows down the momentum of a process that conceivably maintains itself at a lower ebb in the imaginative life of the audience.

8. I define burlesque here as an extreme version of what J. L. Styan terms "non–illusory theatre" in *Drama, Stage, and Audience* (Cambridge: Cambridge University Press, 1975), pp. 180-181.

9. *Cf.* Nicholas Brooke, "Marlowe the Dramatist": "The structure of such a play cannot be considered in simply narrative terms . . . because the rapid changes of theatrical mode which are its chief resource have no narrative significance; still less can it be considered in terms of character, for the actor who takes Barabas' part will have to display a range of theatrical power in which character-definition (though existing) will be quite different things at different times. . . . It seems to me that Marlowe realised the potentialities of this form of play, and that his task was to fulfill them as richly as possible" (pp. 95-96). *Cf.,* also, Howard Babb, "Policy in Marlowe's *The Jew of Malta*," *ELH*, 24 (1957), who contends that the "dramatic standard of reality" in *The Jew* "is completely fluid" (p. 92).

10. The first phrase in quotations is taken from Alfred Harbage, "Innocent Barabas," *Tulane Drama Review*, 8:4 (1964), 51. Harbage adds that "we shall get nearer the truth about the play if we ourselves are less 'terribly serious' about it, and think a

little less in terms of moral philosophy and a little more in terms of native sports" (53). *Cf.* T. W. Craik, ed., *The Jew of Malta* (London, 1966): *"The Jew of Malta* is essentially a play for the theatre . . . it is in the theatre that it must be judged, not according to preconceived notions of tragic dignity and tragic depth" (p. xviii). The second phrase in quotations is borrowed from J. L. Styan, *Drama, Stage, and Audience* (p. 190), who employs it in describing how a play like *Bartholomew Fair* should be approached.

11. I am indebted to Michael Warren (University of California, Santa Cruz) for allowing me to quote these remarks from his unpublished essay, "Marlowe's Prologues."

12. Quotations from the text of the play are taken from Irving Ribner, ed., *The Complete Plays of Christopher Marlowe* (Indianapolis: Bobbs-Merrill, 1977).

13. See Harbage, 55-58.

14. Harbage instructively compares Barabas's speech with Volpone's hymn to gold, and concludes that "the *poetry* of Barabas's speech expresses aspiration, the *poetry* of Volpone's, *perversion*" (57).

15. Identifying Ferneze as the play's only genuine practitioner of Machiavellian policy has become standard in most recent articles on *The Jew.* See, *e.g.,* Bob Hodge, "Marlowe, Marx and Machiavelli: Reading into the Past," in *Literature, Language and Society in England 1580-1680,* eds. David Aers *et al.* (Dublin: Gill & Macmillan, 1981), and Catherine Minshull, "Marlowe's 'Sound Machevill'," *Renaissance Drama,* N. S. XIII (1982), 35-53.

16. Steane calls it "the Machiavellian key-word" (p. 183).

17. Greenblatt, 302. Whereas Greenblatt envisions audience response to Barabas in terms of "the silence of the passive accomplice, winked at by his fellow criminal" (302), I see it more in terms of the active engagement of the aroused participant.

18. Holland, p. 92.

19. Holland, p. 74.

Marlowe as Experimental Dramatist:
The Role of the Audience
in *The Jew of Malta*

EDWARD L. ROCKLIN

Thirty years ago, Raymond Williams explained both the title and the program of his book on *Drama in Performance* by pointing out that while there was an abundance of studies treating plays as literature, and a growing body of work treating plays as theater,

> we have very few examples of the necessary next stage: a considera-
> tion of the play in performance, literary text and theatrical repre-
> sentation, not as separate entities, but as the unity which they are
> intended to become.[1]

Many critics, having noted this problem, have proceeded to develop a number of effective, if quite diverse, methods to analyze the constitut-ive features of what Thomas Van Laan calls "the idiom of drama." Behind the diversity of their methods, however, we can discern a shared perception that to consider drama in performance is to consider the play as a communicative act; and a common recognition that we can best answer the question "What does this play mean?"—the traditional question of criticism in the last one hundred years—by first asking the question "What does this play *do*?"[2]

Asking "What does this play do?" has also entailed shifting attention from the text to the audience since, as Williams later pointed out,

> An audience is always the most decisive inheritance of any art. It is the way in which people have learned to see and respond that creates the first essential condition of drama.[3]

This focus on the audience, in turn, has led critics to formulate new ways of understanding the collective action we call "a performance," so that, as Oscar Lee Brownstein and Darlene M. Daubert remark,

> It is clear that the role of the spectator has been quietly (often unconsciously) reconceived: once seen as an onlooker who was to be pleased, and then . . . as an intruder to be ignored, the spectator is generally considered by contemporary theorists *as a participant in a creative dialogue.*[4]

The spectators participate, indeed, in two ways, for not only do their responses at any single showing influence how the actors perform, but it is in their minds that, as Thomas Van Laan notes, the onstage spectacle is transformed into a vision:

> Since the dramatist works in a medium that denies him the use of a controlling interpretive voice, dramatic point of view is located not in the group of signs presented directly on the stage but in the consciousness of the audience that perceives them.[5]

The performed play and the responsive audience, then, can be seen as producing a virtual, as distinct from an actual, dialogue, aimed at having the spectators recreate the vision embodied in the written script.

This change in our theory has also meant that we are reconceiving the elements of drama in dynamic rather than static terms. As an example, we can take the concept of a *convention*. From the spectator's point of view, to speak of a convention or conventional device is to speak of the ways he has "learned to see and respond" to plays; and such conventions manifest themselves as the *expectations* that spectators bring to the theater. From the writer's point of view, to speak of a convention is to speak of the *practices* he has inherited in the dramaturgy of his day, and thus of the patterns by which he can generate and shape the action recorded in the script—and thereby, of course, seek to shape or control the reaction of his audience. For a dramatist to experiment, then, means for him to modify such practices in ways that, by playing with the audience's expectations, enable him to communicate his vision more precisely. What we are developing are methods of criticism that, by looking at drama as a communicative act, allow us to study how meaning emerges from the experience of spectators responding to what the play does.

These developments in dramatic theory and criticism obviously have not taken place in a vacuum. Rather, they have been spurred on by, and been influential in, the evolution of current theatrical practice, including such movements as the Elizabethan Revival and, even more recently, the resurrection of medieval drama that has brought us two stagings of the complete Chester Cycle in the spring of 1983 (one at Leeds, England, the other at Toronto, Canada). That is, as critics recovered an earlier, more presentational dramaturgy, their work encouraged those in the theater to mount productions of plays in their original staging; and the increasing number of such productions, in turn, by demonstrating the actualities of such production, has impelled critics to refine and expand their understanding of how medieval or Elizabethan drama functioned. This spiraling refinement of theory and practice has also meant that we are revising our images of those who wrote these plays, to see them much more clearly as dramatists. This revision has been most thorough in the case of Shakespeare, while the revision of our image of Marlowe has started later and proceeded more slowly—in part, I think, because Marlowe's plays, unlike Shakespeare's, disappeared from the theatrical repertory, and in part because when he was rediscovered, editors and critics in the nineteenth and early twentieth centuries presented him as a supreme poet of subjectivity and transcendental aspiration, and as a man who, while he wrote plays, was a poetic, not a dramatic, genius.[6]

Two pivotal works in the reformulation of our image of Marlowe as a dramatist have been Bernard Spivack's *Shakespeare and the Allegory of Evil* (1958), with its powerful demonstration of the importance of the Vice figure in early Elizabethan drama, and David Bevington's *From "Mankind" to Marlowe* (1962), with its lucid depiction of the dramatic structure inherited by the Elizabethans from the popular repertory. A limitation of both these essential studies, noted by critics such as Irving

Ribner, is that Spivack and Bevington both tend to present Marlowe as the prisoner of his heritage rather than its master.[7] Only in subsequent work have we begun to see Marlowe as being, in the words of Eugene Waith, "a vastly ambitious and gifted experimenter," who sought to transform that inheritance, and whose experiments with that dramaturgy (as distinguished from his well-recognized revolution in subject matter and his innovative use of blank verse) were an integral, not an accidental, element in his tremendous popular success.[8] The point has been made with especial clarity and vigor by Nicholas Brooke in his seminal essay, "Marlowe the Dramatist," in which Brooke neatly stands the old stereotype on its head:

> Marlowe was not a poet who lacked dramatic talent, he was the reverse; a dramatist who had the resources of a great poet at his command, when required.[9]

In this essay, I want to amplify this image of Marlowe as an experimental dramatist by analyzing his innovative use of the inherited dramaturgy in *The Jew of Malta,* which transformed both the way in which the play was framed and the functions of the Vice-like protagonist's relation with the audience. Put most briefly, my argument is that Marlowe used the prologue spoken by Machiavel to establish both the play's framing question and the role of the audience; that he used Barabas not only to generate the action but also to maintain control of the audience's perspective on that action, particularly at three crucial moments when that perspective is transformed by arousing expectations, then fulfilling them with a surprising twist; and that through these maneuvers he also insured that the spectators would, at the end, have to choose among three primary interpretations of the protagonist's fate.

Toward the end of his prologue, and as if he were seeking to dissociate himself from the traditional moral prologues of earlier plays, Machiavel interrupts himself to remark "I come not, I, / To read a lecture here in Britanie."[10] But this retroactive apophasis serves to alert any spectator who may have missed the fact that a lecture is just what Machiavel has delivered—although the content of that lecture is hardly traditional. For Machiavel's vision is atheist and naturalist, it defines success in the secular terms of wealth and power, and it recommends achieving such success through histrionic manipulation. Addressed to the inhabitants of a Christian society, these propositions act as goads impelling the spectators to articulate their own opposing beliefs in God, in a transcendental moral order, and in supernatural intervention designed to rectify worldly injustice. Machiavel's rhetoric thus serves to define the spectators as an audience of adversaries, hostile not only to himself but to the protagonist he finally introduces with the cunning request that they "grace him as he deserves, / And let him not be entertained the worse / Because he favors me" (ll. 33-35). The rhetoric of the prologue, then, uses, yet inverts, the morality-play frame, for while the members of the audience are assigned their traditional role as judges between the different ways of life presented, they must watch the play over the shoulder of a figure who has just challenged the very world view in which they would ordinarily make that judgment.

Having prepared the audience to reject an avaricious, dissembling protagonist, Marlowe contrives that his first two scenes shall overthrow these expectations. Barabas's first two soliloquies echo the precepts of Machiavel, but what really establishes his allegiance to his mentor is the fact that when three of his fellow Jews arrive, he seizes the opportunity for some Machiavellian dissembling. To the three Jews, he speaks words of reassurance, arguing that while the Turks have indeed come to collect a decade's tribute, and while the Jews have indeed been summoned to appear before the Maltese Governor, they have nothing to fear. To the spectators, however, he utters asides which prove he is hiding his true assessment of the situation. The spectators will stir as Barabas speaks to them, their attention will sharpen at the scent of duplicity, and the soliloquy that follows will produce the intimacy that comes from sharing a secret. Whereas the first two soliloquies of Barabas are spoken *at* the spectators, here Barabas turns *to* them, and engages them by sharing the very process of his thought.

As he confides in the spectators, furthermore, Barabas also establishes their expectations for the next scene. These expectations, as Howard Babb has shown, are phrased in terms of two key ideas, *policy* and *profession*, so that the audience presumes that Malta's Governor, Ferneze, who represents the true profession of Christ and the legitimate policy of a public ruler, will oppose the false, worldly profession and illicit private policy of the Machiavellian Barabas.[11] Ferneze, however, betrays both his offices, as he simply confiscates the wealth of Barabas under cover of religious duty. Answering the charges of Barabas, which point up these betrayals, Ferneze claims that "to stain our hands with blood / Is far from us and our profession" (I.ii.147-148), but bloodshed is precisely what his occupation demands, and in refusing to honor his worldly profession to fight the enemies of Christ, Ferneze reveals the emptiness of his spiritual profession. The indictment is driven home when Barabas, responding to the First Knight's complacent approval of the Governor's policy, bursts out bitterly, "Ay, policy? that's their profession, / And not simplicity, as they suggest" (ll. 163-164). This time, Barabas does not speak *at* the spectators, or even *to* them, but rather *for* them, voicing their sense of having been betrayed by those they expected to favor as representing their own point of view against the play's ostensible Machiavel. Thus they not only share the perspective of Barabas but now sympathize with him as well.

Yet this sympathy, though momentarily quite intense, is sharply qualified by the rapid series of reversals that follow. In response to the First Jew's request that he "remember Job" (l. 183), Barabas unleashes a tirade that, despite grotesque elements of quantification, rises to a tragic pitch in its echoes of Job's own cadence and phrasing:

> For only I have toiled to inherit here
> The months of vanity and loss of time,
> And painful nights have been appointed me.
> (ll. 199-201)

Yet as in the previous scene, so here at the departure of the Jews, Barabas drops his mask, mocks "the simplicity of these base slaves" (l. 218), and reveals his "ecstasy" as pretense. This time, however, since he has not warned them, the spectators find that *their* simplicity has also been abused. Their surprise is intensified, furthermore, when they learn that, even before obeying the Governor's summons, Barabas has hidden much of his wealth in his house. The spectators thus discover that they were not, as they assumed, completely in his confidence. And this reversal is followed by others: for Barabas, stunned by the news that he will not have access to his house, plunges into genuine despair, recovers, and persuades his daughter to feign a conversion as the means to enter their house-turned-nunnery to recover his gold.

By having Barabas deceive the audience only to find himself over-reached, Marlowe subjects the spectators to a direct experience of being gulled as all the characters are gulled by the Machiavellian protagonist, yet he insures that the alienation from Barabas that naturally follows this experience shall be temporary, followed in turn by a renewed intimacy as well as assent to his plot. At the same time, by demanding such a swiftly modulating series of responses from the spectators, the scene functions to teach them the mental and emotional agility they will need to perform their role: it demonstrates, first, that ironic reversal is the fundamental principle of the play's universe; second, that anyone, even the protagonist or, more radically, the spectators, may be subjected to such ironic reversal; and third, that the spectators' business is to assume the detached point of view exemplified by Barabas so as to appreciate the pratfalls and lethal pranks that constitute the rest of the action.

From the middle of the second scene until the end of the third act, the spectators continue to share the perspective of Barabas as he contrives three events: first, the ruse by which Abigail recovers his hidden wealth; second, the stratagem by which Abigail's two suitors, one of them the Governor's son, are lured into a mutually fatal duel, in a scene that Barabas oversees and comments on as if it were a sporting event; and third, the device by which, in order to eliminate Abigail after her sincere conversion to Christianity, he poisons the entire convent in which she has taken refuge. What shocks the spectators here is not only Barabas's murder of his daughter but also the speed with which he decides to act, and the remorselessness with which he carries out his plot. Yet throughout these scenes, even as their sympathy for Barabas wanes and is abruptly wiped out by his filicide, the spectators are encouraged to see these events as what Barabas's slave and accomplice, Ithamore, calls "*brave sport*" (III.i.30), and to share his delight in the gleeful execution of devices.

The murder of Abigail, by producing this second major shift in the relationship between Barabas and the spectators, sets the stage for what follows up to the middle of the last scene. This segment repeats what has gone before in a harsher key and a faster tempo: as Barabas earlier destroys his daughter's two suitors, so now he destroys the two Friars who seek to blackmail him for that crime; as he earlier poisons his first accomplice, Abigail, so now he poisons her replacement, Ithamore; and as he was earlier driven to wholesale slaughter of the nuns, so now he delivers the entire Maltese garrison to the Turks—and, as it were in passing, pulls off the *coup de theatre* by which he stages his own resurrection. These scenes are indeed, as critics from Eliot onwards have declared, farce, but they are farce with a difference: throughout these actions, the emphasis consistently falls on the irony that, with the exception of Abigail, all of these victims follow the lead of Ferneze in becoming objects for destruction because they betray the values or codes they profess to live by (for even Ithamore betrays the code of villainy he claims to follow). Thus the spectators discover that it is Machiavel's vision, not their own, that the characters validate, for it is Machiavel's values, not Christ's, that they live by, and Machiavel's program of action, not Christ's, that they enact. The spectators experience the peculiar sensation of witnessing indignities such as blackmail, treason, and murder, without being asked or, indeed, allowed to feel any indignation. Marlowe thus induces the spectators to assume not only the point of view but also the state of mind embodied by Machiavel at the beginning of the play, adding to his dry irony the glee with which Barabas pursues his evil designs.

And it is this state of mind, at once emotionally detached and intellectually engaged, that is crucial for the final reversal of Marlowe's design, in which Barabas overreaches himself and becomes the last and most splendid victim of the sort of ironic destruction he has hitherto inflicted on others: as they laugh at what is now the horrible (but neither terrifying nor tragic) spectacle of a man boiling to death, the spectators are witnessing and, indeed, participating in a final instance of the "*brave sport*" that they have been taught to enjoy. This comedy, however, is complex, not so much because of *what* happens to Barabas as for *how* it happens.

Barabas falls because he makes the incredible mistake of trusting his worst enemy, Ferneze—but the crucial point to note is that Marlowe dramatizes the event precisely so as to emphasize that Barabas's maneuver *is* a mistake. At the very moment when he commits this blunder, Barabas is boasting about his "policy," and his use of the key word emphasizes how *un*-Machiavellian he is in failing to imagine that others might likewise dissemble—a point that was forecast in the prologue, where Machiavel notes that

> Though some speak openly against my books,
> Yet will they read me, and thereby attain
> To Peter's chair: and when they cast me off,
> Are poisoned by my climbing followers.
>
> (ll. 10-13)

Moreover, even as Barabas fails Ferneze succeeds, and succeeds by being perfectly Machiavellian, dissembling until he can cut the rope that drops his enemy into the pot. Thus even as Ferneze takes over the role of Machiavellian *performer* the spectators are induced to take over the role of Machiavellian *commentator*, which is now theirs alone.

Ferneze, of course, does not define his success as a triumph of Machiavellian duplicity. Rather, after expressing pious horror at "the unhallowed deeds of Jews" (V.v.94), he presents his success as God's triumph:

> So march away, and let due praise be given
> Neither to fate nor fortune, but to heaven.
>
> (ll. 127-128)

The problem here is not with what is said, which is perfectly orthodox, but rather with *who* is saying it, and in what circumstances. For as he watches Barabas boil to death, Ferneze explains to the Turks,

> For he that did by treason work our fall,
> By treason hath delivered thee to us.
>
> (ll. 113-114)

Like his earlier disclaimer that "to stain our hands with blood / Is far from us and our profession" (I.ii.147-148), this moralizing draws attention to what it attempts to conceal, namely that Ferneze has once again cast Barabas as the scapegoat while profiting from his crime, and then rationalized his maneuver by attributing it to God. This time, however, it is the spectators, and only the spectators, who can ironically remark "Ay, policy! *that's* their profession, and *not* simplicity, as they suggest!"

Marlowe concludes, then, by inviting the spectators to provide the epilogue he does not have Machiavel return to pronounce. Furthermore, Marlowe makes this task more complex by putting into the play precisely the sort of speech that his Christian auditors would *like* to deliver in rebuttal of the prologue—but he does so in such a way as to make these claims questionable. The epilogue each spectator articulates, therefore, will be shaped in terms set by the opening challenge of Machiavel, and by their response to the equivocal ending which implicitly refers them back to that prologue.[12]

Marlowe places the audience in an ironic situation not only because Machiavel speaks ironically but also because their role as judges has been framed in a play-encompassing irony. And in such a situation, it is the case that there must be at least two possible interpretations, since genuine irony, as Jonathan Culler reminds us, operates by offering contrasting patterns:

> No sentence is ironic *per se*. Sarcasm may contain internal inconsistencies which make its purport quite obvious and prevent it from being read except in one way, but for a sentence to be properly ironic it must be possible to imagine some group of readers taking it quite literally. Otherwise there is no contrast between apparent and assumed meaning and no space of ironic play.[13]

In the case of *The Jew of Malta* this irony leads to three main perceptions of its design.

For those who take Ferneze literally, all the irony is at the expense of the Turks, Barabas, and Machiavel, and the ending is a simple but complete rebuttal of the prologue. For these spectators, Ferneze's last speech adequately sums up a satisfying action in which the Christian God has contrived that Christian virtue shall triumph over both Jewish and Turkish infidelity. In effect, such spectators respond to the challenge of the play's opening by taking labels such as "Machiavel" and "Jew" not merely as presumptions of evil in those so labeled, but rather as guarantees that everything such creatures do *is* evil. From this perspective, indeed, there is no need to make a new judgment at the end of the play, since the application of labels has been the only judgment needed.[14]

For those who perceive Ferneze as the play's final and most successful Machiavel, but who also distinguish between Christianity and Catholicism, their mental epilogue will focus on the discrepancy between profession and practice as revealing the ineradicable potential for sin in both institutions and individuals. For these spectators, Machiavel's irony is powerful but limited to the human betrayal of what remains the true faith, and the play functions as a satiric defense of Christianity against those earthly folk who become the very "worldlings" that Barabas, unlike his mentor, so confidently assumes the audience to be (V.v.50-51).[15]

However, Machiavel, the notorious atheist, does not limit his challenge in this fashion, and thus for those spectators who see the irony as encompassing Christians, Jews, and Turks alike, Christianity (or, more generally, religion) would be mocked as the "childish toy" the prologue proclaims all religions to be. The atheist interpretation is obviously not one that the play insists on, nor, given the censorship controlling the Elizabethan stage, could it have been made explicit, since the authorities would have suppressed both the play and its author, but the invitation to take the irony in a subversive fashion is built into the complex interaction between play and audience.[16]

But if the play offers both a literal and an ironic interpretation, and if it leaves implicit the scope of that irony, this does not make Marlowe's design "ambiguous" in the sense that some critics mean, who employ the word as a polite synonym for "flawed" or "incoherent"—as Bevington does, for example, when he argues that Marlowe's failure (as he sees it) to fuse older and newer dramaturgies not only explains "the play's characteristic ambiguity," but also renders it "morally neutral."[17] For the spectators of the 1590s, however, whether they took it straight or ironically, the play would not have been morally neutral, but rather would have presented a clear meaning whose significance would be based on one of the potential patterns inherent in Marlowe's design. Obviously, a major part of the play's appeal resided in the melodramatic career of its sensational protagonist. But the play was a theatrical success also because it explored, even as it exploited, one of the major intellectual debates of its time, giving play to the older Christian vision, which provided a security that could come to be experienced as constraint, even as it gave play to the newer vision of an emergent naturalism, which induced a sense of liberation that could also be felt as vertigo.

Marlowe's experiment was also, I would suggest, followed up by his successors. At the conclusion of his fine essay, "Dangerous Sport: The Audience's Engagement with the Vice of the Moral Interludes," Robert C. Jones argues that in our eagerness to prove the continuity of drama in the late 1590s we are neglecting "an obvious but crucial difference between [the later villains] and their morality forebears":

> Though the Shakespearean villain and the Jonsonian knave appeal to us theatrically, they do not openly interact with us or even overtly acknowledge our response as audience. . . . He may still play *to* us, but he does not make us participating actors in his play; he does not make us self-consciously act out our conspiratorial engagement with him . . . or our dissociation from him.[18]

The distinction is important, but I believe it is overdrawn: for in *The Jew of Malta,* at least, Machiavel *does* make us articulate our dissociation from (or, finally, our concurrence with) his ideas, while Barabas not only engages us as co-conspirators but also, in duping us, leads us to discover our role as unwitting participants in a momentarily unified world. And it is precisely by making us undergo this combination of detachment and engagement, overtly rejecting Machiavel yet conspiring with his disciple, that Marlowe induces the central tension through which he shapes our responses. Marlowe's experiment, then, helped later dramatists discover how, as Jones puts it, to "make the audience's engagement with a vicious schemer . . . even more 'dangerous' than it had been with the interlude Vice" (p. 63). In his innovative play, Marlowe used vital elements of the older morality-play dramaturgy to challenge the very beliefs that at once helped to create and were embodied in the earlier form. The brave sport of *The Jew of Malta* was thus a critical event in the emergence of the newer dramaturgy, and it marshalled the way to knavery for a host of villains, including Shakepeare's Richard III, Iago, and Edmund, creatures whose plots produce in their victims the pity and fear appropriate to tragedy, but whose performances induce in themselves and, in varying degrees, their audiences, the laughter and detachment appropriate to comedy.[19]

NOTES

1. Raymond Williams, *Drama in Performance* (London: Frederick Muller, Ltd., 1954), pp. 11-12.

2. Two critics who have argued for this shift in focus are Stephen Booth, in his essay "On the Value of *Hamlet*," which appeared in *Reinterpretations of Elizabethan Drama*, ed. Norman Rabkin (New York: Columbia University Press, 1969), p. 138; and Alan C. Dessen, in his introduction to the 1981 volume of *Renaissance Drama*, N. S. 12 (1981), Editoral Note, n.p.

3. This is from Williams's revised edition of *Drama in Performance* (Harmondsworth, England: Penguin, 1968), p. 176.

4. O. L. Brownstein and D. M. Daubert, eds., *Analytical Sourcebook of Concepts in Dramatic Theory* (Westport, Conn.: Greenwood Press, 1981), p. xiii, italics mine.

5. Van Laan, *The Idiom of Drama* (Ithaca, N. Y.: Cornell University Press, 1970), p. 319.

6. The claim that Marlowe's contributions were essentially poetic (blank verse and passionate heroes to utter that verse) dominates late nineteenth and early twentieth century criticism, and can be found, for example, in such standard works as those of Courthope (*A History of English Poetry*, II, 420-421) and Ward (*A History of English Literature to the Death of Queen Anne*), I, 360-363); but it appears at least as late as 1950, surprisingly, in the very fine work of A. P. Rossiter, *English Drama from Early Times to the Elizabethans* (London: Hutchinson University Library, 1950), p. 174. Like Rossiter, a number of these writers make their point by arguing that Marlowe's poetic genius shows up when compared with the essentially dramatic genius of Kyd.

7. Irving Ribner, "Marlowe and the Critics," in *Tulane Drama Review*, 8:4 (1964), 224.

8 Waith, "Marlowe and the Jades of Asia," *Studies in English Literature*, 5 (1965), 245.

9. Brooke, "Marlowe the Dramatist," *Elizabethan Theatre*, Stratford-upon-Avon Studies 9, ed. John Russell Brown and Bernard Harris (New York: St. Martin's Press, 1967), p. 91.

10. All quotations from *The Jew of Malta* come from T. W. Craik's New Mermaid edition (New York: Hill and Wang, 1967). This passage is ll. 28-29; subsequent citations are given in the text. It is also a pleasure to acknowledge that Craik's introduction, with its emphasis on the theatrical power of the play, has influenced this essay.

11. Babb, "Policy in Marlowe's *The Jew of Malta*," *ELH: A Journal of English Literary History*, 24 (1957), 85-94, particularly 86-89.

12. For a similar analysis of the function of the prologue in the *beginning* of the play, see Don Beecher's "*The Jew of Malta* and the Ritual of the Inverted Moral Order," *Cahiers Elisabethains: Etudes sur la Pre-Renaissance et la Renaissance Anglaises*, 12 (October, 1977), 45-48. Beecher, however, argues that the spectators always keep an ironic distance from and perspective on Machiavel. Brooke, in the essay cited in note 9 above, argues, as I do, that Marlowe's design impels the spectators to remember the prologue.

13. Culler, *Structuralist Poetics* (Ithaca, N. Y.: Cornell University Press, 1975), p. 154.

14. The most forceful advocates of the literal interpretation are Bernard Spivack, *Shakespeare and the Allegory of Evil* (New York: Columbia University Press, 1958),

pp. 348-350, and Alfred Harbage, "Innocent Barabas," *Tulane Drama Review*, 8:4 (1964), 47-58.

15. Among the critics who take this point of view the most important are Douglas Cole, *Suffering and Evil in the Plays of Christopher Marlowe* (Princeton, N. J.: Princeton University Press, 1962), pp. 123-144; G. K. Hunter, "The Theology of Marlowe's *The Jew of Malta*," *The Journal of the Warburg and Courtauld Institutes*, 27 (1964), 211-240: W. L. Godshalk, *The Marlovian World Picture* (The Hague: Mouton, 1974), pp. 203-222; and the article by Beecher cited in note 12 above.

16. Major works in this line of criticism include: Harry Levin, *The Overreacher* (1952; rpt. Gloucester, Mass.: Peter Smith, 1974), pp. 56-80; J. B. Steane, *Marlowe: A Critical Study* (Cambridge: Cambridge University Press, 1964), pp. 166-203; J. L. Simmons, "Elizabethan Stage Practice and Marlowe's *The Jew of Malta*," *Renaissance Drama*, N.S. 4 (1971), 93-104; and the articles by Babb (note 11) and Brooke (note 9) already mentioned. Robert P. Adams's "Opposed Tudor Myths of Power: Machiavellian Tyrants and Christian Kings" is also relevant: for in dealing with *Tamburlaine* and *The Massacre at Paris*, Adams uses evidence from responses to public punishments and executions to show that the original audiences would have been alive to the subversive challenges of these plays. The article appears in *Studies in the Continental Background of Renaissance English Literature*, ed. Dale B. J. Randall and George Walton Williams (Durham, N. C.: Duke University Press, 1977), pp. 67-90.

When an earlier version of this paper was read at the First International Marlowe Conference (University of Sheffield, July, 1983), several of my colleagues pointed out the intriguing possibilities for response by Catholics in the original audience. David Lake, in particular, suggested two options: such spectators might, of course, simply see the play as attacking Catholicism, and doubtless the response of the largely Protestant audience would have confirmed this idea; but such spectators could *also* have equated the postion of the Jews in Malta with that of the Catholics in England, and seen in Ferneze's Machiavellian behavior a portrayal of their experience of Tudor government. Such spectators would still be in my second category, since they would take the irony at the expense of the Protestant mal-practice of the true religion. That Ferneze is indeed the play's most complete Machiavel is the point made by Catherine Minshull in her "Marlowe's 'Sound Machevill,' " *Renaissance Drama*, N.S. 13 (1982), 35-53—an article I read only as I was revising this essay for publication.

17. David Bevington, *From "Mankind" to Marlowe: Growth of Structure in the Popular Drama of Tudor England* (Cambridge, Mass.: Harvard University Press, 1962), pp. 232-233. Waith, in the article cited in note 8 above, also finds the effect of the play puzzling, and he suggests that the ironies cancel each other out.

18. Jones, "Dangerous Sport: The Audience's Engagement with the Vice of the Moral Interludes," *Renaissance Drama*, N.S. 6 (1973), 63.

19. Some of the arguments presented in this essay have been developed from my earlier work, "The Disabler: Formation and Transformation of a Stage Figure in Plays of Marlowe and Shakespeare," Diss. Rutgers University, 1981, chapters 2 and 3.

Lies and Lying in *The Jew of Malta*

COBURN FREER

It is a commonplace that Marlowe's Machiavel has a somewhat limited grasp of the historical Machiavelli's political and social philosophy.[1] But it still may be useful to point out that the peculiar limits
Marlowe has imposed upon that philosphy are given a most consistent
and logical expression in dramatic form. The principal action and
dramatic structure, the characterization, even the mixture of verse
styles, all flow from the assumptions of the Machiavel who greets us in
the Prologue. From the present point of view, the most interesting
thing about the Machiavel is that he condenses a complex system of
observations and deductions about the nature of man and the powers
of the Prince into a single doctrine summed up by the term "policy,"
and that by this term he appears to embrace chiefly verbal deceit and
lying all its forms. Considering the limits and definitions that Marlowe
imposes at the outset, it may be no exaggeration to say that *The Jew of
Malta* works out a comprehensive theory of lying and all its aesthetic
implications.

It might be best at the outset to make some distinctions between lies
and fictions. For our purposes, we may say that fictions require the
mutual (if occasionally grudging) consent of all members of a community, and they tend generally to reaffirm established social structures. I
continue, for example, to cast my vote in local elections, whatever reservations I may have about the proclaimed differences between the

candidates; I shake hands with a person from whom I would never contemplate buying a used car; and I sign all my letters "Yours truly." Lies, in contrast, are by definition the expression of attitudes that stand behind or apart from our mutual consent; they are offered by individuals with individual motives, usually involving personal gain of either a tangible or intangible sort, frequently at the expense of others; and in their most extreme form they would destroy the social fabric altogether.[2] The individual character and secrecy of lies distinguish them from communally accepted fictions; lies we all abhor, just as we accept fictions as the outcome of balance and experience. We tend to regard those who are unable to accept social fictions as immature and overly demanding, and often the radical critique of social fictions is in itself the subject of tragedy.

Now the point of all this for *The Jew of Malta* is that Barabas consistently collapses the distinction between social fictions and lies, and uses the existence of social fictions to justify lying. Most of the other characters also blur the lines between the two, but Barabas is endowed with a greater awareness of how the process works, and is of course given more time to show this awareness in front of us. This is not to say that the difference between lies and fictions is always clear even in his own mind, nor is there realistically any reason why they should be, for by blurring the lines between them he has a ready-made justification for doing whatever he wants. In this tendency toward intermittent awareness too he is not of course alone in the play, and the Machiavel "presents" the drama because its plot revolves around whole sets of lies told by different groups of liars. There is no one in the play who does not lie except the Turks, and it may be one sign of Marlowe's fine cynicism that a group whose very name at this time was synonymous with duplicity should, in this play, always mean exactly what they say and act directly upon it. They present an unequivocal demand for their ten years' tribute, give the Maltese a month's grace to raise it, return as promised, and, when the demand for tribute is rejected a second time, invade the city as promised, seizing its governor and, most astonishingly (and consistently) of all, yielding to Barabas the power they had promised. Throughout the play the Turks are the only straight dealers.

The strength of the play, however, its status as Marlowe's most coherent artistic success, rests upon something far more solid than our own gathering curiosity as to who tells the fastest lie in Malta. If we look at the way Marlowe treats lying as a metaphor, not simply for the development of his central character, but also for the form and structure of the play, we can go far toward an understanding of Marlowe's conception of the dramatist's art. It is important to note at this point that Marlowe is more interested in false saying than in false seeming in its more elaborate forms; the combination of pantomime, disguise, and stage management of groups of people that, say, Richard III practices, for example, is of less interest in this play, where the characters usually confront each other with bald lies delivered with speed and directness. Indeed the Machiavel makes it quite clear at the outset that he is concerned with explicitly verbal falsification, announcing that "such as love me, gard me from their tongues" (Prologue, 6), and adding that he "weigh[s] not men, and therefore not mens words" (Prologue, 8).[3] His opening speech refers to tongues, books, speaking, reading, telling, hearing, talking, writing letters, writing in blood, bellowing, and finally lecturing, a fairly complete compendium of verbal activity. As this catalogue might imply, the duties or pleasures of lying are distributed among nearly all the characters of the play: there is no single liar as impresario in *The Jew of Malta*; no one person or group has a monopoly on lying, and all practice it with uninhibited zeal. (In *Richard III*, by contrast, we see one principal and effective group of liars, with one leader, whom the body politic is in the process of expelling.) When a majority of characters in a play lie to each other and themselves, their verbal behavior will not only shape the action but will also give that action a multiplicity of meanings, some of them inevitably contradictory.

I

It is after all easy enough to see how the scenic structure of the play hangs together on a series of connected lies. As if schooled by the Machiavel's emphasis, Barabas begins the first scene by lying to his fellow merchants, saying that he will come to their aid when he actually plans to look out for himself. When he attempts to act upon this lie in the next scene his goods and money are confiscated by the governor through some lies of his own, and that seizure is qualified in turn by the discovery that Barabas had been lying when he said that the Maltese had totally dispossessed him, for he still has a large quantity of cash and gems hidden in the house. The revelation of this lie then requires the lie by which Abigail asks to be admitted to the nunnery, and the action that follows out of her lie in turn exposes a larger lie, the one behind Barabas's protestations that he loves Abigail; the final exposure of his lie comes later when Barabas sets up her poisoning. In the meantime the lies in the political background begin to surface, as Martin del Bosco reveals that up till now, Malta has been resisting the Turks, not giving in to their threats and extortion. Here del Bosco offers as an inspiring example the siege of Rhodes, where the townspeople "fought it out, and not a man surviv'd / To bring the haplesse newes to Christendome" (II.755-756). Marlowe's inspired change from his source—in fact the Knights surrendered Rhodes—underlines not only the cowardice of the Maltese but also their earlier lie to Barabas. (Marlowe's reversal of his source might also be considered a kind of lie in its own right, a point to which we shall return later.) The Knights are ready enough to assert the Christian principles of honor and freedom when someone else seems likely to take charge, and their new-found (and expedient) moral concerns appear in the kangaroo court they arrange for Barabas. Both these scenes of high moral resolve are shown later to hinge upon lies: Abigail's repentance lasts about two scenes, by which time she is back with her father in a new and more sumptuous palazzo; and when the political plot next returns in Act V, the Knights are all shown as having abjectly surrendered.

Although lying may be the mainspring of the plot, this is not to say that all the play's lies are plot-related. Particularly in the middle of the play, after the main action has been initiated, whenever Barabas speaks he is ready to lie in a way that is very nearly gratuitous. In Act II, for example, when he lies to Lodowick and Mathias about his affection for them, he picks up the language that Lodowick's father had used to justify his promotion of Abigail's cause; Barabas thus creates one lie within the context of another. In the same scene he also recites to Ithamore a catalogue of his own villainy, which may be just as much a creation of the moment as his earlier expression of repentance to the Friar. Part of the problem in deciding about the character's veracity is that Barabas so obviously enjoys lying we cannot refer with any confidence to any past he might have.

Drawing together the middle action, when Ithamore tells Abigail that her father's lies made Lodowick and Mathias kill each other, she determines to enter the nunnery, and with another lie Barabas immediately binds Ithamore to him as his heir in order to induce him to poison all the nuns. Since in the meantime Abigail has revealed the lies about Lodowick and Mathias, Barabas now has to lie to the two priests, who in turn lie to each other and set up another mutual murder.

The brief subplot involving Ithamore, Bellamira, and Pilia-Borza is also built upon their lies to each other, and there is a perfect logic in the way that Barabas puts on a disguise (the visual equivalent of a lie) and a wretched stage-French accent (the verbal equivalent of a very poor lie) to kill them for their lies to him, and then creates the greater lie of his own feigned death, the lie in this case being labeled as the justice of the heavens (V.2057). But this deceit in turn leads back to his telling one final lie to Calymath, whom he betrays to Ferneze, whose own last lie of amity to both Barabas and the Turk concludes the action. Every incident in the play bears a causal or consequential relation to a lie, because in Marlowe's Malta the exposure of one lie invariably leads to the creation of another, and with the triumph of Ferneze at the end there is no suggestion that the process will be halted.

It might be claimed—certainly the Machiavel claims it—that this chain of causality in lying falls within some predictable patterns in human behavior, but at the same time Marlowe frequently sets up the action in such a way as to emphasize that the narrative thread of the play itself is a kind of lie. The premises of the action in the drama show this clearly and often. The initial exposition, the sudden arrival and equally sudden departure of the Turks, the instant dispossession of Barabas and his speedy return to power, the unexpected arrival of Martin del Bosco and the immediate reversal of Maltese foreign policy, the purchase of Ithamore, the liberation of Abigail and the gulling of the two suitors—these turns all occur within the first two acts. The extreme condensation and arbitrariness of event in the play, Marlowe's very evident determination to get on with it, is a form of narration we are more used to in fairy tales and dreams; something of this abruptness appears in *The Merchant of Venice,* but in Shakespeare such narrative condensation is more usually found in the late plays, with their enigmatically compressed openings and sudden, precipitate springs into action. By these means Marlowe constantly reminds us that the action of the play is a fiction which is not bound to the laws of time and causation.

Throughout the play happy violations of probability abound, and in almost every case they are linked to sharp condensations of time or sequence. Act V alone can provide numerous illustrations of the practice, beginning when the order is given to fetch Ithamore in one line and he arrives in the next (ll. 2020-21). Barabas exits and "dies" seven lines later (the comments between del Bosco and Ferneze emphasize the arbitrariness of this), but then revives from an apparently deep coma only seven lines after being discovered. An especially artful ellipsis both involves and avoids a change in scene: for when the first scene of Act V began we were apparently in the Governor's chambers (one edition proposes "The Council-House"),[4] but when Barabas revives at the end of the scene, he is outside the city walls.[5] Examples could be multiplied: from one line to the next, the Turks have taken the town; the town is described as being in ruins at line 2120, but has been completely rebuilt by line 2227; and so forth. Through countless such details, Marlowe reminds us constantly of the fictiveness and schemes of control behind the play; clearly we are intended to keep at a distance the kind of close empathy and identification that writers such as Heywood were claiming about this time for serious drama,[6] and the resulting effects are far more self-conscious and many-layered than contemporary dramatic theory could account for.

II

Nowhere is Marlowe's lack of interest in mere verisimilitude more evident than in the thinning and reduction of Barabas's motives in the conclusion of the play. As shrewd as Barabas has been shown to be time and time again, it strains one's credulity to imagine that he would trust the Governor after he has already betrayed him once. All evidence suggests that since the earliest Greek drama, playgoers have never hesitated to give characters advice, mentally (and sometimes vocally, on the Elizabethan stage) urging them to avoid the imminent catastrophe. Even the densest base mechanic in Marlowe's audience could advise Barabas now to avoid this colossal misjudgment of Ferneze. Marlowe even emphasizes this shallow spot in Barabas's character by giving him a speech praising deep policy (ll. 2137ff.) at the very time he most lacks it. A similar contradiction is apparent in Barabas's histrionic refusal of payment from the Turk before the planned massacre, when many of his speeches throughout the play show a revulsion at this kind of public show of machination and power. And finally, on any level of plausibility, Barabas's system of gunshot signals is obviously a blunder, as the plan could so easily be foiled or jammed.

It is customary to rationalize these shifts in the characterization of Barabas by saying that he overreaches himself or becomes, as a protagonist, his own comic or ironic antithesis, descending like Faustus from high ambitions to low schemes and shortsighted plots. Such an argument attempts to assimilate the condensations in narrative and the disjunctions in motive to the apparent moral design of the play; its advantage is that it accommodates the comic tone of much of the writing, explains the shifting depth of much of the characterization, and establishes a structural parallel with Marlowe's more frequently admired tragedy.

But such a reading is purchased at a very high price, for it overlooks an element in Barabas's character which sets him firmly apart from Faustus, and which helps deepen our own sense of the play as an extended lie. This element is simply the figure's visual appearance onstage, with his grotesquely exaggerated nose and cheekbones, his hat from the Great Cham, and, by some accounts, a red wig or beard and long gabardine coat. Even if the old stage tradition of the makeup and costume originated only in the one performance described by Rowley, the nose and hat are firmly proclaimed by the text itself.[7] If we overlook this powerful visual element in the characterization we will miss much that Marlowe is doing with the theme of lying, for frequently Barabas's words and actions are contradicted or commented upon by his ludicrous stage appearance.[8]

By ignoring the stage history of the character we may even go so far as to make Barabas a Renaissance existential hero of self-fashioning; in this reading, his high audacity is matched only by his readiness to watch his own psyche and further its most powerful impulses wherever they may lead.[9] And certainly that element of *virtù* is present, as in his opening soliloquy with its grand evocation of infinite wealth and growth. On a somewhat more complex level, the same impulse is evoked when, after being robbed of what we think to be a lifetime's accumulation of wealth, Barabas comes forward and bursts out of his own despair, saying "No, I will live; nor loath I this my life" (I.501). It is hard not to be moved by this powerful self-assertion, a moment similar in many ways to that which Shakespeare attempts with Parolles in *All's Well*; both characters reach out beyond their own deep humiliation to a vital center in their own energy.

But the difference is that Barabas has been granted a contemptible appearance that makes his heroic self-assertion a visual and conceptual lie. Much of the criticism that has been written on *The Jew of Malta* only makes sense if we ignore the visual presence of the central character and the tension between that presence and the rhetoric the character is given to speak. The interplay between rhetoric and visual presence is not constant; that is, the physical appearance of Barabas is not in itself some intrinsically satiric element that mocks everything he has to say or do; to hold this would reduce the play to a level of buffoonery that clearly was not Marlowe's intent, because many of the speeches show a good deal of engagement on the part of the poet. The physical appearance of Barabas does, however, affect a number of the play's various implausibilities in character and motive.

If we bear in mind the presence of Barabas on the stage, we can see that the appearance of the character makes many of the play's apparent discontinuities understandable. Consider for example that soon after all of Barabas's known property has been seized, he has managed to restore himself and Abigail to a grand palazzo. The odd part in this is not that he should have been able to do this, for we know about his hidden fortune, but rather it is that no one in Malta—including particularly the son of the Governor—appears to notice the change or regard it as surprising. And more puzzling yet, Barabas's restored wealth plays no significant role in advancing the further action or shaping the dramatic structure of the play. (Later Barabas is appalled by Ithamore's demands for money, but he is really more alarmed about being exposed as a murderer, and it is that fear that leads on the plot.) Again, it is not so implausible that Barabas might regain his wealth in a matter of days (the financial pages of the daily paper can show how these miracles are wrought) as it is that after he has done this no one notices the transformation. From one point of view, the characters thus appear to move with the instant acceptance and bracing illogic of the gulls in Feydeau.

But in this case the physical appearance of Barabas helps explain why his transformation is readily acceptable to both the audience and the characters around him. Seeing him on the stage we are distinctly aware of his existence as a dramatic creation, and this is a type of awareness we are usually persuaded to drop, however intermittently or fully, when a character is costumed in a naturalistic manner. That Barabas should suddenly become wealthy again and live like a grandee is the more acceptable for his appearance, suggesting as it does that he is a product of artifice existing on a plane different from that of the characters around him. Whether the audience consciously reflects upon this awareness is not at issue; what matters is that Marlowe has chosen to make these very large jumps in character and motive more plausible by linking them to a character whose appearance calls attention to the presence of dramatic artifice.

From the first, Barabas's appearance prepares us to accept a narrative that will work at a certain remove from reality; the condensations and gaps in the plot, though, are only one set of adjustments that the costume encourages. A more complex matter involves the tone and substance of the passages dealing with legal and ethical questions. Given Barabas's appearance, how are we to take, for example, his assertions of righteousness, of ethically scrupulous positions? Consider his protest to Ferneze:

> say the Tribe that I descended of
> Were all in generall cast away for sinne,
> Shall I be tryed by their trangression?
> The man that dealeth righteously shall live.
> (I.346-349)

Now although we are not far into the play, we already know Barabas to be a cynical quoter of maxims to his own purpose, and we also know the Christians to be hypocrites. But Barabas's physical appearance gives his question a dimension it would lack were he dressed and made up naturalistically. The point is not that these serious ethical judgments are stupid or irrelevant but that they can be adopted by both the plausible-looking representative of order and a creature who is visibly less than human. In the same way, given Barabas's visual appearance, his curse upon the Christians and his lament from Job has an incongruous element, as if we were overhearing a dog utter a curse or an ape offer a prayer. But if we consistently share any one character's feelings in the play, that character is Barabas, and thus his ridiculous and grotesque appearance insists upon a kind of recognition that is distinctly uncomfortable.

It is of course immediately evident that the Old Comedy, with which Marlowe was likely familiar, shows many instances of characters commenting upon their own roles, which Barabas may be said to be doing through his costume and makeup. This kind of distancing is an ancient and honorable source of laughter with numerous modern equivalents, as when Groucho Marx will turn to the camera and ask how he got into this movie. Several instances of this may be found in Marlowe's play, as when Ithamore enters to Barabas with the porridge: apparently he is also carrying an outsize spoon, and he quotes the proverb about "he that eats with the devil." This sort of internalized commentary is much more superficial than the kind that interests Marlowe in the play as a whole, in which the visual appearance of a character may make a comment upon the ethical structure, or the plot, or the origins of the characters' motivation. While an actor's appearance may be a lie—in the case of Shylock, the red wig was a property with its own history and, like Barabas's nose, was a kind of character in its own right—it can still be a way of focusing on other kinds of lies, the lies of ethical consistency, for example, or the lies of art.

III

While Barabas's appearance and shifts in the narrative are two ways Marlowe has of enlarging the fictions of the play-world, another and equally powerful method of suggestion involves his juxtapositions of verse styles. The different poetic modes that Marlowe employs in this play constitute something close to an index of self-parody.[10] Hearing these passages is no difficult matter because in every case Marlowe signals that he is ridiculing the rhetorical display. If, for example, we take the curse over the porridge pot out of its context, it is powerful stuff indeed:

> As fatall be it to her as the draught

> Of which great *Alexander* drunke, and dyed:
> And with her let it worke like *Borgias* wine,
> Whereof his sire, the Pope, was poyson'd.
> In few, the blood of *Hydra*, Lerna's bane;
> The jouice of *Hebon*, and *Cocitus* breath,
> And all the poysons of the Stygian poole
> Breake from the fiery kingdome; and in this
> Vomit your venome, and invenome her
> That like a fiend hath left her father thus.
>   (III.1399-1408)

The effect of hypnotic incantation is heightened by the heavy alliteration throughout the passage—three pairs appear in the last line alone—and the falling rhythms that appear in most of the words that are not monosyllables. The imagery does not require much comment, but it is rhetorically significant that the action described in the passage is delayed to the last three lines, with the next-to-last line describing the strongest action; the last line thus makes the surprising reversal of having the daughter the active agent rather than only the recipient of the action. But the art and fury of the passage is immediately mocked when Ithamore responds by saying "What a blessing has he giv'n't? was ever pot of / Rice porredge so sauc't?" (III.1409-1410). Ithamore's aside deflates the learning and grand perspectives of the curse, and however effectively Barabas's rhetoric may have distracted us from his appearance—and I think it can have this force—that force is withdrawn by the marveling and clownish *riposte*.

Barabas and Ithamore have no monopoly on this sort of schizophrenic self-criticizing verse. In a similar way the grand huff-snuff on political themes that Ferneze offers in the next scene is followed by another abrupt turn. The opening is in the vein of Tamburlaine's Greatest Hits:

> *Bashaw*, in briefe, shalt have no tribute
>   here,
> Nor shall the Heathens live upon our
>   spoyle:
> First we will race the City wals our selves,
> Lay waste the Iland, hew the Temples
>   downe,
> And shipping of our goods to *Sicily*,
> Open an entrance for the wastefull sea,

> Whose billowes beating the resistlesse
> bankes,
> Shall overflow it with their refluence.
> (III.1431-1438)

These are powerful and evocative images, going from the razing of the walls to the destruction of the city to the sacrilege of destroying the temples; the dissolution of the island itself in the formless chaos of the ocean is the sort of thing that would have been good for at least a modest shudder in either of the *Tamburlaines*. But the Bashaw's reply is chatty and relaxed:

> Well, Governor, since thou hast broke the
> league
> By flat denyall of the promis'd Tribute,
> Talke not of racing downe your City wals;
> You shall not need trouble your selves so
> farre. . . .
> (III.1439-1442)

Once again we listen back to the compelling rhetoric and poetry from a perspective that shrinks and undercuts the claims of grand art. We know also that Ferneze has a moral backbone of India rubber, just as we knew in the earlier scene at the start of the play that Barabas, despite all his martyr's rhetoric, is strongly motivated by greed.

The sheer range of Marlowe's style in this play constitutes something like a virtuoso performance.[11] Some years ago Harry Levin pointed out how, in the rising action of the play, Marlowe could suddenly deepen and modulate the tone by allowing his verse to take on an unexpected Old Testament resonance.[12] Perhaps as a result of this intensification, the later development of Barabas is usually held to be a falling-off in terms of Marlowe's technique, but I think this is not really the case, and it is possible to provide some concise exhibitions from the last two acts. Barabas's repentance to Friars Jacomo and Barnardine starts off in a manner worthy of a grand *contemptus mundi* in an early Shakespeare history play:

> To fast, to pray, and weare a shirt of haire,
> And on my knees creepe to *Jerusalem*. . . .
> (IV.1570-1572)

But upon an instant he is rummaging through his accounts in his mind, and the speech turns into a parody of the Marlovian global catalog, the items all tumbled together with what appears to be no regard for cumulative pressure or climax:

> Cellars of Wine, and Sollers full of Wheat,
> Ware-houses stuft with spices and with drugs,
> Whole Chests of Gold, in *Bulloine*, and in Coyne,
> Besides I know not how much weight in Pearle
> Orient and round, have I within my house;
> At *Alexandria*, Merchandize unsold:
> But yesterday two ships went from this Towne,
> Their voyage will be worth ten thousand
> Crownes.
> In *Florence, Venice, Antwerpe, London, Civill,*
> *Frankeford, Lubecke, Mosco,* and where not,
> Have I debts owing; and in most of these,
> Great summes of mony lying in the bancho. . . .
>   (IV.1572-1583)

The heavy end-stoping and the frequency of regular caesuras prevent the gathering expansion in rhythm that Marlowe usually associates with the kind of imagery; and the catalogue of cities runs on rather too long, dropping off in Moscow—never much known as a commercial center—and petering out in "where not." Barabas's dithering allows the next line to drop in, as if by chance, with stunning effect upon the listening friars: "All this I'le give to some religious house . . . " (IV.1584). The fumbling financier in his dotage has been created before our ears, and here again the verse first moves toward a congruence with the speaker's appearance, and then moves rapidly away: Barabas may look absurd, and he may be speaking in an absurd parody of his very first speech, but the control of the character (and his verse) is shown in that one deft, understated stroke.

Often Marlowe will link together a chain of juxtapositions, each commenting on the other. The treatment of Abigail is especially suggestive in this respect, for there is probably little question that her speeches on the deaths of her suitors are meant to be greatly affecting; certainly they show much care in terms of their rhetorical organization. At the same time, all that touching pathos seems designed to lead up to Friar Barnardine's comment on her grievous virginity, after she has confessed to him and died in his arms. Again, Marlowe does not focus the play's verbal contrasts on one particular character; no one figure in the play is the leading poetic liar, and anyone may assume this role at any time: even the innocent Abigail can join these stylistic raiding parties.

Ithamore is at the edge of parody for most of the play, and he makes a definitive stumble over the line once he becomes drunk. His version of "Come live with me and be my love" is madder, more reckless and surreal, than the witty Raleigh or self-regarding Donne ever could have aspired to:

> Content, but we will leave this paltry land,
> And saile from hence to *Greece*, to lovely *Greece*,
> I'le be thy *Jason*, thou my golden *Fleece*;
> Where painted Carpets o're the meads are hurl'd,
> And *Bacchus* vineyards ore-spread the world:
> Where Woods and Forrests goe in goodly greene,
> I'le be *Adonis*, thou shalt be Loves Queene.
> The Meads, the Orchards, and the Primrose lanes,
> Instead of Sedge and Reed, beare Sugar Canes:
> Thou in those Groves, by *Dis* above,
> Shalt live with me and be my love.
>   (IV.1806-1816)

Rising out of prose on both sides, this lyric is the most astonishing mixture of garlic and sapphires; so many touches are correct in themselves—starting off without a rhyme, for example, as the poetry machine begins to crank over—that the piece could hardly be improved. Especially notable are the violence of *hurl'd*, with vineyards spreading over the earth in a nightmare worthy of Comus, the crazy geography in having Jason sail to Greece instead of Colchis, and better yet, Dis seated up in heaven. The rapid enumeration of pastoral clichés comes down nicely on *Sugar Canes*, which helps underscore the childish basis of the fantasy. Metrically the eleven lines are as intricate as their more canonical parent, but perhaps because of its ragtime zest the piece does not seem to have found its way into any of the Elizabethan (or modern) anthologies.

The elements of contrast and surprise in the poetry of the play are heightened by Marlowe's frequent use of English, classical, and biblical proverbs, French, Spanish, and Italian tags, and every manner of classical allusion. The polyglot lexicon of the play is justified by the setting, but it also furthers the sense that the characters love to pursue their verbal masking and seeming. While it may be argued that the verbal discontinuities "reflect the hypocrisy and double standards of Maltese society,"[13] it is also evident that as they thicken the verbal texture of the play, they give the characters a resonance they would otherwise lack. The plays of John Webster have a similar kind of allusiveness and draw even more heavily upon proverb lore, and like them *The Jew of Malta* has at its center a character who makes extreme demands upon others and thinks with impetuous concentration. The presence of the allusions, tags, and proverbs constantly refers the experience dramatized onstage to larger contexts, yet their very density and frequency of occurrence prevent any clear ethical center from taking shape.

Professor Bawcutt, in the Revels edition of the play, has been extremely thorough in tracing Marlowe's allusions and use of proverbs, and working through his annotations one realizes how many times Marlowe has his characters utter expressions that have the stamp of proverbs yet also have no known verbatim source. "Infinite riches in a little room" is only the most memorable of these, but dozens of others aim at that pithy suggestiveness. To cite just a few: "Who is honour'd now but for his wealth?" (I.151); "How ere the world goe, I'le make sure for one" (I.225); "Better one want for a common good, / Than many perish for a priuate man" (I.331-332); "Great iniuries are not so soone forgot" (I.441); "Here's many words but no crownes" (IV.1899; or "[The ass] labours with a load of bread and wine, / And leaues it off to snap on Thistle tops" (V.2142-2143). Best of all these phrases that have the immediate sound of the proverb but no known paternity is Ithamore's drunken exclamation, "Hey, Rivo Castiliano!" (IV.1930), the exact meaning—or even the language—of which cannot be identified, though its perfect appropriateness here cannot be denied. And the number of proverbs that are not quoted directly must be substantial; as with the phrases that have the ring of proverbs but belong to no identifiable currency, they suggest an overwhelming number of appeals to infinitely conflicting authorities.[14]

One point that emerges from study of the language of the play is that its author is not interested in ravishing hearers with grand rhetoric, or casting spells out of the lyric moment, or conveying sententious wisdom through the accumulated weight of moral commonplaces, but rather is ready to show up all these efforts as only illusions. In the context of this particular play, these different styles are not fictions as they were defined earlier, systems of falsehood a community—in this case, an audience—would accept and expect, despite their variance from perceived fact; to be so, the end of the play would have to validate at least one of these stylistic frames of reference, as being necessary even if limited and provisional. This is the pattern that emerges at the end of Shakespeare's romantic comedies, for example, or in the great tragedies, as in Othello's last speech asserting his noble self, or in Albany's dictum that we must "speak what we feel, not what we ought to say." By contrast, *The Jew of Malta* does not stabilize or resolve its artistic discords in this way; it does not return to a dominant key, and thus it remains entirely consistent within the terms of its own aesthetic. In its stylistic multiplicity, especially within the main character, the play refuses to mesh character and voice, event and language. That the drama should be representative of experience becomes, in other words, one more lie.

IV

It was part of Sidney's cagey logic in his *Defense of Poetry* that the poets could easily be exonerated from the charge of spreading falsehoods, because they never set out to tell the truth anyway; as the familiar phrase has it, "the poet . . . nothing affirms, and therefore never lieth." The somewhat disingenuous addition is interesting for our present purpose: "For, as I take it, to lie, is to affirm that to be true which is false."[15] By Sidney's account several different kinds of lies—I would go here by Augustine's basic catalogue of eight—would appear to fall into a special category that might be called not-truth, and I would suggest that this ambiguity might best describe the kind of lying that we find in *The Jew of Malta*. Sidney is talking about the work of art as it exists in relation to a world of perceived fact, but it may also describe the implicit ethical center of this play. What *is* the truth about Malta? about Barabas? In the absence of a single answer, it would be an error to think of the play as setting out to expose lies, as many readers tend to assume.[16]

Marlowe's indifference to this particular task is evident at the play's most serious theological level, on which we encounter the question of Barabas's Jewishness. As G. K. Hunter has shown conclusively, Judaism is, by any orthodox Elizabethan reading, a lie in itself, a delusion bordering at times on the ludicrous and at times on the tragic.[17] But as Hunter points out, even within the terms of his own faith Barabas is untrue; his pretended idealism is fraudulent, as is his stated desire for spiritual as distinguished from material profit.

In carrying this argument further, though, Hunter may err in attempting to posit a too-firm base for Marlowe's theological satire. Noting the ring of personal conviction in a key speech in *Tamburlaine*, Hunter observes in Marlowe "a passionate involvement with the idea of God's purity and transcendence," and sees behind it the poet himself: "At the very best, Marlowe *knew* what it was to worship transcendence, to take the Calvinist view of a fallen world forever tragically defacing a power and a beauty beyond its comprehension."[18] But can the sudden intensification of tone in one speech of a play—even with manifest allusions on the level of theme—justify or establish ground rules for the whole play? Suppose we hear the ring of personal conviction in the speech to Ithamore beginning

> As for my selfe, I walke abroad a nights
> And kill sick people groaning under walls:
> Sometimes I goe about and poyson wells. . . .
> (II.939–941)

The author of this speech had an intention as focused as the author of any other important passage in the play: it carries all the conviction of its own alarming wit, and is a more authentic expression of the character who utters it than are the lines from *Tamburlaine*. Yet even with the play's many allusions to satanic devices, violence, and homicide, we would not be justified in saying that Marlowe would endorse the ethical and theological principles of the Marquis de Sade. This would be as untenable (that is, as unverifiable) as the position that Marlowe writes from a personal conviction of Christian truth. Either way, we would introduce a fundamental confusion between coherent philosophical systems and the *données* of art. The only thing that is certain, assuming that Richard Baines was correct in his testimony, is that Marlowe would gladly have muddled matters thoroughly.

Surely the Christians in the play fall far short of a serious ethical stand on anything, but might that not be because, in this particular Malta, even good Christian ethics may be a lie? The finished and sacred system that Professor Hunter implies as standing behind Marlowe's criticism of life is not "in" the play at all; no one speaks for it or acts upon it in a dramatically convincing way, not the Christian leaders, not the friars, not (least of all) the unreflective Abigail. The orthodox Christian ethical view seems no more to describe this world than do the certitudes of classical or coherent art, which as we have seen, Marlowe rejects with equal firmness.

The little we know of the origins of Barabas and Ithamore suggests that lying is not a condition of their lives but rather a premise of their existence: Barabas, though now a resident of Malta, is still an alien from "another country"; Ithamore, a Thracian brought up in Arabia, is described by Barabas as "the Turk."[19] Each exists outside, or in a critical relation to, the social systems I began by describing as fictions. For these two in particular, the ruthless individualism that is at the base of lying extends to their social and intellectual existence; Ferneze and the others, however, are propped up as much by the fictions of their world as by their own inventive lying. The difference between Barabas and the rest of the characters might be clarified by reference to Augustine's list of the four most grievous lies:

> The first type of lie is a deadly one which should be avoided and shunned from afar, namely, that which is uttered in the teaching of religion, and to the telling of which no one should be led under any condition. The second is that which injures somebody unjustly: such a lie as helps no one and harms someone. The third is that which is beneficial to one person while it harms another, although the harm does not produce physical defilement. The fourth is the lie which is told solely for the pleasure of lying and deceiving, that is, the real lie.[20]

For Barabas, one lie is never enough, not because a lie will never sit still—he never commits the amateur's mistake of giving too many details—but because the *act* of lying is simply more fun than the enjoyment of a static lie. As Augustine says elsewhere in the treatise, "There is a distinction between a person who tells a lie and a liar. The former is one who tells a lie unwillingly, while the liar loves to lie and passes his time in the joy of lying."[21].

Indeed it would not be an overstatement to say that process philosophy might best describe Marlowe's dramatic notion of lying. Re-creation is continuous; the future is really open, and indeterminate even for God; the laws of nature evolve; creative synthesis transcends causal determination in *all* concrete cases of becoming[22]—all the fundamental assumptions are there, and these better describe the tone of the play than do whole batteries of Christian polemic. Barabas, Ithamore, Ferneze, and the rest never pause to debate their choices in the manner of casuists; there is never a moment of suspension or doubt as they move from one lie to another. Plot, theme, and character all coalesce here, for Marlowe has designed everything to emphasize the ongoing, careering course of lying as constant creation. Consider everything he leaves out, which we will find in other literary portraits of liars; the plot never requires, for example, that Barabas remember one of his complicated lies. It is not for nothing that the proverb says a liar should have first a good memory. As Montaigne asks, "What memorie shall suffice [liars], to remember so many different formes they have framed to one subject?"[23] The structure of the play insures that Barabas never has to recall and repeat a lie, backtrack or fill, and he always lives within an ever-moving process of fresh new lies.

If all this is so, what brings about Barabas's downfall and the final catastrophe? Is Marlowe simply manipulating Barabas for the symmetry of the plot?[24] Or is it that Barabas overreaches himself in his most spectacular lie of all? As the present reading would suggest, neither view is faithful to the larger contexts of lies within the play, or to the nature of Marlovian lying as an ongoing process. The origins of the catastrophe are in fact quite simple. It is after his feigned death that Barbabas realizes he does not want direct political control of Malta, and his soliloquy near the start of Act V ("Thus hast thou gotten, by thy policie . . . ") recognizes the social fiction of political command. This soliloquy is immediately followed, though, by Ferneze's entrance, and when Barabas then attempts to recognize the fiction of command, calling it by its true and proper name, he is done for.[25] The best gloss on the conclusion might well be a brief passage from Augustine's *On Christian Doctrine*:

Everyone who lies commits iniquity, and if anyone thinks a lie may sometimes be useful, he must think that iniquity is sometimes useful also. But no one who lies keeps faith concerning that about which he lies. For he wishes that the person to whom he lies should have that faith in him which he does not himself keep when he lies. But every violator of faith is iniquitous. Either iniquity is sometimes useful, which is impossible, or a lie is always useless.[26]

In Marlowe's systematic inversion of these principles, the rationale of the conclusion may be found. Once Barabas abandons lies in his dealing with the Governor (an iniquity is sometimes useless—an impossibility in Malta) and fails to remain committed to the process by which he has lived (a lie is always useful), he violates the principles that have guided him throughout the play, and his end can be set in motion without Marlowe's creating any sense of dramatic double-dealing.

One final problem which remains, though, is the question of whether the play as a whole is thus utterly self-parodic, a kind of ironic game in which all values, those of the Christians, the Jews, and even the Turks, are ultimately exposed as ridiculous. Such a conclusion would be wide of the mark, for it would mistake the fundamental distinction between theme and form that is implicit in the idea of the dramatically embodied lie. To repeat, lying is not so much a theme given discursive treatment in the play as it is a ground assumption of its existence and operation: it is a part of the air the characters breathe, a law that governs the direction and vectors of energy in the play. No one who has read extensively in the criticism and scholarship on this particular play can rest easily in the conclusion that the play is organized around any single theme, any more than it fits clearly into the definitions of any one existing genre. Lying is not the one long-sought theme that can finally integrate an apparently fractious if not chaotic play; rather it is the reason why no such single theme or structural metaphor is ever likely to be found. If one were tempted to think of lying as the fabled unifying critical vision for which the play has long wanted, the critic's golden fleece, one need only recall how Ithamore disposes of such mythical wool. In theme, structure, characterization, the visual imagery of the actor, rhetoric, and verse texture, *The Jew of Malta* attempts to suggest fully all that which is not. The lie told for pleasure is the real lie.

NOTES

1. The fullest analysis of the influences and alterations is that provided by N. W. Bawcutt in "Machiavelli and Marlowe's *The Jew of Malta*," *Renaissance Drama*, N.S. 3 (1970), 3-49. The major critical readings in this line, and their place within Marlowe criticism generally, have been summarised by Kenneth Friedenreich in "*The Jew of Malta* and the Critics," *Papers on Language and Literature*, 13 (1977), 318-335.

2. Especially helpful in the definition of lies is Sissela Bok's *Lying: Moral Choice in Public and Private Life* (New York: Pantheon, 1978). Bok is not responsible for the distinction here drawn between lies and social fictions.

3. Unless otherwise noted, all quotations come from the *Works*, ed. C. F. Tucker Brooke (Oxford: Clarendon Press, 1910). Line references appear in the text. I have normalized *i* and *j*, *u* and *v*, and have supplied some end punctuation.

4. Edd Winfield Parks and Richard Croom Beatty, *The English Drama* (New York: Norton, 1935), p. 469.

5. J. L. Simmons has argued that the actor playing Barabas was probably thrown from the Elizabethan projecting stage into the yard area (see "Elizabethan Stage Practice and Marlowe's *The Jew of Malta*," *Renaissance Drama*, N.S. 4 [1971], 93-104); this would emphasize further that the artful condensation avoids the necessity of an intervening scene.

6. Heywood describes the operation of this empathy in detail, claiming that it is a powerful force for moral correction (see his *Apology for Actors* [1612]); he is of course responding to such earlier critics of the theater as Stephen Gosson, who were equally emphatic in their description of the way playgoers would identify with the personages they saw on the stage.

7. For summaries of the evidence, see N. W. Bawcutt's Introduction to the Revels edition (Baltimore: Johns Hopkins University Press, 1978), p. 2, and H. S. Bennett's additional comments in his edition of the play (London: Methuen, 1931), p. 88 n. 174. The hat is mentioned at IV. 1990.

8. James L. Smith's fascinating review of the play's stage history (in *Christopher Marlowe* [Papers of the York Symposium], ed. Brian Morris [New York: Hill and Wang, 1968], pp. 1-23), shows how the tension between theatricality and realism has been handled in countless ways; but Smith does not comment on the tension between Barabas's appearance and his rhetoric. In *The Dramatist and the Received Idea* (Cambridge: Cambridge University Press, 1968), Wilbur Sanders refers to Barabas's appearance, describing him as "a monster" (p. 38 *et passim*), following Charles Lamb; but here too, Sanders's close analysis makes nothing of the interplay between the monster's appearance and his language.

9. See Stephen Greenblatt, *Renaissance Self-Fashioning* (Chicago: University of Chicago Press, 1980), pp. 203-210 esp. The self-willed nature of Barabas has often been remarked; in an extreme example, and with an emphasis entirely different from Greenblatt's, Sanders refers to the play's "exposure of ferocious egocentricity: (*The Dramatist and the Received Idea*, p. 50).

10. Stylistic parody and contrast in the play have been mentioned by numerous readers but perhaps most fully by Eric Rothstein in "Structure as Meaning in *The Jew of Malta*," *Journal of English and Germanic Philology*, 65 (1966), 260-273.

11. However, there is one obvious parallel in the canon: the stylistic range and free-dom of the poetry resemble that to be found in *The Massacre at Paris*, on which see H. J. Oliver's Introduction to the Revels edition (Cambridge, Mass.: Harvard University Press, 1968), pp. lii and lxxiii-lxxiv.

12. See *The Overreacher* (Cambridge, Mass.: Harvard University Press, 1952), pp. 63-64. The elements of specifically biblical parody in the play are traced by Roth-stein, *op.cit.*, 260-264. In *Christopher Marlowe: Merlin's Prophet* (Cambridge: Cam-bridge University Press, 1977), pp. 22-49, Judith Weil reads the play as a dramatic rendering of wisdom proverbs, in all their learning and darkness; the present essay may complement what Weil says about the obscurity of truth.

13. N. W. Bawcutt, in the Revels edition (p. 35).

14. Greenblatt observes that all these proverbs "are a kind of currency, the com-pressed ideological wealth of society, the money of the mind" (*op.cit.*, p. 207). While this helps explain the characters' movement toward a proverbial habit of mind, it fails to account for the way that the proverbs often contradict each other.

15. In *A Defence of Poetry*, ed. J. A. Van Dorsten (Oxford: Clarendon Press, 1973), p. 52.

16. See, *e.g.*, Irving Ribner's comment that it was Marlowe's intention "to make clear the deficiency of policy" ("Marlowe's 'Tragick Glasse,'" in *Essays on Shakespeare and Elizabethan Drama in Honor of Hardin Craig*, ed. Richard Hosley [Columbia: University of Missouri Press, 1962], p. 104).

17. "The Theology of Marlowe's *The Jew of Malta*," *Journal of the Warburg and Courtauld Institutes*, 27 (1964), 211-240.

18. Hunter, 239-240.

19. See II. 893 and IV. 1620 and 1636.

20. "Lying," in *Treatises on Various Subjects*, ed. Roy J. Deferrari, vol. 16 in The Fathers of the Church (New York: Catholic University of America Press, 1952), pp. 86-87.

21. "Lying," p. 79.

22. These theses are advanced by most process philosophers but particularly by Peirce and Whitehead. *Cf.* D. J. Palmer's view: "Not only do [Marlowe's] heroes refuse to obey any higher law than that of their own wills, but the course of their fortunes, even in death itself, insists only on a naturalistic plane of being upon which man subjectively imposes his own order" ("Marlowe's Naturalism," in *Christopher Marlowe*, ed. Brian Morris, p. 156). For obvious reasons I find it diffi-cult to accept the arguments of those (such as Battenhouse and Cole) who see Marlowe's drama as working within a resolutely Christian framework.

23. "Of Lyers," in *Essayes*, trans. John Florio (New York: Modern Library, n.d.), p. 27.

24. Many readers find the ending unsatisfactory on exactly this point; as a typical reaction, see, e.g., Michael Goldman's comment: "Barabas's refusal of money at any time is surprising, and the reason for it here, I think, is that Marlowe is maneuvering a prop into position" ("Marlowe and the Histrionics of Ravish-ment," in *Two Renaissance Mythmakers*, English Institute Essays, N.S. 1, ed. Alvin Kernan [Baltimore: Johns Hopkins University Press, 1977], p. 33).

25. As D. J. Palmer says, "Barabas's fatal mistake is that he fails to allow to his

enemies the same degree of suspicious mistrust towards him as he holds toward them. He does not come to grief because he is a Machiavel, but because he is not Machiavellian enough" ("Marlowe's Naturalism," p. 174).

26. Augustine, *On Christian Doctrine*, trans. D. W. Robertson, Jr. (Indianapolis: Bobbs-Merrill, 1958), p. 31.

Formulaic Dramaturgy

in *Doctor Faustus*[1]

THOMAS PETTITT

I

For anyone who has struggled with the generic and behavioral characteristics of traditional oral narratives (such as the ballad), much of the scholarly debate on the status and provenance of the Shakespearean "bad quartos," or the respective merits of variant play texts (such as those of *Doctor Faustus*), has an oddly familiar ring. Indeed, it is odd that the two fields of inquiry have not previously been juxtaposed. For an Elizabethan play, like a ballad (or a romance, or an epic), was created for oral performance before a listening and watching audience, and like a ballad, except that the process was collective, the Elizabethan stage play was orally transmitted, retained in the memories of the players until regenerated in performance. Every performance of a play in the Elizabethan theater was, to a significant degree, a memorial reconstruction, with all that this implies for textual and dramaturgical instability.[2] It should not therefore be entirely unexpected that Elizabethan plays sometimes behave like ballads, or that techniques and insights evolved in the study of oral narratives may be usefully applied to the study of early English drama. It is precisely this I propose to do with regard to one particular characteristic of oral narratives which has attracted a good deal of attention in the last two decades, the formula.

The diction of oral narratives—ballads, romances, epics—is marked by a traditional phraseology, a line, couplet or stanza in one text occurring in a recognizably similar form in others. These are the "commonplaces," "stock phrases," or, in current terminology, the "formulas" of traditional narratives;

> Gar saddle to me the black

exclaims the ballad hero—any ballad hero—on hearing news requiring immediate action;

> Gar saddle to me the brown,
> Gar saddle to me the swiftest stead
> That is in a' the town.[3]

Other recurrent ballad events are likewise provided with appropriate formulas. Earlier generations of scholarship, for example German students of the Anglo–Saxon epics, devoted considerable time and patience to tabulating such *Parallelstellen*, often in the attempt to demonstrate the influence of one poem, or one poet, on another, but more recently it has been appreciated that these formulas belong not to the individual poet or work, but to the tradition as a whole. In what follows I shall explore the possibility that Elizabethan drama may be formulaic in a similar manner. To do so is to follow up a suggestion in Peter Burke's excellent study of *Popular Culture in Early Modern Europe* to the effect that:

> Folksongs and folktales, popular plays and popular prints all need to be seen as combinations of elementary forms, permutations of elements which were more or less ready-made.[4]

I suggest that the formula is one such "ready-made" element in early English drama, and *Doctor Faustus,* an indisputably popular play, positively bristling with textual problems, provides excellent material for exhibiting the viability and usefulness of the concept.

In the case of the oral narratives, inevitably, the formulas are exclusively verbal, and certainly verbal formulas do occur in Elizabethan drama, stock expressions such as "I will, my lord . . . ," "I warrant you . . . ," "Leave me alone for that . . . " occurring particularly (and probably significantly) in "bad" play-texts. But since drama consists essentially of action as well as speech a more applicable unit would be what I shall call the "dramaturgical formula," by which I mean a sequence of action, involving movement, gesture, and (although not necessarily) speech, which occurs in recognizably cognate forms in a number of different plays.[5] This concept is related to, but I think distinct from, a number of structural units already current in discussion of Elizabethan drama. Glynne Wickham, for example, has recently urged the importance of what he terms the "device" in the technique of the Tudor playwrights: it being their task "to externalize in sequences of visual and verbal images . . . abstract ideas and arguments," the device was a useful vehicle, being "a concrete image or figure that mirrored the ideas that were to be exhibited and portrayed in action on the stage," "an active incident that gives physical and visible form to abstact concepts."[6] Michael Hattaway, similarly, notes that many early plays evince "a strong architectonic rhythm," based on "moments that must have been realized by bold visual effects, formal groupings that tend towards tableaux . . . frozen moments that would lodge in the spectators' minds." This dramaturgical unit, borrowing a term from Brecht, Hattaway designates the "Gest": a moment "when the visual elements of the scene combine with the dialogue in a significant form that reveals the conditions of life in the play."[7]

Since such devices and gests were (or became) traditional, their formulaic status is evident, but their value for present purposes is limited. Both concepts are based on assumptions about the function of Tudor and Elizabethan drama on which I should hesitate to pass judgement, and certainly I should not like to restrict the dramaturgical formula to moments which were particularly significant, or to actions which were primarily vehicles for abstract messages. Some of my dramaturgical formulas may also be gests or devices, just as some ballad formulas have symbolic, or supranarrative, as well as purely narrative functions.[8] But for the moment at least my notion of the formula is more practical and functional, as a recurrent pattern of action and interaction in which dialogue, if any, may vary between instances, but have a similar import. A closer and more familiar parallel is provided by the *lazzi* and *burla* of the Italian *commedia dell'arte*, a tradition of popular professional drama roughly contemporaneous with the English theater of Shakespeare and Marlowe.[9] These too are conventional routines involving action and speech, with an evidently formulaic status. They seem, however, to be restricted to humorous scenes and characters, and, of course, have a specific function in a dramatic tradition relying to a large degree on improvisation in performance. Whether the presence of formulas in Elizabethan plays similarly argues a degree of improvisation on the part of the common players is a matter to be discussed in due course. In the meantime the formulaic elements in the dramaturgy of *Doctor Faustus* now claim our attention.[10]

II

The simplest and most obvious dramaturgical formulas of *Doctor Faustus* are the many processional entries onto the stage, sometimes accompanied by music or trumpets (or thunder, in the case of devils), the participants often carrying objects of practical use or symbolic import.[11] More complex, but equally conventional, is the dumb show of Alexander and Darius, in which two processional entries collide, leading to more elaborate action.[12] But the dumb show was only one of several formal subdramatic shows which Elizabethan dramatists conventionally inserted into their plays. Masques and mummings were other favorites, these too with their own formulaic dramaturgy, and *Doctor Faustus* provides a couple of examples. On two occasions, when Faustus's resolve is momentarily shaken, the infernal powers put on what the text in both instances designates as a "shew" to divert his thoughts from repentance. The first, represented in the text by only a brief stage direction, is in fact a complete if elementary mumming:

> *Enter* Devils, *giving crowns and rich appeal to*
> FAUSTUS. *They dance and then depart.*
> (sc. v, 82SD)[13]

In the second, Beelzebub presents to Faustus a series of disguised figures representing the Seven Deadly Sins, each of whom in turn delivers a brief speech of comic self-description (sc. vi, 103-169). As I have argued elsewhere, this show, in content and form, reproduces formulaic action familiar from folk drama, *Fastnachtspiele*, and early mummings.[14] Further instances of formalized—and formulaic—action are provided by the several occasions in the course of the play in which Faustus is urged to desist from, or persevere in, his evil ways, by the Good Angel and Bad Angel, respectively:

> *Enter the* Angel *and* Spirit.
> *Good Ang.* O Faustus, lay that damned book aside
>   And gaze not on it lest it tempt thy soul
>   And heap God's heavy wrath upon thy head.
>   Read, read the scriptures; that is blasphemy.
> *Bad Ang.* Go forward, Faustus, in that famous art
>   Wherein all nature's treasury is contain'd:
>   Be thou on earth as Jove is in the sky,
>   Lord and commander of these elements. *Exeunt* Angels.
>   (sc. 1, 67SD-76; see also sc. v, 15-22; sc. vi, 12-16; sc. vi, 81-84.)

In Marlowe's specific rendition of it, this seems to be a morality formula, a particularly illuminating example occurring in the early fifteenth-century *Castle of Perseverance*, where the speeches of the *Bonus Angelus* and *Malus Angelus* are prefaced by Mankind's explanation of their nature and function (as well as their stage positions):

> *Humanum Genus* . . .
>   To aungels bene asynyd to me:
>   þe ton techyth me to goode;
>   On my ryth syde ȝe may hym se;
>   He cam fro Criste þat deyed on rode.
>   Ano þyr is ordeynyd her to be
>   þat is my foo, be fen and flode;
>   He is about in euery degree
>   To drawe me to þo dewylys wode
>   þat in helle ben thycke.
>   (ll. 301-309)[15]

In more general terms, the formula is that of a man (for example a monarch) offered conflicting advice in turn by good and bad counsellors: these being the roles played for example by Ferrex, Dordan and Herman, respectively, in *Gorboduc*, II.i.1 ff.[16]

The instances offered so far have been formalized sequences of action and dialogue whose formulaic status is immediately apparent from reference to similar set pieces of pageantry, dumb show, masque or morality elsewhere, and are rather too obvious to be instructive. But the formulaic quality of *Doctor Faustus* also extends to sequences which consist of what would normally be termed more realistic and representational action. A striking example is provided by the scene (sc. xiii) in which Faustus, walking alone, is attacked by three knights from the Emperor's court, Benvolio, Martino, and Frederick, in revenge for an earlier insult. They draw their swords in readiness, and Faustus enters *"with the false head"* (37SD). They strike him down and Benvolio decapitates him, after which they discuss what to do with the body, devising comic reapplications for the dismembered parts:

> *Ben.* First, on his head, in quittance of my wrongs, I'll nail
>   huge forked horns . . .
> *Mar.* What use shall we put his beard to?
> *Ben.* We'll sell it to a chimney-sweeper: it will wear out ten
>   birchen brooms, I warrant you.
> *Fre.* What shall his eyes do?
> *Ben.* We'll put out his eyes, and they shall serve for buttons to
>   his lips to keep his tongue from catching cold.
> *Mar.* An excellent policy. And now sirs, having divided him,
>   what shall the body do?
>
> (11.55-66)

At this point Faustus rises, and has devils carry the knights off, unimpressed by Frederick's suggestion, "Give him his head, for God's sake!" (1. 68).

The sequence of action and dialogue here is a formulaic complex with the following main components: A group of swordsmen slay their victim; victim decapitated; they discuss disposal of the corpse; discussion involves dismemberment of corpse and reapplication of the parts; revival of victim. The formulaic status of the complex is suggested by its reccurrence, in whole or in part, and in various contexts and arrangements, in popular dramatic traditions. The complete sequence occurs in one of the varieties of the English mummers' play, the so-called Sword Dance Play, traditionally performed during the Christmas–New Year season in the North East of England.[17] Here the victim is the Clown, who is condemned to death, whereupon the other performers—the sword-dancers—"*tighten the Lock*[18] [of swords] *round the Clown's neck and then draw their swords and the clown falls down dead.*" In some performances the Clown's cap is dislodged, evidently to simulate a beheading (already implied by the position of the swords). In the subsequent dialogue the swordsmen fear the consequences of the slaying, deny responsibility for it in turn, and discuss briefly what to do with the corpse:

> Cheer up me lively lads and be of courage bold,
> We'll take him to the churchyard and bury him in the mould.
>
> Bury him! Bury him! How do you mean to bury him when all these people are standing around?

They conclude it would be better to send for a doctor: he duly appears and in the usual folk-play manner diagnoses the Clown's condition, administers some medicine, and the Clown revives. The dismemberment-and-reapplication motif, meanwhile, has already appeared before the execution, when the Clown makes his will and bequeaths not only his possessions but bits of his body as well, for which he proposes suitable uses:

> My son Fiddler, I'll leave thee my backbone for fiddlestick, small bones for fiddle-strings. And as for thou, I'll leave thee the ring-bone of my eye for a jack-whistle.

One of the minor forms of English folk drama, the "Old Tup" tradition, still performed in the North of England,[19] lacks the final revival (except to the extent that the performer playing the Tup gets up at the end to go off[20]), but otherwise presents a similar sequence. The Tup is slaughtered by a "Butcher" wielding a knife (its throat is cut), and falls to the ground. As this is done the other performers sing the "Derby Ram" song, which in its later stanzas describes the dismemberment of the Tup (*i.e.* "Ram" in local dialect) and the reapplication of the parts:

> All the women in Derby came begging for his hide
> To make some leather aprons to last them all their lives.
>
> All the lads in Derby came begging for his eyes
> To kick them up and down the street for footballs and bulls-eyes

> All the ringers in Derby came begging for his tail
> To ring the Derby passing bell that hangs upon the wall.[21]

Very similar is the sequence of action in the "Old Horse," another animal-disguise tradition from the same area of England, although here the slaying is lacking. The performers sing of the Horse's death from old age, of its dismemberment and the distribution of the parts—hide, body, bones—as the Horse lowers its head to the ground. It rises again at the end of the song in response to a command from its leader.[22]

But the parallels to the sequence in *Doctor Faustus* are not restricted to folk drama.[23] The formulaic sequence is incompletely reproduced in Beaumont and Fletcher's *Philaster* (Q2), where in the course of an insurrection a group of citizens, armed with swords and pikes, surround Pharamond, Prince of Spain, threatening to slay him, and anticipating the dismemberment of his corpse:

> *1. Citizen.* Ile have a leg, that's certaine.
> *2. Citizen.* Ile have an arme.
> *3. Citizen.* Ile have his Nose, and at mine owne charge build a
>   colledge, and clap't upon the gate. . . .

Others, like this last speaker, and like the knights in *Doctor Faustus*, anticipate reapplying the parts, using his guts to string a musical instrument, his liver to feed ferrets, his skin to line scabbards, and his shinbones to make "hafts and whistles."[24] The execution is however prevented by the intervention of Philaster (and there is consequently no opportunity for a revival). A more comprehensive, and highly informative, rendition of the sequence occurs spread over two scenes in the (notoriously bad) quarto of Marlowe's own *Massacre at Paris*.[25] In the course of the massacre, in scene v, the Admiral of France is slain by a group of swordsmen, and Anjoy gives instructions for the dismemberment and disposal of the body:

> Away with him; cut off his head and hands—
> And send them for a present to the Pope;
> And, when this just revenge is finished,
> Unto Mount Faucon will we drag his corse,

> And he that living hated so the Cross
> Shall, being dead, be hang'd thereon in chains.
>
> (ll. 42-47)

(If the decapitation ordered in the first line is carried out on stage, then the parallel to *Doctor Faustus* is still closer.) But despite these clear instructions, scene xi opens with a lengthy discussion between two attendants on just what to do with the body:

> *Enter two with the Admiral's body*
>
> 1. Now, sirrah, what shall we do with the Admiral?
> 2. Why, let us burn him for an heretic.
> 1. O no, his body will infect the fire, and the fire the air, and so we shall be poisoned with him.
> 2. What shall we do, then?
> 1. Let's throw him into the river.
> 2. O, 'twill corrupt the water, and the water the fish, and by the fish, ourselves when we eat them.
> 1. Then throw him into the ditch.
> 2. No, no, to decide all doubts, be ruled by me: let's hang him here upon this tree.
> 1. Agreed.
>
> *They hang him.*
> (ll. 1-11)

Thus suspended—the discussion fortunately having reached a conclusion identical with the instructions in scene v—the body is briefly gloated at by the Guise and Queen Catherine, whereupon the former orders the further disposal of the body in a manner already rejected by the attendants: "Sirs, take him away, and throw him in some ditch" (l. 18). The implications of this extraordinary sequence for the functions of the dramaturgical formula will be discussed in due course.

Meanwhile there remain, finally, the formulaic clownage scenes of *Doctor Faustus*, and these are of particular interest since it is generally agreed they were not composed by Marlowe, most owe little to the English *Faust Book*, and some (to judge by variations between the surviving texts of the play) may have been added in the course of the play's theatrical career. One of the earliest of such scenes in the play (sc. iv) involves Faustus's servant, Wagner, hiring the Clown into his service. Roma Gill has perceptively related some of the small-scale units of dialogue in this scene to the *lazzi* of the clowns in the *commedia dell' arte*,[26] but on a broader level, comic dialogue and stage business between master and impudent or lazy servant are conventional in a number of early dramatic traditions, from the religious drama (*e.g.* Cain and Garcio in the Towneley *Killing of Abel*; Herod and Watkyn in the Digby *Herod's Killing of the Children*[27]) to the *commedia dell'arte* itself.[28] Since Wagner here functions as something of a surrogate for Faustus (whose learning Wagner has mimicked in an earlier scene, and whose conjuring he will emulate in this) his exchange with the Clown may be seen in relation to the many Doctor-and-Servant routines of popular drama. This is a familiar feature, for example, of the mummers' plays of the Cotswolds, where the Doctor is accompanied by the impudent Jack Finney.[29] There is a similar relationship between "Meyster Brendyche of Braban" and his servant Colle in the comic interlude in the Croxton *Play of the Sacrament*.[30] More specifically, the action of this scene in *Doctor Faustus* is matched by several German *Fastnachtspiele* of the fifteenth and early sixteenth centuries, in which a quack doctor appears with his servant, and by the related scenes of the German Easter Plays (*Osterspiele*), in which the *Mercator* visited by the three Maries on their way to the tomb of Christ is often represented as a quack, with one or more comic servants.[31] In both genres this Doctor Scene (*Krämerspiel*) typically involves a sequence in which the Doctor engages the servant, their dialogue (as in *Doctor Faustus*) touching on the terms of employment.[32] The hiring-of-the-servant formula (not necessarily by a Doctor) can also be encountered in the *commedia dell'arte*,[33] and there was once (at least in Warwickshire) a semidramatic sketch performed at harvest-homes called "The Hiring," in which a farmer is represented as hiring a man, their discussion turning on the servant's work, the terms of service, and the food he will receive.[34]

Other dramaturgical formulas occur sporadically in the low-comedy scenes of the play. A neat example, involving predominantly physical action, occurs when the two clowns, Robin and Dick, are accosted by a Vintner, who claims (quite rightly) that they have stolen a cup from his tavern. They brazen it out, and pass the cup surreptitiously between them as the Vintner searches them in turn (the stage directions in the following have been supplied by the editor, but reflect adequately the implications of the dialogue in the B-text):

> *Vint.* O, are you here? I am glad I have found you. You are a couple of fine companions! Pray, where's the cup you stole from the tavern?
>
> *Rob.* How, how? we steal a cup! Take heed what you say; we look not like cup-stealers, I can tell you.
>
> *Vint.* Never deny't, for I know you have it, and I'll search you.
>
> *Rob.* Search me? Ay, and spare not. [*Aside to Dick*] Hold the cup, Dick [*To the Vintner*] Come, come, search me, search me. [Vintner *searches him.*]
>
> *Vint.* [*To Dick*] Come on, sirrah, let me search you now.
>
> *Dick.* Ay, ay, do, do. [*Aside to Robin*] Hold the cup, Robin. [*To the Vintner*] I fear not your searching; we scorn to steal your cups, I can tell you. [Vinter *searches him.*]
>
> *Vint.* Never outface me for the matter, for sure the cup is between you two.

(sc. x, 9-23)

A one-man rendition of the same action is achieved by Mouse, the Clown in *Mucedorus*, when an Alewife accuses him of stealing a pot:

> *Mouse* . . . Search me whether I have it or no.
> *She searcheth him, and he drinketh over her head and casteth down the pot.* . . . [35]

Dericke, the Clown of the *Famous Victories of Henry the Fifth*, is less successful in his struggle over a potlid with the wife of John Cobler.[36]

Toward the end of the play, Doctor Faustus is entertaining the court of Vanholt with his talents when he is interrupted by the boisterous entry of all the clowns together. To amuse the court, he uses his powers to strike each of them dumb in turn in midsentence:

> *Carter.* Do you remember, sir, how you cozened me and eat up my load of—   *Faustus charms him dumb*

and so on with Dick, the Horse-Courser, Robin, and the Hostess (sc. xvii, 106ff.). This action derives from the English *Faust Book*,[37] but seems nonetheless formulaic. This is implied by Faustus himself, who when asking the Duke of Vanholt to allow the clowns to enter says, "They are good subject for a merriment" (sc. xvii, 53). "Merriment"

seems to have been the Elizabethan term for a dramatic or semidramatic low-comedy routine, particularly of the kind inserted by the
clowns into a regular stage play. This is the sense of the word in the title
page of *A Knack to Know a Knave*, which is advertised as including
"Kemps applauded Merriments of the men of Goteham," and it is so
used likewise in Nashe's celebrated account (in *Pierce Penilesse*) of a
country justice who chided the audience during the performance of a
play for immoderate laughter "when Tarleton first peept out his head"
as the players were starting "their first merriment (as they call it)."[38]
Parallels which confirm the formulaic status of the action occur in *The
Birth of Merlin*, where Merlin charms a talkative clown so that he can
say only "Hum, hum, hum,"[39] and in *The Great Magician*, a *commedia
dell'arte* scenario, where Zanni is struck dumb in midsentence by the
magician's spell.[40]

   A more extended formulaic sequence, made up of a number of individual components, is provided by Robin's attempt to emulate
Faustus. Robin has stolen one of Faustus's conjuring books (sc. vii),
and impresses his companion, Dick, with boasts of what he can perform with its aid. Later (sc. x—the action is continuous in the A-text)
he makes use of it to scare off the Vintner whose (formulaic) encounter
with Dick and Robin we have just examined. Dick draws a circle and
Robin pronounces a magical incantation, but the trick misfires as
Mephostophilis, angered at being conjured up from a great distance
(he was at Constantinople), punishes their temerity:

> *Meph.* To purge the rashness of this cursed deed, First be thou
> turned to this ugly shape,   For apish deeds transformed to
> an ape.
> *Rob.* O brave, an ape! I pray sir, let me have the carrying of him
> about to show some tricks.
> *Meph.* And so thou shalt: be thou transformed to a dog, and carry
> him upon thy back. Away, be gone!
> *Rob.* A dog! that's excellent: let the maids look well to their
> porridge-pots, for I'll into the kitchen presently. Come, Dick,
> come. *Exeunt the two* Clowns.
>
> (11. 40-49)

I think it is sufficiently implied by the dialogue (at least here in the
B-text) that the transformation of Robin and Dick to dog and ape re-

spectively occurs on stage (probably by using masks and appropriate posture and movements),[41] and that Dick exits riding on Robin's back. Each of the components in this "Clown's Conjuring" sequence is matched elsewhere in early popular drama, and they sometimes occur in strikingly similar concatenations. The fullest parallel perhaps is supplied by the *commedia dell'arte* scenario *The Magician* (*Il Mago*—more familiar for its analogues with *The Tempest*), where two comic figures, Pantalone and Coviello, obtain one of the Magician's magic books and use it to conjure; eventually, however, demons appear and beat them off the stage. There may be a transformation as well, for in the next scene Pantalone is mistaken for "a wild animal." [42] There is a similar sequence in another scenario, *The Three Satyrs*, involving Pantalone and Zanni. Later in the same play two other characters, Gratiano and Coviello, are transformed (on stage) into a mule and oxe, respectively, when they drink from a magic fountain. They go off "gambolling and howling."[43] Thomas Greene, celebrated clown of the Fortune Theatre, seems to have had a comic turn in which he performed as a baboon.[44] The exit of the clowns, the one riding on the other's back, is of course a familiar incident in the moral interludes and later derivatives (*e.g. Like Will to Like*, *The Devil Is as Ass*) where the Vice is carried off on the Devil's back, and similar ridings occur in folk drama (the Doctor and his "horse"). The Clown is ridden in German *Singspiele* (*e.g.* "Der Narr als Reitpferd") and in Heywood's *Lancashire Witches*.[45]

Prior to the transformation of the Clowns and their exit the A-text of *Doctor Faustus* supplies the stage-direction:

> *Enter Mephistophilis, sets squibs at their backs, and then exit. They run about.*
>
> (A. 1012-1013)

As C. R. Baskervill observes, "to set fire on a clownish character was a recognized trick of the stage devil," and the evidence he offers (although this point is not made) offers many striking parallels to *Doctor Faustus*.[46] The Prologue to *The Two Merry Milkmaids*, for example, suggests the formulaic status of this action on the English stage:

> 'Tis a fine Play:
> For we haue in't a Coniurer, a Deuill,
> And a Clowne too; but I feare the euill,

> In which perhaps unwisely we may faile,
> Of wanting Squibs and Crackers at their taile.

The sequence of components of the A-text—conjuring, appearance of Demon, antics with fireworks—is closely paralleled by an early seventeenth-century Dutch *Singspiel*, Jan van Arp's *Van Droncke Goosen*. I quote from Baskervill's summary of the plot:

> When the *singspiel* opens, the host and hostess of a tavern have just dragged out Goosen, who snores in a drunken sleep. They blacken his face and hands, . . . rouse him, and then go in. Goosen, waking, . . . doesn't know what he is, ghost or devil. . . . Deciding finally to conjure the devil up and settle matters, he makes a circle and begins an incantation. When the hostess and . . . host come in, masquerading as the devil and his dam, Goosen is thrown into a panic. . . . the woman fastens a rocket on his breech and lights it. Goosen cries out, . . . running off in terror.[47]

The parallels to *Doctor Faustus* cited in the preceding pages would presumably, in the terms of conventional philology, be classified as "sources and analogues," and might prompt pleasurable speculation about influences and common origins. But the concept of the dramaturgical formula also advanced in these pages makes such speculation unnecessary, and perhaps unwise: there seems rather to have been—as indeed Peter Burke has suggested—a common European stock of dramaturgical formula which might crop up anywhere, without implying the influence of any one play, or any one national tradition, on another.[48]

III

If, as I have now sought to demonstrate, Elizabethan popular drama is formulaic in the manner of ballads and other traditional narrative genres, then a juxtaposition of the two fields of inquiry may be expected to yield some valuable perspectives, although drawing the parallels and making deductions from them is a difficult operation. In the first place, as students of oral traditions have learned to their cost, it is not possible to transfer insights gained in the study of one tradition (say oral epics) directly to another (say ballads): due weight has to be given to differences of matter, form, and context. This awareness will of course be all the more vital in discussing dramatic traditions, which involve action as well as speech, and where performances involve the interaction of several participants. Secondly, there is not at present a widespread consensus among scholars on the precise role of formulas even in oral narrative. In what follows, therefore, I shall mention various theories on the function of verbal formulas in oral tradition (particularly ballads); these will prompt speculations on the role of dramaturgical formulas in dramatic tradition, and the latter must be assessed on their own merits.

Starting at the beginning of the process, formulas are evidently a potential aid in composition. Someone familiar with ballad tradition would be in a position to construct a new ballad by stringing together a sequence of formulas, interspersed with original matter specific to the narrative in hand.[49] It is, correspondingly, easy to imagine the value of formulas for the dramatists of late Elizabethan England scraping a living by the regular provision of plays to the commercial theaters: in the time of Henslowe a dramatist was apparently expected to deliver a play to the actors about three weeks after the initial commission, and sometimes the deadline was as little as one or two weeks.[50] The formulaic quality of the material they were performing would similarly be a considerable advantage to the players, who, as often noted, were obliged to learn their parts quickly, to perform them with limited rehearsal, and to retain in their memories the parts for a constantly shifting repertoire of between a dozen and a score of plays.[51] It is generally accepted by ballad scholars, and sensibly enough, that whatever their other functions and provenance, formulas "serve to relieve the strain upon the memory of the reciter."[52] Since many of the more frequent events occurring in ballads were narrated in standardized formulations, less effort was required to recall them, and in the meantime the singer could devote at least part of his mind to preparing for what came next, or to embellishing his melody, or in other ways (tone, expression, gesture) enriching his performance. Much of this, with proper adjustment, would be relevant to the problems of the Elizabethan players with their crowded repertoires. The dramaturgical formula, which, as we have seen, is not characterized by exact verbal parallels, would not ease the actor's task of learning his lines, although it would assist in recalling their general import. Rather, the dramaturgical formula makes a familiar routine of so much else (stage position, interaction with other characters, use of properties, action and gesture) that the amount of work in producing a play is significantly reduced, and the individual player can devote more of his attention to what he is saying, and how he says it. The dramaturgical formula may have performed some of the work of the modern director, a figure who is conspicuously absent in the Elizabethan theater.[53]

A startlingly revolutionary theory of formula function has been offered by adherents of the so-called oral-formulaic school, who assert that traditional oral singers do not learn the texts of their narratives, but memorize only the outlines of the story, and recompose the text at each performance, using the formulas provided by tradition.[54] The relevance of the theory to one tradition or another remains a matter of controversy,[55] and certainly its application to popular drama would radically upset received notions of the nature of Elizabethan dramatic performances. It is unlikely, however, that we shall need to go this far. It has become a commonplace of the oral-formulaic controversy that while some improvisational traditions (like the Yugoslav epics) use formulas, it does not follow that any other tradition using formulas must necessarily be based on improvisation, which must therefore be demonstrated by other evidence.[56] Such evidence, for early dramatic traditions in England, does not seem to be available. The most celebrated improvisational tradition, which is also characterized by the use of formulas, is of course the Italian *commedia dell'arte*. But the nature and scope of improvisation by its performers, and the role of formulas in the process, need careful attention. Far from being extemporized in any off-the-cuff manner, *commedia dell'arte* performances were carefully organized and planned in advance. The written *scenario* for a play set out clearly the entrances and exits of the players (often specifying a particular door), the import of the action and dialogue of each scene and the role of each character in it, and the exact distribution of any formulaic *lazzi* and *burla*. Improvisation took place within this fairly exact framework, and was largely restricted to speech (and even some of the speeches were conned by the performers from their commonplace books).[57] So whereas in some traditions of oral narrative improvisation takes the form of selecting and combining formulas to construct a text (the selection and patterns varying from one performance to another), the formula of the *commedia dell'arte* seem rather to have been fixed elements in performance whose routine action was accompanied by improvised dialogue. (The dialogue, in turn, may have used *verbal* formulas, but that is another matter.) There is some evidence for a certain improvisational capacity on the part of Elizabethan stage clowns, like Richard Tarleton and Will Kemp,[58] but it is doubtful whether this applies to their performances in plays or to turns offered between acts or as an afterpiece. And in either case, as in the *commedia dell'arte*, the dramaturgical formulas involved would presumably function not so much as interchangeable units of which an improvisation could be constructed, as a framework within which there might be scope for verbal improvisation.

Of more potential significance, I suspect, is the role of the formula in the deliberate or progressive revision of its host form in the course of transmission. This, certainly, is my own view of the role of the ballad formulas. They are narrative units of which any one ballad is in large part composed, and a ballad can therefore be altered by the processes of formulaic addition, subtraction, or substitution (*i.e.* one formula substituted for another), or an original non–formulaic expression can be replaced by a formula. For example, in the ballad "The Lass of Roch Royal" (already used for illustrative purposes above), after the hero has set off on his formulaically acquired horses in pursuit of his sweetheart, some versions have him encounter her corpse with the following formula:

> He had not rode a mile, a mile,
> A mile but barely three,
> (Til that he spyed her comely corps . . .)
> (Child 76A 30)

while others use the equally formulaic:

> Now the first town that he cam to,
> The bells were ringing there;
> And the neist toun that he cam to,
> (Her corps. . . .)
> (Child 76B 24)

In the nature of things it is not possible to determine which of these formulas, if either, is the original, or which came first in the ballad's evolution, but evidently a substitution has taken place at some stage. It is similarly difficult to determine for any one ballad, when some versions lack a formula present in others, whether addition or subtraction has occurred.[59] The replacement of non-forulaic expressions with formulas can sometimes be detected in those instances where we are lucky enough to have variant texts of a ballad from one singer. In the case of "The Lass of Roch Royal," for example, when the celebrated ballad-singer Anna Gordon Brown sang it in 1783, she had the hero awake with the prosaic, "Love Gregor started frae his sleep" (76D 22.1), which is not particularly formulaic, but when she performed this ballad again in 1800 she used the familiar formula:

> When the cock had crawn, and day did dawn,
>   And the sun began to peep,
> Then it raise him Love Gregor. . . .
>   (76E 17.1-3)

Similar roles, I suggest, could be played by dramaturgical formulas in the revision of Elizabethan stage-plays. Something of the kind is suggested by the last of the formulaic sequences from *Doctor Faustus* discussed above, the "Clown's Conjuring" (sc. vii). The A-text, it will be recalled, has a stage direction for the entry of Mephostophilis and his frightening the clowns by setting "*squibs at their backs,*" after which he exits, only to return for the ape and dog transformations shared with the B-text. W. W. Greg has made the interesting and plausible suggestion that the A-text's business with the fireworks (as in some of the parallels cited) was a means of bringing the scene to a close: the clowns run "*off*" *about.*"[60] By some quirk of its textual history the A-text has preserved what are in fact *alternative* endings to the scene, and since each alternative, as the evidence offered earlier suggests, is formulaic, this sequence provides a revealing instance of the utility of the dramaturgical formula in the revision (under circumstances yet to be determined) of dramatic performances by the process of formulaic substitution.

Doctor Faustus also provides at least circumstantial evidence of formulaic addition and subtraction: since the B-text contains some formulas not in the A-text, they must have been added in the course of the B-tradition of the play or subtracted in the A-tradition. As in the case of ballads the unavailability of the original text makes it difficult to determine which process was involved. For the same reason we cannot determine whether any of the formulas in the surviving texts replace non–formulaic material in the original. I suspect, however, the results of the process may be observable in the use of one of the formulas discussed above in *The Massacre at Paris*. Scene xi of this play (which survives only in a bad quarto) opens with a discussion between two attendants on disposing the body of the Admiral of France, slaughtered in scene v, despite the fact that explicit instructions had already been given, and that subsequently further instructions are given which contradict the discussion (see above for quotations). The association of such narrative illogicality with the use of formulas comes as no surprise to the student of traditional balladry, where there seem to be pressures at work other than mere narrative coherence.[61] In the case of *The Massacre at Paris* I suspect the disposal-of-the-body formula was inserted at some stage in the play's evolution to replace an awkward moment of stage management at the opening of the scene, which may originally have read, "*Enter Admiral, hanging in a tree.*"

I have yet to undertake the exercise, but evidently the role of the dramaturgical formula in revision should be observable through the study of plays recorded at various stages of their theatrical careers, just as the study of multiple versions of ballads can reveal the processes of oral narrative transmission.[62] The material for such analysis is available in the case of those plays for which there survives both a "good" text, by which is usually meant one fairly close to the author's original, and a "bad" text, usually taken to be a memorial reconstruction reflecting the state of the play in later performances (typically those of a provincial tour). It may be significant in this respect that "bad" texts also display a number of other characteristics familiar to ballad scholars, particularly omissions, anticipations/recollections, and contaminations, not to mention "incremental repetition." These are often taken to result from faulty memory on the part of the actor(s) participating in the process of memorial reconstruction which produced the "bad" text.[63] But as I noted at the outset of this study, every performance of a play was a kind of memorial reconstruction, and ballad-studies suggest that the textual characteristics just ennumerated are just as likely to be generated progressively in the course of tradition.[64] Something similar may apply, in both ballads and plays, to the role of the formula.[65]

NOTES

1. This is the full text, with documentation, of the paper presented more informally to the International Conference of the Marlowe Society of America, University of Sheffield, 11-15 July, 1983. I take the opportunity of expressing my thanks to Roma Gill for her kind suggestion that I participate in the conference, and of acknowledging my indebtedness to her own work on *Doctor Faustus*. This paper expands and revises the remarks on traditional features of the play offered in my study, "An Elizabethan Gallimaufry: The Dramaturgy of *Doctor Faustus*", contributed to *Papers Presented to Hans Hartvigson*, ed. J. M. Dienhart & Gillian Eilersen (Odense, 1982), pp. 170-184, and parts of it will in turn be incorporated into a more comprehensive study of oral tradition and its impact on Elizabethan popular drama.

2. Michael Hattaway, *Elizabethan Popular Theatre. Plays in Performance* (London: Routledge and Kegan Paul, 1982), pp. 54-55, offers a comment on Elizabethan plays which parallels many accounts of the textual instability of ballads: "their texts did not have the stability of modern printed books . . . and . . . characters and even plots were correspondingly fluid. Certainly it is highly unlikely that any Elizabethan performance would be as similar to another as is the case with a modern play enjoying even a modest run."

3. This is one of the most frequent formulas in Anglo-Scottish balladry, if not the most frequent. My example is from "The Lass of Roch Royal" (B text, st. 23) in *The English and Scottish Popular Ballads*, ed. F.J. Child, 5 vols. (1892-98; rpt. New York: Dover Publications, 1969), No. 76. For other occurrences see, *e.g.*, Nos. 65A, 23; 72D, 8; 75I, 10-11; 81A, 13; 83A, 18; 87B, 10, etc. My thanks to Flemming G. Andersen for this information, and for providing further illustration from ballad tradition used in the ensuing discussion.

4. Peter Burke, *Popular Culture in Early Modern Europe* (London: M. T. Smith, 1979), p. 124, and see also pp. 134-135.

5. Note that I supply not so much a definition of the dramaturgical formula as a practical guide for detecting it. To attempt more would be both premature and presumptious in the absence of a general agreement on defining the formula of oral narratives. The original and most authoritative definition of the (verbal) formula is Milman Parry's: "A group of words which is regularly employed under the same metrical conditions to express a given essential idea"; quoted in A. B. Lord, *The Singer of Tales* (1960; rpt. New York: Atheneum, 1974), p. 30. For a recent review of the scholarship and theoretical problems involved, see Carol Edwards, "The Parry-Lord Theory Meets Operational Structuralism," *Journal of American Folklore*, 96 (1983), 151-169.

6. Glynne Wickham, *Early English Stages 1300 to 1660*, Vol. III, *Plays and their Makers to 1576* (London: Routledge and Kegan Paul, 1981), chapter IV.

7. Michael Hattaway, *Elizabethan Theatre*, pp. 57-59, and *passim.* for illustrations of

the phenomenon.

8. For the connotative functions of ballad formulas (in Danish ballad tradition), see Otto Holzapfel, *Det Balladesque* (Odense: Odease University Press, 1980), English Summary, pp. 102-107.

9. K. M. Lea, *Italian Popular Comedy. A Study of the Commedia dell'arte* (Oxford: Clarendon Press, 1934), pp. 66ff.

10. The textual problems of *Doctor Faustus* are notorious, and indeed are precisely what has prompted the present enquiry. For convenience of reference, my main text cites *The Tragical History of the Life and Death of Doctor Faustus*, ed. John D. Jump, Revels Plays (1962; rpt. Manchester: Manchester University Press, 1978), but where there is need to distinguish closely between the A-text (Quarto of 1604) and the B-text (Quarto of 1616), I refer to *Marlowe's Doctor Faustus, 1604-1616. Parallel Texts*, ed. W. W. Greg (Oxford: Clarendon Press, 1950).

11. *E.g.* sc. viii, 89SD (Pope and train); sc. ix, OSD (Pope's banquet); sc. ix, 99SD (Friars, to exorcise); sc. xii, OSD (German Emperor and train); sc. xiii, 105SD (Devil-soldiers); sc. xviii, OSD (Devils with Faustus's banquet). For comparative material see Alice Venezky, *Pageantry on the Shakespearean Stage* (New York: Twayne, 1951).

12. For a similarly formalized presentation of the Alexander and Darius story in liturgical drama, see Glynne Wickham, *The Medieval Theatre* (London: Weidenfeld and Nicolson, 1974), p. 49. For comparative material in general see Dieter Mehl, *The Elizabethan Dumb Show* (Cambridge, Mass.: Harvard University Press, 1968).

13. On the form of the early mummings, see Enid Welsford, *The Court Masque* (Cambridge: Cambridge University Press, 1927), chapters I-III. *Cf.* p. 3: "From the beginning to the end of its history, the essence of the masque was the arrival of certain persons vizored and disguised to dance a dance or present an offering." On inserted masques and mummings, see Inga-Stina Ewbank, "'These Pretty Devices.' A Study of Masques in Plays," in *A Book of Masques*, ed. T. J. B. Spencer & S. W. Wells (Cambridge: Cambridge University Press, 1967), pp. 407-448.

14. Thomas Pettitt, "English Folk Drama and the Early German *Fastnachtspiele*," *Renaissance Drama*, N.S. 13 (1982), 1-34, particularly pp. 14-15 and 28.

15. *The Macro Plays*, ed. Mark Eccles, Early English Text Society O.S. 262 (London, 1969). See also Nathaniel Woodes, *Conflict of Conscience* (1581), IV.ii, and IV.iii, where Philologus similarly receives conflicting advance from agents of redemption and damnation (Spirit vs. Sensual Suggestion; Conscience vs. Sensual Suggestion, respectively); *English Morality Plays and Moral Interludes*, ed. E. T. Schell & I. J. D. Shuchter (New York: Holt, Rinehart & Winston, 1969).

16. *Drama of the English Renaissance*, ed. R. A. Fraser and Norman Rabkin, 2 vols. (London & New York: Macmillan, 1976), vol. I, *The Tudor Period*. Another morality formula occurs when Faustus, close to despair, is offered a dagger by Mephostophilis (sc. xviii, 56SD) who here, as often, usurps the function of the Vice. *Cf.* Tattle, in the Second Intermean (ll. 11-12) of Jonson's *The Staple of News*, complaining about the Vice in the play proper: "he has neuer a wooden dagger! I'ld not giue a rush for a *Vice*, that has not a wooden dagger"; *Ben Jonson*, ed. C. H. Herford and Percy and Evelyn Simpson, vol. VI (1938; rpt. Oxford: Clarendon Press, 1966).

17. See Alan Brody, *The English Mummers and their Plays* (Philadelphia: University of Pennsylvania Press 1970), chapter 4; Violet Alford, *Sword Dance and Drama* (London, Merlin Press, 1962). My quotations are from the text printed in N. Peacock, "The Greatham Sword Dance," *JEFDSS*, 8 (1956-59), 29-39.

18. Participants in the Sheffield conference will recall the lock of swords held aloft at the conclusion of their performance by the Handsworth Sword Dancers. On the history of this traditional team and their performances (which formerly included a 'beheading' of the type described in my text), see G. Lester, *Handsworth Traditional Sword Dancers* (Sheffield: 1979).

19. See, *e.g.* Ian Russell, "A Survey of Traditional Drama in the North East Derbyshire 1970-1978," *Folk Music Journal*, 3.5 (1979), 399-478.

20. And in two localities (Worksop, Notts., and Ecclesfield, Lancs.) the folk-play Doctor is brought on to cure the Tup; E. C. Cawte, *Ritual Animal Disguise* (Cambridge: D.S. Brewer, 1978), pp. 115-117. My thanks to Hanne Rasmussen for drawing this to my attention.

21. M. Howley, "The Little Tup," *Folk*, 2 (1962), 9-10.

22. Rory Greig, "We have a poor old horse," *Lore & Language*, 1.9 (July, 1973), 7-10.

23. I have discussed this relationship from a more conventional point of view in "The Folk-Play in Marlowe's *Doctor Faustus*," *Folklore*, 91 (1980), 72-77.

24. *Philaster*, ed. Robert K. Turner, V.iv.67ff., in *The Dramatic Works in the Beaumont and Fletcher Canon*, gen. ed. Fredson Bowers, vol. I (Cambridge: Cambridge University Press, 1966).

25. *Dido Queen of Carthage and The Massacre at Paris*, ed. H. J. Oliver, Revels Plays (London: Methuen, 1968).

26. Roma Gill, " 'Such Conceits as Clownage Keeps in Pay.' Comedy and *Dr. Faustus*," in *The Fool and the Trickster*, ed. Paul V.A. Williams (Cambridge: D.S. Brewer, 1979), pp. 55-63.

27. *The Towneley Plays*, ed. G. England & A. W. Pollard, Early English Text Society, E. S. 71 (1897; rpt. London, 1966), No. II; *The Digby Plays*, ed. F. J. Furnivall, Early English Text Society, E. S. 70 (1896; rpt. London, 1967).

28. *Lea, Italian Popular Comedy*, pp. 54-102. Servant-master scenes are in turn a specific form of the clown-and-stooge routine; see Burke, *Popular Culture in Early Modern Europe*, p. 121.

29. For example in the play from Chadlington, Oxfordshire, in *Eight Mummers' Plays*, ed. Alex Helm (Aylesbury: Ginn, 1971), No. 3.

30. *Non-Cycle Plays and Fragments*, ed. Norman Davis, Early English Text Society, S. S. 1 (London: 1970), pp. 74-78

31. Viktor Michels, *Studien über die ältesten deutschen Fastnachtspiels* (Strasbourg:Trübner, 1896), pp. 56ff.; Rolf Steinbach, *Die deutschen Oster-und Passionsspiele des Mittelalters* (Cologne:Böhlau, 1970),chapter 3.

32. *E.g.* "Die Krämerscene aus dem dritten *Erlauer Spiele*," ll. 106-227, in *Das Drama des Mittelalters*, ed. Richard Froning (Darmstadt: Wissenschaftl. Buchges., 1964), pp.64-68; "Ipocras," ll. 63ff., in *Sterzinger Spiele*, ed. O. Zingerle, vol. I, *Fünfzehn Fastnachts-spiele aus den Jahren 1510 und 1511* (Vienna: Carl Voneger, 1886), No. IV.

33. *Lea, Italian Popular Comedy*, p. 645.

34. Lady Alice B. Gomme, *The Traditional Games of England, Scotland, and Ireland,* vol. I (London: D. Nutt, 1894), p. 319.

35. *Mucedorus,* sc. xii, 11. 44-46, in *Drama of the English Renaissance,* ed. Fraser and Rabkin, vol. I.

36. *Famous Victories,* sc. x, 11. 921-927, in *Narrative and Dramatic Sources of Shakespeare,* ed. Geoffrey Bullough, vol. IV, *Later English History Plays* (London and New York: Routledge and Kegan Paul and Columbia University Press, 1966).

37. *Doctor Faustus,* ed. Jump, Appendix II, p. 136.

38. C. R. Baskervill, *The Elizabethan Jig and Related Song Drama* (1929; rpt. New York: Dover, 1965), p. 88 and n. 2.

39. Cited by Louis B. Wright, in "Juggling Tricks and Conjuring on the English Stage before 1642", *Modern Philology,* 24 (1927), 277-278. See also Robert Greene, *Friar Bacon and Friar Bungay,* ed. J. A. Lavin, New Mermaids (London: Benn, 1969), sc. vi, 1.151SD.

40. Lea, *Italian Popular Comedy,* p. 651. Half-finished sentences (broken off through poison, not magic) also feature in *The Jew of Malta,* IV.i.28ff., ed. Richard W. Van Fossen, Regents Renaissance Drama (Lincoln University of Nebraska Press 1965).

41. *Cf.* "be thou turned to *this* ugly shape . . ." (1. 41). The use of masks here is implied by the Vanholt scene discussed earlier, where Dick, before being struck dumb, complains to Faustus: "Do you remember when you made me wear an ape's—" (xvii, 108), and Robin: ". . . Do you remember the dog's fa[? ce]—" (xvii, 112-113).

42. Lea, *Italian Popular Comedy,* p. 614.

43. *Ibid.,* pp. 667-668, and see pp. 653, 654 and 656 for other grotesque transformations (not all of which, however, occur on stage).

44. Baskervill, *Elizabethan Jig,* p. 117.

45. *Ibid.,* pp. 281-282.

46. *Ibid.,* pp. 315-316 and notes.

47. *Ibid.,* p. 314; the full Dutch text is provided in Part II, No. 36, pp. 601-605. There is one further low-comedy scene in *Doctor Faustus* whose formulaic status I suspect but am not yet in a position to document: the business of the Horse-courser who, in an attempt to rouse the sleeping Faustus, pulls off his leg, and retires in confusion (with the leg) (sc. xv, 27-42). The matter is derived directly from the English *Faust Book* (see *Doctor Faustus,* ed. Jump, Appendix II, p. 134), but as a comic routine sure to raise a laugh with simple properties, and eminently flexible (removal of hand, foot, arm, etc.), it would have made a very useful dramaturgical formula.

48. To take a small example; if the cup-concealing business, common to *Doctor Faustus* and *Mucedorus,* is indeed a formula, there is no need (as is sometimes done) to suggest that one play is indebted for it to the other.

49. Given the oral nature of ballad tradition, it is almost by definition impossible to document this process in action. It is suggested as a means of ballad composition by William Entwhistle, *European Balladry* (Oxford: Clarendon Press, 1939), p. 11.

50. For a perceptive review of these pressures on dramatists such as Munday,

Chettle, Drayton, Dekker and Wilson, and their impact on the plays so produced, see John C. Meagher, "Hackwriting and the Huntingdon Plays," in *Elizabethan Theatre*, ed. John Russell Brown and Bernard Harris, Stratford-upon-Avon Studies, 9 (London: Edward Arnold, 1966), pp. 196-219.

51. See for example Hattaway, *Elizabethan Popular Theatre*, pp. 50ff.; Bernard Beckerman, *Shakespeare at the Globe, 1599-1609* (New York: Macmillan, 1962), pp. 5ff.

52. Cecil J. Sharp, *English Folk Song. Some Conclusions* (1907; rpt. Wakefield: EP Publishing, 1972), p. 113. See also Maud Karpeles, *An Introduction to English Folk Song* (Oxford: Clarendon Press, 1973), p. 41.

53. Formulas, as familiar, recurring elements in popular plays, will also have been a help to the audience. The point is often made that the formulaic qualities of oral narratives reduce the demands on an audience which must listen to a performance (with no possibility of reading a line or stanza again) often in a noisy, sociable context; Matthew Hodgart, *The Ballards* (London: Hutchinson, 1950), p. 31. This would be even more relevant in an Elizabethan theater.

54. Originally evolved by Milman Parry to explain the formulaic characteristics of Homeric verse, the theory has achieved widespread influence since the publication of A. B. Lord's *The Singer of Tales* (see above, n.5), which exploits the fieldwork undertaken by Parry and Lord among the epic-singing *guslars* of Yugoslavia. For the application of the theory to other (English) traditions, see for example, Albert C. Baugh, "Improvisation in the Middle English Romance," *Proceedings of the American Philosophical Society*, 103 (1959), 418-454; David Buchan, *The Ballad and the Folk* (London: Routledge and Kegan Paul, 1972); J. H. Jones, "Commonplace and Memorizations in the Oral Tradition of the English and Scottish Popular Ballads," *Journal of American Folklore*, 74 (1961), 92-112.

55. For opposition to the improvisationalist approach to Anglo-Scottish balladry, see, for example, A. B. Friedman, "The Formulaic Improvisation Theory of Ballad Tradition—A Counterstatement," *Journal of American Folklore*, 74 (1961), 113-115; Flemming G. Andersen and Thomas Pettitt, "Mrs. Brown of Falkland: A Singer of Tales?" *Journal of American Folklore*, 92 (1979), 1-24.

56. The point was first made effectively in the debate on the improvisation of Old English poetry by Claes Schaar, "On a New Theory of Old English Poetic Diction," *Neophilologus*, 40 (1956), 301-305.

57. Lea, *Italian Popular Comedy*, chapter I.

58. See J. A. Bryant, "Shakespeare's Falstaff and the Mantle of Dick Tarlton," *Studies in Philology*, 51 (1954), 149-162; Louis B. Wright, "Will Kemp and the *Commedia dell'Arte*," *Modern Language Notes*, 41 (1926), 516-520; W. J. Lawrence, "On the Underrated Genius of Dick Tarleton," in *Speeding up Shakespeare* (London: Argonaut Press, 1937), pp. 17-38.

59. For example, some versions of "The Lass of Roch Royal" open with a sweetheart-dreaming-of-her-lover formula, others do not.

60. Greg, ed., *Marlowe's Doctor Faustus*, p. 360, note to A. 1012-1022 and Introduction, pp. 37-38. Indeed there are a number of other scenes in *Doctor Faustus* itself which conclude with mortals chased off by demons, sometimes to the accompaniment of fireworks (*e.g.* sc. ix; sc. xiii).

61. The hero of "The Lass of Roch Royal," for example, in one version orders the formulaic saddling of horses and rides off in pursuit of a sweetheart who has just

been seen explicitly to depart by sea (Child 76A, 26-29, & *cf.* st. 22).

62. See Thomas Pettitt, "'Bold Sir Rylas' and the Struggle for Ballad Form," *Lore & Language*, 3.6 (Jan., 1982), 45-60.

63. G. Blakemore Evans, "Shakespeare's Text: Approaches and Problems," in *A New Companion to Shakespeare Studies,* ed. Kenneth Muir & S. Schoenbaum (Cambridge: Cambridge University Press, 1971), pp. 229-230; E. K. Chambers, *William Shakespeare. A Study of Facts and Problems* (1930; rpt. Oxford: Clarendon Press, 1963), pp. 156-159.

64. Flemming Andersen & Thomas Pettitt, "'The Murder of Maria Marten': The Birth of a Ballad?", forthcoming in *Narrative Folksong: New Directions*, ed. Carol L. Edwards & Kathleen E. B. Manley (Los Angeles: Trichstes Press, 1985).

65. A useful point of departure would be provided by W. W. Greg's comparative analysis of the 1594 (bad) quarto of Greene's *Orlando Furioso* and the 'part' for the role of Orlando, evidently used by Edward Alleyn and reflecting an earlier stage in the play's evolution. W. W. Greg, *Two Elizabethan Stage Abridgements: The Battle of Alcazar & Orlando Furioso. An Essay in Critical Bibliography* (Oxford: Malone Society, 1923). Greg notes (pp. 305-310) that a number of the low-comedy scenes in the quarto, not present in the part, may have been added to replace other original (perhaps more literary) material. If some of these episodes, as seems very likely, are dramaturgical formulas, this would confirm the process of revision through formulaic replacement, and Greg suggests in general that the bulk of the alterations in the play "represent a gradual adaption of the play to altered circumstances in the course of repeated acting" (p. 134, and *cf.* pp. 321, 353-355). The play, in other words, is behaving remarkably like a ballad.

The Dialectic of Despair in *Doctor Faustus*

KING-KOK CHEUNG

Many critics have called attention to the connection between Faustus's despair and his damnation. Some see despair as the justification of his damnation, others as but a sign of his damnation. The first view insists upon the responsibility and the perversity of the sinner: despair is an evil choice, an obdurate denial of divine mercy. The second view takes for granted the sinfulness of despair, but underlines its inevitable consequence: despair, being a state of mind proper to the reprobate, will necessarily lead to damnation.[1] Both of these views underestimate the dramatic and tragic potential of despair in the play. I wish to suggest that despair and salvational possibility in *Doctor Faustus* are dialectical rather than antithetical, that Faustus's despair, in tormenting him and in evoking the alternative of repentance, works dialectically to keep alive the possibility of salvation.

To insist on seeing Marlowe's treatment of Christian ideas as wholly believing or as wholly ironic, as many critics have done, is to bury evidence on the other side, and both views ignore a third, existential, view which is beyond religion and blasphemy. By "existential" I mean simply a view which proves itself in existence, regardless of an individual's persuasions, though Kierkegaard's notion of despair has admittedly influenced my reading of Marlowe's play. According to Kierkegaard, despair is a condition of being, issuing from the timeless clash between possibility and necessity, between human immortal longings and the fact of mortality. However, because such despair is grounded in the love of life on earth, I believe it cannot, *pace* Kierkegaard, be cured through Christian faith. Hence Faustus sickens unto death despite the nagging possibility of religious salvation. First I will discuss how the dialectic of religious despair operates in the play, and then speculate on why Faustus persists in despair notwithstanding the dialectic.

Since despair has traditionally denoted the despair of salvation, the possibility of salvation presents itself every time the sinner despairs. M. M. Mahood, who feels that "despair dominates the play, and that the word itself recurs with a gloomy, tolling insistence,"[2] fails to notice that this word always appears in conjunction with the possibility of salvation, that despair never tolls without a concomitant ring of hope, that despair keeps the play alive with suspense and tension. Rather than setting the seal on damnation, despair keeps the lines open for repentance and salvation.

Initially Marlowe presents Faustus as an autonomous individual who willfully indulges in self-delusion and who incurs his own damnation through despair. Faustus reveals his proclivity for self-deception when he reads two bleak verses from Jerome's Bible. The first verse threatens: "The reward of sin is death" (i.40).[3] The threat becomes personal in the second verse: "if we say that we have no sin, we deceive ourselves and there's no truth in us" (i.41-43). Many critics have noticed that Faustus overlooks the complementary verse in the Bible which promises salvation to those who confess their sins and which therefore safeguards against despair. Instead he jumps to the conclusion that all "must die an everlasting death" (i.45). For one as erudite as Faustus, the failure to notice the hopeful qualification seems deliberate.

Faustus's damnation attests no more to predestination than to self-determination. In his own words,

> Now, Faustus, must
> Thou needs be damn'd, and canst thou not be sav'd.
> What boots it then to think of God or heaven?
> Away with such vain fancies, and despair;
> Despair in God, and trust in Beelzebub.

> Now go not backward; no, Faustus, be resolute.
> (v.1-6)

Commenting on this passage, Muriel C. Bradbrook remarks: "If it takes so many negatives to stop Faustus's repentance there must be very strong forces working for it." After making this claim for Faustus's chance of salvation, however, Bradbrook undercuts her own claim by following medieval lore in calling despair "the means by which the devils, from the very beginning, secure Faustus's soul, making him incapable of repentance, even though he wills with all his might to repent."[4] Such a definition of despair renders Faustus's spiritual struggle illusory and the periodic appearance of the good and bad angels a meaningless ritual. The reverse of Bradbrook's statement seems to me more plausible: although Faustus wills with all his might to forsake God in favor of the Devil, his despair, in tormenting him and in evoking the alternative of repentance, works dialectically to keep alive the possibility of salvation.

Despair summons God despite itself; no sooner has Faustus decided to banish the "vain fancies" than despair evokes one—the "God" in "Despair in God." Religious despair, though a professed rejection of God, cannot take place in the absence of the divine object of despair.[5] Because despair entails the thought of God, it will not leave Faustus in peace; it puts him in thrall to Christianity and unsettles him with godly thoughts. However, Faustus imputes his mental perturbations to his irresoluteness, which he tries to overcome by confirming himself in sin. Thus, rather than being "the means by which the devils . . . [make] him incapable of repentance," as Bradbrook suggests, despair elicits in Faustus thoughts of heaven, and therefore must be exorcised through greater commitment to sin.

Immediately after Faustus has pronounced his own damnation, exhorting himself to be "resolute" in his evil ways, an inner voice interjects to shake his determination: "Why waver'st thou? O, something soundeth in mine ears, / 'Abjure this magic, turn to God again!'" (v.7-8). Whenever Faustus despairs, the tantalizing possibility of salvation hovers over him. Contrary to Arieh Sach's contention that the play's situation "by its very nature cannot be suspenseful, since Faustus's despair is such as to make his reprobation a foregone conclusion,"[6] the play's power lies in its painful suspense which can be experienced even by an audience that knows the outcome. Despite his despair, or rather because of it, Faustus's spiritual welfare remains in doubt till the final scene.

Before going to the final scene, let me pause for a moment over the comic scenes which continue to puzzle critics. John D. Jump, for instance, notes the discrepancy "between the tragic Faustus, fluctuating between arrogance and remorse, whom Marlowe portrays, and the jaunty anti-papist wonder-worker and court entertainer who bears Faustus's name in the comic scenes."[7] The easiest solution is to say that these scenes are not written by Marlowe. There is, however, a better way to reconcile these scenes with the rest of the play, a way which deepens the tragedy. Disappointed by his pact with the Devil and despairing of salvation, Faustus anesthetizes himself by turning to what Kierkegaard calls "Philistinism," which "tranquilizes itself in the trivial."[8]

Faustus's consciousness of his sorry plight amid trivial diversions is made obvious when he interrupts his practical joke on the horse-courser with the following soliloquy:

> What art thou, Faustus, but a man condemn'd to die?
> Thy fatal time draws to a final end;
> Despair doth drive distrust into my thoughts.
> Confound these passions with a quiet sleep.
> Tush, Christ did call the thief upon the cross;
> Then rest thee, Faustus, quiet in conceit.
>
> (xv.21-26).

While Faustus may be compounding his sin by taking the good thief as a sign that last-minute repentance is acceptable, that the sinner can wait, the theological reference does show that Faustus still can entertain hopes of salvation. His self-imperatives to "Confound these passions with a quiet sleep," to "rest . . . quiet in conceit," betray his spiritual restlessness and disquiet. Since the throes of despair beget thoughts of salvation, the times when Faustus despairs are the times when he seems most capable of breaking through to God.

If Faustus could have abandoned himself completely, rejecting the desirability of salvation, then at least he would have been able to "live in all voluptuousness" (iii.94) during his twenty-four years on earth. But the possibility of salvation continues to be a thorn in Faustus's flesh that disrupts his sensuous enjoyment. Whereas despair is hardly known to Chapman's Bussy D'ambois, Tourneur's Vindici, or Marlowe's own Tamburlaine, all of whom gloat over their crimes, it plagues Faustus recurrently. The despair which puts Faustus above other desperadoes not only stands in the way of his repentance, but also cheats him of sinful pleasure. Because of his deep conviction of sin, Faustus dares not hope for divine mercy. Because of his fear of damnation, his earthly joys are compromised. Whereas moral insensitivity arms the other daredevils for sinful exploits and allows them to wallow in forbidden pleasures, Faustus's despair exacts its own penance and will not leave him even to his buffoonery. Not surprisingly, Frederick S. Boas suspects Marlowe of shortchanging Faustus: "Had Marlowe vouchsafed us a sight of Faustus in his sinful pleasures it would have been a fitter prelude to his fast approaching doom."[9] Had Marlowe granted us such a sight, however, he would have held his tragedy at the level of a morality, meting out simple poetic justice. With incisive irony, Marlowe shows that the rebel who defies the Christian God is nevertheless too steeped in Christianity to relish the fruit of sin. The hair shirt of despair pricks and chafes; even Faustus's greatest pleasure is no more than an anodyne. He admits that he would have committed suicide "Had not sweet pleasure conquer'd deep despair" (vi.25).

Despair and repentance are again entertained together in the Old Man episode. Moved by the Old Man, Faustus agrees to ponder his sin:

> I do repent, and yet I do despair;
> Hell strives with grace for conquest in my breast.
> What shall I do to shun the snares of death?
> (xviii.71-73)

Although Faustus again sees repentance and despair as antithetical, he cannot deliberate on one without invoking the other, just as he cannot contemplate hell without reflecting on grace. Rather than being mutually exclusive, despair and repentance vie with each other in Faustus's spiritual struggle. The more painfully he is torn between despair and repentance, the more vivid becomes the possibility that he may yet be saved. To evade the painful spiritual struggle, Faustus again diverts himself with bodily pleasure, begging Mephistophilis to summon Helen, "whose sweet embraces may extinguish clear / Those thoughts that do dissuade me from my vow / And keep mine oath I made to Lucifer" (xviii.94-96). These lines give the impression that it is just as difficult to follow Lucifer faithfully as to follow God. Far from being a sin "which would infallibly guide the soul to its infernal destination," as Sachs suggests,[10] Faustus's despair makes it hard for Faustus to go to hell.

But why does Faustus work so hard to go to hell despite the dialectical workings of despair? I submit that Faustus's theological despair has its root in existential despair, which is already apparent at the beginning of the play when Faustus complains that for all his natural knowledge,

> Yet art thou still but Faustus, and a man.
> Couldst thou make men to live eternally
> Or being dead raise them to life again,
> Then this profession were to be esteem'd.
> (i.23-26)

This passage has often divided critics. It suggests guilty presumption to some and heroic aspiration to others, eliciting both disapproval and admiration. But there is a third way to read this passage, and that is to see it simply as an expression of the timeless longing to exceed human confinement, to bypass death, to be immortal. Faustus does not crave eternity (which contains and involves God-in-Heaven) but immortality, which is "deathless life on this earth," as Hannah Arendt puts it.[11] At the height of his spiritual struggle, rather than seeking the means to enter heaven, Faustus asks himself, "what shall I do to shun the snares of death?" Just as the thought of overcoming death has driven him to black magic at the outset, so he yearns for immortality to his last day, as evident in his wistful plea to Helen—"make me immortal with a kiss" (xviii.101). The erotic energy which runs through this memorable line is charged with the woe and wonder of human life.

To immortalize mortals is a desperate enterprise. The play resounds with the constant collision of possibility and necessity. Despite his desire for unlimited freedom, Faustus seems constrained, from the beginning, by foreknowledge of his damnation and of God's hatred. His rejection of God is qualified or even prompted by an uncontrollable fear of that God, as Constance Brown Kuriyama suggests.[12] When an inner voice bids Faustus to "Abjure this magic, turn to God again" (v. 7-8), his instinct responds: "To God? He loves thee not" (l. 9). When his arm reveals the words "*Homo Fuge*," all Faustus can think of is "Whither should I fly? / If unto God, he'll throw me down to hell" (v. 77-78).

Faustus turns to Mephostophilis for help, only to double his fear gradually, for Faustus can hardly distinguish God from the Devil at the end. Indeed, the peculiar horror of the last scene is Faustus's hysterical conflation of the two:

> Ah, my Christ!—
> Rend not my heart for naming of my Christ;
> Yet will I call on him. O, spare me, Lucifer!—
> Where is it now? 'Tis gone: and see where God
> Stretcheth out his arm and bends his ireful brows.
> Mountains and hills, come, come, and fall on me,
> And hide me from the heavy wrath of God!
> (xix.147-153)

The direct address and the direct entreaty in the first two lines suggest that it is Christ who rends Faustus's heart—at least till we reach the next line in which Lucifer emerges as the tormentor. However, as soon as Christ is succeeded by Lucifer, the fierce archfiend merges with the fierce God: "O, spare me, Lucifer!— . . . and see where God / Stretcheth out his arm and bends his ireful brows." Now beseeching God, now Lucifer, Faustus recoils as much from the King of Heaven as from the Prince of Hell.

The scene reveals Faustus's metaphysical bondage. In a Christian society, the very word despair, despite its ostentatious apostate implications, tacitly acknowledges the existence of God. Faustus's despair implicates him in the very context from which he tries to extricate himself. Despair leads inevitably to his damnation, not so much in the ways orthodox critics suggest as because despair binds him to the belief in heaven and hell then prevalent, according to which he is damned. The Good and Bad Angels are likewise voices of the social conscience which readily labels people as good *or* bad. While refusing to conform to social norms, Faustus nevertheless has internalized the judgemnt of society and must regard himself negatively as a "spirit." He cannot avoid the Christian frame of reference; he cannot "shun the snares" of Christianity.

In his anguish, Faustus resigns himself to "despair and die" (xviii.56). But even this last hope, this desire to be done with it all, this defiant refusal to be bound by the fetters of religion, is laden with conventional religious significance, so that to die takes on the meaning of to "die an everlasing death." "Despair and die" epitomizes the existential condition of "no exit" in *Doctor Faustus*.

While focusing on one theme inevitably does some injustice to the play as a whole, exploring Marlowe's treatment of despair helps to reveal the play's divergent possibilities. Tragedy constantly frustrates our longing for a definite answer,[13] our persistent desire to know "What means this show." This tragedy confronts us with warring possibilities which qualify doctrinal prescriptions and shake our reasoning. *Doctor Faustus* is tragic not so much because the hero is painfully suspended between good and evil, fate and freedom, as because these opposing categories blur and blend in the play. Despair, an oft-denounced sin, is seen as the strongest force which, for better or for worse, binds Faustus to Christianity, because despair, viewed by many as a sign of inevitable damnation, constantly teases the sinner with the possibility of salvation. Faustus's theological despair may finally be seen as concealing an existential despair, with his particular dilemma reflecting the human predicament. To see the play steadily and to see it whole, one must embrace all these paradoxes, lest one lapse into the same wishful thinking and commit the same foolish sin as Faustus, who would invoke evil spirits to "Resolve . . . all ambiguities."

NOTES

1. For the first view see Lily B. Campbell, "*Doctor Faustus*: A Case of Conscience," *PMLA*, 67 (1952), 219-239; Gerald Cox, "Marlowe's *Doctor Faustus* and 'Sin against the Holy Ghost,'" *Huntington Library Quarterly*, 36 (1973), 119-137; Paul H. Kocher, *Christopher Marlowe: A Study of His Thought, Learning, and Character* (Chapel Hill, N. C.: University of North Carolina Press, 1946), pp. 104-119; John C. McCloskey, "The Theme of Despair in Marlowe's *Faustus*," *College English*, 4 (1942), 110-113; M. M. Mahood, *Poetry and Humanism* (London: Jonathan Cape, 1950), pp. 64-74. For the second view see Helen Gardner, "Milton's 'Satan' and the Theme of Damnation in Elizabethan Tragedy," *English Studies*, 1 (1948), 46-66; Arieh Sachs, "The Religious Despair of Doctor Faustus," *Journal of English and*

Germanic Philology, 63 (1964), 625-647; Joseph Westlund, "The Orthodox Christian Framework of Marlowe's *Faustus,*" *SEL,* 3 (1963), 190-205.

2. *Poetry and Humanism,* p. 67.

3. Citations of Marlowe's play are from *Doctor Faustus,* ed. John D. Jump (London: Methuen, 1965). I am aware of the recent critical preference for the A-text (see Fredson Bowers, "Marlowe's *Doctor Faustus*: The 1602 Additions," *Studies in Bibliography,* 26 [1973], 1–18; Constance Brown Kuriyama, "Dr. Greg and *Doctor Faustus*: The Supposed Originality of the 1616 Text," *English Literary Renaissance,* 5 [1975], 171–197), but the parts of the play which form the basis of my argument are mostly those which appear in both the 1604 and 1616 editions.

4. *Themes and Conventions of Elizabethan Tragedy* (Cambridge: Cambridge University Press, 1935), p. 151.

5. C. L. Barber notes the irony in the characters' use of religious terms such as "heaven," "blest," "canonize" to describe magic: "In repeatedly using such expressions, which often 'come naturally' in the colloquial language of a Christian society, the rebels seem to stumble uncannily upon words which condemn them by the logic of a situation larger than they are." ("The Form of Faustus' Fortunes Good or Bad," *Tulane Drama Review,* 8 [1964], 99.) Nowhere is such recurrent lapse more apparent than in Faustus's despair.

6. "The Religious Despair of Doctor Faustus," 638.

7. Introduction, *Doctor Faustus,* p. 38.

8. *Fear and Trembling* and *The Sickness Unto Death,* trans. Walter Lowrie (1941; rpt. Princeton, N. J.: Princeton University Press, 1974), p. 174.

9. *Christopher Marlowe: A Biographical and Critical Study* (Oxford: Clarendon Press, 1940), p. 216.

10. "The Religious Despair of Doctor Faustus," 628.

11. *The Human Condition* (Chicago: University of Chicago Press, 1958), p. 18.

12. Kuriyama uses Erik Erikson's concept of negative identity to show how "Marlowe can neither conceive of nor define a wholesome rebellion; to him the values, language, and dramatic conventions of self-condemnation are inescapable, yet intolerable." (*Hammer Or Anvil* [New Brunswick, N. J.: Rutgers University Press, 1980], p. 130.)

13. Stephen Booth convincingly argues the elusiveness of tragedy in *King Lear, Macbeth, Indefinition, and Tragedy* (New Haven, Conn.: Yale University Press, 1983), pp. 79–118.

"Within the massy entrailes of the earth": Faustus's Relation to Women

KAY STOCKHOLDER

All images or portrayals of extrahuman figures, gods and devils, ghosts and witches, are necessarily extensions and exaggerations of human characteristics, for human characteristics are all that we know. To isolate a human characteristic and portray it as belonging to a devil, or an angel, is to express an attitude toward that characteristic; to tell, or to dramatize, a story involving supernatural happenings necessarily involves allegorizing human affairs, whether or not the author believes in the literal truth of the supernatural happenings. The imaginations of secular humanists find resonant meaningfulness in such works as the *Divine Comedy* because those works express powerful evaluations through their heightened portrayals of facets of our common humanity. Accordingly, in discussing the role of women in Marlowe's *Doctor Faustus* I am going to naturalize all supernatural events. That is, I will regard supernatural elements as expressions of an attitude toward or judgment of a natural or ordinary version of such an event or figure.

The Faustus that we encounter as the play begins is a man who, having devoted his youth to study, has risen from lowly origins, from "parents base of stock," to eminence in learning. Despite his achievements in enterprises that once "ravished" him, he now feels depleted and restless, wondering at life's lack of savor. It is not clear how old we are to imagine him, but the experience rendered seems easily analo-

gous to those that today might be described as midlife crises. In order
to escape the emptiness that has overwhelmed him he turns to the forbidden, which seems to promise, as the forbidden always does, a deep
and general fulfillment of undefined desire. Faustus expresses this
vague desire initially in terms of a magnified vision of the satisfactions
he has already—of power, praise, and knowledge. His first imagination of the delights to be found in necromancy extends the range of his
past achievements, but does not initiate new realms, except for one
slight suggestion. Faustus's life, as described by the prologue and by
himself, has been notably barren of sexuality, women, and love. His
imagination touches on the realm of the sensuous when he anticipates
that the spirits will "fly to India for gold . . . And search all corners of
the new-found world / For pleasant fruits and princely delicates." He
approaches a slightly more sensual note when he says, "I'll have them
fill the public schools with silk, / Wherewith the students shall be
bravely clad" (I.i.109-113, 117-118).[1] Though most of his dazed
visions are of the power and status he associates with forbidden knowledge, rather than of love, his expression of delight in the magic that is
to realize them is suffused with the aura of the sexual: "'Tis magick,
magick, that hath ravish'd me" (I.i.137). That suffused swoon suggests that we should see Faustus as a man whose sexual and erotic energies have been diverted into the successful pursuit of knowledge and
fame, and who is therefore left with a vague feeling of unsatisfied emptiness, the satisfaction of which he associates with powers that derive
from forbidden knowledge.

One would not expect a person like Faustus to be aware that he seeks
erotic satisfaction through forbidden magic, since if he knew what he
wanted he would not need magic to get it. One would expect, as is so in
the play, evidence of the nature of his desire to come only slowly into
view. Accordingly, in this anticipatory section the sensual notes are
distanced into metaphors and images. Cornelius says that the spirits
will "fetch the treasure of all foreign wrecks, / Yea, all the wealth that
our forefathers hid / Within the massy entrailes of the earth" (I.i.173–
174). The image suggests not only lost sexual potency—the treasures,
hidden within the feminine earthy entrails—but also the deep past,
containing for Faustus parental images, associated with that potency,
that in turn suggest some of the difficulties involved in recovering it.
Faustus responds, with a kind of swooning sensuality, "O, this cheers

my soul! / Come, show me some demonstrations magical, / That I may conjure in some bushy grove / And have these joys in full possession" (I.i.178-180). The image of the "bushy grove" rings in the same range as the "massy entrails," vaguely suggestive of genitalia, but the first images of women appear in a distanced and aestheticized association with diabolical spirits when Valdes says that they will appear "like women, or unwedded maids, / Shadowing more beauty in their airy brows / Than has the white breasts of the queen of love" (I.i.154-156).

The association of women, both in their sexual and aesthetic ranges, with forbidden magic appears more obviously when Faustus succeeds in conjuring Mephistophilis. Faustus's fearful ambivalence toward his enterprise is suggested not only by the ugliness of Mephistophilis's first appearance, but also by the opposition between Mephistophilis's "fainting soul" at the mention of the "everlasting bliss" of which he is forever deprived, and Faustus's scornful dismissal of his futile yearnings. Faustus prescribes "manly fortitude" for Mephistophilis's heart-sickened sense of deprivation, but as though in consolation for his own parallel deprivation, asks for twenty-four years of "all voluptuousness" (I.iii.319-320). Mephistophilis's poignant nostalgia echoes Faustus's yearnings for the joys he anticipated in magic, which will culminate when he foregoes the asexual Christian heaven, for which Mephistophilis yearns, in exchange for the sensuous heaven of Helen's kiss.

Faustus's mind veers sharply from dreams of voluptuousness to the more familiar ones of the power to be found in forbidden knowledge, but the hidden association of that forbidden realm with the sensual is suggested first by the rapidity with which Faustus's mind moves past his first request, and second by the fact that one doesn't generally have to make a pact with the devil in order to live voluptuously. These considerations indicate that Faustus associates sensuality both with forbidden knowledge and power, and with ensuing diabolic punishment, and that, moved by frustration, he has embarked on magic in a desperate effort to achieve the sensual, despite the fear with which he surrounds it. He remains only half aware that the forbidden knowledge he seeks derives, at least in part, from his desire to know, in the biblical sense, a woman. After his first slight motion in that direction he deflects his attention to less problematic fantasies of power, which only extend what he has already achieved in more ordinary ways. He can scarcely entertain images that betray the true nature of his desire.

The issue of women arises a second time in a context similar to the first. Faustus, having signed the pact, questions Mephistophilis about hell only to dispute with him about its existence. Since he is talking to a devil, his dispute seems illogical; and equally illogical seem Mephistophilis's assurances not only that hell exists, but also that he, even at that moment, inhabits it, for a clever devil would be happy for Faustus to doubt his and hell's existence. But the illogic of the sequence emphasizes its emotional content as Faustus's mind moves toward and away from the vision of hellish deprivation that he has already associated with sensuality. That association is deepened when Faustus says,

> let me have a wife,
> The fairest maid in Germany, for I
> Am wanton and lascivious
> And cannot live without a wife.
> (II.i.527-530)

While Faustus might have trouble getting the "fairest maid in Germany" for a wife without a devil's aid, the relative innocence of his demand is striking, even to the association of the "wanton and lascivious" with the legality of marriage. But the degree to which Faustus feels not only the sensual, but also the domestic realm embattled and colored with the diabolical appears clearly when Faustus perceives the "wife" that is brought as a "she-devil" and a "hot whore." In effect, as he approaches his desire for forbidden sensuality he associates it with the familial and domestic in asking for a wife, but an approach to a fulfillment of his embattled desire appears to him in hideous and threatening images from which he again retreats. Faustus finds himself in a dilemma wherein tainted images of women pervade the innocent domesticity by which he tries to avoid the forbidden sexuality. Accordingly, Mephistophilis supports Faustus in his declaration that he will have no wife, saying, "Marriage is but a ceremonial toy: / And if thou lovest me, think no more of it," and promises Faustus sexual satisfaction, but in images that, like those earlier, are remote and aestheticized:

> I'll cull thee out the fairest courtesans,
> And bring them ev'ry morning to thy bed:
> She whom thine eye shall like, thy heart shall have,

> Were she as chaste as was Penelope,
> As wise as Saba, or as beautiful
> As was bright Lucifer before his fall.
>   (II.i.535-542)

The sexual overtones are diminished in part by the mythological removal, but also because the "fairest courtesans" are imagined coming
to Faustus's bed "ev'ry morning," rather than in the darkness of night
in which pacts are made. The issue of women becomes even more remote when women's beauty is expressed in an image of male beauty,
"As was bright Lucifer before his fall," in a way that homosexually
colors the erotic content.[2]

But these floating promises do not emerge from image into action,
for in the next scene Faustus is in the throes of suicidal despair, allevi-
ated only by the "sweet pleasure" he derives from "blind Homer's"
songs of "Alexander's love and Oenone's death." Faustus associates
his despair with regret for the lost joys of Heaven, but actually experiences an intensified form of the same ennui that prompted his efforts in necromancy. The lascivious delights he anticipated have been
so meagerly provided that it is little wonder that Faustus ignores the
good angel's voice, and pursues the course toward Helen's heavenly
kiss. He distracts himself by seeking more knowledge from Mephistophilis, but the deeper drift reappears when Lucifer and Beelzebub
tell him not to call on Christ or think of God, but rather to "Think on
the devil. / And on his dam too" (II.ii.645-646). Once again, an image
of coupling, or of marriage, is associated with the diabolically ugly, in
contrast to the aestheticized and distanced sensual images which are
defined as an alternative heaven. However, this sublimated sexuality is
still thought of as leading to hell, which contains the more immediate,
and therefore uglier, images of closer relationship and sexuality.

Some of the psychological sources of Faustus's estrangement from
sexuality are suggested in the show of the seven deadly sins by which
Mephistophilis diverts Faustus. Somewhat surprisingly, Pride's
speech has more sexual content than Lechery's. The latter says, "I am
one that loves an inch of raw mutton better than an ell of fried stockfish,
and the first letter of my name begins with Lechery" (II.ii.707-710), an
adequate self-definition, but one notably lacking an aura of sensual
delight. When Faustus closely approaches sexuality, it appears to him

in its most debased version. Within the comic debasement of Pride's speech, however, more sensual resonance is allowed. He says,

> I am Pride. I disdain to have any parents. I am like to Ovid's flea; I can creep into every corner of a wench; sometimes, like a periwig, I sit upon her brow; next, like a necklace I hang about her neck; then, like a fan of feathers, kiss her lips, and then turning myself to a wrought smock do what I list. But, fie, what a smell is here! I'll not speak another word, unless the ground be perfum'd, and cover'd with cloth of arras.
>
> (II.ii.663-670)

Pride's claim of parentless self-authorship is traditional, but his disdain, when coupled with the diminutive sexual exploration suggested by the images that follow, suggests a person acting like a small child in order to steal sensuous gratification from a mother-like, because so much larger, woman. The image that suggests the fulfillment of a sexual act—"turning myself to a wrought smock do what I list"—brings with it disgust—"what a smell is here! I'll not speak another word, unless the ground be perfum'd."

When we naturalize the sequence, that is, see it as Faustus's fantasy, it suggests that in order for Faustus to generate images of heterosexuality he has first to eliminate parental images. Only having done so can he make the sexual claim, which for him still involves the sin of pride. But having strategically disdained to have parents, he reintroduces elements of a parent/child relationship in the image of the flea's sexual exploration, which in turn generates the disgust associated with sexuality that he sought to eliminate along with parents. The context in which this episode occurs justifies the significance I have attributed to this passage, for as a precondition to this diversion Faustus has promised Lucifer that he will "never look to Heaven," and never more name God. Since the idea of God extends from an image of paternal authority, Faustus has his glimpse of sexuality only when he declares himself in prideful rebellion from that authority. The sequence reveals that Faustus thinks himself unworthy of making a sexual claim, and fears paternal reprisal for seeking sexual knowledge, in both senses of the word. The sequence anticipates in little the structure of the entire play.

The kind of punishment he fears appears in the events which he encounters on his journey with Mephistophilis, which turn either on delight in ridiculing others or on fear of being ridiculed. The ridicule takes the specific form of jests about cuckoldry, though the emblematic horns first appear disjoined from the wayward women who make them grow. While those jests, which bear on Faustus's relation to paternal authority, occupy the foreground of the action, Faustus's relationship to women continues in the background. There images of women take fuller and more solid shape, but do so in a context of Faustus's demonstration of his necromantic skills to figures of authority rather than in association with his own desire.

The cuckoldry theme takes shape in parodic form when Robin plans to practice conjuring with the help of Faustus's stolen magic books. Dick warns that Faustus will conjure him in punishment, to which Robin boasts "an my master come here, I'll clap as fair a pair of horns on's head as e'er thou sawest in thy life." Dick says he need not bother, for "my mistress hath done it," and then suggests that Robin has been "sneaking up and down after her" (II.iii.737-739).

That episode preludes those that occur after Faustus, having quenched his thirst for more abstract knowledge on a pretechnological flight with Mephistophilis, arrives at the Pope's palace, where he wishes now to be "an actor." In this sequence the theme of cuckoldry intertwines with the challenge to authority, both of which are introduced and brought into alignment with another reference to Faustus's desire.

When Faustus and Mephistophilis are in the Pope's court to witness the celebration of his "triumphant victory" Faustus says,

> Sweet Mephistophilis, thou pleasest me,
> Whilst I am here on earth, let me be cloy'd
> With all things that delight the heart of man.
> My four and twenty years of liberty
> I'll spend in pleasure and in dalliance,
> That Faustus' name, whilst this bright frame doth stand
> May be admitted to the furthest land.
>
> (III.i.836-842)

The reference to pleasure and dalliance has no obvious connection to the Pope's triumph, nor does it logically follow that such dalliance should bring Faustus fame. However, the lapse in ordinary logic emphasizes the emotional links between sexual desire, or dalliance, the desire for fame into which it is deflected, and the connection between both factors and the need to undermine figures of authority through ridicule. For while no appropriate action emerges from the image of dalliance, what emerges instead is the portrayal of a pettily cruel tyrant, who wishes to use Bruno as the foot-stool to his papal throne. The cuckoldry theme, though not expressed through action, is linked to the Pope's humiliation when, after the reference to dalliance, Mephistophilis suggests to Faustus that he may

> . . . dash the pride of this solemnity;
> To make his monks and abbots stand like apes,
> And point like antics at his triple crown:
> To beat the beads about the friars' pates,
> Or clap huge horns upon the Cardinals' heads.
>   (III.i.859-865)

As Mephistophilis and Faustus succeed in rescuing Bruno from the Pope,[3] and mock his spiritual power, Faustus temporarily asserts his superiority to this version of paternal authority, separated as it is from women and sexuality. However, that authority will overwhelm him most fully at the time he most closely approaches women and sexuality.

The cuckoldry theme reappears, still separated from, but now juxtaposed to, an image of women when Martino announces Faustus's intention to show the emperor all his progenitors, and to "bring in presence of his Majesty / The royal shapes and warlike semblances / Of Alexander and his beauteous paramour" (IV.i.1167-1172). This mention of a heterosexual couple brings immediately in its wake a reference to Benvolio, through whom the cuckoldry theme will be most fully articulated. As Faustus dares to "pierce through / The ebon gates of ever-burning hell" (IV.i.1224) in order to entertain the Emperor, the thrice-repeated line, "Great Alexander and his paramour," resonates through the dumb-show in which the shade of Alexander kills Darius, places his crown upon his paramour, and embraces her; it echoes as well in the Emperor's longing to see the mole on her neck. Though doubly distanced, this action represents the closest approach so far to that pleasurable dalliance Faustus has so desired. This distanced satisfaction is linked to cuckoldry when Benvolio, who has mocked, "and

thou bring Alexander and his paramour before the Emperor, I'll be
Actaeon and turn myself into a stag" (IV.i.1256), wakes to find his
now enhorned head caught in the window-frame.[4] The cuckoldry motif
acquires menacing tones by being articulated through the myth of
Actaeon, who was turned into a stag and dismembered by his hounds
for having stolen a glimpse of Diana naked. The association of cuckoldry with dismemberment, which in turn prefigures the hellish punishments Faustus is to incur, explains the tentative and uneven approach
to the issue of sexuality we have observed. As Faustus moves into contact with actual women or female spirits, even though they are distanced from him by being associated with other men, references both to
cuckoldry and to dismemberment develop in crescendo proportions.
This interweaving suggests that Faustus, to approach sexuality, must
encounter an image of himself not only humiliated but also dismembered. The comic sequence here displaces onto other figures the price
which Faustus, in the final tragic action, will pay for his glimpse of
Helen.

All the action between this sequence and the next serious demonstration of Faustus's power turns on these motifs. Benvolio, in revenge
for having been humiliated, cuts off Faustus's "false head," vowing
that he will "nail huge forked horns" on it, and Faustus turns the tables
by enhorning the heads of Benvolio and his companions so that they
must slink into obscurity to hide the disgrace of their "brutish shapes."
This action slides into the episode of the horse-courser, which recalls
the Actaeon image when the horse-courser thinks he has robbed the
sleeping Faustus of his leg. The horse-courser and carter episodes elide
with the Robin and Dick plot line when Faustus disposes of all those
figures in the Duke of Anholt's court, where he also, for the first time,
experiences domestic warmth. When the duke appears with his pregnant wife, Faustus gently attends to her, and seeks to please her by
sending Mephistophilis to fetch grapes from the other side of the world.
As he meanwhile demonstrates his knowledge of the globe's seasons,
that rather charming domestic episode brings him, in the sequence of
the drama, to the brink of his damnation.

Before discussing the last episode, however, I should note that so far
the uses Faustus has made of his pact with the devil have been as innocent as possible. Despite Faustus's desire for twenty-four years of
lasciviousness, there have been neither sexually suggestive episodes

nor references to behind-the-scenes sexuality. Despite his aspiration for power over all worldy potentates, Faustus has only saved Bruno from a tyrannically cruel Pope, entertained the Emperor by showing him a vision of Alexander and his paramour, and brought the Duchess a bunch of grapes. It would seem that the most damnable thing he has done is to anticipate modern technology by getting grapes out of season and by achieving an aeriel view of the world.

The forbidden knowledge and power he so desired has been used either trivially or generously; he hardly seems to have become an evil man, and the last episode in the court of the Duke of Anholt suggests only gentle domesticity. That disproportion between the relatively benign naturalist portrait of Faustus and the aura of the damnable which surrounds him casts into relief the significance of the last episode, which places Helen, the first realization of the long-promised sexual pleasure and the immediate cause of his damnation, not in distant places but in the domestic comfort of Faustus's home. That home is characterized by lovingly attentive friends, at whose request he first raises the apparition of the "peerless dame of Greece." Her appearance takes on an intimacy and an immediacy to Faustus's ordinary life lacking in the other episodes, and that domesticity, in combination with Helen's more than mortal beauty, suggests an alternative to the Christian heaven. But that alternative heaven is also associated with sexually fraught contention: "No marvel though the angry Greeks pursued / With ten years' war the rape of such a queen / Whose heavenly beauty passeth all compare" (V.i.1698-1701).

The association of Helen with strife might be attributed only to the traditional tale were it not that the aura of contention that she carries intensifies and becomes part of Faustus's personal drama.[5] Just as Helen, unlike the other sensual figures, enters into Faustus's domesticity, so now does the warning voice approach Faustus not in the relatively abstract form of a good angel, but in the unexplained but quite naturalistic form of the Old Man. With his appearance the elements previously suggestive of Faustus's fears of woman and sexuality take dramatic shape. The Old Man's words, their force increased by the lack of circumstance to explain his appearance, carry tones of affectionate paternal concern—he calls Faustus "gentle son." Though he does not mention Helen, his entry immediately after her first appearance suggests that his intense description of Faustus's evil flows from

Helen's appearance. He says,

> O gentle Faustus, leave this damned art,
> This magic, that will charm thy soul to hell,
> And quite bereave thee of salvation.
> Though thou hast now offended like a man,
> Do not persever in it like a devil.
>   (V.i.1706-1709)

Though he refers to magic in general, the image of its power to "charm thy soul to hell" carries forward the resonance of the images surrounding Helen, and the last quoted lines suggest that all that has gone before can be regarded as ordinary, or manly, offense, but that only Faustus's traffic with Helen makes him "like a devil."

The aura of diabolic sexuality associated with Helen comes into sharper focus when the Old Man says,

> For, gentle son, I speak it not in wrath,
> Or envy of thee, but in tender love,
> And pity of thy future misery.
> And so have hope, that this my kind rebuke,
> Checking thy body, may amend thy soul.
>   (V.i.1719-1723)

Since Faustus is not at the moment satisfying his bodily desires, the warning words, "checking thy body," can only function to highlight Faustus's sexual desire for Helen. The vision generated by the Old Man's words centers the play's most extreme polarity around the figure of Helen. On the one hand, she is associated with the most dire imaginings of unspeakable hellish pain, while on the other hand she is associated both with the bliss of an alternate heaven and with a kind of domestic peacefulness. That ironic disparity heightens the portrait of Faustus as a man for whom the sexual has become so permeated by a sense of evil and fear of punishment that it has swept into its orbit all related areas of life—all association with women and the comforts of domesticity. The drama can be seen in this light as Faustus's uneven efforts to reclaim that lost area of his humanity, interpreted by him as diabolical. His approach to Helen, his most daring and most direct

approach to the sexual, consequently releases the most horrendous images of inner corruption and of avenging fury, both in the Old Man's
distinctly paternal appearance, and in supernatural threats.

Since for Faustus the theological heaven excludes so much that is
ordinarily human, it is small wonder that he cannot quite manage a
repentence that would leave him in the state of emptiness implied at
the play's beginning. Though he is moved by the Old Man's words,
which "comfort [his] distressed soul," instead of remaining in the
protective presence of this seemingly benevolent figure, he sends him
away, leaving himself more vulnerable to Mephistophilis's powers. In
a sense he chooses Helen along with the fearful punishments and the
self-loathing he associates with her. Mephistophilis threatens that if
Faustus should revolt from Lucifer he will "in piecemeal tear thy
flesh," as Actaeon was dismembered by his hounds, and as Faustus
will finally be dismembered, but for having claimed rather than for
having disclaimed Helen.

Faustus's vision of Helen finally fulfills the promises of "four and
twenty years of dalliance." Once again signing a pact in blood, this
time Faustus explicity trades his soul for Helen's kiss:

> One thing, good servant, let me crave of thee,
> To glut the longing of my heart's desire—
> That I may have unto my paramour
> That heavenly Helen which I saw of late
> Whose sweet embraces may extinguish clean
> Those thoughts that do dissuade me from my vow,
> And keep my oath I made to Lucifer.
> (V.i.1759-1765)

If one leaves aside the moral obliquy that surrounds necromancy, and
if one sees the supernatural and diabolic contexts in which she appears
as expressive of Faustus's interpretation of his sexual longings as diabolic, and of his consequent inability fully to actualize an image of a
woman's body, the scene itself renders heightened erotic passion with
an almost Lawrentian mystique. Helen's incredible beauty suggests an
alternative to Christian immortality, and to her kisses is attributed a
kind of sexual transcendence: "Her lips suck forth my soul: see where it
flies." The line may have been intended to show the demonic power of
the spirit, but naturalistically it renders an orgasmic passion that

Faustus immediately associates first with the challenge of another man, and then with a heroic version of courtly love. He says,

> Come, Helen come, give me my soul again.
> Here will I dwell, for heaven is in these lips,
> And all is dross that is not Helena.
> I will be Paris, and for love of thee,
> Instead of Troy, shall Wittenberg be sack'd;
> And wear thy colours on my plumed crest:
> Yea, I will wound Achilles in the heel,
> And then return to Helen for a kiss,
> O, thou art fairer than the evening's air
> Clad in beauty of a thousand stars;
> Brighter art thou than flaming Jupiter
> When he appear'd to hapless Semele;
> More lovely than the monarch of the sky
> In wanton Arethusa's azured arms:
> And none but thou shalt be my paramour!
>
> (V.i.1772-1787)

After expressing his love in the image of her encompassing beauty, he imagines himself struggling for her. But he seems also to imagine himself in struggle with paternal images to achieve her, since he thinks of himself as Paris fighting Menelaeus. Aside from the fact that Menelaus, as a king, becomes an elevated paternal image, and that Paris is a king's son, such a reading is supported by two details. First, Faustus adds rather needlessly that "Instead of Troy, shall Wittenberg be sack'd." Since at the beginning of his necromantic career he envisioned himself as Wittenberg's protector, directing spirits to "wall all Germany with brass, / And make swift Rhine circle fair Wittenberg," his desire now to see Wittenberg destroyed places his desire for Helen in opposition to the service of his city. The implication is that he equates himself with the son-like prince Paris, whose violation of the older man's marital rights resulted in Troy's destruction. Second, his desire for Helen is further linked to his challenge to paternal authority when the Old Man, who has already acquired paternal force, re-enters just as Faustus declares his love. Though the Old Man previously claimed that it was not from envy that he warned Faustus against Helen's enchantments, his reappearance at just this moment suggests exactly that.[6] These details together suggest that Faustus's desire for

Helen is embedded in the oedipal fears earlier suggested by Pride's speech, which he momentarily overcomes in his vision of an heroic courtly union with her. He envisions himself wearing her colors on his crest, and returning to her for a kiss, a kiss which elides with the domestic when he compares her beauty to that of the "evening air"—a contrast to the morning in which he previously envisioned beautiful paramours coming to his bed. Though the heterosexual vision is distanced by Helen being defined as spirit rather than as body, and by her beauty being compared to Jupiter's rather than to Semele's (as in the previous image of the fairest courtesans), the passage as a whole overcomes the psychological barriers to an imaginative knowledge of heterosexual love.

Faustus has won his moment of freedom, the one kiss that is all that he realizes of the limitless sensual pleasure he anticipated. He has challenged but not dispersed the fears and dark associations that cling to images of heterosexuality. The naturalistic rendering of the scholars, who maintain their loving friendliness toward Faustus even when told of his pact with the devil, and his benevolent concern for them, contrast startlingly with the aura of damnation, highlighting the disparity between the sense of evil evoked by the good and bad angels, and the naturalistic portrayal of a genially benevolent man who has broken out of his scholarly monasticism to kiss a girl. Since most of the action is supernatural, to naturalize it is necessarily to see it as representing the psychic consequence of Faustus's association of evil and guilt with the sexuality he has chosen.[7] He does not experience himself as having chosen Helen and the domestic aura that she brings in her wake, but rather as being compelled by unknown forces that pull him down when he thinks he wants to "leap up to my God." Either way, he experiences himself as castrated, impotent, dismembered; Lucifer will tear him apart if he submits to God or if he does not, and submission to God represents a filial abasement to a paternal authority that equates sexuality of any kind with forbidden knowledge, civic destruction, and eternal torment. He tries to find a middle way between a heaven occupied by an angry father and the gaping jaws of a hell that contains the "devil and his dam"[8] by seeing himself absorbed into an undifferentiated mist.

He struggles to evade the polarities evoked by his desires for and his fear of women by retreating from the impossible alternatives of an oedipal struggle to an infantile, preindividualized, state. After the angels show him visions first of the heaven he has lost, and then of the torments of hell, which must be "[his] mansion, there to dwell," he sees Christ's blood streaming in the firmament. That disembodied air-born vision still carries the restrictive definitions of heaven, and so he experiences himself pulled down by an unknown force. Next he pleads to become a "foggy mist" drawn "Into the entrails of yon lab'ring cloud" so that his soul might, like smoke, rise to heaven. He abandons the compromise flight toward the father when he imagines first his soul dispersed into the great round of metempsychosis, then the insensibility of beasts, and finally the total loss of self when he desires that his soul "be changed into little water-drops, / And fall into the ocean, ne'er be found!" (V.ii.1927-1980). But that strategy fails, for his sense of himself, a self that has risen from peasant origins to high prestige, will not succumb to a de-individuating oral merger. Instead he chooses hell and heterosexuality rather than yield to a heaven that contains only a forbidding God. Thought of in this way, the tragedy is not that Faustus is damned, but that he thinks himself damned for his desires, even as he claims them.

I am not arguing that Marlowe intended Faustus's damnation to be perceived in this way, though it is quite possible that he did so. I am arguing that a naturalized version of events that are defined as supernatural makes the contrast between the fierce supernatural condemnation of Faustus and the relatively benign figure that emerges when we see Faustus naturalistically revelatory of the psychological consequences of holding such beliefs. The play remains a rendering of those consequences whether Marlowe himself held those beliefs, wrote the play to expose them, or was hampered in the latter project by remnants of the former.

NOTES

1. All citations are to *Doctor Faustus* in *The Complete Works of Christopher Marlowe*, 2, ed. Fredson Bowers (Cambridge: Cambridge University Press, 1973). Though I have used the B text, the A text bears out substantially the same interpretation. Most of the passages on which I rely appear in both texts, but in subsequent notes I will indicate where the variations in the texts alter the emphasis (For the A text I

use *The Works of Christopher Marlowe,* ed. C. F. Tucker Brooke [Oxford: Clarendon Press, 1910]).

2. Constance Brown Kuriyama, in *Hammer or Anvil, Psychological Patterns in Christopher Marlowe's Plays* (New Brunswick, N. J.: Rutgers University Press, 1980), pp. 95-136, uses evidence like this to argue for a previously homosexual association with necromancy. While I do agree that homosexual elements are strong in the play, I believe the strongest struggle depicted is toward the heterosexual.

3. This reference, based on a story in Foxe's *Book of Martyrs,* to a rival for the papal diadem might, as has been suggested, also be seen as a veiled reference to Giordano Bruno, whose challenge to church authority in general could be expressed in this way. If that is what Marlowe intended, then the action in which Faustus and Mephistophilis rescue Bruno from the Pope might be seen as Marlowe's devious way of supporting the magic for which Faustus seems condemned, against orthodoxy as represented by the Pope. If one reads the sequence that way, it augments the argument that the tragedy is not that Faustus was damned, but rather that he succumbed to conventional attitudes toward damnation. To read the play in this way involves supposing that Marlowe constructed the play as a psychomachia. Many aspects of the play make that thesis plausible, particularly the appearances of the good and bad angels, and of the Old Man, and it would make the play into a very sophisticated psychological analysis of the mechanisms by which institutional authority maintains itself through engendering deep-seated guilt. That is the direction in which this reading tends, but I think it more likely that Marlowe's ambivalence appears in the two readings that the end makes possible. The reference to Bruno, however, does not appear in the A text, and its authenticity has been questioned, but the argument for the psychomachiac reading remains plausible on the other grounds.

4. In the A text the cuckoldry motif appears more subtly; while Benvolio's counterpart grows horns, he is not stuck in the window frame, and Robin says to Rafe that "my master and mistress shall find that I can read, he for his forehead, she for her private study: she's borne to beare with me, or else my Art fails" (938-940). On the other hand, the theme of dismemberment gets greater emphasis. Robin, while using Faustus's conjuring books to make "al the maidens in our parish dance at my pleasure stark naked before me," tells Rafe to "keep out, or else you are blowne up, you are dismembered, Rafe" (933-935). Also, Wagner echoes Pride's speech when he says to the Clown that he will "turn al the lice about thee into familiars, and they shal teare thee in peeces" (378-380).

5. It might be said that when Faustus brings a woman into his all-male but tranquil domestic life, all hell breaks loose.

6. The Old Man might be seen as appropriately punished for prying into Faustus's sexual life when he says that Satan begins to "sift me" in his pride.

7. Seen in this way, the two theolgoical puzzles that emerge from the final action appear in a different light. Those puzzles are, first, that despite the doctrine stated in the play that repentance can never be too late, Faustus's damnation after his glimpse of Helen seems inevitable. The old man, after witnessing that scene, gives up on him, declaring "Accursed Faustus, miserable man, / That from thy soul exclud'st the grace of Heaven, / And Fliest the throne of his tribunal-seat!" (V,i,1739-42), and the good angel, though in a tone of sad lament rather than of glee, concurs with the bad angel in the inevitability of Faustus's damnation. Sec-

ond, the doctrine of free will is undermined by hints of determinism when Mephistophilis reveals that he "damned up" Faustus's passage to heaven, that he actively sought Faustus and was not passively called to him, a deterministic suggestion that is echoed when Faustus blames "the stars that reign'd at [his] nativity," the parents that "engender'd [him]" and Lucifer, as well as himself, for his damnation. These disparities show the theological concerns of the play warped by the psychological pull of the protagonist who, confronted with a vision of Heaven void of women and inhabited by an angry, father-like God who seems an extension of the Old Man, and a Hell full of torture and torment but nonetheless containing images of women, chooses the latter.

8. The A text omits the "devil and his dam," making slightly less overt the link between hell and heterosexuality, but it includes a passage that gives a much more emotionally full sense of self-disgust and loathsomeness in association with Helen when the Old Man, pleading with Faustus to mend his ways, says,

> Break heart, drop blood, and mingle it with tears,
> Tears falling from repentent heavinesse
> Of thy most vilde and loathsome filthinesse,
> The stench whereof corrupts the inward soule
> With such flagitious crimes and hainous sinnes
> As no commiseration may expel.
>
> (1277-1282)

Sex, Politics, and Self-Realization in *Edward II*

CLAUDE J. SUMMERS

In *The Dramatist and the Received Idea,* Wilbur Sanders excoriates both the "manifest crudities" of *Edward II* and the "unholy fascination" that the play exercises on many readers. Ostentatiously cloaking himself in the mantle of morality and mental health, Sanders accuses those critics who admire the play of succumbing to a "fascination with disease," of indulging their "curiosity about the fringes of human sanity." As a critical tactic, Sanders's demagoguery is deeply offensive yet amusingly provincial. The provinciality is apparent when he deplores "the fascination exercised by a psychological aberration which is also intelligent and articulate" in order to dismiss Tennessee Williams as well as Marlowe.[1] The critical reductiveness of Sanders's argument is made obvious simply by juxtaposing against his fulminations the more receptive responses of such sensitive readers as Harry Levin, Clifford Leech, Eugene Waith, Irving Ribner, Purvis Boyette, and Judith Weil.[2] Nevertheless, there is a sense in which the excessiveness of Sanders's reaction to *Edward II* is instructive. In Sanders's passionate unease with Marlowe's play, one can detect symptoms of that neurotic condition known as homophobia, the fear and loathing of homosexuality. Awareness of homophobia enables us not only to place in perspective the morality-mongering that characterizes Sanders's response and that colors the work of some other critics,[3] it also allows us to understand an important subtext of *Edward II* and to redefine those "manifest crudities" that Sanders deplores as contributory elements in the play's revolutionary vision.

The radicalism of *Edward II* resides in the play's intersection of sex and politics and in Marlowe's refusal to moralize either. Critics have long noted that Marlowe's history play differs significantly from those by Shakespeare in its failure to promulgate a political lesson compatible with Tudor orthodoxy. As Ribner observes, "Marlowe sees no pattern in history simply because . . . he does not see in history the working out of a divine purpose, and therefore he cannot see in it any large scheme encompassing God's plans for men and extending over many decades."[4] Although Marlowe skillfully uses conventional sixteenth-century religio-political concepts and beliefs for specific dramatic effects, the political world of *Edward II* simply is not the divinely ordered state envisioned by *The Mirror for Magistrates* or the Elizabethan Homilies. The world of the play is one where to succeed politically, "You must be proud, bold, pleasant, resolute, / And now and then, stab as occasion serues" (ll. 762-763).[5] The failure to envision a providential history has been seen by some readers as a serious defect in *Edward II*, while it has been excused by others on the grounds that what engaged Marlowe's imagination was not politics but the personal tragedy of an individual who happens to be a king.[6] It seems to me that both views are wrong. Rather than constituting either a flaw or an irrelevancy, the refusal to moralize history is at the heart of both the play's profound political heterodoxy and the personal tragedy of the king.

More heterodox even than the play's refusal to subscribe to a comforting Tudor political myth is its resolute failure to condemn homosexuality. Marlowe's presentation of homosexual love in casual, occasionally elevated, frequently moving, and always human terms is unique in sixteenth-century English drama. Marlowe's daring in this regard can be appreciated only in the context of the deep horror aroused by homosexuality in Renaissance England. Written in a period during which homosexual practices were invariably denounced as unspeakable and as the source of corruptions that threatened church and state alike, when sodomy was routinely linked with heresy and sorcery and considered a violation of natural order and treason "against the King Celestial or Terrestial," and when sodomy was punishable by death and the confiscation of property, *Edward II* is remarkable precisely because it fails to echo such condemnations.[7] Indeed, while the word "unnatural" occurs frequently in the play to describe rebellion and anarchy and dissembling, it is never applied as a sufficient definition of homosexuality; and in appending the names of Edward and Gaveston to a roll-call of famous homosexual lovers—Alexander and Hephaestion, Hercules and Hylas, Patroclus and Achilles, Cicero and Octavius, Socrates and Alcibiades, Jove and Ganymede—the play counters its Christian context with a classical locus in which homosexuality is accepted as part of the wholeness of personality. By humanizing homosexuality, Marlowe implicitly attacks the hysteria that characterizes the religious, legal, and popular attitudes of his day. Seen against the normative values of the age, Marlowe's play is, as Purvis Boyette has persuasively argued, "seditious and demonic," designed to "make an enemy of every dogmatic moralist."[8]

It is difficult to overstate the significance of *Edward II* in the history of literary depictions of homosexuality, yet it is equally important not to regard the play as simply a liberal defense of sexual freedom. While Marlowe refuses to condemn homosexuality, he complicates the relationships of Edward and his lovers, presenting them ambiguously rather than merely sympathetically. The king's willful attachment to his lovers clearly accounts for his failure as a king and culminates in his gruesome murder, making him finally a martyr to his passion. But Edward's martyrdom encompasses more than his victimization as a lover or even his failure as a king. By redefining received ideas about both sex and politics, Marlowe's history play resonates with implications that transcend neat categories and question comfortable assumptions. On the surface, Edward's tragedy seems simple enough, rooted as it is in the conflicts between the roles an individual must play in the world. What complicates the tragedy and gives it radical significance is that Marlowe depicts a universe whose meaning is gradually contracted into solipsism. In *Edward II*'s world of egotism and opportunism, value finally inheres only in self-realization, a process complicated by the tyranny of circumstance and the conflicts of identity. In the play, characters are torn not merely between the private and public roles that they are called upon to play, but by a fundamental confusion of their social and real identities.[9] And it is in this insight that sex and politics intersect, for the king's tragedy is neither simply personal nor yet providential. Ultimately, it is a tragedy of existential loneliness, in which the king's conflicting identities are reconciled only in his brutal murder.

Marlowe systematically devalues social relationships of all kinds by depicting in *Edward II* an unstable world of competing wills. Indeed, the word *will,* rich in connotations of sexuality as well as unbridled political power, resounds throughout the work. "Ile haue my will" (l. 78), Edward declares upon his first appearance, "I will haue *Gaueston*" (1.96). When he humiliates the Bishop of Coventry, Edward enjoins Gaveston to "make him serue thee as thy chaplaine. / I giue him thee, here vse him as thou wilt" (ll. 195-196); and when he installs his lover in the Queen's royal chair, Edward announces, "It is our pleasure, we will haue it so" (l. 304). Regarding his kingdom as his personal property to dispose of as he chooses, he throws open the national treasury to his friend and gives him the royal seal, authorizing him to "commaund, / What so thy minde affectes or fancie likes" (ll. 169-170). Rather than lose his will, Edward declares, "This Ile shall fleete vpon the Ocean, / And wander to the vnfrequented Inde" (ll. 344-345). His concept of sovereignty is simply to "triumph . . . with his friends vncontrould" (l. 1697). But what is more remarkable even than the fact that the King's absolutism is foreign to English political ideals is that it is actually a mirror of the willfulness that characterizes everyone in the play, nobles, bishops, and commoners alike. Edward's willfulness is tellingly echoed by Mortimer at the peak of his power: "Mine enemies will I plague, my friends advance, / And what I list commaund" (ll. 2398-2399).

The political conflict in *Edward II* does not grow from a philosophical difference as to the proper balance of power exercised by the monarch or the peers in an ideal commonwealth. Instead, the conflict is a more restricted, even petty competition of egos. For all their patriotic speeches, the nobles are actually concerned only with the triumph of their own narrowly conceived self-interest, which is consistently defined in terms of jealousy and pride. In their rebelliousness, Marlowe's barons are, as in Holinshed's orthodox account, "quite estranged from the dutifull loue and obedience which they ought to haue shewed to their sovereigne, going about by force to wrest him to follow their wils, and to seeke the destruction of them whom he commonlie fauoured, wherin suerlie they were worthie of blame."[10] As Mortimer tells his compatriots early in the play, "My lords, now let vs all be resolute, / And either haue our wils, or lose our liues" (ll. 340-341). Similarly, the Archbishop of Canterbury's support for the peers' plan to "banish or behead that *Gaueston*" (l. 250) has little to do with abstract issues or idealism. It too is clearly motivated by self-interest, as the Archbishop acknowledges: "What els my lords, for it concernes me neere, / The Bishoprick of Couentrie is his" (ll. 251-252).

The political instability centered in the competition of king and peers is itself part and parcel of a larger social instability that mirrors a fundamental identity crisis. In *Edward II* the elaborate map of the English class system, with lines drawn to separate the peasant from the commoner and the gentleman from the noble and all from the monarch, is in the process of erosion. Thus, the barons' objection to Gaveston (and, later, to Spencer) has nothing to do with morality and everything to do with class. Most simply, they are determined not to be "ouerpeerd" (l. 314). As Mortimer confesses to his uncle, Edward's sexual infatuation for Gaveston "greeues not me, / But this I scorne, that one so baselie borne / Should by his soueraignes fauour grow so pert" (ll. 699-701). He resolves that "whiles I haue a sword, a hand, a hart, / I will not yeeld to any such vpstart" (ll. 719-720). The nobles repeatedly refer to Gaveston's "baseness"; they characterize him and the Spencers as "upstarts" and "flatterers"; and they self-servingly urge the king "To cherish vertue and nobilitie, / And haue old seruitors in high esteeme" (ll. 1476-1477). In conflict with the peers' disdain for one who is "hardly a gentleman by birth" (l. 324) is the king's will: "Were he a peasant, being my minion, / Ile make the prowdest of you stoope to him" (ll. 325-326).

The class-consciousness of the barons is a reactionary response to the threat of social mobility as epitomized in the precipitous rise of a "night-growne mushrump" (l. 581). In the brave new world of class conflict mirrored in the play, Gaveston mocks Lancaster, who "hath more earldomes then an asse can beare" (l. 292), and scorns the "Base leaden Earles that glorie in your birth" (l. 876), taunting them to "Goe sit at home and eate your tenants beefe" (l. 877). Similarly, the scholar Baldock announces that his gentry is "fetcht from Oxford, not from Heraldrie" (l. 1046), prompting the king's response, "The fitter art thou *Baldock* for my turne" (l. 1047). In fact, the entire concept of nobility is attacked by Edward's insistence that "The head-strong Barons shall not limit me. / He that I list to fauour shall be great" (ll. 1065-1066), and by the self-seeking that motivates all manner of men to attempt the main chance. Thus, Edward promiscuously drapes his friends with titles and honors, even providing money for Spencer Senior to purchase land, the traditional power base of the nobility; thus, everyone in the play sniffs the prevailing currents to determine how they may "aduance vs while we liue" (l. 729). In *Edward II*, the promise of social mobility challenges the traditional assumptions of a natural congruence between social and real identity.

Marlowe's interest in depicting a world of social fluidity and class conflict compels his deliberate departure from Holinshed and history in making Gaveston a commoner and Spencer a servant. The historical Gaveston was "the son of a loyal and prominent Gascon knight and a natural born liegeman of the Crown,"[11] while the Spencers were members of the secondary nobility who eventually came to lead the royalist party. By reducing their origins and presenting their rise in stark contrasts, Marlowe effectively captures a dizzying sense of freedom in the escape from a prescribed social status. Gaveston exults as the play begins, "Farewell base stooping to the lordly peeres, / My knee shall bowe to none but to the king" (ll. 18-19). Moreover, the low origins of the favorites help explain the element of self-seeking that clouds their relationships with Edward. Gaveston's potential for manipulation is obvious in his plan to recruit "wanton Poets, pleasant wits, / Musitians, that with touching of a string / May draw the pliant king which way I please" (ll. 51-53), while Spencer graphically outlines his program for advancement in his conversation with Baldock, whom he advises to "learne to court it like a Gentleman" (l. 752). Significantly, however, the ambitiousness of the king's favorites is no different from the self-seeking that characterizes everyone. Most important of all, the reduced state of the favorites makes vivid the play's insistent contrast of social identity and real identity, and its concomitant elevation of the latter at the expense of the former. Hence, the homosexual attraction that makes plausible the king's attachment to a low-born "dapper jack" and a servant is finally revealed as the most constant emotion in the play even as it endangers Edward's social identity as king.

Another index of the instability of social roles in *Edward II* is the importance paid to appearance. Throughout the play, reference is made to the necessity of "seeming." Because social status is based on no real substance, clothing becomes a defining characteristic of social identity. Spencer tells Baldock that his "curate-like" attire and demeanor are not likely to "get you any fauour with great men" (l. 761), and urges him to "cast the scholler off" (l. 751). Baldock confesses that his puritanical garb is merely a mask, that he is "inwardly licentious enough" (l. 770), focusing attention on the discrepancy between social and real identity in the play. Mortimer, who bitterly complains that the king and his favorite "laugh at such as we, / And floute our traine, and iest at our attire" (ll. 714-715), tellingly objects to Gaveston's extravagant dress on the grounds that it violates his sense of reality: the "proud fantastick liueries" of Gaveston and his friends "make such show, / As if that *Proteus* god of shapes appearde" (ll. 707-708). He also ridicules as incongruous Edward's appearance in the field: "thy souldiers marcht like players, / With garish robes, not armor, and thy selfe / Bedaubd with golde, rode laughing at the rest" (ll. 985-987). Most poignantly, the metamorphosing power of clothing is evoked when Edward, imprisoned in the sewers of Berkeley Castle and clad in tattered robes, remembers his earlier costume: "Tell *Isabel!* the Queene, I lookt not thus, / When for her sake I ran at tilt in Fraunce" (ll. 2516-2517). The defining quality of clothing is also attested by the disguises of Mortimer, Edward, Spencer, and Baldock, all of whom don "fained weeds" in an attempt to escape unfeigned woes (l. 1964). Precisely because social status is conceived as a merely arbitrary circumstance of birth, unconnected either with virtue or accomplishment or providence, superficial appearance becomes both a temptation to protean aspiration and a telling reminder of the insubstantiality of social identity in a rootless society where rigidly prescribed roles are under attack.

The social instability that Marlowe depicts in *Edward II* infects relationships and institutions that might be thought of as intimate, and therefore insulated from the political turmoil. The church, for example, is secularized into a foreign power allied with the nobles for its own worldly ends. The intervention of the papal legate prompts Edward's question "Why should a king be subiect to a priest?" (l. 392) and inspires his fierce but ineffectual threat against "Proud Rome" (l. 393):

"Ile fire thy crased buildings, and enforce / The papall towers to kisse the lowlie ground" (ll. 396-397). Similarly, the institution of marriage is robbed of any sacramental sanctity by Edward's planned union of his niece and his lover and by the nature of his own marriage, a relationship that the king and Isabella both exploit for political advantage. Indeed, the conventional familial attachments—husband and wife, brother and brother, and even mother and son—are all questioned in the play, despite the elaborate lip-service they receive.

The familial roles are revealed to be other manifestations of social identity at variance with real identity. For all her protestations of love for Edward, Isabella betrays her husband and finally endorses his murder. Edmund, who is significantly both the least selfish and most unstable character in the play, perhaps both a choric weathervane and a trimmer,[12] turns against his brother ("No maruell though thou scorne thy noble peeres / When I thy brother am reiected thus" [ll. 1019-1020], he fumes when Edward refuses to banish Gaveston) only to reverse himself later and to pay with his life for his belated loyalty. And, finally, the young Edward III orders his mother's imprisonment, pointedly remarking "If you be guiltie, though I be your sonne, / Thinke not to finde me slack or pitifull" (ll. 2649-2650). While Edward III's refusal to be swayed from duty by personal considerations functions primarily to contrast with his father's failure in this regard, the imprisonment of his mother also symbolizes the collapse of even the most intimate of socially sanctioned attachments. The world of *Edward II* is one in which all social, political, and familial relationships are called into doubt. The social identities defined by such roles as husband and wife, brother and son, and king, queen and lord are insufficient to summarize the real identities of complex individuals.

It is precisely because the world of *Edward II* is so unstable that the language of the play so frequently rings hollow. The hollowness of language becomes a measure of impotence when Edward's histrionic assertions of absolutism are followed by meek capitulations to the demands of his enemies. "Ye must not grow so passionate in speeches" (l. 1763), the self-consciously politic Mortimer warns Isabella. But language is equally devalued when it becomes merely a medium for dissembling. "But yet it is no paine to speake men faire, / Ile flatter these, and make them liue in hope" (ll. 42-43), Gaveston remarks of the three poor men who accost him in the first scene, voicing a sentiment that is repeated throughout the play. "It bootes me not to threat, I must speake faire" (l. 358), Edward comments upon assessing the power of the nobles and the Archbishop; "I must entreat him, I must speake him faire" (l. 479), Isabella echoes in reference to Edward. The king's niece requests her uncle to "speake more kindly to the queene" (l. 1029), an injunction Gaveston seconds: "My lord, dissemble with her, speake her faire" (l. 1030). This web of dissembling culminates finally in the treachery of Mortimer and Isabella, who prove to be the play's most accomplished hypocrites, the characters who most successfully clothe their "policy" in fair speaking. Again, the contrast between what individuals say and what they do reflects the identity crisis in which everyone in the play participates, as they are torn between what is socially acceptable and what is self-fulfilling.

An important function of the pervasive hypocrisy in *Edward II* is to rob ideals of patriotism and social concern of any meaning. Characters frequently appeal to ideals that they habitually violate, transforming such concepts as honor and duty and allegiance into mere catchwords to color the truth. Mortimer acknowledges this fact when, following a *pro forma* genuflection to the "realms behoofe" (l. 540), he confesses that "howsoeuer we have borne it out, / Tis treason to be vp against the king" (ll. 577-578). Thus, when Mortimer explains Isabella's sinister plan to recall Gaveston in order to have him murdered, his words reek of hypocrisy and devalue the very concepts to which he appeals: "This which I vrge, is of a burning zeale, / To mend the king, and do our countrie good" (ll. 553-554). The emblems prepared by Mortimer and Lancaster, adorned with Latin mottoes threatening Gaveston, eloquently contradict their pretense of reconciliation ("Can you in words make show of amitie, / And in your shields display your rancorous minds?" [ll. 834-835], Edward asks pointedly), just as their execution of the favorite "flatly against law of armes" (l. 1430) belies their pretense to honor. Similarly, the stirringly patriotic appeals of the elder Spencer, who leads an army "Sworne to defend king *Edward's* royall right" (l. 1344), are undercut by his admission of self interest. Indeed, all the patriotic slogans mouthed in the play are mere "preachments," and none are more hollow than those of Isabella, whose cynical evocations of Tudor orthodoxy reveal her rank opportunism rather than any faith that "Succesfull battells giues the God of kings / To them that fight in right and feare his wrath" (ll. 1805-1806).

In the unsettled world of *Edward II* traditional values are meaningless and force and violence are the ultimate realities on earth. In this
world where social identity habitually contradicts real identity, where
dissembling is the norm, the most powerful preaching is the silence
that emanates from bodyless heads set upon poles "for trespasse of
their tongues" (l. 118) and the incoherent shriek of pain that issues
from the hapless king and raises the town. From the very beginning of
the play, the hollow appeals to empty ideals are punctuated by brutal
threats that eventually find fruition in violence. On his first appearance, Edward tells Lancaster, "The sworde shall plane the furrowes of
thy browes, / And hew these knees that now are growne so stiffe" (ll.
94-95), a threat to which the baron replies in kind:

> Adew my Lord, and either change your minde,
> Or looke to see the throne where you should sit,
> To floate in bloud, and at thy wanton head,
> The glozing head of thy base minion throwne.
> (ll. 130-133)

Later, Edward conjures his own vision of dismembered body parts
floating in a sea of blood when he is roused to action by the murder of
Gaveston:

> I will have heads, and liues for him as many
> As I have manors, castels, townes, and towers.
> Tretcherous *Warwicke*, traiterous *Mortimer*:
> If I be Englands king, in lakes of gore
> Your headles trunkes, your bodies will I traile.
> (ll. 1441-1445)

Echoing the advice earlier proffered by Edmund, Spencer urges the
king to attack the nobles: "Strike off their heads, and let them preach
on poles" (l. 1326). In the conflict of wills depicted in the play, concern
for "Englands honor, peace and quietnes" (l. 1670) actually figures not
at all. Edward vows that "rather then thus be braude, / [I will] Make
Englands ciuill townes huge heapes of stones" (ll. 1522-1523). The
promiscuous threats and pervasive images of dismemberment finally
yield their fulfillment in the beheadings of Gaveston, Warwick, Lancaster, the Spencers, Baldock, and Mortimer, and in the unspeakable

murder of the king performed "a brauer way" (l. 2369).

In this world of social instability and corruption, where traditional sources of meaning are bankrupt and violence is the ultimate reality, the imagination strains to escape the limitations of circumstance. As Sara Munson Deats notes, *Edward II* "abounds with implicit and explicit allusions to metamorphosis."[13] Throughout the play, characters imagine alternatives to the petty world in which they are trapped, seeking fervently if impotently to transform realities that impinge on their happiness or safety or sense of self. Gaveston conceives elaborate, Italianate spectacles designed to translate the dour English court into a homoerotic theater in which pages become nymphs and men satyrs. Warwick compares him with Phaeton, who "Aspir'st vnto the guidance of the sunne" (l. 312). Edward, according to his enemies, wastes the realm's wealth in "idle triumphes, maskes, lasciuious showes" (l. 959). Complaining of her husband's attachment to a male lover, Isabella wishes "That charming *Circes* walking on the waues / Had chaungd my shape" (ll. 468-469). When Edward is defeated on the battlefield, he entertains the possibility of a "life contemplatiue" (l. 1887), while Leicester enjoins him to "Imagine Killingworth castell were your court, / And that you lay for pleasure here a space" (ll. 1988-1989). The motif of attempted metamorphosis encompasses as well Edward's investiture of his friends and enemies with titles and offices. "I here create thee Lord high Chamberlaine" (l. 154), the king declares as he attempts by force of will to transform a peasant into an earl. The fervent desire to alter reality expresses the need to make congruent the social and real identities that are at war within the characters.

But in *Edward II*, such congruence is impossible. The concept of the protean self—so pregnant with possibilities—becomes finally a measure of limitations rather than aspiration, of entrapment rather than freedom.[14] For despite all the attempted metamorphoses, whether through willfulness, imagination, clothing, or social fluidity, reality prevails and individuals are unable to reconcile conflicting identities. Characters remain entrapped in the prisons of their own circumstances and their own selves. It is here that sex and politics intersect in the personal tragedy of Edward II, for he can escape neither his real identity as expressed most fully in his love for Gaveston nor his social identity as defined by his hereditary role as king. When Edward tells the peers that "none but rude and sauage minded men, / Would seeke the ruine of my *Gaueston*, / You that are noble borne should pitie him" (ll. 373-375), Warwick retorts: "You that are princely borne should shake him off" (l. 376). But Edward can no more shake off Gaveston than he can abdicate the throne, though were the choice available, there is no doubt that he would choose love before monarchy, as he indicates several times in the play. Yet even after he is deposed, Edward remains a king, and hence a threat to his enemies and the target of their wrath. Central to Marlowe's tragic vision is the irony that the man who would not be king is imprisoned and murdered precisely because he cannot escape being king. Edward's fantasy of discarding the kingdom for "some nooke or corner left, / To frolike with my deerest *Gaueston*" (ll. 367-368) finds its ironic fulfillment in the hellish reality of a dungeon where he is the object of Lightborn's sadistic lust, and all because of the circumstances of his birth.

If the tragic dilemma faced by Edward can be seen in terms of the familiar conflicts of duty and pleasure, honor and love, Marlowe complicates these choices and radicalizes his play by devaluing such concepts as duty and honor even as they unavoidably frame his protagonist's catastrophe. Although Edward's failure as monarch is a direct result of his devotion to love and pleasure, it is even more clearly a result of his lack of interest and skill in the brutal game of "policy" practiced so well by Mortimer and Isabella. In the deposition scene, Edward asks "yet how haue I transgrest, / Vnlesse it be with too much clemencie" (ll. 2109-2110), a question that at once reveals his lack of political astuteness and also acknowledges his refusal to practice the brutality necessary to maintain power (as in his failure to execute Mortimer when he had the opportunity). Because the political world of *Edward II* is an amoral arena in which conflicts pivot on the manipulation of raw power, the failures of the protagonist account for his fall without providing a sufficient context for assessing his character. Edward's tragedy is rooted not merely in his political defeats, but most profoundly in his confused identity. By the end of the play, the notion of the sacredness of kingship has been robbed of whatever force it may have possessed in the beginning, but in divesting Edward of his royal robes, Marlowe revels a suffering individual whose existential loneliness and divided self haunt the imagination.

Edward's confused identity is apparent in the questions he persistently asks: "Am I a king and must be ouer rulde?" (l. 135); "shall the crowing of these cockerels / Affright a Lion?" (ll. 1005-1006); "Rebels, will they appoint their soueraigne / His sports, his pleasures, and his companie?" (ll. 1483-1484). These questions, and many similar ones throughout the play, reveal not only Edward's political naïveté and frustration, but also how uncertain he is of his own identity. Moreover, they pinpoint the discrepancy between his social identity as a king and his real identity as a man. The conflict between these identities coalesce in his devotion to his favorites, who are inappropriate companions for him as a king, but essential for him as a man.

In the identity confusion of the protagonist, Marlowe locates in homosexual love the world well lost, for the play pivots on Edward's choice of love "Despite of time, despite of enemies" (l. 1456). The necessity of choosing between love and a hostile world is explicitly evoked. At the beginning of the play, Gaveston declares his love for "The king, vpon whose bosome let me die, / And with the world be still at enmitie" (ll. 14-15). Later, Mortimer asks, "Why should you loue him, whome the world hates so?" (l. 371), and Edward replies in a beautifully simple affirmation: "Because he loues me more then all the world" (l. 372). This is not mere hyperbole, for Gaveston does love Edward more than all the world. He rejects the invitation to "share the kingdom" (l. 2), finding "bliss" and "felicitie" only in the king's embraces.[15] Gaveston's lack of interest in political power makes ironic the objections of the nobles, but by devaluing the political world (and social identity in general), he intensifies the king's identity confusion.

Significantly, Edward's love for Gaveston is conceived as a project of self-discovery, for however inescapably Edward is a king, his kingship cannot fully define who he is. His attachment to Gaveston represents freedom from responsibility and escape into a world of eroticism at variance with his social identity, but it is also, and more fundamentally, a quest for selfhood and wholeness. For Edward, self-realization is inextricably linked to communion with another, specifically with Gaveston, to whom his soul is knit (l. 1535). Thus Gaveston is both a person of sacred worth and a mirror in which the king sees reflected his own possibilities of selfhood. The function of the men as mirror images of each other is suggested by the emphasis on sight in their love-making. "I haue my wish, in that I ioy thy sight" (l. 151), the king exults. Later, when they are forced to part, the men exchange portraits, and

Edward requests "leaue to looke my fill" (l. 435). When the barons capture Gaveston, they render him "deuorsed from King *Edwards* eyes" (l. 1170); and the king fervently pleads to "see him before he dies" (l. 1205). In Gaveston's eyes, Edward finds not a mirror for magistrates but a reflection of his own deepest self. The completeness of the lovers' identification with each other is obvious at the beginning of the play when the king asks of Gaveston, "Why shouldst thou kneel, knowest thou not who I am?" (l. 142). He answers his own question: "Thy friend, thy selfe, another *Gaveston*" (l. 143). When his friend is exiled, Edward tells him, "Thou from this land, I from my selfe am banisht" (l. 414). Clearly, Edward's love for Gaveston defines his inner reality more fully than does his hereditary role as king.

In the terrifying and pitiful conclusion of the play, when Edward is bereft of both his crown and his friends, he is reduced to the bare, forked animal, unaccommodated man. In his incessant preoccupation with his crown and his friends in these final scenes, he attempts to analyze himself, to understand the conflicting facets of his identity and how he has come to his harrowing place. He is tormented by his failed kingship and the pathos of his suffering is intensified by the fact that "a king brought vp so tenderlie" (l. 2453) should be subjected to such mental and physical anguish. "The greefes of priuate men are soon allayde, / But not of kings" (ll. 1994-1995), he exclaims, and compares himself to a gored lion, who rends and tears his wounded flesh. Pressed to abdicate, he rages, lapsing into madness, signifying the collapse of an integrated self.[16] Upon the threat that "the prince shall lose his right" (l. 2078), he resigns the crown, the symbol of his social identity. "Make me despise this transitorie pompe" (l. 2094), he prays, and adds: "if I liue, let me forget my selfe" (l. 2097). Having been deprived of his friends, his kingship assumes greater importance than ever, and he never ceases thinking of himself as "Englands king," marveling that "Within a dungeon Englands king is kept, / Where I am steru'd for want of sustenance, / My daily diet is heart breaking sobs, / That almost rents the closet of my heart" (ll. 2284-2287). The tenacity with which he clings to his social identity in his final hours is directly related to the loss of real identity he feels in the execution of his friends.

More terrifying for Edward than deposition is the loneliness resultant on the loss of his friends. When Spencer and Baldock are arrested, he offers his life for theirs. "Here man, rip vp this panting brest of mine, / And take my heart, in reskew of my friends" (ll. 1933-1934), he pleads. His offer spurned, he requests his captors to take him away in a hearse, so meaningless does life seem to him without friends, and "friends hath *Edward* none, but these, and these, / And these must die vnder a tyrants sword" (ll. 1958-1959). Even his poignant acknowledgment in the deposition scene of the play's harsh political reality—"what are kings, when regiment is gone, / But perfect shadowes in a sun-shine day?" (ll. 2012-2013)—acquires intensely personal resonance, highlighting the division within his personality, for it echoes his early devaluation of kingship in favor of love for Gaveston: "for but to honour thee, / Is *Edward* pleazd with Kinglie regiment" (ll. 164-165). And as he is cruelly shaved with cold puddle water, his mind wanders to his friends:

> O *Gaueston*, it is for thee that I am wrongd,
> For me both thou and both the *Spencers* died,
> And for your sakes, a thousand wronges ile take.
> (ll. 2306-2308)

Edward's murder is indeed a martyrdom for his friends, and for his choice of passion over power. Approached by Lightborn, as intimate and solicitous as a lover, the lonely king offers his visitor his sole remaining jewel in a pathetic attempt to save his life. "Know that I am a King" (l. 2537), he whispers, and then surrenders with dignity to the inevitable. "I am too weake and feeble to resist" (l. 2556), he acquiesces, resigning himself to his fate. In yielding to Lightborn's sadism, Edward concurs in the bleak perception voiced earlier by Gaveston "that heading is one, and hanging is the other, / And death is all" (ll. 1198-1199). But in the sensational manner of Edward's death there is something different, for in his murder the king's divided self is finally unified and an extraordinary catharsis is effected.

Neither merely gratuitous violence nor simply a grotesque parody of homosexual lovemaking and still less the embodiment of a moralistic and "ferocious concept of justice,"[17] the debasement of the king meaningfully joins the opposed worlds of eroticism and political violence, crystallizing in a single act the divisions of Edward's personality. The execution brilliantly illuminates the conflict between Edward's real identity as a lover and his social identity as a king, and validates

his choice of love over power. The "anal crucifixion" combines elements of sexual desire and violent "policy" into a horrible triumph of
the will. In so doing, it forcefully juxtaposes the world of erotic freedom
and sexual fulfillment represented by Edward's love for Gaveston and
the cynical world of power politics symbolized by the union of
Mortimer and Isabella, whose love "hatcheth death and hate" (l.
1801). As Boyette writes, "the fiery apocalypse of Edward's execution
'purifies' the King in the brutally violated image of his sexual
pleasure. . . . For its psychological insight, this image may be the
most important Marlowe ever constructed."[18] In the intersection of sex
and politics in his murder, Edward is transformed into a tragic victim
of his divided self. Yet he is not merely a victim, for his agonizing cry
raises the town and helps effect the restoration of order and distribution of justice on which the play ends.

But despite the fall of Mortimer and the rise of Edward III in the
final scene, Marlowe's play offers little consolation. His depiction of
the world as a solipsistic universe challenges received ideas too
completely to be ideas to be displaced by the perfunctory restoration of
order in the final scene. In his refusal to moralize either sex or politics,
Marlowe subverts conventional attitudes, presenting a world without
anchors in a divinely ordained commonwealth or in traditional social
values. As J. B. Steane notes, in Marlowe's play "the self is all there
is."[19] In this existential world, individuals define themselves, and yet
they are not free, limited as they are by circumstance and divisions
within their own personalities. Marlowe's dramatization of the search
for self within a universe divorced from providential aid and shaped by
the ferocious conflict of wills is deeply disturbing.

But the obstacles to self-fulfillment make the quest all the more ur-
gent, and herein lies Marlowe's positive vision. In his struggle for self-
realization and in his tragic suffering, Edward attains a human dignity
that robs the play of any potential nihilism. Although Marlowe mocks
the moralists who would justify a ruthless competition of wills with
preachments or who would choose power before love, he also goes beyond mockery to make us, as Leech notes, deeply conscious of a shared
humanity.[20] There is in fact nothing in *Edward II* to justify Sanders's
accusation that Marlowe is motivated by an "impulsion to 'do dirt on
humanity'."[21] In exploring the dilemma of the divided self, Marlowe
discovers value in the frustrating quest for individual wholeness. For

all his radical iconoclasm and brutal honesty, the playwright places himself in a venerable humanist tradition. However unsettling *Edward II* is to dogmatic moralists, and indeed to everyone, its portrayal of the divided self cannot be smugly dismissed as a manifestation of disease. The pathos of Edward's fully human dilemma and the courage of his struggle are at once affecting and disturbing and enlightening.

NOTES

1. Wilbur Sanders, *The Dramatist and the Received Idea* (Cambridge: Cambridge University Press, 1968), p. 141. Presumably, Sanders would also discount the work of such artists as Proust and Forster, to mention only two among dozens of writers whose explorations of homosexuality have similarly been distorted by moralistic critics into expressions of pathology.

2. Harry Levin, *The Overreacher* (Cambridge, Mass.: Harvard University Press, 1952), pp. 82-105; Clifford Leech, "Marlowe's *Edward II*: Power and Suffering," *Critical Quarterly*, 1 (1959), 181-196; Eugene M. Waith, "*Edward II*: The Shadow of Action," *Tulane Drama Review*, 8 (1964), 59-76; Irving Ribner, *The English History Play in the Age of Shakespeare* (London: Methuen, 1965), pp. 123-133; Purvis Boyette, "Wanton Humour and Wanton Poets: Homosexuality in Marlowe's *Edward II*," *Tulane Studies in English*, 12 (1977), 33-50; and Judith Weil, *Christopher Marlowe: Merlin's Prophet* (Cambridge: Cambridge University Press, 1977), pp. 143-169.

3. Homophobia vitiates the discussions of *Edward II* in, for example, the following books: Douglas Cole, *Suffering and Evil in the Plays of Christopher Marlowe* (Princeton, N.J.: Princeton University Press, 1962); Charles G. Masinton, *Christopher Marlowe's Tragic Vision* (Athens: Ohio University Press, 1972); John P. Cutts, *The Left Hand of God* (Haddonfield, N. J.: Haddonfield House, 1973); and William L. Godshalk, *The Marlovian World Picture* (The Hague: Mouton, 1974). The recent psychoanalytic study by Constance Brown Kuriyama, *Hammer or Anvil: Psychological Patterns in Christopher Marlowe's Plays* (New Brunswick, N. J.: Rutgers University Press, 1980), is not explicitly homophobic in its discussion of *Edward II*, but its naïve and inacccurate concept of homosexuality (based on a discredited 1962 study of psychiatric patients) is fundamentally homophobic. See my review in *Journal of English and Germanic Philology*, 81 (1982), 254-258.

4. Ribner, *The English History Play in the Age of Shakespeare*, p. 128.

5. All quotations from *Edward II* follow the text of C. F. Tucker Brooke, ed., *The Works of Christopher Marlowe* (Oxford: Clarendon Press, 1910).

6. On Marlowe's use of religio-political beliefs for dramatic effects, see Claude J. Summers, *Christopher Marlowe and the Politics of Power* (Salzburg: Universität Salzburg, 1974), pp. 155-186. In a recent essay, James Voss argues that the type of state depicted in *Edward II* is fundamentally incompatible with the traditional order, a view with which I am in full agreement. See James Voss, "*Edward II*:

Marlowe's Historical Tragedy," *English Studies,* 63 (1982), 517-530.

In additon to Sanders, J. B. Steane also seems to regard the play's refusal to envision a providential history as a defect; see Steane, *Marlowe: A Critical Study* (Cambridge: Cambridge University Press, 1965), pp. 222-223. Among recent studies that stress Marlowe's interest in the personal tragedy of an individual who is only coincidentally a king are the following: Levin, *The Overreacher;* Leech, *"Edward II:* Power and Suffering"; and Cole, *Suffering and Evil.* A better position is that of Voss, who writes: "The tragic pattern of *Edward II* both shapes and is shaped by fundamental political forces which seize control of the English state and begin to transform it. . . . The tragic confrontation which destroys Edward is not the collision of individual personalities alone, but also the clash of incompatible ways of life, opposing types of state order, and contrary systems of values and ideas" (*"Edward II:* Marlowe's Historical Tragedy," pp. 518-519).

7. The quotation is from Edward Coke, *The Third Part of the Institutes of the Laws of England* (London, 1644), p. 37, as cited in Alan Bray, *Homosexuality in Renaissance England* (London: Gay Men's Press, 1982), p. 117. Bray's book, though brief and sometimes debatable in its details, is the best survey yet attempted of Renaissance attitudes toward homosexuality. Bray is especially good in documenting the disparity between the myths about sodomites and the commonplaces of homosexual behavior, and the discrepancy between sexual action and psychological awareness which was particularly glaring in the absence of a homosexual subculture. As Bray points out, in the Renaissance sodomy generally did not denote a specific sexual identity or relate to a particular kind of person, but was considered a temptation to which all men were subject and a symptom of universal dissolution. In this context, Marlowe's intuition of sexuality as a defining characteristic of personality is all the more remarkable.

Other books that trace medieval and Renaissance attitudes toward homosexuality include John Boswell, *Christianity, Social Tolerance, and Homosexuality: Gay People in Western Europe from the Beginning of the Christian Era to the Fourteenth Century* (Chicago: University of Chicago Press, 1980); and Derrick Sherwin Bailey, *Homosexuality and the Western Christian Tradition* (New York: Longmans, Green, 1955). Boswell's masterful history demonstrates that ecclesiastical and civil hostility toward homosexuality becomes dominant only in the twelfth century, but that by the end of the Middle Ages, it is almost unchallenged. The casualness of Marlowe's portrayal of homosexuality has misled many readers into thinking that Renaissance attitudes toward the subject were "broadminded" (see, for example, John M. Berdan, "Marlowe's *Edward II,"* *Philological Quarterly,* 3 [1924], 197-207). While it is true that classical influence led to some positive depictions of homoeroticism in the final decade of the sixteenth century (*e.g.,* the sonnets of Richard Barnfield and William Shakespeare) and that non-hysterical references to homosexuality abound in the works of some seventeenth-century dramatists and poets (usually, in a satirical context), the nonmoralistic tone of Marlowe's play is unique. Drayton's attitude, for example, is strikingly different in his "Peirs Gaveston" and *Mortimeriados.* For a comparative study, see Scott Giantvalley, "Barnfield, Drayton, and Marlowe: Homoeroticism and Homosexuality in Elizabethan Literature," *Pacific Coast Philology,* 16 no. 2 (Nov. 1981), 9-24.

8. Boyette, "Wanton Humour and Wanton Poets," p. 33. For a discussion of homosexuality in the context of Marlowe's evolving concept of love, see Leonora Leet

Brodwin, "*Edward II*: Marlowe's Culminating Treatment of Love," *ELH*, 31 (1964), 139-155. The following two essays focus on Marlowe's treatment of sex roles: Sara Munson Deats, "*Edward II*: A Study in Androgyny," *Ball State University Forum*, 22 no. 1 (Winter 1981), 30-41; and Barbara J. Baines, "Sexual Polarity in the Plays of Christopher Marlowe," *Ball State University Forum*, 23 no. 3 (Summer 1982), 3-17.

9. In using the terms *social identity* and *real identity*, I am borrowing from the Jungian approach to identity used by James P. Driscoll, *Identity in Shakespearean Drama* (Lewisburg, Pa.: Bucknell University Press, 1983). Driscoll distinguishes four categories of identity: social, real, conscious, and ideal identities. Conscious identity refers to a character's ruling conceptions about himself; real identity encompasses a character's actual strengths and weaknesses and the values and drives that actually motivate him and constitute his unique individuality; social identity includes the conceptions the society within a play holds of a character and is frequently defined by social roles, family obligations, class expectations, and political offices; ideal identity subsumes the tensions between conscious, real, and social identity and constitutes wholeness, a willingness to live—consciously and authentically—the real identity. In *Edward II,* the identity crisis centers largely on the conflict between social and real identity, and to simplify terminology, I use those terms to the exclusion of conscious and ideal identity; obviously, however, the more elaborate schema could also be employed and applied.

My intent is not so much to relate Jungian concepts of identity to *Edward II* as to locate the play's identity confusions (and depiction of homosexuality and political turmoil) within a context of the new Renaissance interest in the integrity of the self. The following two essays focus on the issue of self-realization in Marlowe: Stephen J. Greenblatt, "Marlowe and Renaissance Self-Fashioning," in *Two Renaissance Mythmakers: Christopher Marlowe and Ben Jonson*, ed. Alvin Kernan (Baltimore: Johns Hopkins University Press, 1977), pp. 41-69; and Henry Herring, "The Self and Madness in Marlowe's *Edward II* and Webster's *The Duchess of Malfi*," *Journal of Medieval and Renaissance Studies*, 9 (1979), 307-323. Relevant, too, is Voss's view of *Edward II* as embodying a conflict between a traditional way of life and a "nontraditonal lifestyle consciousness" that "makes subjective experience and the pursuit of inner fulfillment—in this case pleasure for the most part—and personal achievement the central categories of individual orientation in the world" ("*Edward II*: Marlowe's Historical Tragedy," p. 523).

10. Raphael Holinshed, *Chronicles of England, Scotland, and Ireland* (London: J. Johnson et al., 1807-08), II, 587.

11. A. R. Myers, *England in the Late Middle Ages* (Baltimore: Penguin, 1952), p. 2. Holinshed describes Gaveston as "an esquire of Gascoine" (*Chronicles*, II, 539).

12. Levin describes Edmund as "a sort of weathervane whose turnings veer with the rectitude of the situation" (*The Overreacher*, p. 98); Boyette, on the other hand, writes that Edmund "appears more and more to be something of a trimmer" ("Wanton Humour and Wanton Poets," p. 38). Steane finds Edmund a "weathercock" without the authority to fill the office, since he shares in the "general littleness" of the play (*Marlowe: A Critical Study*, pp. 214-215). I find Boyette's and Steane's analyses more in keeping with the tenor of the play than Levin's.

13. Sara Munson Deats, "Myth and Metamorphosis in Marlowe's *Edward II*," *Texas Studies in Literature and Language*, 20 (1980), 315. Deats's article is especially useful

in its careful analyses of the implications of the mythological allusions in the play.

14. Eugene Waith notes that "the most powerful feelings in *Edward II* are aroused by the desire to break out of some constriction—a desire which increasingly seems doomed to disappointment" ("*Edward II*: The Shadow of Action," p. 179). Marjorie Garber writes persuasively of the dramatic tension that results from "the dialectic between aspiration and limitation" in Marlowe's plays ("'Infinite Riches in a Little Room': Closure and Enclosure in Marlowe," in *Two Renaissance Mythmakers*, pp. 3-21; the quotation is from p. 3).

15. For a stimulating discussion of this point, see Michael Goldman, "Marlowe and the Histrionics of Ravishment," in *Two Renaissance Mythmakers*, p. 25.

16. See Herring, "The Self and Madness in Marlowe's *Edward II* and Webster's *The Duchess of Malfi*," especially pp. 307, 313-315.

17. Sanders, *The Dramatist and the Received Idea*, p. 124. For a similar, crudely moralistic interpretation of the murder, see Masinton, *Christopher Marlowe's Tragic Vision*, pp. 108-112.

18. Boyette, "Wanton Humour and Wanton Poets," p. 49. The term "anal crucifixion" is also Boyette's, p. 47.

19. Steane, *Marlowe: A Critical Study*, p. 223. Steane voices this conclusion with an air of disappointment, but Marlowe's concern with the integrity and strength of the self can be seen more positively, as in Herring's essay, "The Self and Madness in Marlowe's *Edward II* and Webster's *The Duchess of Malfi*."

20. Leech, "*Edward II:* Power and Suffering," p. 174. On the play's tragic effect, see also Glynne Wickham, *Shakespeare's Dramatic Heritage* (London: Routledge and Kegan Paul, 1969), pp. 204-212; Weil, *Merlin's Prophet*, pp. 167-169; and Elizabeth S. Donno, "*Admiration* and *Commiseration* in Marlowe's *Edward II*," *Neuphilologische Mitteilungen,* 79 (1978), 372-383.

21. Sanders, *The Dramatist and the Received Idea*, p. 140.

Marlowe's Fearful Symmetry
in *Edward II*

SARA MUNSON DEATS

Critics have almost universally praised the structure of *Edward II*, al-though they differ concerning the dramatic principle controlling the events.[1] Yet, few commentators have noted that the play opens and closes with two similar rituals, the funeral of an older Edward and the assumption of royal power by an heir of the same name.[2] (Although Edward III has been crowned earlier, until the final scene his authority is titular rather than actual.) In this essay, I seek to demonstrate that the funerals of the two older Edwards and the ascensions to power of the two younger Edwards provide a frame within which events occurring in the first half of the play (Acts I and II) are repeated with variations and altered emphases in the last half of the drama (Acts IV and V). Moreover, like a mirror image, the structural progression of the drama is reversed in the second half of the play; and the series of parallels and contrasts developing in obverse order create a dramatic chiasmus,[3] as demonstrated in the diagram on the following page. Through this symmetry, the falls of Edward, Mortimer, and Isabella are anticipated in their rises, and the events of the last movement of the drama are bound by a chain of causality to the actions and words of the opening movement. Fortunately, this symmetry is not rigidly procrustean.

A	I.i.	Funeral, Ascension, Confrontation
B	I.i.	Foreshadowing of Edward II's death, associated with bribery, shows
C	I.i.	Stripping, Imprisoning, Humiliation of the Bishop
D	I.iv.	Edward II cannot prevent Gaveston's banishment
E	I.iv.	Mortimer and Isabella conspire to kill Gaveston
F	II.ii.	Edward II loses political support
G	II.iv.-III.i.	Edward II flees from Mortimer and the Barons Edward II is separated from Gaveston Gaveston is taken away to execution
X	III.iii.-IV.iii	Period of victory for Edward II
G	IV.v.-vi.	Edward II flees from Mortimer and the Queen Edward II is separated from Spenser Spenser is taken away to execution
F	V.i.	Edward II loses his crown
E	V.ii.	Mortimer and Isabella conspire to kill Edward II
D	V.iv.	Edward III cannot prevent Kent's execution
C	V.i.-iii.	Stripping, Imprisoning, and Humiliation of Edward II
B	V.v.	Edward II's death, associated with bribery, shows
A	V.vi.	Funeral, Ascension, Confrontation

Marlowe avoids the tyranny of diagrammatic reduction by the flexibility with which he varies his juxtapositions through both comparision
and contrast, counterpoising not acts or scenes but scenic sequences or
units.[4]

This symmetry of antithetical or parallel sequences correlates with a
simultaneous movement of alternating rises and falls, whereby Edward's ascent and descent are augmented by a series of additional *de
casibus* exempla:[5] the rise and fall of Gaveston (first section of the play),
the rise and fall of Spencer and Baldock (middle section), the rise and
fall of Mortimer and the Queen (final section). These multiple ascensions and declensions balance one another, particularly those of Edward and Mortimer: Edward's initial increase in power is counter-
pointed by Mortimer's corresponding loss of authority
—although until III.iii the struggle between the two adversaries
more closely resembles a tug-of-war than a ride on a rotating
wheel—whereas later, as Edward plummets, Mortimer mounts. An
ancillary movement further complicates this pattern; throughout the
play, temporal success proves antithetical to spiritual growth.[6] Political authority—in Edward, Gaveston, Spencer, Baldock, Mortimer,
and Isabella—invariably engenders ruthlessness; only when they decline from power do some of the figures—Edward, Gaveston, Spencer,
Baldock—begin ethically to ascend. Although the young Edward III
provides an optimistic exception to this grim rule, generally in the play
all rise temporally to fall spiritually, and only in falling from worldly
success do they rise to a limited ethical maturation. In analyzing
Marlowe's careful, even awesome fashioning of historical events in *Edward II,* I do not wish to ignore this traditionally accepted design.
Rather, I postulate a symmetrical arrangement of parallels and antith-
eses complementing the larger pattern of ascent and descent.

Marlowe's great history play opens with Edward II's joyous,
epistolary welcome to Gaveston—"My father is deceased. Come, Gaveston, / —And share the kingdom with thy dearest friend" (I.i.1-2)—and
closes with Edward III's dolorous lament:

> Sweet father, here unto thy murdered ghost
> I offer up this wicked traitor's head,
> And let these tears, distilling from mine eyes,

Be witness of my grief and innocency.
                          (V.vi.99-102)[7]

The dénouement of the play deftly parallels and contrasts with the opening scene, the drama concluding as it begins, with the obsequies of a deceased King Edward and the assumption of royal power by a young King Edward. Furthermore, in both the initial and final scenes, a young King Edward, surrounded by his nobles, confronts a Machiavellian overreacher (Gaveston, Mortimer) who attempts to control the presumedly pliant young monarch, thereby threatening the order of the realm. But here the likeness ends, for although the circumstances may be similar, the two Edwards reflect reverse images of kingship. Young Edward II rejoices in his father's demise, appears unconcerned about the deceased King's funeral, wrangles with his nobles, defies his dead father's fiats, and allies himself with the presumptuous overreacher against his peers. Conversely, young Edward III mourns his father's death, honors the former king with appropriate services, and seeks the "aid and succor" of his nobles in executing the hubristic Machiavel, thus demonstrating his allegiance to his murdered father's cause. In the initial scene, the obsequies of Edward I (like the distorted rites so deplored by Hamlet) are replaced by a kind of mock marriage between Edward and Gaveston; the final scene re-establishes decorum as Edward III extirpates the source of rebellion and, attired in funeral robes, commemorates his dead father with appropriate rites. Between the violation of ceremony in Act I, scene i, and the restoration of proper ritual in Act V, scene vi, there unfolds a drama of blatant remissness, usurpation, war, torture, and murder. However, the symmetry discernible beneath the apparent anarchy of the play's kaleidoscopic action reminds the audience of the pattern underlying the chaos and adumbrates the ultimate reinstatement of order.

The similarities and differences in the two framing scenes might be effectively accentuated through duplicate staging.[8] Edward III and his retinue might assume the identical posture and placement of Edward II and his nobles, with Mortimer imitating Gaveston's initial position and stance. Similarly, the antipodal responses of the two Edwards to their fathers' deaths might also be highlighted through stage action, gesture, and posture. Edward III's mourning robes, if donned onstage, would not only symbolize the young monarch's *rite de passage*,[9] but would also contrast vividly with his father's lavish, perhaps Italianate garb, so scorned by the very masculine Mortimer.[10] Moreover, Edward III's rejection in the final scene of his supplicating, probably kneeling mother reverses Edward II's passionate welcome in the opening sequence of the kneeling Gaveston. More significantly, the tableau of the grieving young king, probably bowing with bent knees before his father's bier, perhaps even kissing his murdered father's lips as he did in Toby Robertson's moving TV production,[11] sharply inverts Edward II's initial embrace, and probable kiss, of the returning Gaveston. In shaping to his own dramatic ends the material rough-hewed by history, Marlowe frequently telescopes historical time. By juxtaposing Edward II's murder with Mortimer's arrest—events actually separated by three years—and counterposing these events with the funeral and confrontation in Act I, Marlowe clearly delineates the contrast between the two reigning Edwards.[12]

Not only the resolution but the penultimate scene of the drama is forecast in the rich, resonant opening sequence. The Actaeon-Dian masque described in Gaveston's second soliloquy (I.i.50-73), one of the most provocative passages in the play, emblemizes the entire action of the drama as well as foreshadowing Edward's death. The sensuously evocative soliloquy reverberates with innuendoes of sexual and generic ambiguity—the epicene pages clad as sylvan nymphs, the transvestite Dian, the human animal satyrs, the metamorphosed Actaeon—presaging both the regression of human into bestial and the inversion of sexual roles occurring in the play.[13] Bent Sunesen, in an important essay on the symbolic significance of the Actaeon allusion in *Edward II*, interprets Actaeon "peeping through the grove" as prefiguring Edward, who in punishment for his violation of sexual norms is "hounded to death" by the predatory barons.[14] The imagery of the drama—particularly the recurrent metaphors depicting Edward as a hunted animal[15]—does associate the King with Actaeon who, according to tradition, suffered a similar transformation from predator to prey. The action of the play, however, links only one of the fractious nobles (the ruthless Mortimer Junior) with the "hounds" who attack and dilacerate the King. The other nobles may "bark and bite" (IV.iii.13), but they are either unable or unwilling to harm their monarch physically; instead, Edward beheads a number of the barons. Nevertheless, although the analogy is not rigidly exact, the foretelling by the mythological masque of Edward's macabre murder does stress the causal relationship between the King's Actaeon-like excesses and his Actaeon-like catastrophe. Moreover, the passage may ironically presage not only the event of Edward's murder but the actual type of death he will suffer. Gaveston's use of the phrase "seem to die," suggesting the Elizabethan pun for sexual intercourse, implies that the erotic masque may conclude not with a mock murder but with a dramatized rape, perhaps foreshadowing the mode of Edward's slaying, which many commentators see as a grotesque parody of his forbidden sodomy.[16]

Yet like many of the mythological allusions in the play, this proleptic image elicits contradictory associations. On one hand, the Actaeon-Edward parallel accentuates Edward's *hamartia*—his sexual effrontery, his extravagance, and his psychic destruction by animal passion. On the other hand, the analogy emphasizes *Edward II* as a dramatization of one of mankind's archetypal myths, the cleansing of the kingdom and the restoring of order through the sacrificial dismemberment of the scapegoat king. The same myth that educes our disapproving terror also arouses our pity for the tormented victim-king, thereby anticipating our ultimate ambivalent response to Edward's overthrow.[17]

On two occasions in the opening scene, either Gaveston or Edward explicitly associates their relationship with the word "die" (11. 14, 138), and the reiteration of this ominous term reinforces the pervasive mood of foreboding evoked by the Actaeon allusion. Fantasizing his reunion with the King, Gaveston envisions himself swimming Leander-like to his beloved Hero-Edward and dying, assumedly sexually rather than literally, on the King's bosom. Later (1. 138), Edward employs the term with its literal rather than its sexual denotation, vowing that he will "either die or live with Gaveston." The soldier's curse on the haughty upstart, "Farewell, and perish by a soldier's hand" (1. 37)—a malediction fulfilled when the favorite is slain by Warwick's soldiers—adds a third portent to the tragic adumbrations darkening the initial scene of exuberant welcome.

The sinister premonitions in scene i, like Edward's gruesome death in Act V, are connected by context with acts of bribery. Edward II's early attempt to purchase Gaveston's love with titles and estates (I.i.141–170) is mirrored in his final futile effort to ransom his own life with his one last jewel (V.v.83—87). Throughout the play, Edward views allegiance and affection as commodities to be bought and sold, a mercantile mentality vividly dramatized in three parallel episodes. In the opening scene, the King woos the kneeling Gaveston with a plethora of titles and lands; later, in Act I, scene iv, he rewards the temporarily reconciled, dutifully kneeling peers with multiple honors and offices (I.iv.339-362); still later in Act III, he dispenses to his next favorite, the probably kneeling Spencer, the identical titles earlier awarded to Gaveston (III.ii.143-147). The similar blocking suggested by dramaturgical clues, particularly the visual motif of kneeling, could provide a vinculum linking these three parallel instances of obeisance and reward. On yet another occasion, Edward offers Isabella a golden tongue—instead of the physical embrace she craves—as recompense for her eloquent advocacy of Gaveston (I.iv.326-328), and later the King, through Levune, Jove-like seduces the Danaes of the French court to his cause with showers of gold (III.iii.78-87). Finally, in Act V, scene v, the desperate Edward, perhaps himself now kneeling before his erect assassin, attempts a final, this time abortive, financial transaction to save his life.

Gaveston's description in scene i of the "comedies," "Italian masks," and "pleasing shows" with which he manipulates the "pliant" king (I.i.50-56) introduces another motif that pervades the play, lending pathos to Edward's castastrophe. Edward's preference for spectacles, whether comedies, masques, or tournaments, remains a constant of his nature. Characteristically, he celebrates the recall of Gaveston with "a general tilt and tournament" (I.iv.375), an example perhaps of the lavish entertainments that, according to Mortimer Junior, have drawn his treasure dry (II.ii.155-158). Even when the king marches to war, the scoffing Mortimer pictures him as a bedaubed, spangled actor, playing at soldiering (II.ii.180-185). Edward's preoccupation with appearances, like his materialism a determinant in his downfall, survives his purgation through suffering to be pathetically revealed at the moment of his death, when, reminiscing on past glory, he urges Lightborn:

> Tell Isabel, the queen, I looked not thus,
> When for her sake I ran at tilt in France
> And there unhorsed the Duke of Cleremont.
> (Vv.67-69)

These various links binding the ascendant Edward to the fallen one remind the audience that however diametrically our sympathies reverse at the end of the play—and shift they certainly do—Edward dies much as he lived, seeking vainly to buy affection, tragically confusing show and substance.

The two Vice-figures who help to destroy Edward, the sensual Gaveston and the satanic Lightborn, dominate these two scenes, further strengthening the parallel. Lightborn's name recalls the Satan of the Chester cycle and proclaims his lineage from the medieval mystery play.[18] His delight in the mechanics of wickedness, his finely dissembled compassion for the king, and the relish with which he shares his "brave" stratagems with the audience, immediately revealing himself as an agent of evil, further identify his progenitor as the medieval morality Vice. Gaveston is a very different kind of Vice-figure; although he exerts a destructive influence over the King, his opportunism is ameliorated by genuine passion for Edward.[19] Nevertheless, he does lure the King from the strictures of duty into a world of delight (if not of profit), employing the traditional morality temptations of luxury and lechery, exploiting hypocrisy when expedient, and Vice-like announcing his corruptive tactics to the audience upon his first entrance.[20] In the earlier sequence, therefore, Gaveston assumes the role of the medieval tempter-Vice and directs the mock murder; in the later episode, Lightborn, a much more sinister Vice-figure, masterminds Edward's grisly assassination.

Just as Edward's ghastly murder is verbally imaged in Gaveston's mythological masque, so his degradation in Act V is visually imaged in his impetuous disrobing and humiliation of the Bishop of Coventry in scene i. The casting off of the Bishop's miter, the rending of his stole, the confiscation of his house and goods, and his "christening" in gutter water graphically foreshadow Edward's uncrowning, stripping, loss of kingdom, and shaving in ditch water, and the term "channel-water" (*cf.* I.i.188; V.iii.27) provides a verbal nexus connecting these two violent infractions of order and degree.[21] In both instances, a dignitary is first denuded of his headgear and robes, emblems of his regimen, later dispossessed of his actual property, and finally humiliated by an inverted ritual.[22] Although Edward II's protest against the rule of the state by the church (I.iv.96-105) would doubtless have elicited a sympathetic response from an anticlerical Elizabethan audience, in retrospect they should realize that Edward's rash assault upon authority and his sacrilegious distortion of ritual not only anticipate but to some degree precipitate the later, more horrendous violation of established hierarchy.

Another example of royal incapacity in Act I prepares the audience for the turbulence of Act V. Vacillating between defiant willfulness and fretful weakness, Edward II is unable to command his peers and in Act I, scene iv, is overruled by his nobles and cowed into approving Gaveston's banishment. Edward's flagrant negligence in deliberately alienating his barons and prodigally showering titles and estates on his ambitious minion in no way exonerates the equally egregious presumption of the peers, who continually bait the King, insulting him and blatantly disobeying his commands. On several occasions, Kent chorally comments on both of these infractions of order and degree (I.i.116-118, 158-159; I.iv.22; II.ii.94, 144, 206-209). In Act V, scene iv, young Edward III, inheriting from his ineffectual father an unstable rule, is intimidated by the same belligerent baron who bullies his father in Act I. Just as Edward II, impotent before the aggressive peers, proves incapable of protecting his beloved friend Gaveston from exile, so Edward III, equally helpless before Mortimer, the Queen, and their cohorts, cannot save his beloved uncle Kent from execution. Earlier Kent had warned against royal debility; now he experiences the fatal results of his brother's infirm purpose. In dramatizing Kent's arrest and decapitation, Marlowe again adapts history to the demands of dramatic economy and structured symmetry, for historically Kent was not apprehended and executed until three years after Edward II's murder.[23]

Another close parallel counterpoises the conspiracy of Isabella and Mortimer to assassinate Gaveston (I.iv) with their later decision to commit regicide (V.ii). In Act I, scene iv, Isabella solicts Mortimer for the repatriation of Gaveston with "reasons of such weight" that the seemingly intransigent hothead, to the astonishment of everyone (including the audience), agrees to grant her appeal. Mortimer never discloses the import of Isabella's weighty argument, but her private parley with Mortimer results in a plan clandestinely to murder Gaveston on his return, a subterfuge "not thought upon" before Isabella's tête-à-tête with the irate baron. The implication seems clear: the decision to stoop to secret murder is first suggested by Isabella.[24] Toby Robertson's TV film perceptively interprets this scene for its audience, high-lighting Isabella's crucial role in this episode. During much of the bar-ons' deliberation, the camera focuses not upon the anxious peers but upon the conspiratorial conference between Mortimer and the Queen. Later, when Mortimer responds to Lancaster's bemused query, "Ay, but how chance this was not done before?" with the explanation, "Be-cause, my lords, it was not thought upon," the camera again shifts to focus on Isabella, standing on a raised platform, presiding over the ac-tion. During the King's entrance, Isabella continues to direct the scene, superbly performing her role as Patient Griselda, while coach-ing Edward on his appropriate dialogue and the nobles on their proper stage posture: "My gentle lord, bespeak these nobles fair / That wait attendance for a gracious look / And on their knees salute your majes-ty" (ll. 336-338). The startled nobles, their knees, at least according to Edward II (I.i.95), stiff from disuse, perform on cue, kneeling in proper homage before their sovereign. Robertson's camera thereby makes explicit what is only implied in Marlowe's text—Isabella's com-plete control of events.

Similarly, the audience should be aware, although Mortimer is not, that Isabella also orchestrates the latter scene of plotting. Just as the Queen first hints that Gaveston be secretly dispatched, so she first insinuates the necessity of Edward's assassination, warning, "as long as he survives, / What safety rests for us or for my son?" (V.ii.42-43). And just as she directs the staging of the earlier collusion scene, so she later prompts Mortimer's response to Kent as well as to Edward, "Use Edmund friendly as if all were well" (V.ii.79). A quick study, Mortimer "speaks fair" on cue: "How fares my honorable Lord of Kent?" (l. 80). Replicated staging, with Mortimer and Isabella assum-ing similar positions and postures in both conspiracy scenes and Kent imitating Edward's earlier entrance, could clarify the inherent sym-metry of the two episodes, a symmetry easily overlooked by a reader of the play.

Ultimately, therefore, despite Mortimer's boast, "The prince I rule, the queen do I command" (V.iv.48), and the kindly Leicester's similar perception, "What cannot gallant Mortimer with the queen?" (IV.vi.50), in both the earlier and later movements of the play, Isabel-la instigates and dominates the action. Conversely, Holinshed stresses Mortimer's suzerainty over the Queen, and the chronicler's evaluation perhaps provided the source for Leicester's misconception in the play.[25] Although Isabella's second complicity is much less defensible than her first—self-preservation and desperate jealousy motivate one murderous scheme, whereas vindictive spite and perhaps ambition inspire the other—in Marlowe's drama a similar strategy unites the two intrigues. In both cases, Isabella uses others as agents of her revenge, making certain that the murders are performed by hands other than hers. Although her callousness and deviousness increase as the play progresses, demonstrating the corrosive effect of malice on the human spirit, her motivation (spurned love), her goal (revenge), and her techniques (duplicity and insinuation), remain the same. Thus, although Marlowe portrays his rejected and abused Queen sympathetically, he also presages the Machiavellian villainess of the last acts by the early Isabella's dissembling tactics, her skill at manipulating people, and her alacrity in advocating secret murder.[26] The careful symmetry of the two conspiracy scenes further implies a causal connection. In Act I, scene iv, Mortimer and Isabella embark on a career of criminality that leads inevitably to the atrocities of Act V. Moreover, both the causal nexus and the balanced structure derive from Marlowe, not Holinshed. Historically, neither Mortimer nor Isabella participated in the capture and decapitation of Gaveston. In the play, Isabella betrays her rival's whereabouts to the barons (II.iv.37-39) and thus becomes directly responsible for his capture, if not for his execution. Mortimer also participates in Gaveston's capture, although the favorite's actual death is arranged by Warwick. Marlowe departs from his source, implicating Isabella and Mortimer in Gaveston's capture, in order, I suggest, to associate the downfalls of Gaveston and Spencer Junior, as well as to link the conspiracy to assassinate Gaveston with the planned murder of the King.[27]

The open rebellion against Edward II erupting in Act II, scene ii ignites the explosive chain of events that culminate in the King's forced abdication in Act V, scene i, and the stripping process introduced in this scene and continuing throughout the second act parallels Edward's final, painful uncrowning. Following the King's pillorying by the nobles for his egregious failures both to maintain internal order and to defend his country against foreign invasion (II.ii), Edward suffers a series of excruciating losses. In the second scene of Act II, he is stripped of the political support of his peers and presumedly also of the overtaxed commons, whose loyalty to Mortimer shields the Baron from the King's vengeance; in scene iii, he is divested of the allegiance of his brother, the heretofore faithful and wise counselor Kent; and finally, in scene iv, he is deprived of the fealty of his previously adoring if possessive Queen.

These earlier forfeitures are balanced against Edward's final deprivation—the loss of his crown. The King's deposition lament (V.i) resonates with ironic echoes from previous scenes. Earlier, Edward had disregarded his magisterial role, assuring his lover Gaveston: "For but to honor thee, / Is Edward pleased with kingly regiment" (I.i.164-165); now, his royal prerogative becomes the *sine qua non* of his being: "But what are kings when regiment is gone, / But perfect shadows in a sunshine day?" (V.i.26-27). Earlier, he had sworn either to die or live with Gaveston (I.i.138), his second self (I.i.143; iv.118); now his crown replaces Gaveston as the symbol of his identity (V.i.110-111), and its loss becomes a type of psychic murder (ll. 55-57, 145-146).[28] Earlier, the King had virtually ignored the young Prince, relegating the boy to the Queen's care, dismissing his heir more than once as Isabella's son (III.ii.70; IV.iii.41);[29] now *his* son becomes a central concern, at least the ostensible impetus for his abdication.[30]

Despite these glimpses of *anagnorisis*, however, Edward's education through adversity remains incomplete. He never accepts responsibility for his fall. He continues to view himself through a glass darkly, seeing only the hapless victim with his "guiltless life" and "innocent hands" (V.i.73, 98) rather than the culpable agent, sporting in the dalliance of love while the state is overturned. He attributes his destruction primarily to the malice of heaven rather than to his own flaws (ll. 96-97), protesting his loss of kingdom "without cause" (l. 52), acknowledging only one fault, "too much clemency" (l. 123). Moreover, although he denounces the "unconstant queen" who spots his nuptial bed with infamy (ll. 30-31), he appears oblivious of his own adulterous stains. Finally, he never recognizes his irresolution as a critical determinant in his loss of power—clemency and indecision are hardly synonymous. Holinshed's King proves a more apt pupil in adversity's schoolroom, as the very different response of the chronicler's contrite Edward demonstrates:

> after he was come to himselfe, he answered that he knew that he

was fallen into this miserie through his owne offenses, and therefore he was contented patientlie to suffer it, but yet it could not (he said) but greeve him, that he had in such wise runne into the hatred of all his people: notwithstanding he gaue the lords most heartie thanks, that they had so forgotten their receiued iniuries, and ceassed not to beare so much good will toward his sonne Edward, as to wish that he might reigne ouer them.[31]

Iterative imagery combines with source alteration to accentuate the limited awareness of Marlowe's Edward II. In both parallel scenes of divestiture, Edward ironically associates himself with the imperial lion. His initial bravado:

> Yet, shall the crowing of these cockerels
> Affright a lion? Edward, unfold thy paws,
> And let their lives' blood slake thy fury's hunger,
> (II.ii. 201-203)

resounds in his later pathetic vaunt:

> The forest deer, being struck,
> Runs to an herb and closeth up the wounds,
> But when the imperial lion's flesh is gored,
> He rends and tears it with a wrathful paw.
> (V.i.9-12)

By likening himself to the fierce king of the beasts, primate of the animal world, symbol of bestial puissance, the King unconsciously magnifies his own ineffectuality while simultaneously highlighting the lack of self-knowledge demonstrated in these two episodes of impotence and dispossession. Moreover, despite Edward's denial of responsibility, these corresponding scenes, like the balanced sequences discussed above, imply both causality and similarity, inasmuch as Edward's loss of political support leads ineluctably to his deposition.

The series of defections chronicled in Act II, in which Edward in rapid succession loses the fealty of the peers, Kent, and Isabella, culminate in the King's parting from Gaveston in Act II, scene iv, the Gascon's capture in Act II, scene v, and his death in Act III, scene i. This bereavement balances Edward's defeat in Act IV, scene v, and his separation from his second favorite Spencer in Act IV, scene vi. These remarkably parallel episodes of parting and death dramatize several similar events: Edward's flight from Mortimer and his allies (the barons, the Queen) introduces each sequence; the King's separation from a love subject (Gaveston, Spencer) follows each retreat; a plangent lamentation (by Gaveston, by Edward) accompanies each repulse; treachery (by Warwick, by the Mower) delivers each favorite to his enemies; and each episode concludes with the King's beloved friend (Gaveston, Spencer) conveyed away to execution. Surprisingly, each opportunistic self-seeker dies admirably while staunchly affirming his genuine devotion to Edward.

Linguistic reverberations further punctuate the parallelism of the two sequences. Edward's frantic warning in Act II, scene iv:

> Fly, fly my lords, the earls have got the hold,
> (1.4)

is echoed in Spencer Junior's desperate admonition in Act IV, scene v:

> Fly, fly, my lord, the queen is over-strong.
> (ll. 1-2)

Furthermore, Gaveston's lament in Act II, scene i:

> O, must this day be period of my life?
> Center of all my bliss!
> (ll. 4-5)

verbally anticipates Edward's complaint in Act IV, scene vi:

> O, day! The last of all my bliss on earth,
> Center of all misfortune! O, my stars.
> (ll. 61-62)

Character replication reinforces structural and linguistic similarity to unite these two corresponding episodes. The play stresses Spencer's role as a surrogate Gaveston through action, dialogue, and stage gesture. Spencer's stage debut, his colloquy with Baldock (II.i.4-43), imitates Gaveston's second soliloquy (I.i.50-73), both speeches Vice-like announcing the speakers' moral turpitude while revealing their Machiavellian power drives and skill in manipulation. Edward's embrace of the kneeling Gaveston and his dispensation of titles to his French favorite in Act I (i.140-156) is re-enacted in his embrace (III.ii.176) and granting of the very same titles to the probably kneeling Spencer in Act III (ii.143-147).[32] Similarly, Edward's defiant embrace of Spencer before the messenger from the nobles (ll. 176-177) reiterates the King's earlier cruel taunt and embrace of Gaveston in the presence of his spurned spouse (I.iv.167), and similar staging could effectively underscore the dramatic counterpoint.[33]

Marlowe again alters his source to buttress the parallel between the two favorites. First, he deviates from history by involving Isabella and Mortimer in the capture of both Gaveston and Spencer Junior. Secondly, he compresses historical time through Edward's immediate adoption of Spencer Junior as his confidant and lover. Historically, although the younger Spencer very soon replaced Gaveston as the King's Chamberlain, he did not assume close intimacy with the King until some time later. Indeed, according to Holinshed, Spencer Junior was originally preferred through the influence of Edward's nobles and the mourning King "bare no good will at all to him [Spencer] at the first."[34] Holinshed does not clarify how quickly the new Chamberlain insinuated himself into Edward's favor, but he dates the barons' demand for the exile of both Spencers nine years after Gaveston's death.[35] Moreover, the historical Spencers were of noble birth, not the self-made careerists depicted in the play.[36] In portraying Spencer Junior as an unscrupulous social climber, Marlowe further strengthens the resemblance between the two self-serving *parvenus*. These numerous correspondences, although deflating the uniqueness of Edward's affection for Gaveston, also emphasize the King's bereavement. Both beloved friends are taken from him and both are slain.

Wedged between the two central movements of the play—one chronicling the rise and fall of Gaveston, the other, the rise and fall of Mortimer, both detailing the struggles and failures of Edward—occurs a brief period of martial success for the beleagured King (III.iii to IV.iii). During this fleeting ascendancy, his flaccid will temporarily firmed by the power of his grief and the exhortations of Spencer, Edward uncharacteristically chooses the martial over the histrionic, for one brief moment becoming both lion and fox. He displays forcefulness in overcoming his enemies, guile in bribing the French king, and brutality in the mass extermination of his adversaries. Only once in this middle sequence does Edward's determination falter and this crucial failure to insure his triumph over the barons by executing Mortimer dooms him to final defeat.[37] Although the King gives no explanation for his failure to decapitate Mortimer along with Warwick and Lancaster, Edward's earlier dialogue with Gaveston comments on the lack of nerve responsible for this strategic error in judgment. When Gaveston urges Edward to imprison Mortimer in the Tower, the King demurs, "I dare not, for the people love him well" (II.ii.232-233). When faced with a similar dilemma later in the play, as pity impels the support of the Commons to oscillate back to Edward (V.iv.1-5), Mortimer, in many ways Edward's polar opposite, resorts to "secret means" and Machiavellian cunning to remove the threat to his sovereignty. Edward III's resolute, public beheading of Mortimer exemplifies the correct royal response—the honorable ruler need not placate the people nor resort to intrigue—foiling both Edward II's irresolution and Mortimer's treacherous machinations. Again, therefore, Edward II's momentary faltering in Act III, like his fluctuations between weakness and willfulness in Acts I and II, leads directly to the catastrophe of Act V.

Act IV, scene v introduces the third movement of the play, the dramatization of Edward II's lamentable fall and catastrophic death, a movement accompanied by a realignment of audience empathy. Earlier, in Act II, scene ii, the censorious recitation of Edward's royal remissness should decisively estrange audience sympathy from the feckless monarch, with Kent, the spokesman for traditional values, controlling the spectators' response. The period from Act III, scene iii to Act IV, scene iii correlates Edward's political zenith with his moral nadir (like Mortimer's similar equation of temporal ascent with moral decline in Act V), as the King demonstrates both pusillanimity in failing to decapitate Mortimer, the ringleader of the rebellion, and ruthlessness in his great execution through the realm (IV.iii.6-7) of his more vulnerable defectors. Kent again directs audience reaction, condemning Edward as an "unnatural king," who slaughters noblemen and cherishes flatterers (IV.i.8-9). Act IV, scene v effects a countermovement whereby audience support swerves back to Edward. This final alteration is once more guided by Kent, who strips away the patriotic personae of Mortimer and Isabella, revealing a pair of conniving, dissembling solipsists, and the Earl's final change of allegiance is accented by the repetition of the resonant term "unnatural": "Rain showers of vengeance on my cursed head, / Thou God, to whom in justice it belongs / To punish this unnatural revolt" (ll.16-18). Thus introduced, the third movement of the drama will reenact the errors and infractions of the first movement, shifting the stigma of "unnaturalness" from the vanquished King to the compromised Earl and the triumphant Queen and Baron.

The wheel of fortune looms over *Edward II*. Its rotating movement is reflected in the multiple ascents and descents of the various *dramatis personae*; references to its vicissitudes reverbrate throughout the play (IV.vi.53-54, 111; V.v.59-63). Similarly, the glittering sun, primate of the heavenly bodies, traditional symbol for kingship, illumines the play's imagery, its rising and falling carefully coordinated with the ascensions and declensions of the leading historical players. Finally, the royal golden round also glimmers through the play's poetry, offering an apt metonymy for the power so many of the characters desire. The structure of the drama reflects the concentric form of the play's dominant emblems. The final funeral, ascension, and confrontation of Act V will restore the precarious balance violently fractured in the opening scene. A father's funeral will be re-enacted, this time with proper filial mourning; a rebellious upstart will receive appropriate punishment; order will be reinstated. The action of the drama thus brilliantly comes full circle, like the turning wheel of fortune, like the rising and setting sun, like the shining golden round.

NOTES

1. Robert Fricker ("The Dramatic Structure of *Edward II*," *English Studies*, 34 [1953], 204-217) discusses the play in terms of musical themes and rhythms (sostenuto, rubato, etc.), favoring a tripartite structure that begins with the conflict over Gaveston, continues with Edward's revenge, and concludes with a struggle for power in which Edward's fortunes decline as Mortimer's destiny rises and falls. J. B. Steane (*Marlowe: A Critical Study* [Cambridge: Cambridge University Press, 1964], p. 205) praises the symmetry of the play, interpreting *Edward II* as two plays with a middle intermission: the first half tells the story of the homosexual king and his favorite, the second, the rise of Mortimer and the fall of Edward. The two halves, each of which chronicles the failure of Edward, are marked out by a period of success for Edward. Eugene M. Waith ("*Edward II*: The Shadow of Action," *Tulane Drama Review*, 8:4[1964], 60-64) focuses on the *de casibus* motif as

the controlling principle of the play: "A graphic representation of the structure of *Edward II* would show the intersections of at least five lines, each corresponding to the rising and falling fortunes of a major character." Constance Brown Kuriyama (*Hammer or Anvil: Psychological Patterns in Christopher Marlowe's Plays* [New Brunswick, N. J.: Rutgers University Press, 1980], pp. 176-177), while endorsing the traditional pattern of rise and fall, is the first commentator to identify antithesis as the basic pattern of the play. A minority voice amid all the commendation of Marlowe's well-made play, Wilbur Sanders (*The Dramatist and the Received Idea: Studies in the Plays of Marlowe and Shakespeare* [Cambridge: Cambridge University Press, 1968], p. 122) demurs that "the shape of the dramatic movement does not in any obvious way reveal a general conception lying behind the plotting."

2. As far as I am aware, David Bevington, in a paper presented at the Modern Language Association convention in New York, 1982 ("What are kings, when regiment is gone?": The Decay of Ceremony in *Edward II*"), is the only commentator to focus on the distortion of ceremony as a central motif of the play, although he does not relate this recurrent inversion to the drama's symmetrical structure. [This "paper" appears in its final form as the next essay of this collection. Eds.] Kuriyama (p. 193), on the other hand, does comment on the play's elaborate antithetical or symmetrical motifs, although she does not refer specifically to the two framing funerals or to the balanced distortion and reinstatement of ceremony.

3. This structure of reverse parallelism is certainly not without precedent. Cedric H. Whitman (*Homer and the Heroic Tradition* [1958; rpt. New York: Norton, 1965], p. 257) discovers a precise numerical reverse parallelism in Homer's *Iliad*, which he relates to the principle known as "ring composition," in which "enclosure by identical or very similar elements produces a circular effect" (p. 253), like that of the concentric circles of Protogeometric art. R. G. Peterson ("Critical Calculations: Measure and Symmetry in Literature," *PMLA*, 91 [1976], 367) discusses this ring composition in terms descriptive of the structure of *Edward II* (see diagram):

> A narrative line, thus, is imagined to intersect a group of concentric circles, a visual metaphor for the repetition in reverse order of particular elements: ABCD . . . DCBA. Carried out over the whole or large parts of a long work, this scheme becomes very complex . . . but the beginning and end will be in some obvious way the same, and a midpoint or center (either a single element, an X, or the coming together of two similar elements, D and D) will be clear.

Clyde Murley ("The Structure and Proportion of Catullus LXIV," *Transactions of the American Philological Association*, 68 [1937], 305-317) shows Catullus LXIV to be concentric in this sense, and George E. Duckworth finds a concentric form to be one of several patterns informing the *Aeneid* (*Structural Patterns in Vergil's Aeneid: A Study in Mathematical Composition* [Ann Arbor, Mich.: University of Michigan Press, 1963] pp. 37-38). Andrew Fichter ("Tasso's Epic of Deliverance," *PMLA*, 93 [1978], pp. 267-268) argues persuasively for a similar "mirror" symmetry in Tasso's *Gerusalemme Liberata*: the first ten cantos dramatize the steady deterioration of the moral and political fabric of the Christian camp and the ascendancy of the pagan forces; the second ten reverse the double movement of ascending pagan and declining Christian fortunes, with Canto i parallel to Canto xx, Canto ii to

Canto xix, and so forth. Although Fichter does not specifically relate this design to the "ring composition" noted by Peterson, the paradigm he describes is clearly concentric. Maren-Sofie Røstvig ("Canto Structure in Tasso and Spenser," *Spenser Studies*, I [1980], 179-182) develops Fichter's argument, relating the concentric pattern of Tasso's epic to the structure of many of the cantos of *The Faerie Queene*. Perhaps the most familiar example in English literature of this concentric form is *Sir Gawain and the Green Knight*. In his perceptive study, *Art and Tradition in Sir Gawain and the Green Knight* (New Brunswick, N. J.: Rutgers University Press, 1965), p. 162, Larry Benson demonstrates this composition, whereby the poem both opens and closes with reference to Troy and descriptions of happy celebrations at Arthur's court, and develops through mirroring episodes of beheadings, armings, and journeys, with a center section balancing parallel hunts and exchanges. For a fuller discussion of the classical provenance of this concentric pattern and its development in modern literature, see Peterson, pp. 367-375. The prevalence in classical, medieval and Renaissance literature of this symmetrical and circular structure supports my contention that this design is not only operative in Marlowe's play, but probably deliberate.

4. Fricker, pp. 214-215.

5. See Fricker, p. 214; Irving Ribner, "Marlowe's *Edward II* and the Tudor History Play," *ELH*, 22 (1955), 243-253; Waith, pp. 60-64; Kuriyama, pp. 176-177.

6. Charles G. Masinton (*Christopher Marlowe's Tragic Vision: A Study in Damnation* [Athens: Ohio University Press, 1972], p. 88) describes the play's dominant structural plan as follows:

> . . . as the adulterers gain political power, they lose their humanity and with it our sympathies; and as Edward travels the road to his doom, he develops into a character worthy of our feelings of fellowship. At the point where Edward's worldly descent is intersected by the rising fortunes of Mortimer and Isabella, our favorable emotional responses are subtly but safely shifted to the King.

7. All citations from Marlowe are to Irving Ribner's *The Complete Plays of Christopher Marlowe* (New York: The Odyssey Press, 1963). All references will henceforth be included within the text.

8. This discussion, and indeed the entire approach of my essay, is indebted to Alan C. Dessen's seminal work on Elizabethan dramaturgy, *Elizabethan Drama and the Viewer's Eye* (Chapel Hill, N.C.: University of North Carolina Press, 1977).

9. The donning of new robes is an archetypal symbol of personality transformation. One prototype for this association is the Ishtar myth, since Ishtar's descent into Hades was accompanied by a seven-stage disrobing, her resurrection by a seven-stage adornment (See John F. Haskins, "The Whore of Babylon," *Human Sexuality in the Middle Ages and Renaissance*, ed. Douglas Radcliff-Umstead [Pittsburgh, Pa.: University Publications on the Middle Ages and Renaissance, Vol. IV, 1978], pp. 189-190, 193, nn.23, 24). In Greek initiation ceremonies, a cloak, or *epheboi*, black or dun, was worn at initiation rites to symbolize the death of the child and the birth of manhood (*An Illustrated Encyclopedia of Traditional Symbols*, ed. J. C. Cooper [London: Thames and Hudson, 1978], pp. 38, 104). Dramatic precedents for this sartorial symbolism include *The Castle of Perseverance*, in which Mankind's seduc-

tion by Covetousness is emblemized by his coin-festooned robe (*Medieval Drama,* ed. David Bevington [Boston: Houghton Mifflin Co.], p. 819, 11. 700-701, and *Everyman,* in which the penitent protagonist dons a gown of contrition (*Medieval Drama,* p. 956), as well as Marlowe's own *Tamburlaine* (I.ii.41). Examples from contemporaneous and subsequent plays are too numerous to cite, but Shakespeare offers particularly provocative instances in *Hamlet, Lear, Antony and Cleopatra,* and *The Tempest,* all of which conclude with a dramatic change of garments by the protagonists.

10. Clothes are mentioned frequently in *Edward II.* Mortimer scoffs at Gaveston's sartorial splendor, denigrating him as a "dapper Jack" and a "jetting" Midas, somewhat enviously belittling his Italian cloak and Tuscan cap (I.iv.406-414). Although no explicit reference is made here or elsewhere to Edward's Italian apparel, it is probable that the King, scornfully laughing with his Gascon favorite at the barons' plain, unfashionable English garb, would imitate the foreign style of his "second self." Later, Mortimer ridicules the gold-bedaubed King's "garish robes" and "spangled crest," flowing with women's favors (II.ii.180-185), which recall the fallen Mankind's coin-encrusted attire in *The Castle of Perseverance* (see n. 9 above).

11. This television version of *Edward II* was produced in 1975, under the auspices of the National Endowment for the Humanities, for the series entitled *Classic Theatre: The Humanities in Drama.*

12. *Holinshed's Chronicles of England, Scotland, and Ireland,* Vol. II (London, 1577; rpt. New York: AMS Press, Inc., 1965), pp. 587, 597-598. H. B. Charleston and R. D. Waller in their Introduction to *Edward II* (*The Works of Christopher Marlowe,* gen. ed. R. H. Case [1930; rpt. New York: Gordian Press, 1966], pp. 33-35) enumerate the numerous examples of Marlowe's compression of the events of twenty-three years into the brief two-hour traffic of the stage.

13. The soliloquy hints of a number of sexual perversions—transvestism (l. 60), homosexuality (l. 65), voyeurism (l. 67), and sadism (ll. 69-70)—although how many of these innuendoes are deliberate is difficult to ascertain.

14. For Sunesen's excellent explication of the Actaeon allusion, see "Marlowe and the Dumb Show," *English Studies,* 35 (1954), 241-253. For other analyses of Actaeon as an emblem for Edward, see Masinton, pp. 90-91; John P. Cutts, *The Left Hand of God: A Critical Interpretation of the Plays of Christopher Marlowe* (Haddonfield, N.J.: Haddonfield House, 1973) pp. 206-207 and Sara Munson Deats, "Myth and Metamorphosis in Marlowe's *Edward II,*" *Texas Studies in Literature and Language,* 22:3 (1980), 310-311, 319, n. 23. Conversely, W. L. Godshalk in *The Marlovian World Picture* (The Hague: Mouton, 1974), pp. 60-63, stresses the possible analogy between Gaveston and Actaeon.

15. Sunesen (pp. 247-248) examines the hunt imagery in some detail.

16. Since the method of Marlowe's brutal murder derives from history and from Holinshed rather than from Marlowe's imagination (Holinshed, p. 587), it is difficult to know whether this ironic parody is deliberate or adventitious, originating from Marlowe, Matreuers, or Mortimer. However, ever since the publication of William Empson's influential article, "Two Proper Crimes," *The Nation,* 163 (1946), 444-445, commentators have tended to postulate an intentional parody in Marlowe's account of Edward's harrowing assassination. Probably Marlowe rec-

ognized the ironic implications of this historical act and exploited them dramatically.

17. For an examination of the traditional ambiguous associations of this myth, see Deats, "Myths and Metamorphosis," pp. 319, nn. 23-26. See also, Arthur Golding, *Ovid's Metamorphoses* (1567), ed. W.H.D. Rouse (Carbondale, Ill.: Southern Illinois University Press, 1961), Bk. III, 11. 164-165, 305-308; Florence McCullock, *Medieval Latin and French Bestiaries* (Chapel Hill, N.C.: University of North Carolina Press, 1960), pp. 172-174; Martha Hester Golden, "The Inconography of the English History Play," Ph.D. Dissertation (Columbia University, 1967), p. 215.

18. As far as I am aware, the first scholar to comment on Lightborn's diabolic derivation was Harry Levin in *The Overreacher: A Study of Christopher Marlowe* (Cambridge, Mass: Faber and Faber, 1952), p. 101. Levin also observes that "Lightborn is an Anglicization of Lucifer."

19. See my discussion of Gaveston's often-ignored complexity in *"Edward II*: A Study in Androgyny," *Ball State University Forum*, 22:1 (1981), 37-40.

20. I refer the reader to Bernard Spivak's examination of the homiletic self-exposition of the medieval Vice, *Shakespeare and the Allegory of Evil* (New York: Columbia University Press, 1959), pp. 178-193. The Vice's typical strategies of deceit, manipulation and pretended love or compassion (p. 176), are also relevant to both Gaveston and Lightborn (as well as to Spencer and Mortimer).

21. As many scholars have remarked, Marlowe derived the shaving episode not from Holinshed but from John Stow's *The Annales of England* (1580; rpt. London: Ralfe Newbarry, 1600), p. 350, which recounts the shaving of Edward's beard in cold ditch water. The term "channel-water" appears to be Marlowe's addition.

22. The ironic ritual implications of the Bishop's "christening" in channel-water are obvious and the shaving of Edward's beard can be interpreted as a kind of emasculation, an inverted *rite de passage*. Although Edward's shaving is historical, Marlowe departed from his primary scource (Holinshed) to include this event. The shaping power of Marlowe's imagination appears more saliently in the episode with the Bishop of Coventry. Although the imprisonment and deposition of the Bishop derive from Hollinshed (p. 546), the stripping and "christening " are Marlowe's own inventions, additions that clarify the parallelism of the two episodes as well as stressing Edward's violation of both the secular and sacred hierchies; see Jocelyn Powell's discussion of the morality play analogues to Edward's desecration of the Bishop's sacerdotal garments ("Marlowe's Spectacle," *Tulane Drama Review*, 8:4[1964], 198).

23. Holinshed, p. 597.

24. See Claude J. Summers, "Isabella's Plea for Gaveston in Marlowe's *Edward II*," *Philological Quarterly*, 52 (1973), 308-310, and Purvis E. Boyette, "Wanton Humor in Marlowe's *Edward II*," *Tulane Studies in English*, 22 (1977), 46, n. 10.

25. *Cf.* Holinshed, p. 584.

26. Fredson Bowers documents this association of subterfuge and hypocrisy with the Elizabethan stage Machiavel in *Elizabethan Revenge Tragedy, 1587-1642* (1940; rpt. Princeton N. J.: Princeton University Press, 1971), pp. 48-49, 51, 54-55.

27. *Cf.* Holinshed's account of Gaveston's capture and death, pp. 58-59, 51, 54-55.

28. Douglas Cole perceptively comments on Edward's limited recognition and his pain at the loss of his crown in *Suffering and Evil in the Plays of Christopher Marlowe* (1962; rpt. New York: Gordian Press, 1972), pp. 183-187.

29. Earlier, Edward II does on one occasion use the term "our son" III.ii.82), and once before his abdication scene even refers to Edward III as "my little boy" (IV.iii.48), but such paternal tenderness from Edward II is rare before his deposition scene in Act V.

30. This frequently neglected aspect of Edward's limited maturation is examined by Marion Perret, "Edward III: Marlowe's Dramatic Technique," *Review of English Literature*, N.S. 7:4 (1966), 88-91.

31. Holinshed, p. 585; see also, Charlton and Waller, pp. 37-38; Cole, pp. 177-178.

32. Although no stage direction requires an embrace to accompany the dispensation of titles to Spencer, Edward's earlier demonstrativeness to Gaveston (I.ii.20-24, 50-53) offers implicit support for such a physical salute at this point. Later in the scene, of course, Edward flaunts his affection before the barons' herald. Edward's verbal endearment—"Spencer, sweet Spencer"—also suggests a corollary physical caress.

33. Robertson's TV production effectively employed kisses as a visual link connecting the two parallel actions. It is highly unlikely, however, that such an overt expression of homosexual passion would have been enacted on the Elizabethan stage.

34. Holinshed, p. 552.

35. Holinshed, pp. 559-562. Charlton and Waller (p. 40) argue that historically Spencer Jr. was not "in any invidious sense" a favorite at all, at least "not until 1321."

36. Charlton and Waller (p. 46) attribute this important deviation from history to Marlowe's desire for "dramatic economy," whereby Spencer and Baldock become mere appendages to Gaveston. I suggest that dramatic counterpoint may have been an even more important determinant.

37. Edward's fatal error in judgment—imprisoning rather than executing Mortimer—occurs in Act III, Scene iii. Marlowe's structuring of his rising and falling action around a mid-point climax anticipates the form of many of Shakespeare's tragedies, including *Romeo and Juliet, Richard II, Hamlet,* and *Othello.* Moreover, in dividing his play in the middle between two sets of mirroring sequences, Marlowe adapts to the dramatic genre the concentric structure reflected in the works of Homer, Catullus, Vergil, Tasso, and the Gawain poet (see Note 3 above).

"What are kings, when regiment is gone?" The Decay of Ceremony in *Edward II*

DAVID BEVINGTON and JAMES SHAPIRO

Recent work on stage imagery in Shakespeare's *Richard II* invites a similar investigation of Marlowe's theatrical practice in *Edward II*.[1] There are fundamental differences in the ways in which Shakespeare and Marlowe handle theatrical space, properties, emblematic tableaux and groupings in these plays. A comparison of their visual vocabularies provides insight into the ways they related word to image in their drama, and clarifies their conception of historical drama and their representation of the personal and political conflict at the heart of this genre.

In *Richard II*, the verbal image patterns of the rising and falling sun, the two buckets in a well, Phaethon, and the like, examined by Caroline Spurgeon and other New Critics to the exclusion of stage imagery, are in fact complemented in the theater by a no less extensive and subtle set of visual signals of rising and falling, making obeisance, and inversion.[2] Visual imagery in Shakespeare's play is often a matter of physical ascent and descent, as when Richard appears on the "walls"—that is, in the gallery above the main stage—to his besiegers, who are on the main stage below, which represents the "grassy plain" before the battlements of Flint Castle. The theater façade, with its doors, gallery, and impressive architecture, gives a spatial rendition of a castle under siege, and Richard, its chief occupant, plays the central role of one who is under attack. Richard speaks of Phaethon, while his stage gesture connoting surrender is that of descending into the "base court." His descent behind the scenes transforms the theater space into an interior courtyard, for when Richard emerges through the stage door below into the "base court" he is imagined to be within the walls of the castle.

Kneelings are crucial visual images throughout *Richard II*, enabling us to follow the transfer of power from Richard to Bolingbroke, and culminating in a wryly comic scene in which the Duke and Duchess of York and their son Aumerle all kneel to King Henry IV and are reconciled by him. The crown is of course a central property, and is physically the center of dispute in the play's harrowing scene of deposition. Physical occupation of the throne is a matter of visual concern. Costumes mark the decline of Richard from one who presides over a fashion-conscious court to one who is a prisoner, poorly attended. Ceremonies are visually impressive but are characteristically aborted or marred, as in the breaking off of the tournament between Bolingbroke and Mowbray or, most notably, in the deposition scene—a coronation in reverse. The final procession for the dead King Richard is marred by the circumstance that the chief mourner is also Richard's murderer.

Marlowe's *Edward II* does less than Shakespeare's play with vertical movement, and indeed makes less use of the architectural environment of the theater as a means of suggesting location. His earlier plays do make occasional use of the vertical. *Tamburlaine Part II*, for example, displays a captain above (III.iii.15)[3] and then the Governor of Babylon "upon the walles" (V.i.1 S.D.), where he is subsequently shot. *The Massacre at Paris* shows us the body of the Admiral hurled down from above (v. 306), though Marlowe does little with the thematic possibilities of such an abrupt descent. Despite his familiarity with this stage idiom, Marlowe does not use the gallery for appearances on the walls in *Edward II*. Nor does Marlowe simulate a siege onstage in *Edward II*, as Shakespeare repeatedly does in the *Henry VI* plays and *King John* as well as in *Richard II*. Though a siege is in progress at Tynemouth Castle(when Gaveston is removed from King Edward for the last time) the siege is not visually simulated by an assault on the tiring house façade or by a parley at the "gates." And while the rebel lords assemble somewhere in the vicinity of the castle, talk of advancing upon and scaling these "castell walles" (II.iii.24), and order their drummers to strike an alarum, by the next scene we are within the walls with Edward's party while the battle is fought through offstage sound effects. "Flie, flie, my lords, the earles have got the holde" (II.iv. 4), warns the King, speaking of some imagined offstage space where the fighting has been going on. Later, when Mortimer escapes from the Tower of London and joins the waiting Earl of Kent, the stage doors and façade do not signify the Tower as they do in Shakespeare's *1 Henry VI* and *3 Henry VI*. We would not know the scene to be the Tower at all but for a mention in the previous scene that Mortimer is to be imprisoned there.[4]

Generally, then, Marlowe does not visualize exterior architecture or geographical location in *Edward II*. Editors' attempts to provide names of places for scenes are frustrated by Marlowe's conflating or altering his sources. In fact, the rebel barons' determination to meet at the New Temple in order to confirm the banishment of Gaveston, announced at the end of scene iii, does not square with some indications in scene iv that the gathering actually occurs in the royal palace. Location is occasionally established by verbal means, as when Edward welcomes the returned Gaveston to Tynemouth, or is urged to imagine Killingworth Castle to be his court, or is informed by Lord Berkeley that "Your grace must hence with mee to Bartley straight" (V.i.144). The "Welsh hooks" borne by Rice ap Howell's followers assure us that Edward is apprehended in west country; but, lacking the historical information supplied by editors from Marlowe's sources, we simply do not know while viewing the play that the abbey where Edward is arrested is that of Neath in Glamorganshire, or that the action two scenes before is located "near Harwich," or that Edward learns of the death of Gaveston near Boroughbridge, in Yorkshire. Marlowe seems less interested than Shakespeare in the theater as an English battleground encompassing the whole nation. Nor in this play does he invoke the idea of a *theatrum mundi* as often as Shakespeare does in his history plays, with a strong vertical sense of a cosmic and hierarchical world existing multidimensionally above and below the sphere of human action. Marlowe's theatrical vision is very much directed to the middle ground of human conflict.

On that plane of human history represented by the main stage, Mar-

lowe's visual artistry is concerned above all with images of confrontation and juxtaposition. His juxtaposition of groups of characters is accentuated by a sharp visual contrast between the extravagant and
martial styles of these contending factions. The extravagant style is
epitomized by Gaveston. In the opening scene, having dismissed the
ragged "three poor men" (I.i.24 S.D.), he rhapsodizes upon his ideal of
courtly life:

> I must have wanton Poets, pleasant wits,
> Musitians, that with touching of a string
> May draw the pliant king which way I please:
> Musicke and poetrie is his delight,
> Therefore ile have Italian maskes by night,
> Sweete speeches, comedies and pleasing shows.
>   (I.i.51-56)

Gaveston's Italianate spectacle includes homoerotic fantasies of a
"lovelie boye in Dians shape" (I.i.62) bathing in a spring, and his men,
dressed as "Satyres," dancing "an antick hay" (I.i.60). Confident that
"such things as these best please his majestie" (I.i.71), Gaveston imagines a spectacular Roman triumph. Beloved by Edward, he thinks
himself "as great / As Caesar riding in the Romaine streete, / With
captive kings at his triumphant Carre" (I.i.172-174). This icon of political domination recalls Tamburlaine's chariot, drawn by other captive kings—the "pampered Jades of Asia"—across the London stage.
Gaveston and Edward create an image of king and court that is visually hyperbolic, an illusion of power. Gaveston's costume must be particularly noticeable in the theater. Mortimer's observation of him as a
"dapper jack" (I.iv.412) is unfriendly but no doubt accurate in sartorial detail when he complains that Gaveston "weares a lords revenewe
on his back, / And Midas like he jets it in the court / With base out-
landish cullions at his heeles" in "proud fantastick liveries" (I.iv.407-
410). Gaveston wears "a short Italian hooded cloake, / Larded with
pearle, and, in his tuskan cap / A jewel of more value than the crowne"
(I.iv.413-415). The barons rail at Edward for the "idle triumphes,
maskes, lascivious showes / And prodigall gifts bestowed on
Gaveston" (II.ii.157-158). They jeer at the King's inappropriate and
luxurious mode of dress when defeated in battle at "Bannocks borne":
"thy selfe / Bedaubd with golde, rode laughing at the rest, / Nodding

and shaking of thy spangled crest, / Where womens favors hung like labels downe" (II.ii.184-187). The barons respond to such effeminacy with what Mortimer describes as a "homely" (II.ii.12) style: direct, blunt, unembellished. Their bluntness is conveyed visually as well as verbally. They are of course richly dressed as aristocrats, but they pointedly separate themselves from Gaveston's Italianate prodigality.

This close attention to physical appearance ultimately engenders a cynicism about the manipulation of visual signs. Spencer tells the ambitious Baldock that he must "cast the scholler off, / And learne to court it like a Gentleman" (II.i.31-32). He adds that "Tis not a black coate and a little band, / A velvet cap'de cloake, fac'st before with Serge, / . . . Can get you any favour with great men" (II.i.33-34,41). Baldock agrees: "thou knowest I hate such formall toies, / And use them but of meere hypocrisie" (II.i.44-45). His plain attire is "precise" and "curate-like," with a black coat and small buttons, effectively conccaling an inward licentiousness and ambition in the hypocritical style of a Tartuffe.

Occupying as it does a dual world of visual splendor and of secret hypocrisy, *Edward II* alternates visually between large scenes of aborted ceremonial, involving sizable groups of contending factions, and contrasting scenes of isolation when we are virtually alone with a soliloquizing figure in prison or some sort of adversity. An essential figure in this alternating rhythm is the outsider whose estranged position on stage comments ironically on the political world at court. The opening scene, for example, juxtaposes the solo appearance of Gaveston with two interrupted ceremonial occasions: a procession from a gathering of parliament and the funeral obsequies for Edward I. Gaveston speaks of the ceremonial forms with which he is impatient, claiming he will have no more of "base stooping to the lordly peeres" (I.i.18). Gaveston's standing aside for the entry of the King and members of parliament emphasizes his separation from this world and affords him an opportunity to comment upon it adversely in asides.

This juxtaposition through grouping is visually expressive of the political state of affairs, for Gaveston's presence occasions a massive breakdown in public order that is realized on stage as interrupted or inverted ceremony. Members of parliament jar with one another and refuse the forms of obeisance due their king. The knees of "aspiring Lancaster," the King notes, "now are growne so stiffe" (I.i.95) that he will not kneel. Instead, he and his fellow peers "brave the king unto his face" and threaten to parley with their "naked swords" (I.i.116, 126).

King Edward's own alliance with anti-ceremonial behavior is prominent from the beginning, especially in his behavior toward Gaveston. "What, Gaveston, welcome: kis not my hand, / Embrace me Gaveston as I do thee: / Why should'st thou kneele?" (I.i.140-142) are the first words with which he greets the man in whom he sees a mirror of himself. The barons view these anti-ceremonial signals not so much as an offense against conventional sexual morality, which might be overlooked as a common failing of royal persons, but as an offense against the hierarchical structure upon which they depend no less than the King. We are informed in detail of the gestures that openly flaunt the orderly ceremony of the court. The King first showers aristocratic titles on Gaveston—Lord High Chamberlain, Chief Secretary to the state and king, Earl of Cornwall, King and Lord of Man—then marches everywhere "arme in arme" (I.ii.20) with his favorite. The guard waits upon the new earl, "And all the court begins to flatter him" (I.ii.21-22). "Thus leaning on the shoulder of the king, / He nods, and scornes, and smiles at those that passe" (I.ii.23-24). The King dotes upon Gaveston, "claps his cheekes, and hanges about his neck" (I.ii.51).

These reports come from the unfriendly mouths of the barons and Queen Isabella, but they clearly match the gestures of the actors of Edward and Gaveston, whose roles violate all expected visual forms of royal and courtly behavior. When Edward occupies the throne on stage, Gaveston is at his side. "What? are you mov'd that Gaveston sits heere?" (I.iv.8) asks the King, underscoring his awareness of the grave consequences of such a visual signal. Mortimer concurs from his opposite position: "What man of noble birth can brooke this sight? . . . / "See what a scornfull look the pesant casts" (I.iv. 12,14). Later, the King makes a political point through the gesture of embracing Spencer: "See how I do devorce / Spencer from me" (III.i.176-177), he sardonically answers those demanding that he banish his new favorite. Pointedly, his embracements are not for the Queen. "From my imbracements thus he breakes away" (II.iv.16), she laments. "These hands are tir'd, with haling of my lord / From Gaveston, from wicked Gaveston, / And all in vaine" (II.iv.26-28). Edward thus flaunts in gesture his hostility toward ceremonial order. We can understand his motive for doing so, but we also perceive that in so doing he alienates himself from the forms that nourish his claims to authority. In stage gesture Edward isolates himself, taking the part of the outsider and parvenu, and thereby anticipates visually his own deposition and increasing isolation at the end of the play.

Decay of ceremony is reinforced by a series of visual signals that mark a shift from order to disorder. In Act III, scene i, for instance, Edward enters ceremoniously with Spencer and Baldock to the martial sounds of "Drummes and Fifes" (III.i.1S.D.). Their subsequent joint entrances, contrastingly, grow more and more visually chaotic. Stage directions describe "Alarums, excursions, a great fight, and a retreate" (III.i.184 S.D.), until at last Edward, Spencer, and Baldock are seen "flying about the stage" (IV.v.1 S.D.) in desperate, unceremonious retreat. When they re-enter together in Act IV, scene vii, the seeming order and dignity of their procession is vitiated by their disguise as monks in the train of an abbot. The King's donning of clerical robes is pointedly ironic, not only for its austerity, but also because he had earlier ordered the desecration of the Bishop of Coventry's ecclesiastical robes.

The rapid, turbulent stage action described in the battle scenes (and elsewhere, such as the tugging to and fro of the young prince by Kent and Mortimer in Act V, scene ii) are characteristic of much of the play's alternating visual rhythm. This turbulence has led critics like Wolfgang Clemen to distinguish Marlowe's visual technique in *Edward II* from Shakespeare's practice in *Richard II*. Clemen argues that "the restless movement on the stage which characterized most scenes" in *Edward II* contrasts sharply with the dramatic rhythms of *Richard II*, in which Shakespeare creates "scenes in which progress is arrested, and the significance of these 'still' scenes is deepened and elaborated by speeches rich in imagery or by symbolic gestures and actions."[5] This claim, insightful as it is, undervalues the frequency and effect of the emblematic in Marlowe's play, as well as its function in reinforcing the sense of disrupted ceremony.

Perhaps the most powerful visual image of disrupted ceremony occurs in Act II, scene ii, through the use of emblems onstage. Edward has called for a celebratory tilt and tournament, a "triumphe" honoring Gaveston's return from exile. The barons' response is emphatically less decadent and more politically pointed in its visual signs, disrupting both the spirit and the purpose of Edward's decree. To the royal command that he display the "device" he has prepared "Against the stately triumph," Mortimer reveals a painted shield featuring a device or emblem. Mortimer's description of his device as "homely" is double-edged: on the one hand it reinforces the blunt directness characteristic of him at this point in the play; on the other it implies that the message of his martial emblem is meant to strike home. Lancaster's emblematic shield similarly underscores this subversion of Edward's ceremonial plans. Lancaster describes his device as follows:

> Plinie reports, there is a flying Fish,
> Which all the other fishes deadly hate,
> And therefore being pursued, it takes the aire:
> No sooner is it up, but thers a foule,
> That seaseth it: this fish my lord I beare,
> The motto this: *Undique mors est.*
>
> (II.ii.23-28)

Marlowe probably adopted this emblem from a version of Alciati's popular and influential *Emblemata*.[6] The woodcut of emblem 170 in Alciati's collection depicts a small fish harried from both sea and air; the verse ominously concludes, *"undique debilitas,"* translated by Whitney as: "Ah feeble state, on everie side anoi'de."[7] Marlowe's audience may have been familiar with this emblem through Whitney, who had produced the first emblem book in English in 1586, copying Alciati's woodcut almost exactly, and translating his verse into English couplets. Marlowe himself was probably first acquainted with this emblem through a continental edition, however. Despite Lancaster's claim—and to the frustration of Marlowe's editors—Pliny never reports this particular phenomenon, but when we consult sixteenth-century editions of Alciati, we find commentators like Claude Mignault citing Pliny and explaining that the specific fish and fowl Alciati names (Auratus and Mergus) can be found in scattered references in Pliny's *Natural History*.[8] The evidence suggests that Marlowe is probably doing what he did so often in his translations: consulting commentators along with the original text itself.

Marlowe's use of Lancaster's emblem is striking in its multiple dramatic function: as decoration for a literal shield, as scarce-veiled political allegory, and as signal of the duplicity and ambiguity that figure so largely in later scenes of the play. The emblem's allusion to the sea (recalling Edward's fear that Gaveston is "wrackt upon the sea" (II.ii. 2) in his return from Ireland) is perhaps meant to exacerbate the King's anxiety. Gaveston—likened earlier to a fish: "that vile Torpedo" (I.iv.223)—is endangered both in his crossing of the Irish Sea and upon his arrival upon English soil. Critical views of Marlowe as essentially a lyric or poetic dramatist surely underestimate the extent to which Marlowe's dramatic imagination derives from the visual and emblematic, especially in the ways in which he conceives and constructs particular scenes.

The barons' emblematic shields may be the most ornate and expensive properties in the play. Marlowe keeps them onstage and integrates them into the action of the scene for two hundred lines. They must have provoked curiosity; emblems demand interpretation. Our curiosity is whetted when Mortimer first refuses to display and explain them. By line 80 of the scene, when Lancaster assaults Gaveston, the devices function as literal shields. Since Lancaster and Mortimer remain onstage throughout Act II scene ii, moreover, we can assume that they are still carrying their shields when they subsequently burst in upon King Edward at court. It is with shields in hand, then, that Mortimer and Lancaster condemn the "idle triumphes, maskes, lascivious showes, / And prodigall gifts bestowed on Gaveston" (II.ii.157-158). Their emblematic art-turned-armor reinforces thematic and dramaturgic ends: Edward's desire to transform war into spectacle—"When wert thou in the field with banner spred? / But once, and then thy souldiers marcht like players" (II.ii.182-183)—is countered by the barons' transformation of spectacle and show into arms, exposing the illusion of Edward's power. Lancaster's final words in the scene confirm the shift from obscure to blunt signs; he warns the King, "If ye be moov'de, revenge it as you can, / Looke next to see us with our ensignes spred" (II.ii.198-199). Because his actions and those of his favorite so visibly violate ordered hierarchy, Edward is drawn into ever more direct conflict with his peers.

The confrontation at Tynemouth introduces two further stage actions that would signal grave disorder to an Elizabethan audience: first, the drawing of weapons in the presence of the King as Mortimer wounds Gaveston with his sword and sends the royal party scurrying for shelter, and then the forced interruption of Edward's privacy, despite the guard's warning to the barons that "His highnes is disposde to be alone" (II.ii.135). The barons want to question Edward about ransom for Old Mortimer, taken prisoner by the Scots, but the real issue is the forcing of an audience. After these broachings of custom, the unchivalrous overwhelming of Gaveston, "flatly against law of arms," and the seizure of the King in an abbey despite the promise of the Abbot to "keepe your royall person safe with us" (IV.vii.3) are almost anticlimactic.

The borrowing and direct application of a specific emblem is unusual in *Edward II*. More generally, the emblematic impulse is conveyed through static tableaux or groupings of characters forming a stage picture. In Act IV, scene vii, the symbolic arrangement of characters onstage is even accompanied by a Latin motto, reiterating its visual message. Edward here abjures his kingly responsibility in favor of "this life contemplative" (IV.vii.20) and despairs of worldly success. His lament is accompanied by symbolic action. As he speaks he puts his head, "laden with mickle care" (IV.vii.40), upon the Abbot's lap. Spencer, alert to the implication of this visual symbol, warns Baldock: "This drowsines / Betides no good" (IV.vii.44-45). The stage image also foreshadows a similar tableau in the play's final act, where the drowsy Edward lies down to sleep only to be "overwatchde" by the villainous Lightborn.

Marlowe expands the tableaux in Act IV, scene vii, to include another symbolic figure, the Mower, who directs Rice ap Howell to the reclining King. As Clifford Leech and others have observed,[9] the Mower serves as an image of death, the grim reaper. Leicester, who arrives onstage with this party, hangs back, momentarily disengaged from the action, and considers the unhappy tableaux—sleeping King, gloomy Mower—before him. The scene illustrates the emblematic quality of Marlowe's stage imagery. "[S]ee where he sits," Leicester exclaims, "and hopes unseene, / T'escape their hands that seeke to reave his life" (IV.vii.51-52). Leicester, a dispassionate observer, interprets the scene emblematically, providing the appropriate Latin motto: "Too true it is, *quem vidit veniens superbum, / Hunc dies vidit fugiens jacentem*"—a Senecan tag translated by Ben Jonson as "For, whom the morning saw so great, and high, / Thus low, and little, 'fore the 'even doth lie."[10] We encounter here the kind of emblematic scene ascribed by Clemen to Shakespeare's *Richard II* (but denied by him to

Marlowe), containing "moments of repose in which the action seems to be suspended, as if it were to be reviewed and reflected from a distance."[11]

The decay of ceremony we encounter so repeatedly in *Edward II* gives special prominence to ceremonial mourning and the ways in which it is violated. The play opens with the announcement of Edward I's death. Gaveston enters "reading on a letter brought to him from the king" (I.i.1 S.D.) that begins, "My father is deceast" (I.i.1). We might expect that this important statement would be expanded into the characteristic Marlovian verse paragraph. Instead, the subject shifts in midline, and Edward's note passes from the comment that his father has died to more immediate concerns: "come, Gaveston, / And share the kingdom with thy deerest friend" (I.i.1-2).

From the outset, then, the play concerns not only the decay of ceremonial mourning, but its absence as well. While it is a dangerous critical maneuver to criticize a play for what it omits, we might note that Marlowe is fairly insistent elsewhere in *Edward II* about the significance of ceremonial mourning. It is prominent, for example, in the confrontation in the second scene when Edward and Gaveston confront the Bishop of Coventry. This scene is usually read as an attempt by Marlowe to play upon anti-Catholic sentiments. Yet the confrontation has a ceremonial significance as well. When Edward demands, "Whether goes my Lord of Coventrie so fast?" (I.i.175) the Bishop admonishes him: "To celebrate your fathers exequies" (I.i.176). Our attention to this issue is diverted when the Bishop sees Gaveston and demands to know if "that wicked Gaveston is returnd" (I.i.177). Having impeded the Bishop's performance of his father's exequies, Edward next orders Gaveston to desecrate the Bishop's robes: "Throwe off his golden miter, rend his stole, / And in the channell christen him a new" (I.i.187-188). The violent treatment of the Bishop and the wry jest about rechristening foreshadow Edward's own violent treatment and mock-ceremonial anointing at the hands of Gurney and Matrevis, when they "wash him with puddle water, and shave his beard away" (V.iii.37 S.D.).

This kind of visual parallel and foreshadowing is frequent in Marlowe's presentation of ceremonial observation and its decay. Alan Dessen points out a visual parallel between the horseboy who cannot save Gaveston's life from Warwick's treachery and the other young boy in the play, Edward III (perhaps, as Dessen suggests, played by the same child actor), who similarly cannot prevent an adversary (here, Mortimer) from haling Kent to his death.[12] If, as Stanley Wells argues, the drums beaten by Gurney and Matrevis are to be incorporated in the play itself and not merely in Edward's description,[13] then Edward's entrance in Act III, scene i, to the sounds of drums and fifes sets in motion another contrast that will reinforce the decay of ceremony onstage. Similarly, the huge jewel Mortimer describes in Gaveston's "tuskan cap" is recalled in Edward's final moments, when the deposed king vainly tries to appease Lightborn: "One jewell have I left, receive thou this" (V.v.84).

Visual foreshadowing is to be found everywhere in Marlowe's handling of the ceremonies of bereavement. Recalling the reign of the deceased Edward I as a time when duty showed its proper form, the barons insist that their duty to that great monarch now obliges them to resist the desecration that Gaveston represents. "Mine unckle heere," says Mortimer, "this Earle, and I my selfe, / Were sworne unto your father at his death, / That [Gaveston] should nere returne unto the realme" (I.i.82-84). Conversely, the scene in which the King awaits Gaveston's return from exile must be evaluated in light of Edward's unusual gesture and attire, for he is to enter "moorning" (I.iv.305 S.D.). Surely this sign of bereavement inappropriately worn to honor his favorite further accentuates Edward's abuse of proper ceremony. When Gaveston subsequently enters, prepared to be led to his death, the stage direction ironically reiterates in Gaveston the King's own gesture and dress: "Enter Gaveston moorning" (II.vi.1 S.D.).

The close of the play, bringing as it does Edward III's restoration of order and ceremony, thereby places strong visual emphasis on proper mourning. Having commanded Mortimer's execution, the young King asks his lords to fetch his father's "hearse," where Mortimer's head "shall lie" (V.vi.94). The appearance of the hearse recalls Edward's earlier response to the litter brought by Leicester to carry him to Killingworth: "A litter hast thou, lay me in a hearse, / And to the gates of hell convay me hence" (IV.vii.87-88). Once again, visual images parallel and foreshadow subsequent action. In the final lines of the play the hearse slowly transverses the stage, recalling Zenocrate's hearse in the impressive funeral ceremonial of *Tamburlaine Part II*.

Prior to the final restoration of order, the consequences of this decay of ceremony in Edward II's court are twofold, and both take the visual form in the theater of ironic inversion of proper custom: first, a transfer of the signs of obeisance to Mortimer and Isabella; and second, a re-nunciation of pomp by Edward. Virtually all the signs of royal privi-lege once enjoyed by Edward are assumed by those who supplant him. The embracements of Gaveston to which Isabella objected give way to the embracements of Isabella and Mortimer. The kneelings that were such visible tokens of contention between Edward and his peers are now made to the Queen and her son, as when Rice ap Howell and the citizens of Bristol greet Isabella with obeisances "In signe of love and dutie to this presence" (IV.vi.48). Mortimer boasts in soliloquy "that with a lowly conge to the ground, / The proudest lords salute me as I passe" (V.iv. 49-50). The crown is transferred to young Edward III, who demonstrates his virtuous intents by declaring his unwillingness to be thus crowned. Young Edward's coronation procession, full of re-splendent ceremony with sounding trumpets and the naming of a champion to fight in defense of Edward III's true claim to the throne, is made a mockery by the arrest of his uncle Kent at Mortimer's behest and by the young Edward's inability to save the life of one so close to him. The hollowness of ritual in the court of Isabella and Mortimer gives concrete and visible expression to the hypocrisy and to the suborn-ing of secret murder that increasingly characterize their short reign.

Edward II's visual transformation, from the time of his arrest, im-ages forth the fall of princes. "Stately and proud, in riches and in traine, / Whilom I was, powerfull and full of pompe" (IV.vii.12-13) he reflects. But "what are kings, when regiment is gone?" (V.i. 26). Like Richard II after him, Edward makes trial of philosophy and the life contemplative. His abdication becomes more than a coronation in reverse, for, despite Edward's reluctance to resign, the act becomes for him a means to "despise this transitory pomp" and thereby gives posi-tive meaning to the anti-ceremonial thrust of so much stage imagery in this play. For an Elizabethan audience, the image of a king reduced to appalling physical indignity is at once a shocking affront to proper cer-emonial form and a reminder of the impermanence of all worldly pros-perity. The numerous hand properties and movable stage objects of this play reinforce the point. Our vision is fixed at first on crowns, sym-bolically decorated shields, swords, rings, jewels, official documents, and lockets containing portraits; increasingly, we are forced to contemplate such jarring images as the handkerchief wet with Edward's tears, the ring sent by Isabella as a false confirmation of love to Edward, the token by means of which Lightborn gains access to the King, the table, the feather bed, and perhaps a red-hot spit (unless this particularly ugly stage property is kept out of view; it certainly is prominently mentioned). The uneasy and unfinished struggle between savagery and civilization is present until the last in the image of the bloody head of Mortimer lying by the hearse of the man he killed.

Some of the visual method of *Edward II* recurs in *Richard II* and may be part of what Shakespeare admired in the earlier play. Especially noteworthy are the deposition that is so anti-ceremonial, the physical struggle over the actual removal of the crown, the paradoxical inversions of renunciation, and the visual contrast between Henry IV's tarnished glory and the noble sparseness of Richard's end. For Charles Lamb, the "reluctant pangs of abdicting Royalty in Edward furnished hints which Shakespeare scarce improved in his Richard the Second."[14] To make such a comparison, on the other hand, is to see how much more inclined Marlowe is to exploit the brutal circumstances of juxtaposition. Especially in the final scenes of *Edward II*, as we shift our gaze from the scenes of rich panoply at the court of Isabella and her lover to the succession of prisons where Edward is incarcerated, we are forced to confront the most searing evidence of insolent dissembling and obscene secret murder. The verbal imagery that we hear in the play's words conveys some of this, as when Edward speaks of the wren striving against the lion's strength all in vain, thereby reversing the traditional association of the lion with his royalty. Only in the theater, however, can we experience the full assault conveyed by a table and a feather bed. If Marlowe confines his theatrical vision in this play to the middle ground of human history represented by the main stage, he does so in order that he can intensify the brutal personal conflicts, the dismaying juxtapositions and confrontations, and the savage ironies that characterize for him the violent transitions of the political process.[15]

NOTES

1. Three important essays related to stage imagery in *Edward II* appeared in the *Tulane Drama Review*, 8.4 (1964): John Russell Brown, "Marlowe and the Actors," pp. 155-173; Jocelyn Powell, "Marlowe's Spectacle," pp. 195-210; and Glynne Wickham, "'Exeunt to the Cave': Notes on the Staging of Marlowe's Plays," pp. 184-194. Recent studies include David Zucker, *Stage and Image in the Plays of Christopher Marlowe* (Salzburg: Institute für Englische Sprache und Literatur, University of Salzburg, 1972); T. W. Craik, "The Reconstruction of Stage Action from Early Dramatic Texts," *The Elizabethan Theatre* V, ed. George R. Hibbard (Hamden, Conn.: Archon, 1975), pp. 76-91; Felix Bosonnet, *The Function of Stage Properties in Christopher Marlowe's Plays* (Bern, Switzerland: Francke Verlag, 1978); and Michael Hattaway, *Elizabethan Popular Theatre* (London: Routledge and Kegan Paul, 1982), which appeared after most of this article was written.

2. See Caroline F. E. Spurgeon, *Shakespeare's Imagery and What It Tells Us* (Cambridge: Cambridge University Press, 1935); Madeleine Doran, "Imagery in *Richard II* and in *Henry IV*," *Modern Language Review*, 37 (1942), 113-122; Leonard F. Dean, "*Richard II*: The State and the Image of the Theater," *PMLA*, 67 (1952), 211-218; Paul A. Jorgensen, "Vertical Patterns in *Richard II*," *Shakespeare Association Bulletin*, 23 (1948), 119-134; Arthur Suzman, "Imagery and Symbolism in *Richard II*," *Shakespeare Quarterly*, 7 (1956), 355-370; and John Russell Brown, *Shakespeare's Plays in Performance* (New York: St. Martin's Press, 1967).

3. References to Marlowe's work are to Fredson Bowers, ed., *The Complete Works of Christopher Marlowe*, 2 vols. (Cambridge: Cambridge University Press, 1973).

4. Michael Hattaway suggests a possible explanation for the use of a single stage level: the play, acted by Pembroke's company, "seems to have appeared first on provincial stages rather than in the professional playhouses" (*Elizabethan Popular Theatre*, p. 144). A thematic explanation is also possible.

5. See Wolfgang Clemen, "Shakespeare and Marlowe," in *Shakespeare 1971, Proceedings of the World Shakespeare Congress*, ed. Clifford Leech and J. M. R. Margeson (Toronto: University of Toronto Press, 1972), p. 126.

6. The correspondence between Alciati's emblem (and imitations of it) and Lancaster's description has been noted by several generations of iconologists, including Henry Green, A. O. Lewis, Mario Praz, Martha Fleischer, and Peter Daly.

7. Geffrey Whitney, *A Choice of Emblemes* (Leyden, 1586), facs. (Amsterdam: Theatrum Orbis Terrarum Ltd., 1969), p. 52.

8. See, for example, Claude Mignault's edition of Alciati's *Emblemata: Cum Commentariis* (Antwerp, 1577), pp. 547-548.

9. Clifford Leech, "Marlowe's *Edward II*: Power and Suffering," *Critical Quarterly*, 1 (1959), 193.

10. The closing couplet of *Sejanus*, in *Ben Jonson*, ed. C. H. Herford and Percy and Evelyn Simpson, 11 vols. (Oxford: Clarendon Press, 1925-1952), IV, 470.

11. Clemen, "Shakespeare and Marlowe," p. 126.

12. Alan C. Dessen, *Elizabethan Drama and the Viewer's Eye* (Chapel Hill: University of North Carolina Press, 1977), pp. 56-58.

13. Stanley Wells, "Mutations of the 'Gest,'" rev. of *Elizabethan Popular Theatre* by

Michael Hattaway, *Times Literary Supplement*, 17 December 1982, p. 1402.

14. Charles Lamb, *Specimens of English Dramatic Poets*, 2nd. edition, (London, 1813), p. 28.

15. Portions of this article were presented by the authors at the Marlowe Society meetings at the MLA Conventions in Los Angeles (1982) and New York (1983).

Perspective in Marlowe's *Hero and Leander*: Engaging Our Detachment

ROBERT A. LOGAN

In interpreting Marlowe's *Hero and Leander*, twentieth-century critics have changed their perspective markedly. Up into the 1950s, critical reaction was strongly romantic, as if the poem engaged our senses and emotions but seldom spoke to our reason and judgment.[1] *Hero and Leander* was both praised and condemned for what critics variously called erotic passion, libertine naturalism, and "the most shameless celebration of sensuality which we can find in English literature."[2] Whether in praise or condemnation, commentary on the poem was often impressionistic and, both in its romanticized content and intensity of expression, strongly emotional. But since the 1960s, critical reaction has been characterized by intellectual reflection and impersonal analysis, and critics have agreed that, through comedy and narrative aloofness, the poem assumes an ironic, antiromantic posture.[3] This critical response better reflects what I would point to as Marlowe's most pervasive artistic concern in the poem: to keep his readers' responses rational and detached rather than emotional and absorbed.[4]

We are now ready to understand Marlowe's artistic concern as both the subject and object of the poem, and to exploit the interpretive

279

possibilities of responding with rational detachment. Marlowe distances us from his characters and their actions through a portrayal of the effects of eroticism rather than the causes, through intellectualized mythological details and imagery, through comedy, generalizations, abstractions, sententiousness, and a shifting, mercurial narrative perspective. By responding with rational detachment exactly as the poem bids us, we can view in *Hero and Leander* a thematic unity and an integration of content and artistry not yet acknowledged. In particular, we can understand how Marlowe's exploration of the limits of human power gives coherence to even the most irrelevant passages in the poem and explains his fascination with detachment as a poetic device. We can also evaluate Marlowe's strengths as a poet, and, because he has overreached himself in equipping us with the means, his limitations. Our perspective allows us to see, finally, that, for the Marlowe of *Hero and Leander*, rational detachment is more than simply a poetic convention of the Ovidian epyllion; it is something of a credo, as valuable for success in life as it is for success in art.

Broadly speaking, *Hero and Leander* is one of Marlowe's several attempts throughout his works to define human freedom in relation to the amoral restrictive forces within and beyond humankind. Given a universe of fierce energy and violence ("murder, rape, war, lust and treachery"—I. 457), a universe in which all restrictive forces are "deaf and cruel" where they mean to "prey," the chief question that Marlowe's works explore is how much freedom people have to assert themselves.[5] In *Hero and Leander*, Marlowe portrays the restraints imposed upon people by the interacting forces of sexual drives (nature), the gods (whose whimsical actions betray an absence of purpose in the universe), and fate (those fortunes which the Destinies, not always justly, decree). The poem indicates that we are powerless to control the irrational desire ("will") we feel for another person, even powerless to select the person (*e.g.*, I. 167-168 and I. 173-174). The reasons why are largely inscrutable. Apparently, they have nothing to do with the gods whose existence, like ours, is dominated by sexual drives and the desire for power. Physical desire may be restricted from without by what Marlowe calls "fate" (I. 168). This notion is most clear in the allegorical digression on the conflict between Cupid (Love) and the Destinies (I. 377-484). There, Cupid's power is eventually quelled, although not before it has been indirectly responsible for uprooting the hierarchy in

Olympus (I. 447ff). Later in the poem, love is credited with an equally dynamic function: the creation of the world (II. 291-293). The mythological portrayal of the extremes of destruction and creation indicates Marlowe's assurance that, in spite of all restrictions, the power of Eros is immense, even cosmic; and, whether in the human psyche or in the universe operating as a mysterious power, physical love is a force as destructive as it is creative.

Hero and Leander contains passages, apparently irrelevant, in which Marlowe denies the validity of the romantic ideals conventional in pastoral literature. Such passages can actually be understood as part of the poet's multifaceted concern with power and its human limitations. The poem indicates that a desire for power is natural to *all* humankind and that, since this is so, pastoral idealizations of country people have grossly distorted the truth:

> Yet proud she [the country girl] was (for lofty
> Pride that dwells
> In tow'red courts, is oft in shepherds' cells).
> (I. 393-394)

> . . . In gentle breasts
> Relenting thoughts, remorse and pity rests.
> And who have hard hearts and obdurate minds,
> But vicious, harebrain'd, and illit'rate hinds?
> (II. 215-218)[6]

Marlowe rejects the facile faith in natural goodness common to the sentimental ethics of pastorals. For him, country people are proud, insensitive, malicious, unintelligent, and uneducated. His view is consistent with his unromantic attitude toward love and his detached portrayal of it. But his view has deeper roots than the rejection of an unrealistic convention. Hallett Smith has pointed out that "The central meaning of pastoral is the rejection of the aspiring mind. The shepherd demonstrates that true content is to be found in this renunciation."[7] In support of this point, Smith describes four conditions of idealized pastoral existence which invariably receive poetic treatment.[8] Of the four, one can be seen as sharply in conflict with Marlowe's conviction about the reality of human nature: "being content with what you have, however small it is." Smith adds, "this is the way taught by nature," and follows this statement with a parenthesis: "(contrast Tamburlaine's statement that nature teaches us to have aspiring minds)." Smith's observations help to clarify the psychological opposition between the pastoral and Marlovian views of human nature. Moreover, given as corroborative evidence such figures as Tamburlaine (who began as a shepherd) and Doctor Faustus, "the rejection of the aspiring mind" would seem to be alien to Marlowe's works generally. Certainly, any such rejection is alien to the world of *Hero and Leander*, both on divine and human levels, in the court and in the country, and among women as well as men. The aspiring country girl stands as an example. She is a pastoral antiheroine who clearly agrees with Tamburlaine that nature teaches us to have aspiring minds. (One might also consider Hero's natural aspirations as they reveal themselves in the scene in the temple, where she involuntarily encourages Leander.) To stress the point, Marlowe generalizes the country girl's ambition with the statement, "all women are ambitious naturally" (I. 428). This sentiment not only adds force to the poet's unsentimental examination of a basic ingredient of human nature, but also it denies the validity of the idealization of women popular in contemporary Petrarchan and courtly literature.

Marlowe's pervasive interest in the effects of power unifies individual passages as well as the whole of *Hero and Leander*. Material which appears superfluous becomes integral to the poem if one views it as a manifestation of this concern. For example, in the following description of Hero, Marlowe stresses the effects of her beauty on others and, hence, the power of it:

> Nor that night-wand'ring, pale and watery star
> (When yawning dragons draw her thirling car
> From Latmus' mount up to the gloomy sky,
> Where crown'd with blazing light and majesty,
> She proudly sits) more over-rules the flood
> Than she the hearts of those that near her stood.
> Even as, when gaudy nymphs pursue the chase,
> Wretched Ixion's shaggy-footed race,
> Incens'd with savage heat, gallop amain
> From steep pine-bearing mountains to the plain:
> So ran the people forth to gaze upon her,
> And all that view'd her were enamour'd on her.
>   (I. 107-118)

In these lines the power of Hero's beauty is the focus of both mythological comparisons. A second example occurs at the end of the digression on Mercury where the narrator glances with apparent irrelevance at the plight of scholars. In an etiological myth, he states that Learning "and Poverty should always kiss" (I. 470) and that "to this day is every scholar poor; / Gross gold from them runs headlong to the boor" (I. 471-472). He expands this criticism into a prophecy:

> That Midas' brood shall sit in Honour's chair,
> To which the Muses' sons are only heir:
> And fruitful wits that inaspiring are
> Shall discontent run into regions far.
> And few great lords in virtuous deeds shall joy,
> But be surpris'd with every garish toy,
> And still enrich the lofty servile clown,
> Who with encroaching guile keeps learning down.
>   (I. 475-482)

Here, the speaker especially laments that individual power is contingent upon wealth and not merit. In a society where one person's financial power may control and influence the pattern of existence for many, it is patently ironic that such power is merely arbitrary.

Throughout the poem, there are frequent indications of a corollary to Marlowe's views on power. He believes that an assertion of power is inevitably the result of strife (and, often, of violent destruction), and that strife is a pervasive condition natural to humankind and to the universe. Fate asserts its power over Love after strife (I. 441-464), just as Leander asserts his power over Hero after strife (II. 269-298). Leander argues that, in striving for Hero's maidenhead, "all heaven" would "with intestine broils the world destroy" (I. 247-252). Moreover, we are told that there is a considerable strife among the gods (*e.g.*, I. 322). Strife, then, is a major condition which shapes and limits one's power to act.

Marlowe's single-mindedness in probing the boundaries of power enables him, as well as us, to consider detachment itself as a form of mental power. Detachment is for him the most powerful of perceptual modes (in the sense of control, not intensity). Whereas engagement brings on a loss of control, detachment, being voluntary, consolidates power. This concept applies equally to the poet and to his readers. Seen from Marlowe's perspective, detachment not only gives the poet control over his material; it also enables him to understand the power of style and to use it effectively to govern the readers' responses. Through detachment, readers are able to understand the chief idea of the poem—that ultimate reality for human beings lies in their relation to the controlling forces within and beyond them. The style of the poem is thematically important, because it enables readers to become aware of the perceptual mode which Marlowe is advocating even as they experience that mode. Ultimately, detachment performs a moral service for readers: it gives them the distance and control necessary to perceive the wisdom of a detached perspective in themselves.

Detachment serves still another important function: it enables readers to understand and appreciate the full artistic achievement of the poem and the freedom and power of the poet. Although there is no Prologue to *Hero and Leander* to explain its artistry, as there is to *Tamburlaine,* a detached reading reveals that the poem is as much of a manifesto. First, through devices of detachment Marlowe calls attention to his manner of expression, often a means of self-advertisement. In his initial descriptions of Leander, for example, he inserts between the subject and verb of the sentence an important parenthesis: "Amorous Leander, beautiful and young, / (Whose tragedy divine Musaeus sung) / Dwelt in Abydos . . . " (I. 51-53). The obtrusive irrelevance with which he mentions Musaeus is meant to draw attention to the earlier writer and to invite us to draw comparison with Musaeus's telling of the tale—to see, in effect, how much richer Marlowe's poem is, not only in its greater thematic import but in its more sophisticated artistry.

Another example of the poet's drawing attention to his artistic superiority—in this case, his superiority to convention—occurs when, in describing Leander, the narrator adopts the familiar device of *occupatio*:

> . . . I could tell ye
> How smooth his breast was, and how white his belly,
> And whose immortal fingers did imprint
> That heavenly path with many a curious dint,
> That runs along his back, but my rude pen
> Can hardly blazon forth the loves of men,
> Much less of powerful gods: let it suffice
> That my slack muse sings of Leander's eyes,
> Those orient cheeks and lips, exceeding his

> That leapt into the water for a kiss
> Of his own shadow, and despising many,
> Died ere he could enjoy the love of any.
> (I. 65-76)

In lines 69-71, the comic nonsense of suddenly elevating Leander to an artifact and equal of "powerful gods" points to the false modesty of the convention as a disclaimer, and to the virtue of common sense. In the second half of the passage (I. 71: "let it suffice"), the narrator seems to assume a conventional posture; but he is so long on the comparison and short on his actual subject that we sense Marlowe's mockery of the convention. This satirical device, itself a technique of detachment, marks, in effect, the poet's consistently unsentimental focus and strong artistic control.

Marlowe's varying the tone or mood of the poem also fosters our detachment, and in our detachment we are able to appreciate his innovativeness. One representative example occurs in Leander's speech to Hero just after they have become enamored of one another:

> This idol which you term Virginity
> Is neither essence subject to the eye,
> No, nor to any one exterior sense,
> Nor hath it any place of residence,
> Nor is't of earth or mould celestial,
> Or capable of any form at all.
> (I. 269-274)

The tone is mock serious, as the youth sophistically marshals philosophic reasons why Hero should yield her virginity to him. The more earnest Leander becomes, the more ironic the tone becomes. Less abstract and quite pointedly comic is the initial description of Hero, in particular, her buskins:

> Buskins of shells all silver'd used she,
> And branch'd with blushing coral to the knee,
> Where sparrows perch'd, of hollow pearl and gold,
> Such as the world would wonder to behold:
> Those with sweet water oft her handmaid fills,
> Which as she went would chirrup through the bills.
> (I. 31-36)

The comically outrageous overstatement may well be intended as a satiric thrust against conventional romantic description, but the brash sense of fun in the excess of it all makes the tone playful rather than serious. In the Marlovian world, where hyperbole is the norm, the tone ranges considerably. There are the "mighty line[s]," resonant with "high astounding terms" (*Tamburlaine the Great*, Part One: Prologue, 1. 5), which are meant to make of us, in Hamlet's words, "wonder-wounded hearers":

> For every street like to a firmament
> Glister'd with breathing stars, who where they went
> Frighted the melancholy earth, which deem'd
> Eternal heaven to burn, for so it seem'd,
> As if another Phaethon had got
> The guidance of the sun's rich chariot.
>
> (I. 97-102)[9]

There is the brisk comedy of the description of Hero's suitors, "and many seeing great princes were denied, / Pin'd as they went, and thinking on her died" (I. 129-130). And there is what Keats might have called "a fine excess" (letter to John Taylor, Feb. 27, 1818) in this description of Hero on the morning after her first night of love:

> Thus near the bed she blushing stood upright,
> And from her countenance behold ye might
> A kind of twilight break, which through the hair,
> As from an orient cloud, glims here and there.
> And round about the chamber this false morn
> Brought forth the day before the day was born.
> (II. 317-322)

The tone can be intellectual (*e.g.*, sententious, in I. 167-176, or scientific, in II. 55-60) or emotional (*e.g.*, lyrical, in I. 345-352).

Partly because the tone seldom remains the same for long, the poet always keeps before us a perspective of reason and common sense. Our detachment enables us to see that the tone is often very different from the perspective Marlowe wishes us to take. In the following lines, our delight in Leander's sexual naïveté is undercut by a narrator who, often "in plain terms," is bawdy, voyeuristic, and ironic. We are thereby prevented from becoming completely enmeshed in the characters and

their situation. Instead, we are made to look upon sexual love un-
romantically, without idealizing or sentimentalizing our response:

> Albeit Leander, rude in love, and raw,
> Long dallying with Hero, nothing saw
> That might delight him more, yet he suspected
> Some amorous rites or other were neglected.
> Therefore unto his body hers he clung;
> She, fearing on the rushes to be flung,
> Striv'd with redoubled strength; the more she strived,
> The more a gentle pleasing heat revived,
> Which taught him all that elder lovers know.
> And now the same 'gan so to scorch and glow,
> As in plain terms (yet cunningly) he crav'd it;
> Love always makes those eloquent that have it.
>
> (II. 61-72)

Here, as in other passages, Marlowe manages through devices of detachment to suggest a rational perspective without assuming a rational, unified tone. That he can maintain such variety is clearly a measure
of his control and artistic achievement.

One other manifestation of his control of tone must be mentioned,
because it, too, becomes apparent through detachment and re-
establishes the boundaries of poetic conventions. We have already seen
that Marlowe disappoints expectations by mocking such conventions
as the digression. The list of conventions which he has reworked,
overturned, and twitted could be expanded, beginning with the genre
of the epyllion itself, but let us focus on a single representative example,
the dawn song, so that we may have some idea of how, by distancing
us, he makes us aware of his artistic innovation. The dawn song or
aubade lamenting the intrusion of morning upon lovers is standard fare
for any amatory poet. But Marlowe goes beyond the conventional uses
of it to point up his antipathy to its usual sentimentality:

> Now had the Morn espied her lover's steeds,
> Whereat she starts, puts on her purple weeds,
> And red for anger that he stay'd so long,
> All headlong throws herself the clouds among.
>
> (II. 87-90)

This is the first of three hints of a dawn song in the poem. The domestic drama in this description is comical, burlesquing the dignity and seriousness of the typical *aubade*. After a few more lines of narrative, Marlowe returns to the song. This time, with apparent seriousness, the sun is portrayed as sympathetic and understanding, but the maudlin build-up has been calculated to contrast with a comic let-down:

> And now the sun, that through th' horizon peeps,
> As pitying these lovers, downward creeps,
> So that in silence of the cloudy night,
> Though it was morning, did he take his flight.
> But what the secret trusty night conceal'd,
> Leander's amorous habit soon reveal'd.
>
> (II. 99-104)

Marlowe's second dawn song (II. 301-306) is conventional, except in its brevity. But the third, perhaps more accurately an extension of the second, is unconventional and yet Ovidian in type and function.[10] It closes as much as we have of Marlowe's poem:

> By this Apollo's golden harp began
> To sound forth music to the Ocean,
> Which watchful Hesperus no sooner heard,
> But he the day's bright-bearing car prepar'd,
> And ran before, as harbinger of light,
> And with his flaring beams mock'd ugly Night,
> Till she, o'ercome with anguish, shame, and rage,
> Dang'd down to hell her loathsome carriage.
>
> (II. 327-334)

No one can be sure how this would have fit in with what was to follow, but the cacophonous intensity of line 330, and Hesperus's violent assertion of power, signify that it is as unconventional as it is characteristic of Marlowe.[11] The disparity between the sober, bittersweet lyricism of convention and Marlowe's unconventional mode only emphasizes the hard certainty of tone and the concern with strife and power which runs throughout the poem. Thus, the contrast between the conventional dawn song we expect and the unconventional one we get helps us to separate Marlowe's individual talent from tradition, to see more sharply his originality.

Marlowe's limitations as a poet can also be understood in the light of his concern with power. Evidently for him, power as a poet means an unhampered striving against what has been done conventionally by others in order to beget for his readers "another world" (II. 292), one "of unknown joy" (II. 293). To be sure, the exuberance, the comic flippancy, the outrageousness, and the abundant sheer inventiveness of the poem do keep readers well entertained and in awe of the poet's power. But the detachment that allows Marlowe's imagination to range freely also brings with it at times an insensitivity to the characters and their plights. Instead of projecting into his characters with feeling and allowing himself to examine the psychological, moral, even philosophical implications of their struggles, Marlowe often takes quick refuge in ironies and in marveling at the consequences of power and the contentions for it. Thus, rather than allow his readers to become engrossed in the feelings of the characters as they struggle in a harsh world of strife and instability, he keeps them continually at arm's length. But whereas this detachment gives Marlowe the freedom and security of the poet's god-like control, it can leave his readers feeling empty. A case in point is the episode of Neptune and Leander. Marlowe is venturesome enough to depict a homoerotic incident but, finally, only to sensationalize it; he pulls away from the human issues of the encounter with brisk comedy and, in so doing, points to the boldness of the incident without pointing to anything beyond it. This is also often the case when he portrays Hero and Leander striving to consummate their love.[12] The result is that the detached readers see more than they were meant to: namely, superficiality and mere cleverness, the result of Marlowe's fear or inability to confront the deeper implications of the characters and situations he has portrayed.

Ultimately, Marlowe's assertion of detachment over engagement can best be seen as a realistic reworking of romantic convention and as part of a system of values, both aesthetic and moral. To Marlowe, emotional absorption for readers, like love for the victim of physical desire, "is too full of faith, too credulous, / With folly and false hope deluding us" (II. 221-222). It is the defect in "th' enchanted gazer's mind" (I. 104). Therefore, detachment functions morally to prevent us from deceiving ourselves. It enables us to use our rational faculties to make independent choices, whether in living or writing, and, in so doing, to discover our individuality and supremacy, the sweet fruition of an earthly crown.

The individuality and supremacy of *Hero and Leander* as an epyllion was not questioned during Marlowe's time and is not now. The hyperbolic world which is depicted with alternate drollery and seriousness, the glittering series of impersonal pictures, the exuberant splendor of amplification, the lavish Italianate filigree and adornment, the unsentimental frankness, and the realistic examination of the powers and true nature of physical desire mark the poem unmistakably as a masterwork. *Hero and Leander* is the apotheosis of the Renaissance epyllion because, while relying—as all epyllia do—on Ovidian techniques of expression, it surpasses its Roman source in tone and theme. And we know this, as Marlowe intended us to, because our detachment while reading the poem enables us to perceive it.

NOTES

1. Three representative examples will suffice to show that during the early 1950s the critics were still strongly romantic in their responses to the poem. Louis R. Zocca writes in *Elizabethan Narrative Poetry* (New Brunswick, N. J.: Rutgers University Press, 1950), p. 33, that *Hero and Leander* is "the very embodiment of the romantic mood." Michel Poirier in *Christopher Marlowe* (London: Chatto and Windus, 1951), p. 195, views the poem as "essentially a hymn to sensuality." Muriel C. Bradbrook in *Shakespeare and Elizabethan Poetry* (London: Chatto and Windus, 1952), pp. 58-59, waxes lyrical in describing "the winds that caress Hero" and "the green waves that enfold Leander" as "servants of the servants of love."

2. C. S. Lewis, "Hero and Leander," *Proceedings of the British Academy,* 38 (1952), 24.

3. Just as Marlowe rejected romanticized characterizations of physical love, recent critics have rejected romanticized interpretations of the poem. Although there are signs of a shift in attitude earlier, it was in the late 1950s that critics consistently directed their attention to the range of humor and the antiromantic characteristics of the poem. Most recently, the tendency has been to intellectualize (overintellectualize in some instances) the serious matter of the poem.

4. See Maynard Mack, "Engagement and Detachment in Shakespeare's Plays" in *Essays on Shakespeare and Elizabethan Drama,* ed. Richard Hosley (Columbia, Mo.: University of Missouri Press, 1962), pp. 275-296. Professor Mack's distinction between these two psychological states is useful to describe Marlowe's (and hence his readers') relation to the characters and events of *Hero and Leander.* In talking about Marlowe's plays, Marjorie Garber says that "much of the dramatic tension in Marlowe's plays derives from the dialectic between aspiration and limitation" ("'Infinite Riches in a Little Room': Closure and Enclosure in Marlowe" in *Two Renaissance Mythmakers, Christopher Marlowe and Ben Jonson* [Selected papers from the English Institute, 1975-76], ed. Alvin Kernan [Baltimore, Md.: The Johns Hopkins University Press, 1977], p. 3). Although she does not mention *Hero and*

Leander in her essay, her generalization easily applies to the poem; in fact, Marlowe uses this "dialectic" to give unity to the poem.

6. All citations from *Hero and Leander* are from the Revels Edition of the works of Christopher Marlowe: *The Poems: Christopher Marlowe,* ed. Millar MacLure (London: Methuen & Co. Ltd., 1968).

7. Hallett Smith, *Elizabethan Poetry* (Cambridge, Mass.: Harvard University Press, 1952), p. 10.

8. *Ibid.*, p. 11.

9. This passage can be said to exemplify Marlowe's "mighty line" by virtue of the absoluteness of its statement, the exalted cosmic imagery, the larger-than-life details, the energy and intensity of its verbs, and the heavy, emphatic rhythms.

10. As L. C. Martin, ed., *Marlowe's Poems* (London: Methuen & Co., Ltd., 1931), points out in his notes (p. 66), the "loathsome carriage" of this line is similar to the "hateful carriage" of Marlowe's *Elegies,* I, xii, 38.

11. Some critics view the poem as complete and, therefore, Chapman aside, not in need of being continued. See, for example, Louis L. Martz, ed., *Hero and Leander by Christopher Marlowe: A Facsimile of the First Edition, London 1598* (New York: Johnson Reprint Corporation, and Washington: The Folger Shakespeare Library, 1972), pp. 13-14, who believes the poem is complete, and Gordon Braden, *The Classics and English Poetry* (New Haven, Conn.: Yale University Press, 1978), pp. 149-150 and 209, who sensibly questions this view. Whether the poem is in fact unfinished does not affect my point here.

12. See the excellent discussion of this point by Jane Adamson, "Marlowe, *Hero and Leander,* and the Art of Leaping in Poetry," *The Critical Review,* 17 (1974), 71-75. In a context different from mine—Marlowe's concern with flux in the poem—Adamson treats the success and failure of characterization in "the last 50 or so lines of Sestiad II" (p. 72) and then goes on to enumerate Marlowe's defects as the author of *Hero and Leander* (pp. 75-81).

Hero and Leander:
The Sense of an Ending

W. L. GODSHALK

Hero and Leander has appropriately evoked a variety of responses from its readers. In 1598, Edward Blunt, one of the first readers of the poem, saw it as an *"unfinished Tragedy."*[1] In the nineteenth century, however, Edward Dowden felt that the poem gave evidence of "the Renaissance feeling for sensuous beauty." Following Dowden, A. C. Bradley found that "Nothing of the deeper thought of the time, no 'looking before and after,' . . . interferes with its frank acceptance of sensuous beauty and joy," and Havelock Ellis described the poem as a "free and fresh and eager song . . . full of ideal beauty that finds its expression in the form and colour of things, above all in the bodies of men and women."[2] While the Renaissance reader did not fail to see the tragedy of the poem, the nineteenth-century readers hardly noticed it because of their preoccupation with the poem's sensuous detail. Twentieth-century readers, on the other hand, influenced by Muriel Bradbrook's vision of a Chaucer-like Marlowe who "is both ironically detached and sympathetically identified with the lovers"[3] have often had difficulty seeing the tragedy and the sensuality through the obviously comic presentation.[4]

Indeed, the poem builds its own mysteries and demands the variety of responses chronicled in the first paragraph. Hero and Leander are themselves shrouded in mystery. Few of the questions that we ask ourselves about the lovers can be answered with any degree of certainty, and, of course, the problem is compounded by the fact that we see them only through the eyes and sensibility of Marlowe's dramatized narrator. Although critics have attempted to place the narrator, they have succeeded only in proving that he is a man of here, there, and everywhere.[5] He defies precise definition, and the narrator's elusiveness may be only one aspect of his general unreliability. Can we really trust this shifty, shifting personality? But, of course, the major problem may be the supposedly fragmentary nature of the poem. Had Marlowe completed his poem—so the argument goes—many of the present mysteries would be nonexistent.[6] It is this question of incompleteness that we must address first.

In 1972, Louis Martz argued carefully—and heretically—that the poem is complete as it stands. Basing his description on the first edition of 1598, Martz described *Hero and Leander* as an

> unbroken poem of 818 lines, falling into a symmetrical, triadic design. We have first the leisurely scene of the lovers' first encounter at the feast of Adonis, a section of 384 lines; we have next the tale of Mercury, the country maid, and the Fates, forming a central panel of exactly 100 lines; and finally we have the urgent movement of the lovers toward their consummation, a section of 334 lines, roughly balancing the length of the opening section. (p. 3)

Muriel Bradbrook had briefly anticipated, in 1951, Martz's concept that the poem is completed. Approaching the question from a different direction, she noted: "It is conjectured that the poem was left unfinished at Marlowe's death but this again is pure hypothesis. . . . There was never any need to take the whole of a classical story for literary purposes, but only so much as was relevant to the matter at hand and the literary species in question. . . . There are no loose ends in Marlowe's poem," and Bradbrook succinctly links the various parts of the narrative. "The lovers," she suggests, "are included in the circle of comedy."[7]

Although the combined authority of Bradbrook and Martz has caused some scholars to hedge their bets,[8] most recent critics silently reject their arguments by simply referring to the poem as "unfinished"

or "fragmentary."[9] At this point in literary history, it is distinctly unfashionable to defend the poem as complete, and yet this is precisely
what I intend to do.

To begin, it must be pointed out that some critics who apparently
believe that the poem is incomplete also believe that Marlowe had run
out of options where he stopped writing.[10] They suppose that Marlowe
intended to finish the poem as Musaeus had finished the original *Hero
and Leander,* but that his comic handling of the initial parts of the narrative militated against his concluding it in the manner in which he had
planned. Gordon Braden summarizes this position:

> Marlowe certainly did not intend to change the eventual end of the
> story in the way in which, say, Petowe did, and probably he at least
> set out to cover the whole of Mousaios's plot. Yet it remains in-
> triguing that he stopped writing exactly where he did, at so satisfy-
> ing a close, rather than trailing off, as though he realized that he
> had reached some sort of logical conclusion. Certainly 'finishing'
> the poem with a tragic end after what had gone before would have
> required some poetic strategies that we cannot easily extrapolate
> from what we have.[11]

It strikes me that this argument is a special case of the intentional falla-
cy. We have, after all, no way of knowing—in our present state of
ignorance—that Marlowe "probably . . . set out to cover the whole of
Mousaios's plot." Blunt's statement that *Hero and Leander* is an unfinished tragedy is merely an early critical opinion, and his words
"*Desunt nonnulla*" appended to the end of his edition are only a footnote
to that opinion. If, indeed, Marlowe had run out of options, as Braden
and others suggest, then the poem ends where most poems end: when
the poet has said what he has to say.

Nevertheless, Braden points out, in defense of his position, that
Marlowe has placed in his poem "some clear foreshadowings of the
tragic dénouement" (p. 149) as it is found in Musaeus. In Marlowe's
first line we are told that the Hellespont is "guiltie of True-loues
blood," and as the narrator prepares to bring his lovers together, he
says:

> On this feast day, O cursed day and hower,
> Went *Hero* thorow *Sestos,* from her tower
> To *Venus* temple, where vnhappilye,

As after chaunc'd, they did each other spye.
(ll. 131-134)

Later, when Cupid requests from the Fates that Hero and Leander "might enioy ech other, and be blest" (l. 380), he is (apparently) denied. Moreover, Paul Miller argues that Leander's rejection of Neptune's love also prepares for a tragic conclusion: "Had Marlowe concluded the poem, it appears likely that he would have made Neptune, angered beyond endurance at Leander's repeated crossings of the sea and rejection of divine love [*i.e.*, Neptune's], [take] mortal revenge on the youth."[12] But tragic innuendo, as we know from Shakespeare's comedies and romances, does not necessarily point toward a tragic conclusion.

There are other ways to explain the function of these foreshadowings in the poem. First, it appears that Marlowe wishes to set up a tension between the comic narration and the tragic implications. I take it that this tension helps yield the complexity of tone experienced by most readers of the poem, and that this tension is a function of Marlowe's dramatized narrator. The narrator is not quite sure what attitude he should assume toward his material, nor is he sure precisely where his narrative is going. We will consider this aspect of the poem more fully later. Second, except for the general reference to the Hellespont being guilty of true love's blood, the foreshadowings are not necessarily to the death of lovers. A love affair can end unhappily without the lovers dying, and the Fates do allow if, indeed, they have *any* power over the lovers—Hero and Leander to enjoy each other physically. Paul Miller's suggestion, apparently accepted by Braden,[13] is extremely debatable, and the evidence ambiguous. The narrator tells us that "The god put *Helles* bracelet on his arme, / And swore the sea should neuer doe him harme" (ll. 663-664). The classical tradition has it that Helles drowned in the straits afterward named for her; but, in a later tradition, recorded by Martin,[14] she was rescued by Neptune and bore him a son. Is the bracelet a token of Neptune's redeeming love—or quite the opposite? Is Neptune's vow an indication that Leander will not drown in this recreation of the story? Or is Neptune no more reliable than the other mythological figures in the poem?[15] The homosexual or possibly bisexual god we are introduced to in the poem does not appear to be an uncontrolled killer; he pulls his punches: "He flung at him [*i.e.*

Leander] his mace, but as it went, / He cald it in, for loue made him repent" (ll. 693-694). But the chief point here is that the tragic fore-shadowings noted by Braden do not specifically indicate that Hero and Leander will die in Marlowe's narrative.

One line not pointed out by Braden suggests, perhaps, that Leander, if not Hero, will die in the poem. The narrator parenthetically speaks of Leander "(Whose tragedie diuine *Musaeus* soong)" (l. 52). Why Hero is not included we can not say, but as Martz correctly suggests, the parenthesis may well be "Marlowe's way of telling us that he will leave the singing of the 'tragedie' to other poets" (p. 14). And even though a critic may not accept this reading of the line, he can no longer use the line as unequivocal evidence that Marlowe "intended" his poem—ultimately—to be a tragedy.

One other point made by Braden demands comment. Not all readers of the poem will agree that the ending is a satisfactory close, a logical ending of the story.[16] There is a feeling among some readers that the poem as it now stands lacks closure, a sense of an ending, and, though I agree with Braden that the poem does have a satisfactory conclusion, I acknowledge that the position needs to be defended. The poem ends with daybreak. Earlier in the poem, the narrator aphoristically in-forms us that "darke night is *Cupids* day" (l. 191). Love thrives on dark-ness, not light, and, following Musaeus,[17] Marlowe has night fall as Hero and Leander first fall in love: "The aire with sparkes of liuing fire was spangled, / And night deepe drencht in mystie *Acheron*, / Heau'd vp her head, and halfe the world vpon, / Breath'd darknesse forth" (ll. 188-191). In contrast, the poem ends with daybreak, and the light here is that of a comic reality that does nothing to soften the torture of Hero's embarrassment: "she knew not how to frame her looke, / Or speake to him who in a moment tooke, / That which so long so charily she kept" (ll. 791-793). As she tries to flee from bed—"her naked feet were whipping out" (l. 797)—Leander tackles her and "Meremaid-like vnto the floore she slid" (l. 799). This is surely a peculiarly gro-tesque way to conclude one's first night of love; the emphasis appears to be on the unromantic fiasco.

For Hero, however, misery is piled on misery; the false dawn of her intense blush calls forth the real dawn, and she is displayed "all naked" to Leander's sight. He watches her greedily—a stare that takes us back to the beginning of the poem when "*Leander* was enamoured. / Stone

still he stood, and euermore he gazed" (ll. 162-163) on the elaborately
dressed Hero. But there is an implied contrast between the incipient
lover whose gaze calls forth Hero's love and the voluptuous young man
lying in her bed voyeuristically watching her naked embarrassment:
"his admiring eyes more pleasure tooke, / Than *Dis*, on heapes of gold
fixing his looke" (ll. 809-810). The simile (possibly a reminiscence of
Book II of *The Faerie Queene*) suggests that his is not exactly an innocent
pleasure. And the poem ends, not with the birth of a new day, but with
the death of night—which, as we have seen, for the lovers had been
Cupid's day: "ougly night . . . / . . . o'recome with anguish, shame,
and rage, / Dang'd downe to hell her loathsome carriage" (ll. 816-
818). It seems obvious enough that the dying night takes on the emotions of the naked Hero, and sophomoric readers have informed me
that it is, indeed, Hero who dies at the poem's end. That inattentive
reading is, strangely, perhaps not totally false to Marlowe's vision.
Something more important than night has died here; we are witnessing, among other things, the death of youthful innocence.

Marlowe underscores the importance of this conclusion by ending
his poem much as Vergil had ended the *Aeneid*. The death of
Turnus—"vitaque cum gemitu fugit indignata sub umbras"—is, on
the surface, no appropriate way to end an heroic poem celebrating the
triumphant founding of Rome, just as Marlowe's final image is no way
to end a scene celebrating the triumph of young love over the apparent
prohibitions of fate. Obviously the conclusions of both poems ask, not
for a simple, but for a complex response. Only a certain kind of vision
will allow us to see Marlowe's ending as—in Braden's words—a "satisfying close."

Perhaps the best way to begin developing that vision is by looking at
certain progressions in the poem, that is, the way the poem moves
from, say, an emphasis on seeing in the first 384 lines to an emphasis on
touching in the last 334 lines. These progressions, I think, allow us to
see generally the movement of Marlowe's thinking and, because these
progressions are completed, to see how Marlowe in this way has given
his poem a sense of closure. Let us begin with the movement from seeing to touching, hardly an unexpected progression in a love story, but
one which establishes a recurrent pattern in the poem.

In the first lines, it is established that Hero is the object of men's
gaze; courted by Apollo, she is offered his throne as a dower "Where

she should sit for men to gaze vpon" (l. 8). The concept is reinforced by the embroidery on her sleeve: "Where *Venus* in her naked glory stroue, / To please the carelesse and disdainfull eies, / Of proud *Adonis* that before her lies" (ll. 12-14). As Hero walks through the streets of Sestos to the temple of Venus, she steals "away th'inchaunted gazers mind, / For like Sea-nimphs inueigling harmony, / So was her beautie to the standers by" (ll. 104-106). When Leander sees her, "euermore he gazed" (l. 163), and the narrator steps in to inform us, "What we behold is censur'd [*i.e.*, judged] by our eies" (l. 174). Leander in his *suasoria* (ll. 199-328) draws the obvious conclusion of the impatient lover: "Nor heauen, nor thou, were made to gaze vpon" (l. 223) and indicates where the progression is headed.

In the first section (384 lines) touching is minimal—if significant: "He toucht her hand, in touching it she trembled, / . . . / These louers parled by the touch of hands" (ll. 183, 185). However, when Leander "stoopt, to haue imbrac'd her," Hero casts herself away from "his spreading armes" and admonishes him: "Gentle youth forebeare / To touch the sacred garments which I weare" (ll. 343-344). In the first section of the poem, seeing takes precedence over touching.

The sight pattern is comically reinforced in the digression (ll. 385-484), where on "The selfe-same day that he asleepe had layd / Inchaunted *Argus*" (ll. 387-388), a creature known for its many eyes, Mercury "spied a countrie mayd" (l. 388). Like Leander, Mercury is immediately enamored, but, lacking Leander's restraint, Mercury tumbles his country maid "in the grasse" (l. 406), and the reader surmises the worst. But not so. Mercury is only looking: "he often strayd / Beyond the bounds of shame, in being bold / To eie those parts, which no eie should behold" (ll. 406-408), the narrator comments rather prudishly. It appears that the country maid escapes Mercury's clutches *virgo intacta*. The digression clearly emphasizes the prurient voyeurism of gazing on naked beauty, and thus looks forward to Leander's final stare at the embarassed Hero.

The third section (ll. 485 ff.) begins almost immediately with the first kiss: "He kist her, and breath'd life into her lips" (l. 487), and during Leander's first visit to Hero's tower, the touching becomes extremely erotic:

Albeit *Leander* rude in loue, and raw,

> Long dallying with *Hero,* nothing saw
> That might delight him more, yet he suspected
> Some amorous rites or other were neglected.
> Therefore vnto his bodie, hirs he clung,
> She, fearing on the rushes to be flung,
> Striu'd with redoubled strength, the more she striued,
> The more a gentle pleasing heat reuiued,
> Which taught him all that elder louers know,
> And now the same gan so to scorch and glow. . . .
>   (ll. 545-554)

The very ambiguity (*e.g.,* "the same" points to the increasing physicality of the poem. During their final encounter, in Hero's bed, physical touch dominates. Leander "greedily assayd / To touch those dainties" (ll. 753-754), her sexual parts, and though she struggles, Leander lies "on her quiuering brest" (l. 773), encloses "her in his armes and kist her to" (l. 776). For the moment, in the darkness of the bedroom, seeing is forgotten, but—as we have noticed—Leander returns to gazing on Hero, and the final stare is no longer the innocent gaze of the young lover recorded in Part One. Thus the progression of seeing to touching is also a progression of innocence to experience. If we divorce these terms from their Blakean connotations, we can see that the lovers have moved from sexual innocence to a certain level of sexual awareness, and that that movement has changed the way they experience their world. Hero is filled with shame; Leander, with lust.

The other progressions in the poem are easily explained, for they are set up much like the movement from seeing to touching. There is, for example, a parallel movement of words to actions.[18] In the digression, Mercury quickly moves from words to deeds:

> [Mercury] sweetly on his pipe began to play,
> And with smooth speech, her fancie to assay,
> Till in his twining armes he lockt her fast,
> And then he woo'd with kisses, and at last,
> As sheap-heards do, her on the ground hee layd.
>   (ll. 401-405)

As we have noticed already, the comedy of these lines lies in the fact that our expectations are denied. Mercury's actions cycle back into voyeurism. Leander's words and actions are segregated more completely. In section one, he is the "the bold sharpe Sophister" (l. 197), using the long *suasoria* in his attempt to seduce Hero: in Section Three, Leander moves decisively to actions as we have seen in our description of touching. Leander's words here are passed over rapidly: "*Leander* . . . / Breathlesse spoke some thing, and sigh'd out the rest" (ll. 773-774). The emphasis is clearly not on what he says, but what he does. In general we see a movement away from Artifice—from Leander's rhetoric and Hero's elaborate costume—toward Nature—to Leander's physical seduction and Hero's nakedness. There is a stripping away here of society's restraints, not the awesome stripping of *King Lear,* of course, but certainly its comic counterpart.

In examining these progressions in the poem, what strikes the reader about Hero and Leander is the sketchiness with which their backgrounds are presented. Veselin Kostič describes their mystery: "Hero and Leander are isolated beings, detached from ordinary life and human society in general. They are without any clearly defined context—social, ethical, national, intellectual—that could impose limits on them. The few everyday details . . . which . . . found their way into the poem are distinctly jarring."[19] In Musaeus's poem, Hero is given jealous parents who are mentioned or alluded to throughout. To keep Leander from touching her, Hero tells him: "Shun the wrath of my parents, rich in many possessions" (l. 125). Later, after she has decided to give Leander her love, she explains: "We cannot openly come into a righteous marriage, / For it was not my parents' will" (ll. 179-180). Her tower is apparently some kind of prison forced upon her "by my parents' hateful will" (l. 190). Leander secretly swims to her tower by night to keep her parents from finding out about their love. The fatal lamp is to guide him on his night sea journey. "Hero of the trailing robes, in secrecy from her parents, / Was maiden by day, by night a wife" (ll. 286-287). Musaeus gives a context by which we can understand the human impediments to the love affair; we know why Hero is so reluctant and why Leander must swim to her tower by night.[20]

But Marlowe changes all this. His Hero has no jealous parents; instead "A dwarfish beldame beares" her company (l. 353) and this dwarf conveniently disappears before Leander arrives at Hero's tower—much as Adam disappears from *As You Like It.* She is not missed, and her disappearance usually goes unquestioned. With the

disappearance of family and duenna, the reason for secrecy also disappears, and Marlowe's narrator wryly notes: "what the secret trustie
night conceal'd, / *Leanders* amorous habit soone reueal'd . . . / Which
made his loue through *Sestos* to bee knowne, / And thence vnto *Abydus*
sooner blowne, / Than he could saile" (ll. 587-588, 595-597).

In Marlowe's poem, the love of Hero and Leander is publicly known;
their love is not "the darkling marriage-bond, unseen by deathless
Dawn" (Musaeus, 3; *cf.* ll. 282-283). For Hero's parents, Marlowe
substitutes Leander's lenient father who mildly rebukes his son (l. 621)
and is heard from no more. Leander's reason for swimming to Hero's
tower by night also disappears, and Marlowe's Leander swims by
sunlight (l. 686). But without the reason for secrecy, we wonder why
Leander swims at all. Why doesn't he take a boat? It is part of the
poem's sketchiness that we can come up with no good reason.

However, Kostič's perception is only partially correct. While
Marlowe relieves Hero of inhibiting parents, he provides her with a
strict vow of celibacy to Venus. In fact, what Marlowe does is to dimin-
ish the lovers' human context only to give them a divine one.
Musaeus's lovers have no direct contact with the gods of their world;
Marlowe's lovers do. At the beginning of Marlowe's poem, we hear
that "Apollo courted" Hero for her "haire"[21] offering "as a dower his
burning throne" (ll. 6-7). To balance the sun's attentions to Hero, the
narrator in describing Leander says that "Faire *Cinthia* wisht, his
armes might be her spheare" (l. 59), and that "immortall fingars did
imprint, / That heauenly path . . . / That runs along his backe" (ll.
67-69).[22] We are further told that Cupid "imagyn'd *Hero* was his
mother":

> And oftentimes into her bosome flew,
> About her naked necke his bare armes threw.
> And laid his childish head vpon her brest,
> And with still panting rockt, there tooke his rest.
>   (ll. 40-44)

The possible sexual implications of this passage are hard to miss. The
narrator indicates that Hero and Leander—for all their apparent innocence—have both been rather intimate with the gods before the action of the poem begins. Reflecting back on these passages, the reader

may wonder if they are simply a product of the narrator's hyperbolic imagination, but even so, the narrator in this way gives the lovers a context.

The description of Venus's temple—containing "*Venus* glasse" (l. 142)—is also a Marlovian addition to Musaeus's narrative. Here we find carved effigies of Proteus and Bacchus, and in the "glasse" "there might you see the gods in sundrie shapes, / Committing headdie ryots, incest, rapes" (ll. 143-144). Cupid's active participation in the love affair is also Marlowe's addition. When Hero vows "spotlesse chastitie" (l. 368) to Venus, Cupid

> beats downe her praiers with his wings,
> Her vowes aboue the emptie aire he flings:
> All deepe enrag'd, his sinowie bow he bent,
> And shot a shaft that burning from him went. . . .
> (ll. 369-372)

Cupid's abortive journey to the Destinies introduces the explanatory digression which in turn reinforces the concept of human and divine interpenetration: Mercury's wooing of the shepherdess looks forward to Neptune's pursuit of Leander. Kostič is surely correct in pointing out that Hero and Leander are "detached from ordinary life and human society in general," but he is just as surely wrong in suggesting that they are "isolated." They get more attention than they desire from the gods.

But why does Marlowe introduce this divine context? It has been suggested that the immorality of the pagan gods in the poem is an implied criticism of divinity.[23] In reading the poem, I do not find this criticism, but I do find a marked difference between the gods and the humans. The difference is that the gods have no sense of morality, whereas the humans do. The gods are totally uninhibited; they have no conscience, no sense of sexual taboo. Hero and Leander just as surely do. By placing the lovers in the context of the pagan deities, Marlowe has set them off as different, moral creatures who are not in tune with the amoral universe in which they exist.

Hero and Leander express their moral sensibilities in quite different ways, and we must begin our analysis of this difference with their initial portraits. As Brian Morris notes (pp. 116-117), their portraits are strangely inverted; in Renaissance pictorial tradition, the man should be clothed, the woman nude,[24] but quite the reverse is true here. Hero's portrait is essentially a detailed description of her costume:

> The outside of her garments were of lawne,
> The lining, purple silke, with guilt starres drawne,
> Her wide sleeues greene . . .
>
> . . .
>
> Her kirtle blew . . .
>
> . . .
>
> Her vaile was artificiall flowers and leaues,
> Whose workmanship both man and beast deceaues.
>   (ll. 9-11, 15, 19-20)

But most surprising are her elaborate boots:

> Buskins of shels all siluered, vsed she,
> And brancht with blushing corall to the knee;
> Where sparrowes pearcht, of hollow pearle and gold,
> Such as the world would woonder to behold:
> Those with sweet water oft her handmaid fils,
> Which as she went would cherupe through the bils.
>   (ll. 31-36)

Yeats no doubt would have approved, and Morris aptly comments that the main point of this description is "the triumph of Art over Nature" (p. 116). But Hero's emphasis on the artificial further suggests that her costume is being used as a device to insulate her from the world of nature. She wishes to remain in the totally human world of art. Her vow of chastity points in the same direction. As Leander hints in his *suasoria*, Nature abhors a virgin, and only humans place any value on the virgin state. That Hero has made her vow of chastity to Venus serves to underscore her ambivalence. Though she has consciously chosen art over nature, a part of her still owes allegiance to the natural world ruled over—in this poem—by the pagan deities. For the moment, she elects to be totally human.

In contrast to the overdressed Hero, Leander begins the poem as he ends it—nude. The narrator focuses on his hair, arms, hand, neck, breast, belly, back, eyes, cheeks, and lips—the kind of description we expect of the beloved woman in a sonnet sequence. The orientation of the description itself indicates an androgynous Leander, but the narrator goes on:

> Had wilde *Hippolitus, Leander* seene,
> Enamoured of his beautie had he beene,
> His presence made the rudest paisant melt,
> That in the vast vplandish countrie dwelt,
> The barbarous *Thratian* soldier moou'd with nought,[25]
> Was moou'd with him, and for his fauour sought.
> Some swore he was a maid in mans attire.
>   (ll. 77-83)

We learn that, just like Hero, Leander is the object of a great deal of hypothetical and real masculine attention. However, unlike the portrait of Hero, the portrait of Leander does not seem to reveal a preference for art or nature. In other words, these do not seem to be contrasting portraits in which Art triumphs over Nature in the first, Nature over Art in the second. In fact, the major point of Leander's portrait seems to be his extreme androgyny: "in his lookes were all that men desire" (l. 84).

The homosexual attention indicated in the portrait of Leander looks forward to his encounter with Neptune as he swims toward Hero's tower. I would like to suggest that Neptune's attempted seduction of Leander is purposefully juxtaposed to Leander's successful seduction of Hero, and further that these two last scenes are imaginatively linked with the opening portraits. In these two scenes, Hero and Leander reveal their different, and yet strictly human, moral sensibilities.

The gods, as we have seen from "*Venus* glasse" (the mirror that allows us a vision of the amoral cosmos), have no sexual taboos. Jove is incestuously married to his sister, carries on a homosexual dalliance with Ganymede, has a bestial affair with Europa, and so on. With the gods, anything goes, including the sadism implied by the reference to burning Troy (l. 153). As one of the celestials, Neptune is of course not subject to any human restrictions, and, initially mistaking Leander for Ganymede, he falls immediately in love with him:

> He clapt his plumpe cheekes, with his tresses playd,
> And smiling wantonly, his loue bewrayd.
> He watcht his armes, and as they opend wide,
> At euery stroke, betwixt them would he slide,

And steale a kisse, and then run out and daunce,
And as he turnd, cast many a lustfull glaunce.
                                        (ll. 665-670)

Leander's response is a strictly human one: "You are deceau'd, I am
no woman I" (l. 676). Neptune smiles at this naive response. Now what
I find interesting here is the way in which Leander tries to ward off
Neptune's unwanted attentions. He does not, for example, say that he
is in love with Hero and that he wishes to remain faithful to that love.
Instead he rejects Neptune's advances in terms of taboo against homosexuality. His feelings of homophobia, in terms of the poem, are very
human, but not very natural. Moreover, taking into account Leander's
extreme androgyny as indicated in his initial portrait, I think Marlowe
is also suggesting that Leander is denying an essential part of his own
nature in his rejection of Neptune. Although Leander is, ironically, not
at all morally troubled by his seduction of a young virgin, he finds it
unthinkable to have a homosexual affair with Neptune. Marlowe's
point, I judge, is that Leander is limited by his moral sensibility and
cannot get in touch with an essential part of himself: the homosexual.

   In the final scene, Leander plays Neptune's role of the sexual aggres-
sor; Hero, Leander's role of the reluctant sexual object. The seduction
is not presented as a tender affair:

        Loue is not ful of pittie (as men say)
        But deaffe and cruell, where he means to pray.
        So that the truce was broke, and she alas,
        (Poore sillie maiden) at his mercie was.
        Euen as a bird, which in our hands we wring,
        Foorth plungeth, and oft flutters with her wind.
                (ll. 781-782, 779-780, 783-784)

Although Hero's ambivalence toward her seduction is fully suggested,
her final reaction, as we saw in our consideration of the poem's final
lines, is one of shame. Unlike the goddess whom she worships, Hero
cannot deny the moral implications of her acts. Seen in the nude by her
lover, she blushes, and that blush pays tribute to her abiding moral
sense.

   The poem ends on a dissonant note. The amoral gods of a naturalistic universe do not understand man's moral nature, but man cannot

live in a world that is not tinged with the colors of morality. The universe demands a natural response—in the case of the poem, copulation—and the humans insist on a moral one. Hero, caught between the two worlds—the world of natural sexuality and the world of human morality, is an emblem for all humanity, and her blush is our blush. For the reader, it is Hero who chiefly exemplifies the paradoxes inherent in the human condition. "Born under one law, to another bound," she is torn between her moral nature and her erotic drives. To her problem, to our problem, there is no resolution.

But the poem also presents another, quite different problem to which there is no resolution: the reader perceives this love story through the sensibility of a dramatized narrator. The narrator stands between us and the lovers, and we tend to read *Hero and Leander* in much the same way we read Ring Lardner's "The Haircut." The narrator cannot be trusted. Part of his vision we may accept, but a good deal of his interpretation seems to miss the point. David Farkas hears two voices in the narrative: the genuine Marlovian voice and the narrator's.[26] But this distinction, which must in reading be very subtly applied, seems to add an unnecessary complexity. How ultimately do we distinguish between Marlowe and the narrative voice? Is it Marlowe or the narrator who is so taken with Leander's physical beauty *and* with Hero's preposterously clashing color scheme? Of course, the usual, quite glib answer is that Marlowe is taken with Leander's nude body, while his insensitive narrator glories in the absurdities of Hero's costume. But this distinction is completely arbitrary, and one might just as well claim that Marlowe had an inordinate interest in exotic dress. It seems to me that we are, ultimately, stuck with the narrator. It would be helpful to see certain passages as Marlowe's own guideposts to the reader; the guideposts are, however, simply not there.

The narrator is intrusive and often, it appears, misleading. His conclusion to the Mercury digression (ll. 465-482) is, in fact, a second digression, and these lines might be cut from the poem without any loss of logical continuity. Line 483 follows logically, not from line 482, but from line 464. The reader surmises that this brief digression-within-a-digression relates more to the narrator and his preoccupations than it does to the love story:

And but that Learning, in despight of Fate,

Will mount aloft, and enter heauen gate,
And to the seat of *Joue* it selfe aduaunce,
Hermes had slept in hell with ignoraunce.
Yet as a punishment they [the Fates] added this,
That he and *Pouertie* should alwaies kis.
And to this day is euerie scholler poore,
Grosse gold, from them runs headlong to the boore.
Likewise the angrie sisters thus deluded [by Mercury],
To venge themselues on *Hermes*, haue concluded
That *Midas* brood shall sit in Honors chaire,
To which the *Muses* sonnes are only heire:
And fruitfull wits that in aspiring are,
Shall discontent, run into regions farre;
And few great lords in vertuous deeds shall ioy,
But be surpris'd with euery garish toy.
And still inrich the loftie seruile clowne,
Who with incroching guile, keepes learning downe.

                                        (ll. 465-482)

We notice immediately that Mercury, who throughout the digression is simply an anthropomorphic god, has become allegorized as Learning, and that the narrator is no longer explaining why the Fates have rejected Cupid's plea. He is more interested in pointing out why scholars are poor, rejected, and unhonored. For a moment we may be puzzled by what seems like an excrescence, but we soon realize that the narrator is consciously revealing something about himself: he is a poor scholar; he needs money. And the passage may be seen as a fairly subtle plea to those "few great lords" who joy "in vertuous deeds" to honor with a monetary gift this narrative. Further, we realize that this passage, as far as narrative technique is concerned, is inept. Of course, from the point of view of the fictional narrator, this ineptitude is unconscious—even though his final statement on the Mercury digression is a misinterpretation in almost any reader's eyes. Preoccupied with his own feelings, the narrator misses the point. And, finally, his inability to keep to his story and its proper interpretation, in light of his pretensions to scholarship, is ironic. Indeed, the narrator takes on the convential image of a Gabriel Harvey.

The major point to be made here is that we have a narrator whom we cannot quite trust. He glories in the parade of truisms, aphorisms, and hyperboles. Bringing his lovers together much as Chaucer brings

Troilus and Criseyde together—with the meeting of eyes—Marlowe's narrator stops the action with an aphorism: "*Such force and vertue hath an amorous looke*" (l. 166), and then continues with a longer editorial comment:

> It lies not in our power to loue, or hate,
> For will in vs is ouer-rul'd by fate.
> When two are stript long ere the course begin,
> We wish that one should loose, the other win.
> And one especiallie doe we affect,
> Of two gold Ingots like in each respect,
> The reason no man knowes, let it suffise,
> What we behold is censur'd by our eies.
> Where both deliberat, the loue is slight,
> Who euer lov'd, that lov'd not at first sight?
>   (ll. 167-176)

O, reason and impertinency mixed! On one hand, the narrator belabors a truism: there's no accounting for taste. On the other, in his final question, he seems to carry that truism to its hyperbolic extreme so that the answer to his question is: many people. The majority of the narrator's comment then is comic because of his blithe assurance that what he's giving his reader is a fresh perception and that his final inference is valid. We smile at the narrator as we smile at any pompous ass.

However, the first two lines of his commentary indicate, possibly, a more profound vision of the poem, that Hero and Leander are powerless in the narrative, that they are "ouer-rul'd by fate."[27] It has been argued that "will" (l. 168) does not mean "free will," but "amorous desire, or its opposite"—an acceptable Elizabethan reading.[28] But even if we accept this narrowing of meaning, given the sexual orientation of the poem, it still means that Hero and Leander are significantly fated; predestination in this one aspect would govern all of the poem's action. This *is* a poem about sexual will.

But does the narrator's assertion give us a valid way to see the lovers? Are they ruled by fate? And if they are, how do we interpret that fate? It seems rational to begin our inquiry by looking at Cupid's mission to the Destinies and at the digression that involves them. Cupid, we know, "to those sterne nymphs humblie made request, / Both [lovers] might enioy ech other, and be blest" (ll. 379-380). The Fates apparently answer in the negative, for, hating Cupid, they will not vouchsafe him "one poore word" (1. 384). But, from the end of the poem, we know that the lovers have enjoyed each other, though whether they are blest or not is another question. The main point is that the Fates have not kept Hero and Leander apart, and this fact certainly calls in question their absolute power.

Turning to the digression itself, we find several clues that the Fates are not so "Adamantine" (1. 444) as the narrator suggests. First, Cupid "wounds [them] with loue, and forst them equallie, / To dote vpon deceitfull *Mercurie*" (ll. 445-446). Second, in love with Mercury, the Destinies

> granted what he crau'd, and once againe,
> *Saturne* and *Ops*, began their golden raigne.
> Murder, rape, warre, lust and trecherie,
> Were with *Joue* clos'd in *Stigian* Emprie.
> But long this blessed time continued not.
> (ll. 455-459).

Finding that Mercury is simply using them for his own ends, they "*Iupiter* vnto his place restor'd" (1. 464). What we learn here is that the Fates can be—at least, in the past they were—controlled by love in the guise of Cupid, and that what the Fates decree can be changed again and again. A close reading of the digression questions the narrator's assertion that "will in vs is ouer-rul'd by fate." In fact, very few readers see Marlowe's poem as a story of love controlled by destiny, unless, of course, we define destiny as the inability to transcend the human condition. What our analysis indicates is that we cannot accept at face value the commentary of the narrator. His dicta must be evaluated in the context of the rest of the poem.

Moreover, I think we must also question the narrator's descriptions, the way he sees, not just how he evaluates what he sees. As our first example, let us look at his opening description of Hero: her kirtle, he tells us, was blue, "whereon was many a staine, / Made with the blood of wretched Louers slaine" (ll. 15-16). Keach believes that these lines make sense when, later in the poem, we find "*Hero* sacrificing turtles blood" (1. 158).[29] The blood of the wretched lovers is the blood of the sacrificed turtle doves. If so, the first allusion to blood becomes one of the narrator's ineptitudes, for most readers do not make the connection between lines 15-16 and line 158, and, indeed, see the blood on Hero's kirtle as a sign that she is both an experienced and a cruel woman. But the narrator goes on to make it relatively clear that she is neither. Finally, we must conclude that this descriptive detail supplied by the narrator is merely misleading, a fault in his vision.

We meet the same problem of the narrator's ambiguous descriptions at the end of the poem. When Leander enters Hero's tower after his swim across the Hellespont, Hero "scriecht for feare" (l. 721) upon seeing him, and "The neerer that he came, the more she fled, / And seeking refuge, slipt into her bed" (ll. 727-728). David Farkas analyzes these lines carefully:

> The literal meaning . . . cannot be reconciled to the story since it conflicts with human behavior. Even the purest and most innocent of virgins could not imagine her bed a good place to hide from an insistent lover. . . . The reader recognizes that the dramatized narrator has given a mistaken account of this part of the poem.
> (pp. 142-143)

Farkas goes on to suggest two possible reconstructions: (1) "Hero's 'flight' may be no such thing, but rather a thoroughly purposeful removal to her bed in expectation of sex." (2) "Hero's fleeing may be an act of self-deception. In this case, the literal sense dramatizes . . . Hero's attempt to convince herself that her removal to her bed is an act of resistance when, in fact, it is a step in the other direction" (pp. 143-144). Farkas finds the second reconstruction preferable. However, he leaves out one further possibility: the narrator is being consciously ironic. I mention this possibility only to reject it. This kind of poignant irony would seem to be beyond the narrator's meager abilities, and I also find the second reconstruction gives the best reading of the line. Marlowe uses the narrator's mistaken vision to indicate a quality in Hero herself.

To read *Hero and Leander* is to be forced to make a series of choices—both simple and complex. The narrator is no adequate guide to the poem, and the reader must constantly challenge the narrator's descriptions, interpretations, and evaluations. The story gets told in spite of him, and when he speaks of his "slacke muse" (l. 72), he may think that he is being conventionally modest, but the evidence of the poem suggests otherwise.

But why does Marlowe wish to filter his story through the eyes of such an inept narrator? The first thought that strikes a thoughtful reader is that this narrator would not be appropriate for a tragic poem. He is a comic narrator, and his ineptitudes tend to distance us from the action. The primary function of the narrator, then, is to give Marlowe a comic—burlesque, if you will—handle on the story. But I think there is a further function. The ineptitude of the narrator is mirrored in the ineptitude of the lovers—and *vice versa*. This is not a poem about suave Leander and self-assured Hero. Instead it is about Leander "rude in loue, and raw" (l. 545) and an almost equally innocent Hero. The poem is Marlowe's human comedy, and the bumbling artist merely rounds out his picture of the human condition.

From this perspective we must return once more to the end of the poem. As we have seen before, the poem does not end with resolution, but with dissonance. The two lovers, no longer virgins, are exposed in the garish light of day, Leander lustfully staring, Hero shamefully blushing. The ending strikes me as terribly modern, very much like the end of a movie I vaguely remember seeing a few years ago. With the exception, perhaps, of *Astrophel and Stella*, Renaissance poems do not usually end this way. They tend, generally, to have a stronger sense of closure, of things being wrapped up, completed. Part of the reason, I suspect, we do not get that closure here is because of Marlowe's fiction of the inept narrator who just couldn't bring it off. But I further believe that we must approach the end of the poem in much the same way that David Farkas approaches lines 727-728. On the surface, the narrator presents an inadequate conclusion, but the reader, forced to reconstruct and reinterpret the scene, comes to understand that this conclusion is perfect for the poem. The poem stresses that humans are caught in the no man's land between two worlds: the world of human morality which they cannot fully escape; and the world of naturalistic sexuality which they can only partially accept. There is no resolution, and the poem, honest to its vision, leaves the lovers stranded together, and yet supremely alone. The final grace note—the death of night—is perfect. For these lovers there is no longer any escape into the dark night of thoughtless love. Hero stands, the scales fallen from her eyes, in the light of a new—and hopeless—day.

NOTES

1. *Hero and Leander by Christopher Marlowe: A Facsimile of the First Edition*, London 1598, ed. Louis L. Martz (New York: Johnson Reprint Corp., 1972), sig. A3ᵛ. This edition (slightly modernized) is used throughout.

2. The nineteenth-century evaluations are found in Millar Maclure, ed., *Marlowe: The Critical Heritage, 1588-1896* (London, Boston and Henley: Routledge & Kegan Paul, 1979), pp. 104, 130, 167.

3. Muriel Bradbrook, "'Hero and Leander,'" *Scrutiny*, 2 (1933-34), 63.

4. J. B. Steane, *Marlowe: A Critical Study* (Cambridge: Cambridge University Press, 1964), p. 331, is a notable exception.

5. See, *e.g.*, Paul M. Cubeta, "Marlowe's Poet in *Hero and Leander*," *College English*, 26 (1964-65), 500-505; Robert E. Knoll, "The Narrator in *Hero and Leander*," *Christopher Marlowe*, TEAS 74 (New York: Twayne, 1969), 127-139; and Chinmoy Banerjee, "*Hero and Leander* as Erotic Comedy," *Journal of Narrative Technique*, 3 (1973), 40-52.

6. See Louis R. Zocca, *Elizabethan Narrative Poetry* (1950; rpt., New York: Octagon, 1970), pp. 234-236.

7. M. C. Bradbrook, *Shakespeare and Elizabethan Poetry* (Cambridge: Cambridge University Press, 1951; rpt. 1965), p. 60. Steane in 1964, pp. 302-333, also seems to accept the poem as complete.

8. See *e.g.*, William Keach, *Elizabethan Erotic Narratives* (New Brunswick, N. J.: Rutgers University Press, 1977), pp. 115-116. Keach's excellent study deserves and repays a careful reading.

9. See, *e.g.*, William E. Sheidley, "The Seduction of the Reader in Marlowe's *Hero and Leander*," *Concerning Poetry*, 3 (1970), 51: "Marlowe's fragment"; Elizabeth Bieman, "Comic Rhyme in Marlowe's *Hero and Leander*," *English Literary Renaissance*, 9 (1979), 75: "The Marlovian fragment breaks off."; Gordon Williams, "Acting and Suffering in *Hero and Leander*," *Trivium* (St. David's University College), 8 (1973), 25: "It is commonly noted that Marlowe succeeds in telling much of the story in two unhurried sestyads whilst Chapman requires twice that space to conclude;" S. Ann Collins, "Sundrie Shapes, Committing Headdie Ryots, Incest, Rapes: Functions of Myth in Determining Narrative and Tone in Marlowe's *Hero and Leander*," *Mosaic*, 4, no.1 (1970-71), 107: "the unfinished epic." The list might be expanded.

10. See Zocca's comment, p. 234.

11. Gordon Braden, *The Classics and English Renaissance Poetry: Three Case Studies*, YSE 187 (New Haven and London: Yale University Press, 1978), p. 150. David Kalman Farkas, "Problems of Interpretation in Malowe's *Hero and Leander*," Unpublished Ph. D. Dissertation, University of Minnesota, 1976, pp. 16-36, discusses the fragmentary nature of the poem at length and concludes that the poem was resisting completion at Marlowe's hands. Although I do not concur with Farkas's conclusion, his dissertation is essential reading for any one studying *Hero and Leander*.

12. Paul W. Miller, "A Function of Myth in Marlowe's 'Hero and Leander,'" *Studies*

in Philology, 50 (1953), 166.

13. See Braden, p. 269, note 95.

14. L. C. Martin, ed., *Marlowe's Poems* (1931; rpt. New York: Gordian Press, 1966), p. 59, note to line 179.

15. See Myron Turner, "Pastoral and Hermaphrodite: A Study in the Naturalism of Marlowe's *Hero and Leander*," *Texas Studies in Literature and Language*, 17 (1975), 402-404, who cogently makes this point.

16. See, *e.g.*, Farkas, p. 27, who feels that "the abrupt ending gives little sense of a planned conclusion."

17. I use the Loeb text edited by Thomas Gelzer, trans. Cedric Whitman (Cambridge, Mass.: Harvard University Press, 1975), lines 110-111, pp. 358-359.

18. Brian Morris, "Comic Method in Marlowe's *Hero and Leander*," in *Christopher Marlowe*, ed. Brian Morris (New York: Hill and Wang, 1969), p. 119, notes this movement in another context: "Marlowe shows the diminishing power of words, and the increasing efficacy of action as the means to achieve the right true end of love."

19. Veselin Kostič, "Marlowe's *Hero and Leander* and Chapman's Continuation," *Renaissance and Modern Essays, Presented to Vivian de Sola Pinto*, ed. G. R. Hibbard (London: Routledge and Kegan Paul, 1966), p. 27. Farkas, pp. 192-231, fully defines the concept of "sketchiness" as it relates to the poem.

20. It would be wrong to say that Musaeus gives his lovers a full and circumstantial context. As Gelzer (p. 308) notes, "No secondary character is individualized" in Musaeus's poem. In fact, Marlowe's own sketchiness may ultimately derive from Musaeus's presentation.

21. I suspect a joke here. I believe the line should be read with a pregnant pause after "her," so that "haire" will be heard as an anticlimax. Obviously we do not expect Apollo to be wooing Hero for her *hair*. There is also a possible pun on "heir."

22. Nigel Alexander, ed., *Elizabethan Narrative Verse* (Cambridge, Mass.: Harvard University Press, 1968), p. 12, points out the ambiguity of the immortal fingers imprinting Leander's back. This is either "the act of creation" or "the act of love."

23. Farkas, pp. 163-180, explains this position.

24. The tradition extends beyond the Renaissance, and is vividly illustrated in Ian Donaldson's *The Rapes of Lucretia: A Myth and its Transformations* (Oxford: Clarendon Press, 1982), plates 1, 2, 4, 12, 13, 14. Thomas Rowlandson's naked Tarquin (plate 3) is unusual.

25. There is a pun here on "nothing" and "naughtiness."

26. See, *e.g.*, Farkas, pp. 161-162, and pp. 112-162 *passim*.

27. Musaeus does emphasize the rule of fate in his version. See, *e.g.*, lines 307-308.

28. Steane, pp. 315-316, discusses the passage, identifying F. S. Boas as the first to define "will" as sexual appetite or its opposite.

29. See Keach, p. 97.

"Metre meete to furnish Lucans style": Reconsidering Marlowe's *Lucan*

JAMES SHAPIRO

Marlowe scholarship, long focused upon discovering the man in the work—as iconoclast, overreacher, atheist, or machiavel, or more recently as orthodox Christian, troubled homosexual poet, or detached ironist—has, with few exceptions, ignored Marlowe's efforts as translator. Marlowe's rendering of Lucan's *Pharsalia*, when discussed at all, has been dismissed as peripheral, described as a juvenile exercise, even ascribed to others.[1] This critical response often seems motivated by a desire to reaffirm preconceived notions of Marlowe's role as Elizabethan poet and dramatist. How else can we account for L. C. Martin's tenuous claim that we should attribute the translation to Chapman;[2] or C. S. Lewis's curious statement that "if it were ever reasonable to reject contemporary ascription on purely internal evidence I should be tempted to deny this work to Marlowe."[3] This critical bias has resulted in a self-perpetuating and distorted image of Marlowe's accomplishments and artistic ends, in this poem and in general.

I would like to fashion or reconstruct a different Marlowe: one who saw himself working within the humanist program of setting "the end of scollarisme in an English blank verse," one who may well have turned to this translation as an established dramatist, who had Lucan in mind while composing *Edward II* (which may, in turn, have stimulated Marlowe to direct his energies at rendering into English the

most famous poem on the nature of civil war). To this end, I am interested in why Marlowe translated Book One of Lucan's *Pharsalia*, why
he did so in a line-for-line blank verse, and what the defining features of
that blank verse style are. Marlowe's metrical decisions seem to me
especially significant in a discussion of a translation: when a poet
renders the verse design, syntax, diction, and rhythm of one language
into another, meter is a crucial concern. For it is largely on the basis of
rhythmic range and effect, the capacity to evoke for an audience the
experience of the original, that a translation is judged and valued. The
very choice of blank verse—and what Marlowe does within the formal
constraints of this meter—provides a basis for examining Marlowe's
position within the humanist movement of translating classical works,
and identifies his interests in and conception of Lucan's stylistic qualities.

The laurel for first translating the *Pharsalia* proved an elusive prize: if
Marlowe was familiar with the preface to Turberville's 1576 edition to
the *Tragical Tales*, he knew that Turberville had attempted—and failed
to complete—an English translation of the *Pharsalia*. Turberville was
not the first Elizabethan poet-humanist to have tried and failed. Fifteen years earlier Barnabe Googe, another master of the rhymed four-
teener, had also tried, and also given up. Their self-deprecating and
apologetic prefaces tell us much about how Elizabethans conceived of
Lucan, the topical significance of this poem on the horrors of civil war,
and the difficulties encountered in trying to translate it. The pressure
to account for failure to translate the work is telling: almost alone
among the classical texts taught in the grammar school curriculum,
the *Pharsalia* remained unavailable in an English version. Googe ex-
cuses himself by explaining that he was accosted in his study by the
Muses, where Melpomene, muse of tragedy, ordered him to "Reduce
to English sence . . . the lofty Lucanes verse."[4] Her sister Muses overruled her, though, and the task was postponed. Turberville, undoubtedly familiar with Googe's preface—and the need for an Englished
Lucan—apologetically related that his own translation was already
underway when he too was visited by the muse of tragedy. This time
Melpomene begged him to stop: his verses were "all too vyle," his "pen
too playne"; Turberville acquiesced, admitting that he lacked "metre
meete to furnish Lucans style."[5] Melpomene suggested instead that the
swelling vein of Sackville (who had recently coauthored *Gorboduc* in

blank verse) better suited Lucan's lofty style. For these Elizabethan poets Lucan's poem was tragic, topical, as yet untranslated, and difficult to render metrically. In the ensuing fifteen years the *Pharsalia* continued to gain in popularity. Recommended by Erasmus and Elyot, required in grammar schools based on the Eton system, the first English edition was published in 1588.[6] The mid-1590s saw a remarkable renaissance in literature based upon the *Pharsalia*: Daniel published his *Civil Wars* modeled upon Lucan in 1595; a year later Drayton would publish his *Mortimeriados*, also based upon the *Pharsalia*; Shakespeare's Brutus would speak of the spirit of Julius Caesar which "walks abroad, and turns our swords / In our own proper entrails" (*Julius Caesar* V.iii. 93-95), in the latter phrase rendering the familiar opening of the *Pharsalia*. This renewed interest in Lucan again raised the problem of finding a metrical equivalent and a suitable literary form in which to convey the work.

   For the Elizabethan translator, the choice of meter was neither arbitrary nor free of ideology: witness the debate between adherents of the Cambridge-led movement who argued that classical works should be rendered into quantitative measures, and those who preferred, in the words of the quantifiers, "rude beggarly rime."[7] Marlowe eschewed "jygging vaines of riming mother wits," but he likewise avoided quantitative versification. Within the context of this controversy, Marlowe was a promulgator of the position which found in blank verse a valuable compromise between the dissatisfying alternatives of quantitative and rhymed verse. Indeed, the first printed criticism of Marlowe's work is directed in part at his choice of meter: Robert Greene (sometime quantifier) attacked Marlowe for having "set the end of scollarisme in an English blank verse."[8] Marlowe's metrical practice was paradoxically tied to, yet freed from, the ends of scholarship. For the Elizabethans, as Tucker Brooke observed, blank verse seemed to capture the feel of Latin verse; the first dozen or so uses of this meter appeared in Latin translations and imitations.[9] This perceived resemblance or correspondence between blank verse and the Latin hexameter was short-lived, and marks a change in poetic sensibility in the English Renaissance. If Googe and Turberville contemplated poulter's measure or rhymed fourteeners in their translations of the *Pharsalia*, and Marlowe accomplished his in blank verse, by the early seventeenth century Sir Arthur Gorges would turn instead to jingling octosyllabic couplets, and Thomas May would deem smooth heroic couplets most proper.[10]

In light of Turberville's suggestion about Sackville's swelling vein, Marlowe, a master of blank verse, may have seen himself as ideally suited—technically and temperamentally—for the task of translating the *Pharsalia*. The poem undoubtedly held other attractions for him, not the least of which was that, according to Quintilian, Lucan provided a better model for orators than for poets,[11] and that the *Pharsalia* was written specifically for public declamation. The poem's oratorical possibilities are complemented by other features with inherent dramatic potential: descriptions of battles, speeches ranging from calculated oratory to inspired rant, an overreaching Caesar, sharp juxtapositions, and much violence. Sulpitius's dedication to his edition of the *Pharsalia*—which, Roma Gill has shown, Marlowe consulted—may further have attracted an accomplished dramatist seeking a challenging and stylistically compatible vehicle for his poetic skills. James Welwood's eighteenth-century translation of this dedication in the Rowe edition of the *Pharsalia* emphasizes these theatrical possibilities:

> [Lucan's] style is so masterly, that you rather seem to see than read of those transactions. But for the enterprises and battles, you imagine them not related but acted: towns alarmed, armies engaged, the eagerness and terrour of the several soldiers, seem present to your view.[12]

Having provided some suggestions on Marlowe's motives for translating Lucan, and why he did so in blank verse, I would now like to consider the defining features of that verse style. There is no question, from the point of view of metrical practice, that this work shares the major features of Marlowe's inimitable mighty line.[13] In its broader contours, Marlowe's verse observes his usual—and idiosyncratic—rules governing the relation of stress and syntax to an underlying metrical pattern. The matching of syllables to metrical positions is likewise typical, as is his treatment of compounds, phrases consisting of monosyllabic adjectives and nouns, and particles. The meter is more rigidly constrained than his dramatic blank verse, lacking such variations as nine syllable and shorter lines, extrametrical syllables in the middle of lines, or line—initial extrametrical apostrophes, which generate more rhythmically flexible and dramatically suitable speeches.

Unique to this work, however, is Marlowe's complex treatment of poetic closure, and it is upon this that I wish to focus my discussion. The familiar paradigm for Marlovian blank verse consists of decasyllabic end-stopped lines, built up into a grammatically and syntactically suspended verse paragraph. The rhythm generated at the outset of the poem confirms this powerfully felt sense of suspension and resolution:

> Wars worse then civill on Thessalian playnes,
> And outrage strangling law and people strong,
> We sing, whose conquering swords their own breasts launcht,
> Armies alied, the kingdoms league uprooted,
> The affrighted worlds force bent on public spoile,
> Trumpets and drums, like deadly threatning other,
> Eagles alike displaide, darts answering darts.
>
> (ll. 1-7)[14]

In the absence of either rhyme or quantities, the strong syntactic break at the end of each line—resolving lexical and phrasal stress—gives integrity to the individual line units, and produces rhythmically satisfying closure.

But as in *Hero and Leander*, Marlowe, having established this metrical expectation, subjects it to marked variation. The most notable departure in this translation from his usual blank verse practice is the preponderance of eleven syllable lines: statistically, fourteen percent, or one in seven lines, contain an extrametrical syllable; in comparison, *Tamburlaine* contains fewer than two percent, *Edward II* fewer than four percent. In *Hero and Leander* Marlowe used such lines to great effect in creating deflating, comic rhymes. Their different function here is twofold: they help re-enforce closure, notably at the end of sententious speeches; but more importantly, they enable Marlowe to approximate more closely the familiar pattern of stresses marking the end of a Latin hexameter, especially the unstressed final syllable. Vergil's "*Arma virumque cano, Troiae qui primus ab oris*" provides a typical example of this pattern; my Latin teacher called it the "shave-and-a-haircut" rhythm, "*primus ab oris.*"

If at one extreme we find this strongly pronounced closure, at the other we find great fluidity and variety at the end of lines through enjambment. Roughly a quarter of all lines in the poem are, to varying degrees, enjambed. One result of this enjambment is the creation of a richer rhythmic texture in the speeches which comprise fully a tenth of the poem. And, not surprisingly, both extrametrical syllables and enjambment occur disproportionately in these speeches. The Centurion's speech swearing blind obedience to Caesar illustrates the way in which enjambment, in conjunction with extrametrical syllables (particularly monosyllabic ones at the end of lines) delineates highly individualized and rhetorically effective speaking styles:

> Love over-rules my will, I must obay thee,
> Caesar, he whom I heare thy trumpets charge
> I hold no Romaine; by these ten blest ensignes
> And all thy several triumphs, should thou bid me
> Intombe my sword within my brothers bowels;
> Or fathers throate; or womens groaning wombe;
> This hand (albeit unwillingly) should perform it.
> (ll. 373-379)

Extrametrical syllables occur here at the ends of lines 373, 375, 376, 379, and possibly 377 as well, while lines 374, 375, and 376 are successively enjambed. The rushing quality of this impassioned outburst is slowed and brought back to the established pattern, in part, by the strongly end-stopped decasyllabic line 378, a parenthesis, repeated semicolons, and a final line which concludes with an extrametrical monosyllable.

A valuable explanation for this frequency of enjambed lines is provided by Marlowe's contemporary, and student of Lucan, Samuel Daniel. Daniel writes of enjambment and Lucan that

> sometimes to beguile the ear with a running out, and passing over the Ryme, as no bound to stay us in the line where the violence of the matter will breake thorow, is rather gracefull then otherwise. Wherein I finde my Homer-Lucan, as if he gloried to seeme to have no bounds, albeit he were confined within his measure, to be in my conceipt most happy.[15]

For Daniel, the texture of Lucan's verse is defined by its enjambed quality, a comment akin to Dr. Johnson's less admiring observation that the "variety of pauses, so much boasted by the lovers of blank verse, changes the measures of an English poet to the periods of a declaimer."[16]

I want to emphasize that Marlovian enjambment in this translation is highly constrained: in the passage quoted above—and with one exception in the first 684 lines of a 694 line poem—Marlowe carefully observes both lexical and phrasal boundaries when enjambing. Milton, in comparison, requires only lexical boundaries when enjambing (*e.g.*, "Great joy he promis'd to this thought, and new / Solace in her return"), while Shakespeare in his late work relaxed his constraints so that only phrase boundaries are required to separate the lines of his blank verse (*e.g.*, "Thy mother was a piece of virtue, and / She said thou wast my daughter").[17]

But metrical rules are made to be broken, especially by confident artists, and Marlowe does so four times in the closing nine lines of the poem, where context and speaking style demand it. This violation of established constraints occurs in the frenzied speech of the Roman Matron, who runs through the streets, terrifying the "quivering Romans" with her prophecies of the destruction that awaits them. Here, truly, enjambment conveys Daniel's sense of "violence of the matter" breaking through. It is mimetic, too, of the Matron's disorienting and rapid flights through time and space. By violating his metrical constraints in these lines Marlowe captures her speech's rhythmically erratic style:

> This headless trunk that lies on Nylus sand
> I knowe: now throughout the air I flie,
> To doubtful Sirtes and drie Affrike, where
> A fury leades the Emathian bandes, from thence
> To the pine bearing hils, hence to the mounts
> Pirene, and so back to Rome againe,
> Se impious warre defiles the Senat house.
> New factions rise; now through the world againe
> I goe; O Phoebus show me Neptunes shore,
> And other Regions, I have seen Philippi.
> (ll. 684-693)

The enjambment in lines 689 and 691 overrides phrase boundaries; that in 687 overrides a lexical boundary; and the enjambment of line 686 ["where / A fury"] overrides both—that is, it would not occur in either Milton or the later Shakespeare. The overall effect is mimetic of the rhythms of the corresponding lines (ll. 685-694) of Lucan's original:

> . . . fluminea deformis truncus harena
> qui iacet, agnosco. dubiam super aequora Syrtim
> arentemque feror Libyen, quo tristis Enyo
> transtulit Emathias acies. nunc desuper Alpis
> nubiferae colles atque aeriem Pyrenen
> abripimur. patriae sedes remeanus in urbes,
> concurgunt partes iterum, totumque per orbem
> rursus eo. noua da mihi cernere litora ponti
> telluremque nouam. uidi iam, Phoebe, Philippos.[18]

The Matron's speech resembles neither the cool and deliberate style of the Roman orators, nor the exhortatory rhythms of many of the poem's narrative passages. By subtle changes in the constraints governing the relation between syntax and line endings, Marlowe departs from his established pattern, and the resulting disruption of our metrical expectations is striking and appropriate. Imitating his original, he evokes a disconcerting climax in the closing lines of the poem, a site where poetic convention usually demands a reaffirmation of metrical regularity and closure.

Perhaps the most powerful illustration of this metrical skill is provided by comparison. If we set Marlowe's translation of this speech alongside Thomas May's 1627 version, we get a stronger sense of the technical range and dramatic qualities of Marlowe's work:

> There, there alas I know what man it is,
> That on Nile's banke a trunke deformed lyes.
> Ore Syrtes sands, ore scorched Libya,
> Whether the reliques of the Pharsalia
> Erinnis carry'd ore th'Alps cloudy hil,
> And high Pyrene am I carried still.
> Then back againe to Rome, where impious,
> And fatall warre defiles the Senate house.
> The Factious rise againe; againe I goe
> Ore all the world; show me new Kingdomes now,
> New Seas; Philippi I have seen. . . .[19]

May's rhythmically regular assignment of stress and the equally regular closure of his decasyllabic and rhymed couplets efface these rhythmic dynamics and signal a change from Elizabethan to Jacobean conceptions of metrical decorum. This change in sensibility extends further: Marlowe was content to translate just the first book of Lucan's long and unfinished poem; we might recall in this regard Ben Jonson's admonition that "Lucan taken in parts was Good . . . read alltogidder merited not the name of Poet."[20] In contrast to Marlowe, the Jacobean May not only translated all ten extent books, but produced a Latin conclusion of his own creation.

In closing I would like to return to my original speculation that Marlowe might have turned to this work at the close of his career and life, possibly during the long period in which London's playhouses were closed because of plague in 1592-93. *Hero and Leander* is generally attributed to this period, and it is perhaps worth noting that these works were posthumously entered together in the Stationers' Register.[21] Consider, too, the evidence provided by a Lucanic passage in Act IV, scene iv of *Edward II*. The scene begins with Isabella's long soliloquy following the crossing of her own Rubicon, the English Channel. In the speech she tries to justify civil war against Edward. Like the conflict in the *Pharsalia*, family bonds make this war "worse than civill." Before her speech is interrupted by Mortimer, who derides her "passionate" speech as inappropriate to a warrior, Isabella's words recall the opening lines of Lucan's poem:

> . . . a heavie case,
> When force to force is knit, and sword and gleave
> In civill broiles make kin and country men
> Slaughter themselves in others and their sides
> With their owne weapons gorde, but whats the helpe?
>   (IV. iv. 4-8)

Stylistic affinities—especially enjambment, a defining feature of Lucan's style for the Elizabethans—help signal Isabella's thematic evocation of the *Pharsalia*.

Passages like this remind us of how much remains to be done towards clarifying the ways in which Marlowe turned to Lucan—and other classical models—in his plays. The passage also raises the difficult question of whether Marlowe translated the *Pharsalia* before or after he composed *Edward II*. In dating *Lucan*, neither internal nor external evidence points conclusively to either early or late periods of Marlowe's brief but productive career. And while this issue cannot presently be resolved, it nevertheless remains important in determining how we conceive of Marlowe's artistic development.

I confess to dissatisfaction with the prevailing view that the work is juvenilia; the arguments for this position assume—wrongly, I believe—that Marlowe necessarily moved from the apprenticeship of translation to the freedom of more original compositions. Such a view presupposes a Romantic conception of originality, one not necessarily shared by Elizabethan humanist translators. It also ignores a tradition—which extends from Chaucer to the present day—of poets undertaking laborious translations in their maturity. My own impression is that the translation followed the play. I imagine a Marlowe stimulated by his interest in civil war in *Edward II* (and perhaps in *Tamburlaine* and *The Massacre at Paris* as well), undertaking the translation in 1592 or 1593, a period which saw a renewed interest in Lucan by contemporaries like Daniel and Drayton. At such a point an accomplished and ambitious poet might well have decided to turn his hand to the archetypal and as yet untranslated work on civil war, confident of his powers, confident, too, of providing meter meet to furnish Lucan's style.

NOTES

1. Notable exceptions are Roma Gill, "Marlowe, Lucan and Sulpitius," *Review of English Studies*, N. S. 24 (1973), 401-413, and J. B. Steane, *Marlowe: A Critical Study* (Cambridge: Cambridge University Press, 1964), pp. 249-279.

2. L. C. Martin, "Lucan—Marlowe—? Chapman," *Review of English Studies*, 24 (1948), 317–321.

3. C. S. Lewis, *English Literature in the Sixteenth Century* (Oxford: Clarendon Press, 1954), p. 486. Lewis adds: "it is of very great merit." He is also "inclined to put it late."

4. Barnabe Googe, *Eglogs, Epytaphes, and Sonettes* (1563), ed. Edward Arber (London: Constable and Co., 1910), p. 486. The "Preface" is printed from the 1561 edition.

5. George Turberville, *Tragical Tales, and Other Poems*, rpt. from ed. of 1587 (Edinburgh: Edinburgh Printing Co., 1837), p. 17.

6. See T. W. Baldwin, *William Shakespere's "Small Latine and Lesse Greeke,"* 2 vols. (Urbana: University of Illinois Press, 1944), I, 103, and II, 550-551.

7. For the standard work on this subject see Derek Attridge, *Well-Weighed Syllables: Elizabethan Verse in Classical Metres* (Cambridge: Cambridge University Press, 1974).

8. Robert Greene, *Works*, ed. Alexander Grosart, 15 vols. (London: Hazell, Watson, and Viney, 1881-1883), VII, 8.

9. See C. F. Tucker Brooke, "Marlowe's Versification and Style," *Studies in Philology*, 19 (1922), 186-205.

10. Sir Arthur Gorges, *Lucans Pharsalia* (London, 1614), and Thomas May, *Lucans Pharsalia* (London, 1627).

11. Quintilian, *Institutio Oratoria*, 10. 1. 90.

12. Cited from *The Words of the English Poets*, ed. Alexander Chalmers (London, 1810), XX, 16.

13. The analysis which follows is based upon my "Marlowe's Metrical Style: 'Infinite Riches in a Little Roome,'" Diss., University of Chicago, 1982.

14. Marlowe's works cited from *The Complete Works of Christopher Marlowe*, ed. Fredson Bowers, 2 vols. (Cambridge: Cambridge University Press, 1973).

15. From his *A Defense of Rhyme*, cited from *Elizabethan Critical Essays*, ed. G. Gregory Smith, 2 vols. (London: Oxford University Press, 1904, rpt. 1971), II, 382.

16. In his essay on "Milton" in *Lives of the Poets*, as cited in John Hollander, *Vision and Resonance* (New York: Oxford Univeristy Press, 1975), p. 91.

17. For this distinction (and these examples) see Paul Kiparsky, "Stress, Syntax, and Meter," *Language*, 51 (1975), 600-606.

18. References to Lucan's *Pharsalia* are cited from *De Bello Civili: Liber I*, ed. R. J. Getty (Cambridge: Cambridge University Press, 1940).

19. May, sig. B3ª.

20. Ben Jonson, *Works*, ed. C. H. Herford and Percy and Evelyn Simpson, 11 vols. (Oxford: The Clarendon Press, 1925-1952), I, 134.

21. See *The Works of Christopher Marlowe*, ed. C. F. Tucker Brooke (Oxford: The Clarendon Press, 1910), pp. 642-643.

Marlowe and the Art of Translation

ROMA GILL

The first volume of the forthcoming Oxford edition of Marlowe's *opera* will contain four major works: *All Ovids Elegies, Lucans First Booke, Dido, Queene of Carthage* and *Hero and Leander*. Three early pieces will be bound up with the late poem *Hero and Leander*; and three non-dramatic ones will be printed with the play of *Dido*. Linked by neither time nor form, the works find their common denominator in the fact that all are translations from a classical language into English. But the translations are not all of the same kind. The poet Dryden recognized three separate methods when, prefacing a collection of Ovid's *Epistles* translated by divers hands, he meditated on the art of translation, and suggested a tripartite division of the topic into "metaphrase," "paraphrase," and "imitation"[1]—three "heads" which serve admirably to distinguish Marlowe's translations from each other.

> "First, that of metaphrase, or turning an author word by word, and line by line, from one language into another."

This, of course, is the technique we all learn at school as soon as we begin the study of a foreign language, and it is immediately adequate for the first simple sentences that we translate. But Ovid's *Amores* are far from simple, and Marlowe must have learned—very quickly—the truth that Dryden was later to articulate: "Tis almost impossible to

327

translate verbally, and well, at the same time." Two lines from the fifth poem of Book III of the *Elegies* can illustrate the shortcomings of the metaphrastic method. The lover in Ovid's poem, recalling the amorous adventures of various river deities, includes Alpheus, whose love for the nymph Arethusa caused him to flow through many distant lands:

> quid? non Alpheon diversis currere terris
> virginis Arcadiae certus adegit amor?
> (ll. 29-30)[2]

Marlowe returns word for word, in almost the order of Ovid's inflected language:

> What? not *Alpheus* in strange lands to runne,
> Th' *Arcadian* Virgins constant love hath wunne?
> (ll. 29-30)[3]

Perhaps the subject failed to inspire!

The rendering of the compulsive "*adegit*" with the gentler persuasion of "hath wunne" serves at the present to draw attention to the verse form. In the *Amores* Ovid brought the Latin elegiac couplet to a peak of perfection; and like the other Roman elegists (Propertius, for example, or Tibullus), he could easily comment on the form in the poems themselves:

> Sex mihi surgat opus numeris, in quinque residat.
> (I.i.31)

Marlowe translates the words correctly; but the English is meaningless without a better knowledge of the foreign tradition than the poem supplies:

> Let my first verse be sixe, my last five feete.

The delicate Latin meter seems to defy the English language—although Coleridge achieved momentary success in an adaptation of Schiller, "The Ovidian Elegiac Metre described and exemplified":

> In the hexameter rises the fountain's silvery column;
> In the pentameter aye falling in melody back.

Marlowe cleverly substitutes the rhymed heroic couplet, with its potential for satire (developed by him, later, in *Hero and Leander*). On occasion this makes a poem surprisingly effective—although Marlowe cannot quite reproduce Ovid's calm sophistication. A case in point is the fourth elegy of Book I, where the lover instructs his mistress on the way to behave in the presence of her husband at a banquet where all three are guests. Ovid's lover suggests that the lady should reject food that has been tasted (and therefore recommended) by his rival:

> si tibi forte dabit, quod praegustaverit ipse,
>   reice libatos illius ore cibos.
>   (I.iv.33-38)

A modern English translation renders the lines quite felicitously:

> Refuse all food he has tasted first—
> it has touched his lips.[4]

The conduct urged by Marlowe's lover, however, is far less ladylike; and the snap of the couplet's rhyme adds force to the gesture:

> If hee gives thee what first himself did tast,
> Even in his face his offered Goblets cast.

Dyce's emendation of "Gobbets" for "Goblets" makes the couplet, and the lover therein characterized, very much nastier. The *dramatis personae* of Marlowe's poem are, clearly, the forebears of the characters in Donne's elegy "Jealosie," whose satiric comedy takes the couplet another step away from the subtlety of the Roman elegiac mode.

Even when it is far from the scornful laughter at the banquet conspiracy in Elegy I. iv, there is usually a certain smile in Marlowe's couplet. When he refers to Semele in III. iii, Marlowe's lover seems to show a wry amusement which is expressed even in the clumsiness with which the rhyme is achieved:

> But when her lover came, had she drawne backe,

The fathers thigh should unborne *Bacchus* lacke.
(ll. 39-40)

Perhaps there are traces of this in Ovid's attempts to justify Corinna's infidelity, but the flexible elegiac couplet also voices a tenderness which is quite absent from the English:

at sī | ventū | rō | se | subdūx | īssĕt ămantī,

nōn pătĕr | īn Bāc | chŏ | mātrĭs hă | bērĕt ŏ | pūs.

Ovid's couplet is remarkable for the spondees of its hexameter, which seem to enact a shrinking from the approaching lover, and for the delicate assonance of "*pater*" / "*matris*" in the pentameter speaking of the father who bore the mother's labor in the birth of Bacchus. Perhaps Marlowe thought it necessary to remind his readers of the circumstances of the birth—hence the addition of Jupiter's thigh; but it is hard in such cases not to agree with Robert Frost that "Poetry is what gets lost in translation."[5]

Although Marlowe's *Elegies* sometimes show surprising ability—first of all in the bold choice of the *Amores* for translation—it must, I think, be admitted that the venture as a whole is not a great success. Two main reasons suggest themselves. In the first place, the technique of metaphrase is hopelessly inadequate for the *Amores*, where the most accomplished of the Latin lyric poets is at his brilliant best with the inflected language. And it is not only linguistic craftsmanship that makes the elegiac Ovid an unsuitable companion for Marlowe at what appears to be a very early stage in his career: the Roman has a sophistication foreign, at this time, to Marlowe—but which becomes his own towards the end of his life and produces the masterpiece that is *Hero and Leander*. The advice of the Earl of Roscommon is pertinent:

> Examine how your Humour is inclin'd,
> And which the Ruling Passion of your Mind;
> Then seek a Poet who *your* way do's bend,
> And Chuse an Author as you chuse a friend:
> United by this Sympathetick Bond,
> You grow Familiar, Intimate and Fond;
> Your thoughts, your Words, your Stiles, your Souls agree,

No longer his Interpreter, but He.[6]

Marcus Annaeus Lucanus became such a friend to the young Marlowe. Born in 39 A.D. into a provincial family in Spain, Lucan was educated entirely in Rome, where he died in 65 A.D. at the age of twenty-six. Nothing of his writing has survived except the massive epic poem, *De Bello Civili*, whose ten Books recount the events in the struggle between Julius Caesar and the Roman Senate.

Here I think I must confess my own misapprehension of Marlowe's translation of *Lucans First Booke*. I have been looking too closely at the work, comparing it with the original and with the Latin Commentary that Marlowe used for his bright, but erratic, metaphrase.[7] This pedantic approach was of some use in preparing an edition of the poem; but for some time it prevented me from seeing the importance of the translation, not merely in its adumbration of the "mighty line." It now seems to me that Marlowe's encounter with *Lucans First Booke* is comparable to Gavin Douglas's meeting with the *Aeneid* or Ezra Pound's with the *Cathay* poems—all three experiences of the kind which Charles Tomlinson has described as the "confrontation deepened by history between the personal and a text in a language distant in time and place".[8] Marlowe recognized the grim topicality of *De Bello Civili* and responded to this, just as he responded to Lucan's formal rhetoric, in his act of translation.

Lucans First Booke is both illuminating to, and illumined by, the events of its historical and literary contexts. Historically it seems to belong to the period of national tension surrounding the disclosure of the Babington Conspiracy to dethrone the monarch, with the execution of Mary Queen of Scots (1587), and the threat of invasion from the Spanish Armada (1588). In its literary context, pride of place is held by Shakespeare's *Henry VI* trilogy with the famous stage direction (in the Folio text) from Part III:

> *Enter a Sonne that hath kill'd his Father, at one doore:*
> *and a Father that hath kill'd his Sonne at another doore.*

Whether or not the direction is authorial, this piece of dramatic symbolism indicates the greatest disorder in the little world of men—the same disorder that threatens when Lucan's Centurion promises to wage civil war at all costs, even though Caesar's command forces him to

> Intombe my sword within my brothers bowels;
> Or fathers throate; or womens groning wombe.
> (ll. 376-376)

Like the history plays, the epic poem could speak to the English people
at a time when the unity and harmony of their country was in danger,
issuing the stern warning that all this has happened before, and could
happen again: only the names need be changed.

> Roome if thou take delight in impious warre,
> First conquer all the earth, then turne thy force
> Against thy selfe: as yet thou wants not foes.
> That now the walles of houses halfe rear'd totter,
> That rampiers fallen downe, huge heapes of stone
> Lye in our townes, that houses are abandon'd,
> And few live that behold their ancient seats;
> *Italy* many yeares hath lyen until'd,
> And choakt with thornes, that greedy earth wants hinds
> Fierce *Pirhus*, neither thou nor *Hanniball*
> Art cause, no forraine foe could so afflict us,
> These plagues arise from wreake of civill power.
> (ll. 21-32)

And Marlowe (a great plagiarist of his own favorite lines) recalled this
passage when the King in *Edward II* threatens to "Make *Englands* civill
townes huge heapes of stones" (III.i. 215).

In *Lucans First Booke* Marlowe demonstrates his mastery of the skills
of metaphrase; and in the writing of *Dido, Queene of Carthage* he essays
what Dryden described as the second kind of translation:

> The second way is that of paraphrase, or translation with latitude,
> where the author is kept in view by the translator, so as never to be
> lost, but his words are not so strictly followed as his sense; and that
> too is admitted to be amplified, but not altered.

The story of Dido and Aeneas occupies Book IV of the *Aeneid*, but
Marlowe, moving now with greater ease and confidence in his Latin
text, picks up and transposes details from the first two Books to serve
his dramatic intentions. With considerable latitude he turns the epic

narrative into dramatic action: Anna and Iarbus are developed into substantial characters, and Marlowe invents the subplot (with its ludicrous climax) of Anna's love for her sister's rejected suitor. But except for this interpolation, Marlowe is true to his original: Vergil is always "kept in view."

Marlowe's major problem (one might expect) was with the presentation of Aeneas. In the twelve Books of Vergil's poem he is undoubtedly the hero, characterized by the single word "*pius*" which carries a multitude of meanings. The momentary lapse from decency, which makes him first love and then betray the Queen of Carthage, can be viewed *sub specie aeternitatis*—and consequently understood with more than human comprehension: when he sets sail for Italy he is still "*pius Aeneas.*"

The play's audience lacks such an overview. Certainly they (or perhaps I should say "we") have witnessed, at the start of the play, the immortal gods who control the lives and destinies of mortal creatures; but it is hard to give serious credence to such deities of shreds and patches, whose conduct in the security of their Olympian home is less than admirable. Consequently an audience can only respond to Marlowe's Aeneas as they would to the rest of the Elizabethan *dramatis personae*: as humans to another human being. That such a human response is achieved can be seen from the different comments made by the play's critics—comments whose variety is itself a tribute to the skill of the young dramatist. John Bakeless saw Aeneas as "an Elizabethan adventurer, a little like Drake and a great deal more like Raleigh"; and for Michel Poirier he is a man of action who leaves Dido "because he wants to resume his active life and carry out heroic deeds which will make his name glorious." Brian Gibbons finds traces of "the Aeneas of medieval legend [who] was a notorious villain," and W. L. Godshalk seems to see a sort of pyromaniac: "One of the first things that Aeneas does after his arrival in Libya is to start a fire."[9] My own view is of a much less resolute character than that envisaged by these critics: *my* Aeneas is an ordinary "man-in-the-street," whose personality was never meant for noble action but who nevertheless, to his own bewilderment, finds himself at the center of one.

But the truth is that to talk of "character" in the modern sense (*OED*, "The sum of the mental and moral qualities which distinguish an individual . . . viewed as a homogeneous whole") is irrelevant in discussing Marlowe's play. *Dido, Queene of Carthage* was, according to the title page of the 1594 Quarto, "Played by the Children of her Majesties Chappell"; and we should consequently try to understand it in the way we appreciate Lyly's *Endimion* rather than comparing it (as J. B. Steane does)[10] with Shakespeare's *Antony and Cleopatra*. In the plays performed by the sixteenth-century children's companies, boys with unbroken voices presented the great figures of classical mythology—"Hercules and his load too," as Rosencrantz tells Hamlet. Verisimilitude is not to be looked for: the emphasis was on artifice, on an imitation that is always ready to draw attention to itself *qua* imitation expecting applause for the excellence of its craftsmanship and for its ingenuity in equalling and, whenever possible, outdoing Nature.

The child actor's voice, however, was his chief asset, being naturally good (hence his selection for the royal choir) and highly trained. Marlowe exploits the children's elocution to the full, most notably in the speeches written for Aeneas and Dido. Aeneas's narration of the fall of Troy has been justly praised,[11] but it is important, I think, to point out that this is in the nature of epic narrative (selecting and condensing that of the early Books of the *Aeneid*) where the identity of the speaker is unimportant. The speech reveals nothing of the character[12] of the speaker, but its length (more than 160 lines) says much for the actor's powers of memory and delivery. Dido's speeches have received no such acclaim; yet they deserve some comment, especially in the context of Marlowe's art of translation.

Although Aeneas is indeed the protagonist of the epic poem, he is ousted from this position for the duration of Book IV of the *Aeneid* where Vergil "creates within an epic of grand historical scope the intimate tragedy of a woman in love."[13] On the English stage—even at this early date, and even when the actors are children—such intimacy cannot be reproduced by the kind of detached narrative appropriate for Aeneas's account of the fall of Troy, and Marlowe seems to have appreciated this. But there was no easy alternative. In the encounter between Dido and Aeneas during the divinely evoked storm, the Queen is made to declare the passion she can neither understand nor control—since, like the storm, it has a supernatural cause. Vergil gives a simple description of her speech—*incipit effari, mediaque in voce resistit* (IV. 76)—which Marlowe takes for prescription. The puzzled Aeneas questions, and Dido struggles to reply:

> Aeneas.   What ailes my Queene, is she falne sicke of late?
> Dido.   Not sicke my love, but sicke, I must conceale
>   The torment, that it bootes me not reveale,
>   And yet Ile speake, and yet Ile hold my peace.
>   Does shame her worst, I will disclose my griefe.
>   Aeneas, thou art he, what did I say?
>   Something it was that now I have forgot.
> Aeneas.   What means faire *Dido* by this doubtfull speech?
>   (III.iv.24-31)

The punctuation of such "doubtfull speech" may be a headache for
modernizing editors; but the gentle commas of the first quarto (the text
used here) give enough direction for the actor to convey the swift and
subtle changes of mood and direction of the character's thoughts.
Marlowe shows himself to be already familiar with the playwright's
technique, himself supplying the words that Vergil left to the imagination.

In the play's final scenes, however, there are two crucial moments
when Marlowe seems to be defeated. When Dido pleads for pity to an
obdurate Aeneas, the most powerful words are those of Vergil:

> Dido.   Si bene quid de te merui, fuit aut tibi quidquam
>   Dulce meum, miserere domus labentis: & istam
>   Oro, si quis adhuc precibus locus, exue mentem.
>   (V.i.136-138)

Such passages have incurred heavy censure from the critics of the
twentieth century. Harry Levin reproaches Marlowe for "an evasion
[that] smells of the university"; and J. B. Steane is even more dis-
missive of the dramatist's efforts in this part of the play:

> his being content merely to quote Virgil shows him not to be taken
> up, involved in the material, as he had been in Aeneas' narrative.
> The impression throughout is that he is in too much of a hurry:
> doing a job, no more.[14]

Comparison of the play with its Latin source, however, precludes any
suggestion that the translator was "in too much of a hurry"—and there
is no known reason why Marlowe should have been "doing [such] a

job" unless the work was intrinsically interesting. Other aspects of the play suggest that he was very interested in his work. The attempted framework of the degenerate Olympians foreshadows his well-known sardonic mockery; the speeches at the banquet reveal his mastery of the narrative art and a keen appreciation of graphic detail; and the scenes in the cave were undoubtedly written by a man with theatrical ability, albeit not yet highly developed. It would be odd if the interest—of which these are surely signs—were to disappear before the departure of Aeneas.

I prefer to think that in retaining some of Vergil's lines Marlowe is betraying a quality not usually attributed to him—modesty. And, of course, an appreciation of the great beauty of those particular lines, which would be familiar to every member of the audience who had experienced a normal grammar-school education in Elizabethan England, where "grammar" referred to *Latin* grammar, which was learned through Latin literature. Aeneas replies to Dido's plea with a finely patterned line followed by one of the most famous half-lines in all literature:

> Desine meque tuis incendere teque querelis.
> Italiam non sponte sequor.

Only an inflected language could achieve the patterning of this first line; and the half-line is too well-known (even today) to admit translation. Marlowe, I think, recognized the beauty of the Latin poetry, acknowledged his own limitations (and those of the English language), and also paid a subtle compliment to the education and understanding of the audience when he retained Vergil's words. *Dido, Queene of Carthage* translates epic into drama; but when the epic poem itself becomes dramatic, there is no need for a translator.

After the paraphrase of Vergil in *Dido, Queene of Carthage*, Marlowe abandoned translation for a few years to write his plays for the public theater. When he returned to the art—perhaps when the theaters were closed during the plague of 1592-93—it was to attempt what Dryden recognized as the third kind of translation: imitation.

> I take imitation of an author . . . to be an endeavour of a later poet to write like one who has written before him, on the same subject; that is, not to translate his words, or to be confined to his sense, but

only to set him as a pattern, and to write as he supposes that author
would have done, had he lived in our age, and in our country.

Marlowe's *Hero and Leander* is a truly rare achievement—when "rare" is
used with the sense of "uncommon excellence or merit" (*OED*); but it
can be considered as a translation of the Greek poem by Musaeus only
when "translation" is used with Dryden's sense of "imitation." And
perhaps "competition" might be even more appropriate! Marlowe's
reference to his predecessor is significant:

> Amorous *Leander*, beautifull and yoong,
> (Whose tragedie divine *Musaeus* soong).

Musaeus sang the *tragedy* of the two lovers; but it was (to use Nashe's
description)[15] "a diviner Muse than hc, Kit Marlowe," who sang their
comedy.

Musaeus was one of the writers of the fifth and six centuries A.D.
who were given thc title *grammatikos*; they were distinguished as

> scholars and teachers learned in the rhetoric, poetics, and philoso-
> phy of their time, and expert in the scholarly interpretation of the
> classical prose and verse authors, in particular of Homer, the
> orators, and the philosophers.[16]

The Greek poem opens with fifteen lines of formal invocation; and then
the narrative proceeds sequentially from the festival when the visitor
from Abydos encounters the virgin-priestess of Aphrodite. Hero at first
resists Leander's seduction, insisting on her vowed virginity and thereby permitting the comedy of Leander's argument (l. 143):   παρθένον
οὐκ ἐπέοικεν ὑποδρήσσειν Ἀφροδίτῃ ["It is not fitting a virgin attend on
Aphrodite"]. An assignation is made, and the union is quickly consummated. Leander regularly swims the Hellespont, to be warmly received by his bride who is content to live "maiden by day, by night a
wife" (l. 287: παρθένος ἡματίη, νυχίη γυνή). The poem climaxes into
tragedy on the winter's night when "Love could not fend off the Fates"
(l. 323): Ἔρως δ᾽ οὐκ ἤρκεσε Μοίρας and Leander's struggle with the
sea ends when his drowned body lies at the foot of Hero's tower,

κὰδ δ᾽ Ἡρὼ τέθνηκε σὺν ὀλλυμένῳ παρακοίτῃ,

ἀλλήλων δ' ἀπόναντο καὶ ἐν πυμάτῳ περ ὀλέθρῳ.
(ll. 342-343)

["And Hero lay in death beside her dead husband, And they had joy of each other even in their last perishing"].

More than twice as long as the Greek poem, Marlowe's *Hero and Leander* was written when the author was at his most mercurial: fluent and witty in his invention, he also shows himself an Autolycus amongst authors—the snapper-up of unconsidered trifles. Maybe this is just another way of calling him, like Musaeus, *grammatikos*.

The English poem is rich in allusion; its simple story is laid out in formal rhetorical schemes, and richly embroidered with classical mythology and Marlowe's own mythopoeic imaginings. There is no time to discuss the work in detail; it must suffice to draw attention to the descriptions of the two protagonists. Either portrait could be taken as a model for the rhetorical scheme called *effictio* or *prosographia* in which, to use Thomas Peacham's definition, a person is "so described, that it may appeare a playne pycture paynted in Tables."[17] Musaeus is the inspiration for the portrait of Hero, but there are few points of contact between the Greek *effictio* and the English. Both Musaeus and Marlowe delight in the comparison of Hero with the goddess whom she serves—but even here the differences are more striking than the similarities. Musaeus is serious, crowning his description of Hero's damasked (διδυμόχροον) radiance with the assertion that "she far excelling among women, Priestess of Cypris, revealed herself Cypris anew":

Ὣς ἡ μὲν περιπολλὸν ἀριστεύουσα γυναικῶν,
Κύπριδος ἀρήτειρα, νέη διεφαίνετο Κύπρις.
(ll. 67-68)

Marlowe is less reverent. He begins his description with the amazing claim (from his personal mythopeia) that "young *Apollo* courted [Hero] for her haire" (l. 6), and proceeds to itemize the sacerdotal vestments, praising the elaborate artifice that rivals Nature. Hero's footwear is a technological *tour de force*:

> Buskins of shels all silvered, used she,
> And brancht with blushing corall to the knee;
> Where sparrowes pearcht, of hollow pearle and gold,

> Such as the world would woonder to behold:
> Those with sweet water oft her handmaid fils,
> Which as shee went would cherupe through the bils.
>
> (ll. 31-36)

Marlowe's verse admires the elaborate luxury, while at the same time revealing its absurdity. Hyperbole topples into comedy at the point where Musaeus is most serious—in the comparison with Venus. Marlowe first offers his own explanation for Cupid's blindness (prefixing it with the pseudoscholarly "Some say"—the *aiunt* of mythographers), and then invokes Venus in her least expected role—as a mother:

> Some say, for her the fairest *Cupid* pyn'd,
> And looking in her face, was strooken blind.
> But this is true, so like was one the other,
> As he imagyn'd *Hero* was his mother.
>
> (ll. 37-40)

The feminine rhyme of "other"/"mother" makes the fun secure.

Having exalted Hero as a masterpiece in which the work of man seems to have excelled that of great creating Nature, Marlowe initiates a second example of the scheme *effictio* with his portrait of Leander. For this Musaeus offers no precedent. The writing here is even more enthusiastic than in the portrait of Hero, as Marlowe ransacks mythology for comparisons, and indulges the senses in a complex interplay of thought and feeling. The description of Leander's neck is remarkable:

> Even as delicious meat is to the tast,
> So was his necke in touching, and surpast
> The white of *Pelops* shoulder.
>
> (ll. 63-65)

The relevance of the first simile is not immediately obvious: taste and touch are, after all, different senses. But the connection becomes clear with the introduction of Pelops, whose celebrated white shoulder was in fact an ivory prosthesis designed to replace the human shoulder which had been served as meat to the goddess Ceres.

Once again the admixture of comedy prevents the mythological and sensual richness of the passage from becoming overindulgent. Following the respectful allusions to Narcissus and "wilde *Hippolitus*" is a sly acknowledgement of Leander's epicene quality:

> Some swore he was a maid in mans attire,
> For in his lookes were all that men desire . . .
> And such as knew he was a man would say,
> *Leander,* thou art made for amorous play.
>
> (ll. 83ff.)

Hyperbole ends in gentle teasing.

Hero and Leander is a lovely comedy, where satire is tempered with gentleness, carrying undertones of ironic pathos through occasional reminders of the lovers' well-known tragic ending. But this is not described in the poem, which ends with glorious and harmonious fulfilment, the apotheosis of comedy.

Yet the publisher Edward Blunt (or some unknown "editor" of the 1598 Q1) appended the words "*Desunt nonnulla*" after Marlowe's last line, giving George Chapman excuse or authority to interfere by adding more than 1300 of his own lines and almost swamping Marlowe's original 818 in order to bring the lovers to their deaths. He takes the further liberty of manipulating a final Ovidian metamorphosis, changing Hero and Leander into

> two sweet birds, surnam'd th'*Acanthides,*
> Which we call Thistle-warps.

Chapman's additions were printed in the second quarto (also 1598) of the poem, and have been included in almost every subsequent edition. But the promised Oxford edition will leave the lovers where Marlowe left them—and, I think, intended to leave them—on the floor of Hero's bedroom in a triumphant, happy, consummated tangle: there will be no thistle-warps.

NOTES

1. "Preface to the Translation of Ovid's *Epistles*" (1680); in *Essays of John Dryden*, ed. W. P. Ker, 2 vols. (Oxford: Clarendon Press, 1926) I, 237.
2. Quotations from Ovid are taken from the Loeb edition of the *Amores*, ed. Grant Showerman (1914); in the passages I quote here there are no variants between the

modern text of the poems and that available to Marlowe.

3. Quotations from Marlowe's poems are taken from the MS prepared for the Oxford edition.

4. *Ovid's 'Amores,'* translated by Guy Lee (1968).

5. *Cit.* George Steiner, *The Penguin Book of Modern Verse Translation* (Harmondsworth: Penguin, 1966).

6. *An Essay on Translated Verse* (1684); *cit.* Charles Tomlinson, Introduction to *The Oxford Book of Verse in English Translation* (London: Oxford University Press, 1980).

7. Some of the findings were published in my essay "Marlowe, Lucan, and Sulpitius" *The Review of English Studies*, N. S. 24 (1973).

8. Introduction to *The Oxford Book of Verse in English Translation*, p. xiii.

9. John Bakeless, *Christopher Marlowe; The Man in His Time* (New York: W. Morrow and Company, 1937), p. 257; Michel Poirier, *Christopher Marlowe* (Hamden, Conn: Archon, 1968), p. 82; Brian Gibbons, "Unstable Proteus: Marlowe's *The Tragedy of Dido Queen of Carthage*" in *Christopher Marlowe* (Mermaid Critical Commentaries), ed. Brian Morris: (London: Ernest Benn, 1968), p. 41; W. L. Godshalk, *The Marlovian World Picture* (The Hague: Mouton, 1974), p. 53.

10. In *Christopher Marlowe: a Critical Study* (Cambridge: Cambridge University Press, 1964), pp. 59ff.

11. By (for example) T. S. Eliot in the essay on "Christopher Marlowe" first published in 1919.

12. This seems to me to be the mistake made by Brian Gibbons (in the essay cited above) when he observes that at the end of the speech "The apparent hero, ancestor of the British race, loyal defender of Troy, founder of Rome, breaks down and betrays his guilty cowardice!"

13. Reuben A. Brower, *Hero and Saint: Shakespeare and the Graeco-Roman Heroic Tradition* (New York: Oxford University Press, 1971), p. 99.

14. Harry Levin, *Christopher Marlowe: The Overreacher* (1954, paperback edition, Boston: Beacon Press, 1965), p. 33; J. B. Steane, *Christopher Marlowe*, p. 48.

15. *Nashe's Lenten Stuffe* (1599); in *The Works of Thomas Nashe*, ed. R. B. McKerrow and revised by F. P. Wilson, 5 vols. (Oxford: Basil Blackwell, 1968), III, 195.

16. Thomas Gelzer, in his Introduction (p. 297) to the Loeb edition of Musaeus's *Hero and Leander*, ed. T. Gelzer (London and Cambridge, Mass: William Heinemann and Harvard University Press, 1978); all Greek quotations (with the English translation by Cedric Whitman) are from this edition.

17. *The Garden of Eloquence* (1577), f. D2^v.

Marlowe's Nemesis:
The Identity of Richard Baines

CONSTANCE BROWN KURIYAMA

In the last serious scholarly compilation of facts and speculations about Marlowe's life and work, *The Tragicall History of Christopher Marlowe,* John Bakeless wrote, "the identity of Richard Baines remains a mystery."[1] Baines, of course, was the author of the notorious list of allegations about Marlowe's "Comon Speeches," at first dismissed by genteel Marlowe scholars as the "Baines libel" until the discovery of more information by F. S. Boas and others lent Baines's testimony increasing credibiltiy.[2] But nothing else was certainly known about Baines. For some years, we have known considerably more about Robert Poley, whose significance relative to Marlowe derived solely from the fact that he happened to be present in the same room when Marlowe died. Admittedly, Poley was a tempting subject for research. He was an important, active government agent and rogue who had left a clear, broad trail of documents behind him. Baines was a relatively obscure figure—and was certain to stay obscure as long as no one made any serious effort to find out more about him.

Apparently, the identity of Richard Baines has remained a mystery for so long partly because the topic has been treated casually by most Marlowe scholars. Why they took so little interest in a man who made such detailed and fascinating claims about Marlowe is at least as great a mystery as Baines's identity. Perhaps certain details of Baines's report were more distasteful than intriguing to them; still, the man's identity had a clear bearing on how seriously they should take his allegations, and identifying him should have been awarded higher priority than certain topics which have been investigated more thoroughly, such as the activities of Nicholas Skeres, or the identities of Humphrey Rowland and Richard Kitchen, who acted as bondsmen for Marlowe when he was indirectly involved in the killing of William Bradley.[3] Only two of Marlowe's biographers have made any serious effort to identify Baines. C. F. Tucker Brooke found traces of three men named Richard Baines living in England and London during and shortly after Marlowe's lifetime. One of these was a wealthy merchant of London, dealing largely in wool, who also owned a considerable amount of property in Shropshire and Montgomeryshire. This Richard Baines (or Baynes, as his name is most often spelled in the documents preserved at the Public Record Office in London) had a son of the same name, born about 1566. The elder Baynes was involved in a number of Star Chamber proceedings, most of them meticulously reported on by Brooke, although Baynes's accusations against his adversaries often have a violent and distinctly paranoid flavor which Brooke does not describe so colorfully as he might. This Baynes evidently was, as some of his opponents alleged, "a troublesome, clamorous, and wilful vexer of divers her Majesty's subjects."[4] In addition to the documents discussed by Brooke (Star Chamber B 6/11, 26/14, 56/13, and 90/7), his affairs are also treated in Star Chamber H 14/15 and 52/22, which concern a dispute between "Ricard Bayns" and Edmond and Phillip Hamond.

However vexatious the merchant Baynes may have been to his neighbors and business associates, he demonstrates an exemplary paternal solicitude for his son, who was admitted to the Middle Temple "specially" in 1582, and in 1583 sent to Oxford, where, like many wealthy scholars, he took no degree. When the elder Baynes died in December, 1588, his son inherited his legal and financial entanglements as well as his estate. Brooke discussed one of these, a dispute with John St. Leger, merchant stranger, in which the younger Baynes seemed to be trying to escape paying his father's debts.[6]

Brooke also found traces of a third Richard Baines, a Cambridge man who had matriculated as a pensioner from Christ's in 1568. Even if this Richard Baines was only twelve or thirteen at the time, as a number of youths entering the university were, especially those from Catholic families, he was at least eight years older than Marlowe. Brooke estimated that he was a dozen years older, and since Brooke knew of no evidence that he was in London in the early 1590s (nor, apparently, looked for any), he concluded that the merchant's son, who was close to Marlowe's age and possibly unscrupulous, was the likeliest candidate for the informer.

Even if we confine ourselves to Brooke's limited evidence, his conclusions seem doubtful. As Conyers Read's *Mr. Secretary Walsingham* makes clear, the principal motive for most informers and government agents in Elizabeth's reign was simple: they needed money. Government service attracted men who were clever, often well educated and well allied, but lacking adequate financial means to sustain themselves. The only agents and informers who were not drawn by money were coerced—many of them Catholics who were offered life and freedom as well as monetary rewards if they turned against their former associates.[7] Since the younger Richard Baynes of London was evidently well off, his only motive for informing on Marlowe would have been pure piety. But neither the elder nor the younger Baynes shows any signs, in the documents pertaining to him, of being notably pious, and zeal, in any case, was never the true motive for supplying information such as the Baines list, however pious the informer might profess himself to be.

Even Brooke's sketchy profile of the Richard Baines of Cambridge makes him seem a likelier candidate for the informer than the merchant's son. This Richard Baines took his B.A. in 1573 and his M.A. in 1576. He was therefore Marlowe's fellow alumnus and intellectual peer, holding a degree which might well lead to chronic unemployment and government service. The fact that he was older than Marlowe is hardly so important as Brooke believed. Robert Poley, as Ethel Seaton speculated, is probably the "Robert Pollye" who matriculated at Cambridge as a sizar in the same year as this Richard Baines, 1568, which would make him Baines's age or close to it, and Poley's acquaintance and occasional association with Marlowe is a matter of historical record.[8] Furthermore, the Richard Baines of Cambridge, according to more than one source, was hanged on December 6, 1594—a fate much more likely to befall an impecunious newsgatherer and intriguer than a wealthy merchant's son.[9]

Nevertheless, Brooke's argument exerted enough influence on F. S. Boas to prevent him from turning his great talent for biographical research into a more productive direction. Instead of trying to learn more about the Cambridge Baines while gathering material for *Christopher Marlowe: A Biographical and Critical Study*, Boas mainly confined himself to collecting more information about the merchant Baynes and his son.[10] Possibly following up a suggestion by Brooke concerning the "injunctions to Ric. Baynes and others" mentioned in the *Calendar of State Papers, Domestic*, and dated January 30, 1591, Boas located a document from the Court of Requests (Requests 2/144/4) recording a suit by Thomas Gell of Hopton, who, like John St. Leger, had found the younger Richard Baynes reluctant to pay his father's debts.[11] Boas does not explicitly connect the Requests document with the injunctions mentioned in the *Calendar*, but they apparently do concern the disposition of Gell's suit, which was filed on November 28, 1590. With Boas's last book on Marlowe, active inquiry into the identity of Richard Baines ended. Bakeless, whose *Tragicall History* was published two years later, was evidently content to leave Baines's identity a mystery.

The two significant discoveries about Baines published after 1942 have been made not by Marlowe scholars, but by researchers pursuing other topics. In 1947, Dr. L. Antheunis of Louvain published a study of English spies in the Netherlands, in which his principal examples were John Nichols and Richard Baines. Information about this article reached Boas through an American, Professor H. R. Hoppe, and Boas, though he was then eighty-seven years old, published Antheunis's findings in *TLS*, motivated partly by his delight in the discovery, and partly by a desire (reflecting Boas's characteristic integrity) to correct the false conclusion he had drawn earlier.[12]

Antheunis's discoveries are startlingly illuminating. Richard Baines, it seems, was an English Catholic or convert to Catholicism who had come to Rheims to study and be ordained. However, according to his confession, he had turned against his fellow Catholics in hope of being rewarded by the English government. He considered the possibility of destroying the entire religious community by poisoning the well or the bath (a meditation in which he not only anticipated Marlowe's Barabas, as Boas pointed out, but perhaps also directly influenced Marlowe's conception of his character). At the very least, he planned to reveal the treasons being hatched at Rheims by this "sorte of English priests," as Marlowe termed them in *The Massacre at Paris*, "gainst their naturall Queene."[13] For this information he expected to receive no less than 3,000 crowns. He even dared to ask the rector at Rheims, Dr. William Allen, for money to finance his trip back to England, on the pretext of carrying the true word of God to the English. Unfortunately for Baines, he was discovered and jailed before his purpose could be achieved. However, he was eventually removed from the city jail because of the expense of keeping him there and confined to a room in the seminary, where he made another confession. Possibly he escaped, as Boas suggests, or was simply released because he had confessed contritely, and his captors had no power to punish him. In either case, Boas speculated that he most likely returned to England to join Walsingham's intelligence service.

For some reason, it did not occur to Boas to connect this Baines with the Cambridge Baines, but almost certainly they were the same man. The Cambridge Baines took his M. A. from Caius in 1576, and, as Austin Gray has pointed our, Caius was one of the four colleges at Cambridge which produced large numbers of Catholic converts, among them John Ballard, a major figure in the Babington plot.[14] Until 1573, the master at Caius was Dr. John Caius, according to Gray "an open and irascible Catholic" who gave asylum to Catholic priests.[15] Although Baines did not proceed to Douai immediately after taking his degree, as was the common practice, he did go to France in 1578, just after the seminary had relocated at Rheims.

The parallels between this Richard Baines and Marlowe are curiously compelling. Both held Cambridge M. A.'s. Both sought employment and financial rewards as government informers or agents. If we believe that Marlowe indeed went to Rheims, and the evidence strongly implies that he did, both he and Baines were engaged in spying on Catholics in the same place. Baines presumably left Rheims in 1583; Marlowe went there in 1587. The only really striking difference between them is that Baines's conversion was seemingly sincere. But, of course, perhaps it was not. Like those of other men engaged in work against the Catholics—Robert Poley, Michael Moody, Thomas Barnes, Gilbert Gifford, Richard Cholmley, even Marlowe himself—Baines's precise sympathies and beliefs, assuming that he had any, are impossible to determine from the surviving evidence. Probably many of these men did not know themselves what they believed. Such lability of identification was only natural, since the differences between Anglicans and Catholics were more political than doctrinal, and authority on both sides had been discredited by the rift. When profit, advantage, or the impulse of the moment dictated, it was easy enough for men caught between two equally corrupt and unscrupulous antagonists to shift allegiances.

After the publication of Antheunis's work, the presumption that this Richard Baines, the spy of Rheims, returned to England, worked for Walsingham, and ultimately informed on Marlowe was tempting, since such unprincipled conduct seemed even more consistent with his character than with that of the merchant's son. The conjecture remained unproven, however, until R. B. Wernham produced the conclusive piece of evidence. Since Wernham's principal research interest, like Antheunis's, was not Christopher Marlowe, he simply published his discovery without extended comment in 1972.[16]

The paper Wernham discovered is a letter from Sir Robert Sidney to William Cecil, Lord Burghley, dated January 26, 1591/2. In this letter Sir Robert, who succeeded Sir Philip as Governor of Flushing in 1588, declares that he is sending back "one named Christofer Marley, by his profession a scholer," and a goldsmith named Gifford Gilbert, to be tried for an abortive attempt at coining in Flushing.[17] Their activities were disclosed by "one Ri: Baines," their chamber fellow and confederate, who, fearing discovery and apparently harboring malice toward Marlowe, divulged the plan to the authorities. Marlowe and Baines, when questioned separately by Sidney, accused one another of plotting to counterfeit English and Dutch money, of intention to go over to the enemy (Spain and Catholicism), and of malicious motives for accusing the other. Marlowe and the goldsmith, on the other hand, were, to quote Dogberry, "both in a tale," swearing that they had only meant to test the goldsmith's skill. Marlowe, evidently anxious to establish his respectability, told Sidney that he was "very well known both to the Earle of Northumberland and my Lord Strang."[18] Sidney, wary of a possible conflict of authority with the Dutch in Flushing, chose to involve himself no further in the matter. Presuming that Burghley, as Lord Treasurer, could best adjudicate the case, he sent the three men to Cecil along with his letter, in which he emphasized his belief that the goldsmith, "an eccelent worckman," had been duped by other two.

Not all of the significance of Sidney's letter is obvious, but it does suggest that Baines and Marlowe were closely associated, and that both were active in government service a year and four months before Marlowe's death, when Baines made his *second* accusation (as the Baines list now appears to be) against Marlowe. To those familiar with Elizabethan newsgathering, the location of the episode in Flushing is immediately significant, for when Flushing became a remote English outpost in Elizabeth's shadowy maneuvers against Spain, it also became a nucleus of intelligence activity. Robert Poley's ciphers, discussed by Ethel Seaton, included a symbol for Flushing,[19] and the records of Poley's movements as a messsenger, described by Eugénie de Kalb, mention his bringing letters "from fflushinge and sundire other places in the Lowe Countries" in July of 1590.[20] In October, 1591, Poley wrote to Sir Thomas Heneage (or, possibly, to Robert Cecil, whose policies Heneage was helping to implement until Cecil was officially appointed Secretary of the Privy Council) of certain instructions that he had given the spy Michael Moody, including the injunction that he bridle "his lavish tongue and indiscreet dealing where he is," and "that he go not too often to Flushing, etc."[21] Marlowe and Baines were most likely sent to or through Flushing in connection with their work, possibly on an intermittent or regular basis, and had decided to develop a profitable sideline. Thus Baines's and Marlowe's lives, which before had followed somewhat parallel paths, had finally converged.

This fortuitous discovery of two critical pieces of information about Baines naturally raised the question of what someone might discover if he tried—especially since we now had a better idea of who Baines was. I began researching the question casually, and without much effort found two leads in a very old reference work, the *Calendar of the State Papers Relating to Scotland*, by Markham John Thorpe (1858), where I found references both to "Baynes" and to "Baines, Dick" in the index. Since the indices to even the most recent *Calendars* are not completely reliable, because not all names occurring in the summaries and transcripts of documents (let alone in the documents themselves) are listed in them, the index to the older *Calendar* seemed well worth checking. Only one of these references, however, appears to have led to the Richard Baines Marlowe knew.

"Dick Baines" appears in a document dated June 20, 1574 and summarized thus by Thorpe:

> Examination of John Steward at Edinburgh before Mr. Kylly-
> grew, respecting his service with Alexander Hamilton under the
> Scottish Queen, letters and messages conveyed to her, the persons
> employed therein, Glover, John the musician, who played the base
> violin, Morgan, Dick Baines, Cuthbert Reid, Hamilton, &c.[22]

At first glance, this Dick Baines seems conceivably identical to the Richard Baines who later defected to Rheims and informed on Marlowe. He would have been working on his M.A. in 1574 and, like Marlowe, might have found time to dabble in political intrigue, in this case for the Catholic side. Unfortunately, an examination of a copy of this document and another closely related one, supplied by the Public Record Office, revealed the boy's or young man's name to be "Baies" or "Bayes," not Baines or Baynes. (The fact that he is called a boy in the document is not significant; John Steward the informer, who claimed to have carried letters himself, is also referred to as a "boye," specifically one "of xviii[th] yeres or thereaboute."[23] We might be tempted to speculate that the last name had been corrupted in oral transmission, since the name "Bayes" is rather uncommon, somewhat more unusual than the name "Baines"; however, the *Dictionary of National Biography* offers a brief account of Joshua Bayes, son of a Reverand Samuel Bayes who was ejected from a living in Derbyshire in 1662 by the Act of Uniformity. Since the name can be documented so readily in the area around Sheffield, "Bayes" is probably correct, to the great loss of Marlowe scholars, for the story of Walsingham's stalking of Hamilton is at least as entertaining as many of the tales surrounding Robert Poley.

The second document, as summarized by Thorpe, seemed equally promising. Thorpe dates it September 21, 1586:

> Letter in cipher, deciphered, respecting a report spread against the
> person addressed, that he was practising a marriage for the son of
> the Duke of Parma with the Lady Arbella Stewart. [Indorsed by
> Phelippes "From Clitherow to Baynes."]

Phelippes was Thomas Phelippes, the most indispensable man in

Walsingham's intelligence operation, since he coordinated the activities of newsgatherers, knew all of the ciphers they used as well as the ciphers used by the Catholics, and performed all of the deciphering. Clitherow was Father William Clitherow, a Catholic exile of the Welsh or anti-Jesuit faction at Paris.[25] Although he never authored a major plot against Elizabeth, the English government was acutely suspicious of him, and followed his movements constantly. He is described as a "Great Practiser" in a list of "sundry Englishmen, Papists, presently abiding in Paris," dated April 27, 1580.[26] Margaret Clitherow, the "martyr of York," who suffered *peine forte et dure* for her refusal to plead on a charge of harboring priests, was his sister-in-law. Baynes, most probably, was the Richard Baines of Cambridge, now active as a Walsingham agent three years after his departure from Rheims.

P. M. Handover has come to different conclusions about this document, transcribing the endorsement as "Clitheroe to Barnes."[27] The endorsement is indeed difficult to read: the third letter of the second name is heavily marked (perhaps marked over or corrected); it does have a tail, though a very short one. Dr. D. Crook of the Public Record Office suggests that it may be an *r* corrected to a *y*. Certainly, in the context of her research, Handover had good reason for taking the name to be Barnes, since a newsgatherer and agent named Thomas Barnes was certainly involved in negotiations to marry the Lady Arbella to the Duke of Parma's son in 1591, and at that time Barnes was also corresponding with Clitherow.[28]

However, we have strong evidence to suggest that Barnes was not active as a Walsingham agent until 1588. As Conyers Read argues, when Barnes became implicated in the Babington plot in 1586, he appears not to have been known to Walsingham's men, and to have been drawn into the conspiracy as a pawn by his cousin Gilbert Gifford, as Barnes himself swears in a letter of confession and supplication for pardon dated March 17, 1587.[29] Presumably, Barnes was arrested in August of 1586, along with the rest of the conspirators. It is not likely, under such circumstances, that he would have been asked to arrange a marriage for Arbella, or even be *rumored* to have such an assignment.[30] As far as we know, he had no correspondence with English Catholics on the Continent at this time. He wrote again to Walsingham on April 30, 1588, offering his services as restitution for his past offenses.[31] In September, 1588, he supplied intelligence to Phelippes,[32] and by August 19/20, 1591, he was corresponding with Clitherow under the name Gerard Bourghet. Quite possibly, Barnes took over Baines's correspondence with Clitherow, just as he took over some of the work with Catholic exiles earlier performed by Nicholas Berden.[33] Such shifts in assignment among government agents were routine, since this was an effective way of preventing them from knowing too much or becoming too powerful.

In September of 1586, Baynes was far more likely than Barnes to be Clitherow's correspondent, and far more likely to have been involved in early negotiations for Arbella's marriage, if indeed any took place. Baynes could conceivably have been the agent whom Read mentions as working in Antwerp and approaching Parma at Walsingham's behest (though not specifically about marriage) in October, 1586 and September through December, 1587.[34] The communications of this agent, identified in the endorsements simply as "B," suggest a person likely to be rumored to be practicing a marriage for Arbella. On October 29, 1586, not long after Clitherow warned Baynes of his rumored matchmaking, "B" reported that he had sounded out the Duke of Parma, and that the Duke was favorably disposed to Walsingham's proposal that Parma take possession of the Netherlands in exchange for breaking his alliance with Spain.

"B's" location in Antwerp in October, 1587, might also suggest his identity as Baynes, since Clitherow, who was living in Paris in 1580, is described in state papers of 1591 and 1594 as living at Antwerp, where he survived on "some allowance from a church . . . , and from Paget."[35] At some indeterminate time between 1580 and 1591, he evidently moved, and if this move occurred in the early 1580s, Antwerp was quite possibly the place where his correspondence with Baynes originated. Baynes would have been employed more effectively in the Low Countries than in France, since he had been exposed in Rheims as a traitor to the Catholic cause. His presence with Marlowe in Flushing in 1591 suggests that he was being sent to the Low Countries at that time, and it is likely enough that he was more or less steadily employed there between 1586 and 1591, on a variety of assignments. In a state paper of 1589, Walsingham writes that he "liked well of B's proceeding," and would furnish him with £20 to cover the cost of his journey.[36]

"B," on the other hand, may well be "A.B.," a "Roman Catholic Priest, generally dwelling at Mr. Henry Drury's house in Suffolk" who was captured and obliged to confess in 1584.[37] Evidently, "A.B." was recruited by Walsingham, and used the pseudonym "Alessandro de la Torre," an alias which Read links to "B." A state paper of 1594 is described in the *Calendar* as an "Answer made to A.B. (Alex. de la Toria)" concerning his proposal to the queen, on the behalf of "certain honorable personages" (presumably Catholics) that she open communications with the Pope.[38] This man seems to me more likely to be the one who negotiated directly with Parma, partly because the style of "B's" letter to Walsingham, quoted briefly by Read, is not like that of the Baines list. Baynes, however, is likely enough to have played a role in the negotiations, or to have acted in such a manner that he was suspected of doing so. Normally, several agents were involved in the same operation, and Baynes's more overt or publicized involvement may have been meant to divert attention from the covert movements of "A.B." The invariable references to the latter man by his initials or pseudonym suggest that his identity was a carefully guarded secret, as if he could work most effectively under these conditions.

Since Clitherow's letter is very probably addressed to "Baynes" rather than Barnes, the content has some interest for Marlowe scholars. The deciphered text reads thus:

> you are sayde to practise a mariage for the sonne of the D. of Parma with Arbella and hit is writen so in the Hage & Spaine for to disgrace and plage you, and one of the Counsell of England gaue out this matter of you as hit is sayd. the Brother of S^r. W^m. Stanley hath broken the heade of M^r. Owen and is in the sanctuary for hit. for the D. taketh hit done in despite for the matter of the lieutenat Co: Conell.

The episode of Mr. Owen's broken head was evidently too trivial to make history, but Sir William Stanley was not. Stanley was a nobleman of Catholic sympathies who, in 1587, openly allied himself with Spain after serving Elizabeth in Ireland and the Low Countries. Like Clitherow, Stanley was a member of the anti-Jesuit faction of exiles. In 1591, he plotted to kidnap Arbella Stuart and establish her as queen of England. His brother presumably preceded him in openly espousing the Catholic cause, and Mr. Owen is doubtless one of the family mentioned in the 1580 list of English Catholics residing in Paris. The Owens were members of the Jesuit faction of exiles, which may explain the hostility between Owen and Stanley. [39] "The D.," judging from the repetition of the cipher, is Parma, but the "matter of the lieutenat Co: Conell" remains obscure.

The rest of the letter is in Latin, with some undeciphered ciphers interspersed in it. I have been able to examine the document only in a photocopy, not all of which is legible. However, the general sense is clear. Clitherow asks for an unspecified book of the latest edition. (He makes a similar request for Stowe's *Chronicle*, on behalf of Sir William Stanley, in a later letter to Barnes.) Apparently in response to a query, he gives news about an unnamed person who, two months before, was in danger of robbers, but escaped "beneficio pedum." Clitherow also reports a betrayal, a siege, and the dire need of someone's sister (ciphers prevent certain interpretation). The Latin portion of the letter is hastily scrawled, cautiously allusive, and in general extremely difficult to construe, but it does suggest that the person addressed was intimately familiar with the Catholic exiles and their affairs, and an old acquaintance of Clitherow's, for the familiar, even gossipy tone of the letter is unmistakable. This letter provides a rarely intimate glimpse of the informal exchanges of information in which Walsingham's agents engaged, and the wary but workable bonds they established with their contacts and correspondents.

After tracing these two leads in the old *Calendar*, I was able to continue my investigation of Richard Baines by working for a few days in the Public Record Office and the Greater London Record Office and History Library. At this time I checked all the Star Chamber references to Richard Baynes, which invariably concerned the merchant. I also found two references to "Richard Baynes" in the *Calendar of Assize Records, Surrey Indictments*, in both cases as the victim of a crime. [40] One of the victims, however, is unlikely to be the Baines who accused Marlowe. On January 20, 1598, at Southwark, the records report that a cloak of cloth worth 11d was stolen from Richard Baynes by Edward Keightley, James Cotmore, and Richard Pressell. Since a cloak worth 11d was a tolerably mean garment by prevailing standards (Some cloaks recorded as stolen in the Middlesex Sessions Records of the late sixteenth century were valued at £40 or more.), it is reasonable to assume that this Baynes was neither Marlowe's acquaintance nor the merchant's son. And if the Cambridge Baines was indeed hanged on December 6, 1594, this document could hardly refer to him. The name

Richard Baines was perhaps somewhat more common than Boas thought.[41]

The other indictment in the Surrey records appears more likely to have involved the agent Baines, though we can hardly be sure of this. On May 23, 1586, John Hartopp of Oxford, gentleman, assaulted Richard Baynes on the highway at Chobham, stealing from him a gelding worth £10 and 15 shillings in money. Since the true bill gives no more information about this Baynes, it is difficult to identify him with any certainly. Both the merchant Baynes and his son were also alive at this time, although the merchant, who was aging, is not likely to have been riding out alone, and probably would have had more to steal if he had been. The younger Baynes was attending Oxford, the specified residence of the assailant, but it is not clear how this fact would lead to his being assaulted and robbed in Chobham. When we consider this document, it is worth recalling that being robbed on the highway was an occupational hazard of government messengers and agents, who traveled extensively, often by circuitous routes. Thomas Walsingham, in the days when he carried messages and letters for his cousin Sir Francis, was stopped by wandering soldiers on his way from Paris to England on November 12, 1581. According to Cobham's letter to Francis Walsingham, "Monsieur's packet" saved Walsingham and Cobham's Italian messenger Paulo from being robbed, but their companion, whose name Cobham recalled as "Skeggs," was less fortunate: he was "spoiled."[42] Another government agent, the musician Dr. John Bull, whom H. A. Shield suggests was brother-in-law to the Eleanor Bull in whose house Marlowe was killed, was assaulted on the outskirts of Tewkesbury in April, 1582, on his way to London from Bristol.[43] It is certainly possible that the Richard Baynes robbed in 1586 was on his way to London from one of the southwesterly ports of England on similar business, and was similarly assaulted. The value of his horse and the amount of money he was carrying are perfectly consistent with our knowledge of regularly employed government agents.

I have discovered no clue as to why Baines was hanged in December of 1594, if indeed he was. The man who suffered this misfortune—who was, according to three sources, the Cambridge Baines—enjoyed at least some notoriety, for two printers attempted to capitalize on his demise the very same day of his execution.[44] On December 6, 1594, the Stationers' Register records the entry by Thomas Gosson and William

Blackwell of "a ballad entitled *the woeful lamentation* of Richard Banes, executed at Tyburn the 6 of December, 1594."[45] Unfortunately, we seem to have lost this doleful composition, which probably contained information about Baines's crime. Since the Richard Baines of Cambridge was an educated man, he could have taken benefit of clergy for a crime for which he had that recourse. Presumably he was hanged for an offense specifically excluded from this provision by act of Parliament, such as murder, poisoning, highway robbery, burglary, rape or buggery. Treason, too, is a distinct possibility, even if he committed no actual treasonous act. Agents indeed lived precarious lives. In 1585, for example, Burghley allowed one of his agents, the self-styled "Dr." William Parry, to be hanged for treason after Parry, acting as an *agent provocateur* by his own account, proposed to an English Catholic, Edmund Neville, that he should conspire to murder Elizabeth.[46] The case was apparently well known, since Marlowe's convert to "Atheism," Richard Cholmley, who also spied on Catholics, reportedly observed that "William Parry was hanged, drawen & quartered but in Jeste, that he was a grosse Asse over-reached by Conninge, & that in trueth he nev[er] meante to kill the Queene more than himselfe had."[47] Baines could have been caught in a similar trap. The major treasonous plot of 1594 was the alleged scheme of Dr. Lopez to poison the queen, but the Lopez case was investigated early in the year, and I have found no evidence that Baines was connected with this or any other plot. How and when Baines's life ended remains to be discovered.

Baines's life, whatever inherent interest it may have, is important mainly because it helps us visualize and interpret Marlowe's life. Apparently, Marlowe was active as a government agent at least through his escapade in Flushing in 1592, and quite probably until the end of his life. His pursuit of such a second career was itself not unusual, as the instances of the composers Dr. Bull and Thomas Morley, and the less well known "John the musician, who played the base violin" while carrying letters for Mary, can testify.[48] Artists had ready access to great men's households, and were unlikely to be suspected of deeper motives than plying their trades. If Marlowe's style of leading such a double life seems to us somewhat more sensational than Dr. Bull's or Morley's, perhaps we may attribute this to a distinct difference in character.

Marlowe may, in fact, have found a highly convenient way to combine his two professions. One of the most provocative details of Sir Robert Sidney's letter to Burghley is his report of Marlowe's claim to

be "very wel known both to the Earle of Northumberland and my lord
Strang." Though we know very well that Sir Thomas Walsingham was
Marlowe's patron, Marlowe, perhaps for good reason, does not mention him to Sidney, but instead evokes the names of two noblemen who
were known both as patrons of the arts and as relative freethinkers.
Strange, of course, lent his name to the players for whom Marlowe
wrote some of his plays, but Ferdinando Stanley, Lord Strange had
two other traits in common with Northumberland, apart from patron-
age and freethinking, which might have brought Marlowe into association with both, in this case by virtue of his undercover occupation
rather than his ostensible one. Strange, like Northumberland, was suspected of Catholic sympathies or inclinations (Strange was a cousin of
Sir William Stanley), and he also, like Northumberland, was a favorite
candidate among Catholic exiles for a match with Arbella Stuart, so
that they might establish a Catholic king. Northumberland was urged
to marry Arbella in 1590; Strange was similarly approached in 1591.[49]
Again, in 1594, Strange was advised of a plot to place him on the
throne, and urged to cooperate. Speculation about Strange ended only
with his death in 1594, while Northumberland finally disappointed the
Catholics by marrying Dorothy, sister to the Earl of Essex, in 1595.
Marlowe, then, who could enter Northumberland's and Strange's
households because of his credentials as a poet and freethinker, would
have been a valuable source of information to the Cecils. Perhaps that
is why his eccentricities were tolerated, and why Sir Robert Sidney's
letter to Burghley about Marlowe's counterfeiting scheme apparently
had no serious consequences.

Marlowe may very well have worked for the Cecils both before and
after Walsingham's death. Although Marlowe's connection with the
Walsinghams is clear, it was Burghley, not Walsingham, who was present at the Privy Council meeting when the letter to the Cambridge
authorities on Marlowe's behalf was drafted in June, 1587.[50] As Read
indicates, Walsingham had agents of his own, but many other agents
worked for the Privy Council at large, and at least some of these continued in the service of the Cecils after Walsingham died, as Robert Poley
evidently did.[51] The emphasis of Marlowe's biographers on Marlowe's
and Poley's obvious links to the Walsinghams have probably prevented us from suspecting the complexity and extent of Marlowe's involvement in government work.

While my investigations of Richard Baines have been limited, I believe they demonstrate that we have a great deal more to learn about

Marlowe, partly by studying his associates. The preoccupation of Marlowe criticism during the last four decades with determining the "right" critical approach to Marlowe has been valuable, but it also appears to have drawn interest away from biographical research. If critics with lingering Romantic tendencies overemphasized the importance of Marlowe's life, post-New Critical work on Marlowe has largely neglected it. The latter extreme seems to me somewhat more pernicious, because facts have, or ought to have, an indisputable claim to scholarly interest and respect, quite independent of disputes over how (or whether) we should use them. We know very little about many junctures of Marlowe's life, as the late Dr. William Urry's fruitful work on Marlowe and Canterbury suggests, and undoubtedly we could learn more by studying not only minor figures like Baines, but also the important men with whom Marlowe was connected, (Thomas Walsingham, the Cecils, Northumberland, and Strange). We could also benefit from further study of his historical and political milieu, particularly the deadly struggle between Catholics and Reformists in Elizabethan England, and even the places where he lived and worked, such as the old theater district north of Bishopsgate (which, I have learned, was a refuge for Catholic priests working in England, a fact which may help explain Robert Poley's residence there between 1586 and 1591).[52] We have nothing to lose, and much to gain, by directing at least some of our efforts back to Marlowe's life, and exploring, with renewed energy and enthusiasm, the possibilities opened up by our expanded knowledge of Richard Baines.

NOTES

1. 2 vols. (Cambridge, Mass.: Harvard University Press, 1942), I, 112.

2. Baines's allegations are printed in full in C. F. Tucker Brooke, *The Life of Marlowe and the Tragedy of Dido, Queen of Carthage* (London: Methuen, 1930), pp. 98-100. The phrase quoted is from p. 99.

3. Skeres has been discussed by Frederick S. Boas, *Marlowe and his Circle*, 2nd ed. (Oxford: Clarendon Press, 1931), pp. 94-102, as well as by Brooke and Bakeless. Rowland and Kitchen occupy an entire chapter of Mark Eccles, *Christopher Marlowe in London* (Cambridge, Mass.: Harvard University Press, 1934), pp. 69-101. Though Eccles Assumes that Kitchen was Marlowe's friend

Kitchens frequently appear in the Middlesex records as bondsmen. Presumably they did this for *money*, not friendship.

4. Brooke, p. 101.

5. *Ibid.*

6. *Ibid.*, pp. 102-103.

7. Conyers Read, *Mr. Secretary Walsingham and the Policy of Queen Elizabeth*, 3 vols. (Cambridge, Mass.: Harvard University Press, 1925; rpt. New York: AMS Press, 1978), II, 321-338. See also P. M. Handover, *The Second Cecil: The Rise to Power, 1563-1604* (London: Eyre & Spottiswoode, 1959), pp. 107-109, for a discussion of Father John Cecil.

8. Ethel Seaton, "Robert Poley's Ciphers," *Review of English Studies*, 7 (1931), 147.

9. Brooke, p. 103; Bakeless, I, 112.

10. (Oxford: Clarendon Press, 1940), pp. 245-249.

11. *Ibid.*, p. 249. Brooke, p. 103.

12. "Informer against Marlowe," *TLS*, September 16, 1949, p. 608.

13. In *The Works of Christopher Marlowe*, ed. C. F. Tucker Brooke (Oxford: Clarendon Press, 1910), ll. 1042, 1044.

14. Austin K. Gray, "Some Observations on Christopher Marlowe, Government Agent," *PMLA*, 43 (1928), 687-688.

15. *Ibid*, p. 687.

16. "Christopher Marlowe at Flushing in 1592," *English Historical Review*, 91 (1976), 344-345.

17. The goldsmith's name is an exact transposition of Gilbert Gifford, one of Walsingham's spies or double agents active in the exposure of the Babington plot. This may be merely a coincidence, but it is an extremely curious one.

18. Wernham, p. 345.

19. "Robert Poley's Ciphers," pp. 139-140.

20. "Robert Poley's Movements As a Messenger of the Court, 1588-1601," *Review of English Studies*, 9 (1933), 15.

21. Ethel Seaton, "Marlowe, Poley, and the Tippings," *Review of English Studies*, 5 (1929), 282. For a glimpse of Heneage's role as intermediary for the Cecils, see Handover, *The Second Cecil*, p. 106.

22. (London: Longman, Brown, Green, Longmans, & Roberts, 1858), II, 916.

23. The papers in question here are S. P. 53/9/22 and 53/9/24.

24. *Calendar of State Papers Relating to Scotland*, II, 1012.

25. Read, II, 428. See also Seaton, "Robert Poley's Ciphers," p. 144.

26. *Calendar of State Papers, Foreign, Elizabeth I*, 14 (1579-1580), 250, #279.

27. *Arbella Stuart: Royal Lady of Hardwick and Cousin to King James* (London: Eyre & Spottiswoode, 1957), p. 305, Chapter V, n. 8. Handover is master of material on Arbella, but less knowledgeable of material on Marlowe. She takes "Poly," for example, to be a pseudonym rather than the actual name of Robert Poley. See *Arbella Stuart*, p. 96.

28. Handover, *Arbella Stuart,* p. 70, ascribes the name Gerard Bourghet to Barnes. Clitherow was corresponding with "Bourghet" in August, 1591. *Calendar of State Papers, Domestic, Elizabeth I,* III (1591-1594), 85.

29. Read, III, 70.

30. Handover, however, believes he was. *Arbella Stuart,* p. 70.

31. *Calendar of State Papers, Domestic, Elizabeth I,* II (1581-1590), 479.

32. *Ibid.,* p. 547.

33. Read, III, 70.

34. *Ibid.,* p. 261. Read, oddly enough, speculates that this agent was Thomas Barnes, a conjecture which contradicts his earlier argument that Barnes was incarcerated in October, 1586.

35. *Calendar of State Papers, Domestic, Elizabeth I,* III (1591-1594), 34, 555.

36. *Ibid.,* II (1581-1590), 594.

37. *Ibid.,* p. 218. On May 2, 1585, "A.B." supplied Walsingham with news of Catholics. *Ibid.,* p. 239.

38. *Ibid.,* III (1591-1594), 577.

39. Seaton, "Robert Poley's Ciphers," p. 144.

40. *Calendar of Assize Records, Surrey Indictments, Elizabeth I,* ed. J. S. Cockburn (London: H. M. Stationery Office, 1980), items 1710 and 2810, referring to Assizes 35/28/6 m. 55 and Assizes 35/40/5 m. 44.

41. "Informer against Marlowe," p. 608.

42. Bakeless, I, 161. Full details can be found in the *Calendar of State Papers, Foreign, Elizabeth I,* 15 (1581-1582), 365.

43. "The Death of Marlowe," *Notes and Queries,* N. S. 4 (1957), 102.

44. Brooke, p. 103.

45. *Ibid.,* p. 67.

46. Gray, p. 691.

47. *Ibid.,* p. 695.

48. Handover, *Arbella Stuart,* pp. 98-99. Morley, like John the musician, worked for the Catholics.

49. *Ibid.,* p. 89. Seaton, "Marlowe, Poley, and the Tippings," pp. 284-285.

50. Brooke, p. 35.

51. Read, II, 323. See de Kalb, pp. 15-17, where one can trace Poley's smooth transition from warrants signed by Walsingham to warrants signed by Heneage and the Cecils.

52. Bakeless, I, 178 notes that Poley is described as living in Shoreditch in 1591. However, a more recent source of information fixes his residence there as early as 1586, during the events leading up to the exposure of the Babington plot. See William Weston, *An Autobiography from the Jesuit Underground,* trans. Philip Caraman (New York: Farrar, Straus, and Cudahy, 1955), p. 79, n. 19 and 21. Weston lived in a house in Hog Lane (the site of Marlowe's later duel with Bradley) lent him by Mrs. Francis Browne in May, 1586. He was arrested just outside Bishopsgate on August 3, 1586, at which time, according to Caraman's note, Babington and Ballard were hiding in Poley's house in the same area.

Marlowe's Endings

KENNETH FRIEDENREICH

This paper provides no exegesis concerning how Marlowe the poet stays his mighty lines, nor how Marlowe the dramatist concludes his plays. My concerns are the endings imagined for Marlowe the man by biographers and would-be hagiographers. After all, Philip Henderson wrote some decades ago, "Marlowe was the kind of man who could not help making enemies and letting off squibs *pour epater le bourgeois.*"[1]

In my own schooling, and subsequently in my own teaching, I blithely assumed that Marlowe was killed by Ingram Frizer in a tavern brawl on 30 May 1593, in the heat of the moment; further, that the event inspired lurid accounts by Beard, Meres, William Vaughan, Rudierde, Earle, Aubrey, and Wood during the next decades. These "moral" versions made even more scandalous reading when compounded by the Baines's Note and Kyd's communications with Sir John Puckering. Supposedly the whole business was put into perspective by Leslie Hotson's discovery of the Marlowe Inquest proceedings in the Public Record Office in 1925.

More than a few commentators, before and after Hotson, have said Marlowe's life is the stuff of great tragedy. We should expect it to resolve like tragedy, with a definite sense of closure. It does not. The right metaphor for Marlowe's ending is no Grecian urn; it is a can of worms. Hotson himself made but modest claims for his own discovery at the time; Marlowe's betters "knew him as discreet and useful for the secret purpose of Elizabethan government. . . . To praise a man as a faithful and effective secret agent is to throw more light on his moral nature than to damn him as a free thinker."[2] But immediately William Danby's report on the death of one Christopher Morley at Eleanor Bull's establishment was attacked not only for what it contains, but for what it does not contain. Hotson thought to allay ghosts; instead, others took advantage of his discovery to raise them. Once the veracity of the inquest document itself was imputed, inquiry could accelerate into wild surmise. Marlowe could have all sorts of endings.

About the time Hotson was poring over documents in the Public Record Office, others were using his evidence to cry foul. Among the first were Samuel Tannenbaum and Eugénie de Kalb. Tannenbaum asked legitmate questions of the inquest account.[3] First, Marlowe and Frizer were violently arguing, then fighting, but the latter's wounds were so slight as to appear self-inflicted. Second, the only witnesses were Frizer's friends, Skeres and Poley. Third, what business kept Marlowe in the company of rogues for upwards of eight hours? Fourth, if Marlowe and Frizer engaged in "acrimonious discussion," why was Marlowe positioned behind his adversary, lying down? Fifth, why could Frizer not deal a deathblow to Marlowe from such a position. Sixth, no other patrons of the tavern were questioned by Danby's inquest. Seventh, the other parties did nothing to stop the fight. Eighth, Eleanor Bull was not questioned. Ninth, the wound described in the report would not have caused Marlowe's death. Items 1, 3, 6, 7, 8 are inferences drawn by Tannenbaum by what he saw as omissions in the report. For item 9, he secured the opinions of eminent physicians from Baltimore and New York. He concludes that Marlowe was assassinated by Frizer, probably while drunk or asleep, and that the Coroner "was influenced by certain powers not to inquire too curiously into the violent death of an 'outcast *Ismael*'." For Tannenbaum, "certain powers" read Ralegh, then out of favor with Queen Elizabeth, afraid Marlowe could reveal too much of the School of Night. In this scenario, Ralegh outMachiavels Barabas the Jew, Aaron the Moor, and Richard III. More than a half-century later, we possess a more balanced view of Ralegh's character than either Tannenbaum or Hollywood then provided.

If we required something even more sinister, then we could join Miss de Kalb in believing the murder of Marlowe came indirectly on orders from the Privy Council. On 29 May 1593, the informer Baines delivered his record of Marlowe's opinions to the Council, promising to name names when the lords wished. Would Marlowe's patron and Ingram Frizer's boss, Thomas Walsingham (nephew to Sir Francis who died in 1590), be named there? Marlowe had been summoned from Walsingham's estate at Scadbury to appear before the Council on 18 May 1593. Walsingham, with his connections to the Council, could have had ample opportunity to discover what winds might blow against his fortunes and decided to act, with the Council's acquiescence. Still, one wonders why it would be necessary to suborn murderers in a conspiracy rather than to allow the machinery of English law to crush Marlowe just like any heretic. We must stretch credulity more if we then imagine this murderous conspiracy was legitimized by an inquest and pardon process within the law. Worse still, the mere fact that Frizer, Poley, and Skeres survived and even occasionally prospered into the seventeenth century is seen by some, beginning with Tannenbaum and de Kalb, as a token of their complicity in a dark cover-up. It stimulates greater invention where Marlowe's endings are concerned. And yet, despite the work of pioneers who sought to undermine the citadel of established opinion that was now shored up by Hotson's discoveries, established opinion prevailed. F. S. Boas acknowledged the irregularities de Kalb and Tannenbaum found in the Coroner's report, but asserted "the evidence from various sources is consistent, and . . . it presents a figure of passionate impulse and restless intellect, quick at word and blow, equally ready with the dagger-point and the no less piercing edge of a ruthless dialectic." [4]

Since Boas wrote in 1929, most biographers and critics have been content to end Marlowe's tale in Deptford that day, pretty much as circumstances appear in Danby's Report. In recent years, though, it has again become fashionable to revise those circumstances, even to suggest that Marlowe's end came at some other time and place. These writers come from diverse backgrounds and work to different ends. In 1978, for example, the British actor Herbert Lom, perhaps best known to us as the zany Inspector Dreyfus in the series of *Pink Panther* comedies, published what had begun as a screenplay about Marlowe's life, *Enter a Spy: The Double Life of Christopher Marlowe*. In response to the evidence compiled by the Coroner, Lom posits three theories that have been recently taken up with varying degrees of fervor. First, that

Marlowe's death occurred as reported; that he met with the trio of Frizer, Skeres, and Poley because the Privy Council wished to intimidate him to silence. The quarrel over the bill was just a manifestation of a deeper rift—unknown to us—between the poet and the serving-man Frizer. Second, Marlowe was assassinated as Tannenbaum and de Kalb thought, because many powerful persons feared Marlowe's defense of any formal charges brought in against him. Third, the most devastating possibility: Marlowe was given a chance to escape and did, but on the condition that Lom quickly adds, facing the horror of it, "but if so, his connection with the theatre was in any case finished."[5]

Holding principally to the first of these theories is Constance Brown Kuriyama, whose study of psychoanalytic patterns in Marlowe's plays was recently published. Hers is a spirited defense of the subjective approach to interpretation, claiming that Marlowe's plays *do* reveal his personality. Kuriyama supports the majority on the Coroner's report, following Boas, but with a twist: Marlowe was a confused, bitter young man, who pursued three careers—theology, theater, espionage—without much direction: "These three occupations were not progressive steps to a clearly defined goal; rather, they were discrete arenas that could supply a compulsive personality with the challenges and spectacular achievements it insatiably craved."[6] She sees Marlowe burdened by a chronic Oepidal condition and sexual ambivalence, the result of his upbringing: his mother was shrewd and determined, his father a hyperactive man who managed his own affairs poorly, a kind of Swiftian Projector. Marlowe's challenges to authority, Kuriyama says, are self-destructive, self-punishing, and guilt-ridden. His behavior at Eleanor Bull's tavern is one final "violent attempt to reassert his dominance, manifesting itself in a sudden attack from behind involving the provocative seizure and use of the prospective victim's weapon (castrating before one is castrated)." At the moment of his ending, Marlowe had reached a "psychological and intellectual cul-de-sac." And so, torn within by fears of success, failure, conflict, impotence, Marlowe conspired and succeeded in his own murder-suicide.

Marlowe's precociousness and aberrant sexuality figure too in Hugh Ross Williamson's 1972 *Kind Kit: An Informal Biography of Christopher Marlowe*. Williamson largely advocates Lom's second theory, implying from the outset that William Danby knew not to pursue the inquest business too far. The major rivals in this story of the poet's ending are

Marlowe himself and Frizer. Both woo Thomas Walsingham, with whom Marlowe fell in love at the time he was recruited by Robert Poley through Thomas Watson into Sir Francis Walsingham's spy system. Williamson imagines the heir to Chislehurst as a restless profligate, not above fleecing gulls for sport and profit with those in his employment. Thus, "Faced with a choice between a temperamental lover and a trustworthy servant who saw to the smooth running of the house and estate and who tactfully superintended the provision of all creature comforts, no one was likely to hesitate long, certainly not anyone of Tom Walsingham's self-indulgent habits."[7] In this ending Marlowe exhibits a curious mixture of naïveté and cyncism, having come to admire John Penry *qua* Martin Marprelate far more than his sometimes sleazy patron. Only at the last moment, however, does he sense and embrace his doom at Frizer's dagger point.

In 1977, Della Hilton published *Who Is Kit Marlowe?* In this version of the ending, Marlowe's summons to the Privy Council in connection with the "Dutch Church Libel" did not cause too much concern for his benefactor at Scadbury. She continues by noting that had Marlowe been with the fatal trio at Deptford for the hours reported in the inquest report, he would not have been able to keep his appointment with the Privy Council that day. What happened, then, was that a spy, Christopher *Morley*, whose name appears throughout Danby's report, was killed at Deptford. Hilton adds that because of a possible hold Frizer had on Walsingham, he was in the position to insist that something be done to get him off the hook for murder. Marlowe could fit the bill. It was his identity—not body—substituted for that of Morley at the inquest. And what of the glorious poet whose name was elevated with his repute? Marlowe could not abide this: "it leads to the awesome speculation that Marlowe took his own life in despair, because of the desolation of anonymity spreading out before him."[8] He was buried at Scadbury, Richard Harvey officiating, and Edward Blount assisting in the obsequies, as glanced at in the Preface to *Hero and Leander*.

The singular end imagined by Herbert Lom is singular because it is defiantly heterosexual, perhaps a concession to the realities of the film marketplace. In his version, Marlowe's work in the Walsingham spy network brings him into close connection with Sir Francis's only child, daughter Frances. It is she, not nephew Thomas, who inspired the line "Who ever loved that loved not at first sight." The complication this time is the powerful Earl of Essex, by whose agent, the hated Poley, Marlowe is lured to Deptford for a meeting with his lady and the promise of subsequent freedom for both. He finds neither, and is slain even as Edward Alleyn delivers the great final moments of Doctor Faustus to a packed house. This is Lom's "history as it might have been," a sanitized, almost operatic ending.

Of course the last speculation Lom offers in his introduction carries the most trepidation for Shakespeare scholars, namely that Marlowe's end occurred much later. We have already noted that Lom can imagine Marlowe surviving the seemingly deadly circumstances leading up to 30 May 1593, but only at the cost of all future writing. Others are more determined. The best-known of these is Calvin Hoffman, who took up the cause of A. N. Ziegler's *It Was Marlowe*, published in the 1890s, and framed his own anti-Strafordian scenario in the 1950s. Few books are sillier than *The Murder of the Man Who Was "Shakespeare"*, which contends that a luckless sailor was lured to Eleanor Bull's tavern at Deptford on 30 May 1593, and that he was killed in order to provide a cover for the escape of the poet. Marlowe went off to Italy where, lacking one shred of detail from Hoffman, we are asked to believe he was contentedly writing the plays of Shakespeare. Of course, Hoffman, gifted with a special insight, discovers the secret allusions in the supposed Shakespeare canon to the career of the plays' true author, Marlowe. Despite initial resistance to his notions, despite the careful surgery S. Schoenbaum performed upon Hoffman's theories in *Shakespeare's Lives*, he persists.[9] The Los Angeles *Times* carried an account of a hastily arranged press conference Hoffman called in 1980, declaring that through computer analysis he would vindicate his theory of Marlowe's authorship of Shakespeare's plays. Naturally such a theory refutes one official report of Marlowe's death at the hands of Frizer. And more recently, The London *Times* carried a signed article by Alan Hamilton, dated 11 August 1981, reporting that as a result of lines missing from every edition of *Hero and Leander* save 1598, referring to "My still obcured estate, my unhappiness of life, my forced obscurity, my painful dumbness," Hoffman found "explosive proof" of Marlowe's exile in Italy. Because they came too close to revealing Marlowe's continued existence, these lines were excised from subsequent editions. Perhaps for Hoffman, Marlowe is *still* living in Italy.

Hoffman's visit to Los Angeles was prompted by his attempt to work

closely with Mr. Louis Ule. It was because of the first newspaper item
that I spoke with Mr. Ule about *his* manuscript, some 773 pages long,
in which he argues that Marlowe did survive Deptford, and that he
resided largely in Britain under the alias "Hugh Sanford" in the service
of the Countess of Pembroke, with whom he was also perhaps romati-
cally involved. A "Henry Sanford" turns up in John Aubrey's *Brief
Lives* as a secretary to the Countess and her assistant in publication of
her late brother's *Arcadia.* The same Sanford appears in a passing reference in E. K. Chambers's *The Elizabethan Stage,* iii, 279, as an assistant
to Samuel Daniel in presenting the masque, *The Vision of the Twelve
Goddesses* in 1604. This would appear to be Ule's man, "Hugh," who
succeeded Daniel as tutor to Phillip Herbert, the nine-year-old son of
the Earl and Countess of Pembroke. Here is a man in the right place in
the right time about whom we know little. The road leading to
Deptford found Marlowe ensnared in the machinery of William Cecil,
a principal on the Privy Council, and only an elaborate scheme culminating with an apparent assassination at a tavern saved Marlowe's
life. He ventured briefly to Italy, an account of which Ule finds deline-
ated in Thomas Nashe's *Unfortunate Traveller*—Marlowe is the character of Surrey. But the real objective leads to Wilton House and, again,
the Shakespeare canon. By the time Hugh Sanford dies in early 1607,
that canon is complete. Moreover, the author dies in bed. Unlike Hoffman's monomaniacal vendetta against Shakespeare's reputation, Ule
offers a wonderful caricature of the Bard, even filling in "the lost years"
of Shakespeare's career in a plausible manner. Shakespeare was the
consummate theartrical opportunist, so it is hardly surprising that he
posthumously provides the cover for publication of Marlowe's plays.
This is an ending for Marlowe quite different from that which was un-
covered by Hotson.

In view of these endings and for those who ponder a Marlowe biography I pose the following and sometimes unanswerable questions: 1)
compare the account of Marlowe's death to other Coroner's reports
contained in the Public Record Office, preferably those inquests led by
William Danby. Just how irregular are they and in what details? Can
the objections raised by Tannenbaum be seen elsewhere, or are they
unique to the Marlowe inquest? 2) To what extent does the testimony
of Baines and Kyd color our inquiries into the character of Christopher
Marlowe as it pertains to the inquest? To what extent are these docu-

ments self-serving statements of individuals with every reason to believe Marlowe was dead or about to be excuted? 3) Is it necessary or prudent to assume that the Privy Council as it was constituted in 1593 care enough about the poet or about his "late service" to "warn" him daily for ten days? 4) If one wishes to speculate that Marlowe survived Deptford—a temptation tantalizing to anyone who admires his writing—why must it also be assumed he wrote Shakespeare's plays as well? Moreover, could a dramatist frequently so resourceful and brilliant be content to let posterity acknowledge another's authorship, merely slipping in occasional, super-subtle hints for the hyperperceptive to decipher only centuries later? 5) If Frizer had been indicted for Marlowe's death, would any other "ending" be necessary? I think the restless ghosts in this tale mock the living, leading to the assumption that Marlowe's life ceased as attested to by the inquest accounts, albeit under circumstances to prompt even the most credulous to ask "Why?"[10]

NOTES

1. Philip Henderson, "Christopher Marlowe" in *British Writers and Their Work*, Bonamy Dobrée and Geoffrey Bullough, eds. (Lincoln: University of Nebraska Press, 1962), p. 7.

2. J. Leslie Hotson, *The Death of Christopher Marlowe* (London: The Nonesuch Press, 1925), p. 43.

3. Samuel A. Tannebaum, *The Assassination of Christopher Marlowe*. New York: The Tenny Press, 1928.

4. F. S. Boas, *Marlowe and His Circle* (1929; rpt. New York: Russell & Russell, 1969) pp. 136–137.

5. Herbert Lom, *Enter a Spy: The Double Life Christopher Marlowe* (London: Merlin Press, 1978), p. 23.

6. Constance B. Kuriyama, *Hammer or Anvil:Psychological Patterns in Christopher Marlowe's Plays* (New Brunswick, N.J.: Rutgers University Press, 1980), especially pp. 226–232.

7. Hugh Ross Williamson, *Kind Kit: An Informal Biography of Christopher Marlowe* (London: Michael Joseph, 1972), p. 238.

8. Delia Hilton, *Who Was Kit Marlowe? The Story of the Poet and the Playwright* (London: Weidenfeld & Nicolson 1977), p. 157.

9. S. Schoenbaum, *Shakespeare's Lives* (Oxford and New York: Oxford University Press, 1970), pp. 622–626.

10. The original version of this paper appeared as part of a presentation at the annual Marlowe Society of America (MSA) meeting in December, 1981.

INDEX

(All literary works with known authors whose names are specified in the text are listed under the author's name.)